THE ROAD TO IMPROVEMENT

CONTEXTS OF LEARNING
Classrooms, Schools and Society

Managing Editors:

Bert Creemers, *GION, Groningen, The Netherlands*
David Reynolds, *School of Education, University of Newcastle upon Tyne, England*
Sam Stringfield, *Center for the Social Organization of Schools, Johns Hopkins University*

THE ROAD TO IMPROVEMENT
REFLECTIONS ON SCHOOL EFFECTIVENESS

PETER MORTIMORE
Director of the Institute of Education
University of London

SWETS & ZEITLINGER
PUBLISHERS

LISSE   ABINGDON   EXTON (PA)   TOKYO

Library of Congress Cataloging-in-Publication Data

Mortimore, Peter.
    The road to improvement: reflections on school effectiveness / Peter Mortimore.
       p.   cm.
    Includes bibliographical references and index.
    ISBN 9026515251. -- ISBN 902651526X (pbk.)
       1. Educational evaluation--Great Britain. 2. School improvement
programs--Great Britain. 3. Educational surveys--Great Britain.
I. Title.
LB2822.75.M67 1998
379.1'58'0941--DC21   98-33633
                                                    CIP

Cover Design: Ivar Hamelink
Typesetting: Red Barn Publishing, Skeagh, Skibbereen, Co. Cork, Ireland
Printed in The Netherlands by Krips, Meppel

Copyright © 1998 Swets & Zeitlinger B.V., Lisse, The Netherlands

ISBN 90 265 1525 1 (Hardback)
ISBN 90 265 1526 X (Paperback)

Contents

Acknowledgements vii

Preface viii

Chapter 1: The Beginning of the Story: Schools, Schooling and Research 1

Chapter 2: The Study of Institutions 9

Chapter 3: Schools as Institutions 23

Chapter 4: Effective Schools for Secondary Students 35

Chapter 5: Effective Schools for Primary Students 49

Chapter 6: Effects of School Membership on Students'
Educational Outcomes 69

Chapter 7: The Reception of Educational Research 97

Chapter 8: The Positive Effects of Schooling 113

Chapter 9: Technical Issues in School Effectiveness Research 137

Chapter 10: Which Way at the Crossroads? 147

Chapter 11: The Management of Effective Learning and Teaching 161

Chapter 12: Value-Added Measures and School Effectiveness 179

Chapter 13: Differential Effectiveness 195

Chapter 14: Current Impact and Future Potential of Effective Schools 235

Chapter 15: The Relationship between School Effectiveness
and School Improvement 257

Chapter 16: The Burntwood School Case Study 269

Chapter 17: The Drive Primary School Case Study 289

Chapter 18: Can School Improvement Overcome the
Effects of Disadvantage? 299

Chapter 19: Criticisms of School Effectiveness 317

Chapter 20: The End of the Story: Policy, Practice and New Directions 329

References 347

Subject Index 379

Dedicated to all who have worked with me over the years on the many different projects and who have shared the excitement of the search for effectiveness and of research in the world of the school

Acknowledgements

Portions of the following chapters were adapted from previously published material, listed below, and are reprinted with permission. Chapter 2: Mortimore, P. (1978) 'The Study of Institutions', *Human Development* 31 (11): 985–99. Chapter 3: Mortimore, P. (1978) 'Schools as Institutions', *Educational Research*, 20 (1): 61–8. Chapter 4: Mortimore, P. (1978) 'Influence of School on Children's Development', *Concern*, 33: 22–7. Rutter, M., Maughan, B., Mortimore, P. & Ouston, J. (1979) *Fifteen Thousand Hours: Secondary Schools and their Effects on Children*. Wells: Open Books. Reprinted 1995, London: Paul Chapman. Chapter 5: Mortimore, P., Sammons, P., Stoll, L., Lewis, D. & Ecob, R. (1988) 'A Study of Effective Junior Schools', *International Journal of Educational Research*, 13 (1): 735–68; Mortimore, P., Sammons, P., Stoll, L., Lewis, D. & Ecob, R. (1988) *School Matters*. Wells: Open Books. Reprinted 1995, London: Paul Chapman. Chapter 6: Mortimore, P., Sammons, P., Stoll, L., Lewis, D. & Ecob, R. (1988) 'Effects of School Membership on Pupils' Educational Outcomes', *Research Papers in Education* 3 (1): 3–26. Chapter 7: Mortimore, P. (1991) 'The front page or yesterday's news: The reception of educational research', in G. Walford (ed.) *Doing Educational Research*, pp. 210–33. London: Routledge. Chapter 8: Mortimore, P. (1995) 'The Positive Effects of Schooling', in M. Rutter (ed.) *Psychosocial Disturbances in Young People: Challenges for Prevention*, pp. 333–63. Cambridge: Cambridge University Press. Chapter 9: Mortimore, P. (1992) 'Issues in School Effectiveness', in D. Reynolds & P. Cuttance (eds.) *School Effectiveness: Research, Policy and Practice* pp. 154–63. London: Cassell. Chapter 10: Mortimore, P. (1991) 'School effectiveness research: Which way at the crossroads?', *School Effectiveness and School Improvement*, 2 (3): 213–19. Chapter 11: Mortimore, P. (1993) 'School effectiveness and the management of effective learning and teaching', *School Effectiveness and School Improvement*, 4 (4): 290–310. Chapter 12: Mortimore, P. Sammons, P. & Thomas, S. (1993) 'School effectiveness and value added measures', *Assessment in Education*, 1 (3): 315–32. Chapter 13: Sammons, P., Thomas, P. & Mortimore, P. (1997) 'Implications for School Improvement', in *Forging Links: Effective Schools and Effective Departments,* pp. 181-215. London: Paul Chapman. Chapter 14: Mortimore, P. (1995) *Effective Schools: Current Impact and Future Potential*. London: Institute of Education. Chapter 15: Stoll, L. & Mortimore, P. (1993) 'School effectiveness and school improvement', *Viewpoint* X, 1–8. London: Institute of Education. Chapter 16: Mortimore, P., Davis, H. & Portway, S. (1995) 'Burntwood School', in M. Maden & J. Hillman (eds.) *Success Against the Odds: Effective Schools in Disadvantaged Areas,* pp. 146-74. London: Routledge. Chapter 17: Mortimore, P. & Harris, A. (1997) 'The Drive Primary School, Gateshead', in Department for Education and Employment *The Road to Success*. London: DfEE/Institute of Education. Chapter 18: Mortimore, P. & Whitty, G. (1997) *Can School Improvement Overcome the Effects of Disadvantage?* London: Institute of Education. Chapter 19: Mortimore, P. & Sammons, P. (1997) 'Endpiece: A welcome and a riposte to criticism', in J. White & M. Barber *Perspectives on School Effectiveness and School Improvement*, pp. 175-87. London: Institute of Education.

I also wish to thank Jo Mortimore and Ranjna Patel for their help in managing the texts and disks and negotiating the permissions for this book.

Preface

I was asked to assemble this book by another long-time researcher—David Reynolds—and by Martin Scrivener of Swets & Zeitlinger Publishers. The proposal was an opportunity 'to tell the story' of my research career through the reprinting of some of my publications from the 1970s onwards. In the busy life of a university professor and administrator, the task of assembling publications—written at different times and in very different formats—and converting them into a contemporary book seemed both daunting and more than slightly self-indulgent. I also feared that it might tempt me to look backwards rather than forwards at a time of great educational change. I thought about the proposal, but was not inclined to accept until Martin Scrivener sent me a copy of *Education For All*, compiled by Robert Slavin of the Johns Hopkins University in Baltimore (Slavin, 1996). As I read this volume I began to realize the value of the opportunity that had been offered to me.

As Bob Slavin notes in his own Preface, researchers are seldom allowed the opportunity to explain *why* they wrote any particular work or to comment on its reception or subsequent impact. I decided to accept Reynolds' and Scrivener's invitation and, as a result, have re-read some of my early publications and tried to weave them into a 'story': partly the story of my research career but, in addition, a much more important narrative. I hope I have also written a story of 'the influence of the school'—for, during the last twenty years, public views of state schools as sources of lasting influence have swung from disparagement to unrealistic over-expectation. Drawing on the findings of the various studies with which I have been involved, I have tried to chart a middle course which asserts the potency of the individual school whilst also recognizing the limitations of its social context.

Research about school effectiveness has been an important part of my life since 1975, when I joined Professor Michael Rutter's research team at the Institute of Psychiatry of the University of London. For nearly four years, I worked with Janet Ouston and Barbara Maughan under the direction of Professor Rutter on what became known as the *Fifteen Thousand Hours* study. It was a challenging project—developing a methodology to enable us to make a series of delicately balanced judgements about the effectiveness of a group of twelve London secondary schools. The privilege of working in schools over an extended period—observing the daily life of the institution, talking to its teachers and students and collecting data—is not conferred lightly and carries a responsibility to analyse, interpret and write up the assembled information with care. This was a stimulating experience for someone who had been a secondary school teacher in the inner city for nine years. It drew deeply on my knowledge of day-to-day school practice and on my research training. As it happens, the experience determined the shape of the rest of my career. Apart from relatively short intervals working as a school inspector and an educational administrator, I have been involved in school-based research ever since.

I learned a great deal from Professor Rutter and my two colleagues about research in the social sciences and, particularly, about the scope for variation which existed both between and within schools which were ostensibly very similar and which, to the eye of those working on the Coleman survey (Coleman, 1966), would probably have appeared identical.

Working in the University of London gave me the opportunity to combine my work as a researcher with study for a doctorate, under the joint supervision of Michael Rutter and the late Jack Tizard, at that time a professor at the Institute of Education and the director of the Thomas Coram Research Unit. I learned much from these two academics and owe them an enormous debt. Chapters two and three stem from the review of research which I undertook as part of my doctoral studies.

In 1978, just before the publication of *Fifteen Thouasnd Hours: Secondary Schools and their Effects on Children*, I applied for the post of Director of Research and Statistics for the Inner London Education Authority (ILEA). Since leaving the Institute of Psychiatry I had worked as one of Her Majesty's Inspectors—a job I would have relished if the opportunity to lead the Research and Statistics Branch had not become available. My applying for a post outside of HMI after less than a year in post was a risk—and was most unusual—but I was aware of the unique opportunity provided by the post of director of 'R and S' (as the Branch was known colloquially) and that it might not become vacant again for several years. I took the gamble and risked the wrath of the then HMI Senior Chief Inspector, Sheila Browne (who, having given me the dressing-down of a lifetime, proved very supportive). I was lucky and got the ILEA job. Selecting a relatively young researcher for this prestigious post was a bold move by the authority and a vote of confidence by the (then) Chief Education Officer, Peter Newsam.

The Research and Statistics Branch had been established in 1964 by the London County Council (LCC), just before the Council was replaced by the ILEA. The LCC's far-sighted action set an agenda for the next 26 years. The Branch had four main responsibilities: the routine monitoring of statistical data; the vetting of external research; undertaking development projects; and carrying out research. The achievements of the ILEA Research and Statistics Branch have been described elsewhere (Mortimore, 1989). During my term as director, I was involved in over 100 studies as diverse as the provision of support centres for disturbed and disturbing children (Mortimore et al., 1983), improving the authority's primary and secondary schools (Mortimore, 1982; Tomlinson et al., 1988), and addressing questions of equal opportunities (ILEA, 1983).

I also had the opportunity, building on the experience of *Fifteen Thousand Hours*, to plan a study of primary schools which, in 1979, the authority agreed to fund. The Junior School Project (JSP)—published under the title *School Matters*—was one of the largest and most complex studies undertaken by R and S. With an excellent team assembled, we scoured the literature, developed our research tools, chose a random sample of schools and appointed the additional four primary teachers needed for the study. An overview of the study is presented in greater detail in chapter five and more detailed findings in chapter six. When the junior school sample reached the age of transfer to secondary schools, we found a research opportunity too good to miss. Accordingly, we developed the Secondary Transfer study in tandem with the later phase of the JSP.

In September 1995, after seven years directing the authority's research programme, I became the education officer with responsibility for the ILEA's secondary schools. This change of role meant that the final analyses and writing up of *School Matters: The Junior Years* had to be overseen from outside the R and S Branch. Such was the devotion of our team that we met on a series of Saturdays in an otherwise empty County Hall in order to complete the task. The study was published in 1988.

Shortly before its publication, I left London to take up the dual post of Professor of Educational Research and Director of the School of Education at the University of Lancaster, a position I held for nearly three years. During that time, in addition to my management and administrative responsibilities, I was involved in a number of small-scale studies to do with appraisal and the quality of schooling, but I undertook nothing on the scale of *School Matters*.

In 1990 I was appointed deputy to the then director of the Institute of Education, Peter Newsam. I returned to London to work for a former boss from the ILEA at the same college of the University of London in which I had studied for my master's degree in the early 1970s.

The Institute of Education

The Institute, initially called the London Day Training Centre, was founded by the London County Council in 1902 '*to prepare men and women to become school teachers and to encourage the study of the theory, history and practice of education*'. That original purpose still holds good today, although the Institute's mission statement is broader and encompasses '*the promotion of new ideas in policy and professional practice grounded in its research and teaching expertise*'. With its excellent record of research and many renowned scholars, the Institute provided fertile ground for my subsequent research.

Despite the numerous demands of a new job, first as the deputy but later as the director of the Institute of Education, I used the opportunity of my return to London to collaborate with former colleagues and undertake new research. The studies I have undertaken at the Institute address a number of different strands of research into policy and practical concerns. They include: with my colleagues, Barbara MacGilchrist, Jane Savage and Charles Beresford, an exciting project concerned with school development planning; with Desmond Nuttall—before his sad and premature death—and with Pam Sammons and Sally Thomas I have continued the detailed exploration of differential effectiveness within schools; with Jo Mortimore and Hywel Thomas (of Birmingham University) I have worked on projects concerned with associate (non-teaching) staff in schools and in city technology colleges; with John MacBeath and his colleagues (from the Quality in Education unit of Strathclyde University) and a group of Institute researchers, I have worked on a large-scale project on school effectiveness in Scotland; with Harvey Goldstein on a critique of inspection; with Geoff Whitty in a review of school improvement and disadvantage; with Peter Blatchford in a review of class size; and with Judy Ireson, Sue Hallam and Sarah Hack I have been involved in a study looking at the way students are grouped in schools. Throughout this time I have worked with Louise Stoll—a long-time collaborator from ILEA days—to develop our International School Effectiveness and Improvement Centre at the Institute.

As is clear from this list of collaborators and projects, I have worked, over the course of my research career, with a group of extremely talented and hard-working colleagues. I have progressed from being a junior researcher—one of the 'et al's'—to the role of project director and principal author. But, in recent years as a busy university administrator, I have demoted myself to the role of collaborator or adviser to colleagues whom I recruited early in their own careers. In the collegial community of the research world, where anyone with appropriate data and a plausible interpretation can challenge anyone else, the shifting of power positions acts as a effective safety check on the ego!

In this book, I have endeavoured to present a selection of my work as it has progressed over the years. It is not the whole story and cannot do justice to the rich detail of so many projects but—I hope—it will give the flavour of what I have called the *Road to Improvement*. Like other odysseys, it may be that the search will never end and that, just when we think we understand 'effectiveness', the realities of time and progress will render its explanation inaccurate. The journey, however, will still have been worthwhile for me and—I trust—for some of the many head teachers and teachers with whom, over the years, I have worked and to whom I have talked during innumerable meetings and conferences; for the policy makers who have listened and, as a result, sometimes changed their minds; and for the research community, which must always be moving forwards.

1

The Beginning of the Story: Schools, Schooling and Research

Most societies insist that children attend school for their formative years. Children are expected to absorb the knowledge, skills and understanding which their societies see as essential for their roles as adults and as future members. Although the teaching of the formal curriculum dominates the life of the school, a substantial part of the learning experience is implicit: pupils learn self-control through having to conform to established rules and they acquire social skills through the experience of living in a mini-society within the school setting.

We expect schools to be places in which the energy and the desire to learn, with which almost all young children are equipped, is harnessed and cultivated. Children do not, however, enter school as *tabulae rasae*! They come after three, four or five years of intensive learning about how the world works in general and with detailed and intimate knowledge of how their families function in relation to them. Children thus enter school with a wide range of skills. The strength of these skills will depend on the way their own individual talents (arising from their genetic inheritance and their constitutional make-up) have melded with the particular family environment in which they have lived. As we know only too well—as much from novels as from social science—families not only vary according to their wealth or poverty and their size and composition but according to the relationships and attitudes of individuals towards each other. It is the combination of individual attributes, home and school that shapes so much of the behaviour and the attitudes of children.

Historically, in most societies, schools have had dual functions: selecting out those with obvious talents to become future leaders and, at the same time, convincing those without such obvious skills and abilities that their likely occupation will be a fair reflection of their talents. Tasks like these are, of course, implicit—head teachers are not given such goals to work towards—but they are inherent in most systems of schooling and are maintained by elaborate processes of selection and competitive examination. This leaves schools in the unenviable position of acting as a sieve for society. Schools are the arenas in which expectations, socializing influences, talents and motivation combine and influence the individual educational outcomes of children. Small wonder that—at times—schools are places of conflict. This situation is made even more difficult when the teachers involved are strongly committed to the progress of students who are disadvantaged by their socio-economic backgrounds or their gender or race. In such situations—where both teachers and pupils are trapped by the demands of a system designed in a different age to achieve different goals—tensions and frustrations can inhibit positive outcomes.

During the twentieth century, popular ideas about individual potential and about the power of social class, gender, race and other influences have changed a great deal. Whereas, at one time, people believed that the aristocracy of a nation was inherently more talented than the ordinary people, the advent of state-supported schooling during the nineteenth century opened up the possibility of progression to the most prestigious occupational roles to those coming from ordinary backgrounds. (Of course, extraordinary advancement has always been possible in exceptional circumstances, as numerous autobiographical accounts reveal.)

Schools are not, therefore, such simple places that, from the outside, they may seem. Furthermore, just having been a student does not provide a full understanding of how they work. Schools are fascinating institutions in which different traditions and cultures develop and in which adults and children are engaged in complex interactions. These interactions can be both positive and negative. Where energy is converted through learning into knowledge, understanding and skills, schools function well. In less happy instances, the energy is used negatively. We will all have read about tragic situations in which children are bullied by their fellows. Many of us will have seen teachers who abuse their authority and act tyrannically towards their charges. Where students feel unfairly treated and resentful, they frequently reject the values of school and, in some cases, go on to abuse the values of the wider society. Those of us who have worked in schools may also have seen the obverse, however, where teachers are bullied by their students. This too is a terrible thing. We need schools where both students and teachers treat each other with dignity. Only in such schools can energy be directed—without distraction—to learning and the pursuit of achievement.

Research on schools and schooling

At the time when my research career was beginning, a commonly-held view amongst researchers was that, despite the hopes and resources invested in national school systems, schools had not given individuals equal chances of achievement nor had they rid societies of anti-social behaviour. Many educationalists in the early 1970s had come to believe that schools made little difference to the life chances of pupils. This negative conclusion stemmed largely from the work of two American social scientists, James Coleman and Christopher Jencks. Coleman (1966) had carried out a large-scale survey examining 'equality of opportunity' and Jencks et al. (1972) had followed this up with further studies which, he argued, showed that, 'if all (American) high schools were equally effective, differences in attainment would be reduced by less than one per cent' (quoted in Ouston et al., 1979).

The findings of Coleman and Jencks were deeply depressing for those with responsibilities for public education. Luckily for them, however, closer examination of the data, on which these researchers had formed their judgements, revealed a more optimistic view. The macro-variables studied by these two researchers and their assistants were to do with the size of the school site, the nature of the facilities available and the resources given to institutions. They did not tell the whole story. Other researchers asked whether, if Coleman and Jencks had been able to collect information on micro variables—such as the patterns of staff behaviour, pupils' attitudes or the 'ethos' or social climates of individual schools—their analyses might have been rather different (Ouston et al., 1979; Edmonds, 1979).

These unanswered questions inspired a second wave of research studies. Researchers working on both sides of the Atlantic—but unbeknown to each other—began studies which focused on the micro-variables that operated in individual schools. It was through my involvement in one of these studies (Rutter et al., 1979a) that I gained an awareness of the potential fascination of research on schooling.

The *Fifteen Thousand Hours* study broke new ground by creating a methodology to identify a set of student outcomes; to measure, in a sample of schools, the range of effectiveness by taking account of the different backgrounds and attributes of pupils entering these schools, and then endeavouring to 'backward map', to identify the characteristics of the seemingly most effective schools in the sample. It was a delightfully elegant research design. Although, with a sample of only twelve schools, the scale of the study was limited, the use of longitudinal data and a broad range of student outcomes attracted considerable interest, as the account in chapter five illustrates. The study was praised for its pioneering approach, its innovative use of outcomes and its challenging of the Coleman/Jencks thesis on the impotence of schooling. It was criticized on account of the limitations of its methodology and, in particular, for the way it sought to take account of pupil intake variation, lack of attention to the curriculum and the absence of parental views on children's schooling.

At exactly the time that we were working on the *Fifteen Thousand Hours* study in England, Ron Edmonds and his colleagues were coincidentally undertaking a similar study in the United States and obtaining broadly comparable results. At the macro level, the British and the American systems of education are similar in some respects. Students in both systems are grouped in dedicated institutions staffed by adults trained in instruction. Both students and teachers are constrained by a curriculum which deals both with subject knowledge and with attitudes and values. The aims of the institutions are to foster the quality of learning yet, in both countries, success for some has to be set against the failure of others.

In Britain, until quite recently, there has been a tendency to 'blame the individual' and to see the role of the school, as opposed to family background, as peripheral to the success of the student (Reynolds, 1988). Recent changes, however, may be revising this view and replacing it with an equally biased one in which the individual bears no responsibility for his or her own success or failure, which is seen as the result of the quality of schooling. As will be argued later, I believe that both views are wrong: successful schooling depends on a positive interaction between the individual and the school.

In North America, the 'American dream' of individuals reaching their potential—and the implications for the school she or he attends—is striking. The systems of assessment in the two countries are imbued with quite different cultural values. Thus, in Britain the formal public examinations were traditionally constructed to have high failure rates. Even though there have been recent changes in the organization of the examinations, the reality in Britain is that less than half of all students reach a level deemed to represent academic success—five A*–C grades in the General Certificate of Secondary Education (45.1% according to DfEE *News* 386/97). In these circumstances it is perhaps not surprising that until very recently many students chose to drop out of full-time education at the age of 16. In contrast, many 'average' students in America leave school feeling successful and the school drop-out rate is far lower than in England.

Edmonds' work dominated the field in the United States for most of the decade following publication of his ground-breaking study of effectiveness. I shared a platform with him on at least six occasions. These were always exciting events: Edmonds was a powerful orator. As a black American, he was fired by a passion for equity and he believed that the United States had the capability to make all schools effective. Despite his tragic early death, his idea that *'all children can learn'*—and that all sections of society are educable if there is political will to make them so—still resonates in many countries beyond North America.

In like manner, the debates which followed the publication of the *Fifteen Thousand Hours* study raised questions about the size of pupil effects, the best methods of controlling for intake differences, and the extent of variation within any one school. Furthermore, the studies undertaken in this country over the last twenty or so years have built on the *Fifteen Thousand Hours* model but have not, fundamentally, changed it. Some of the questions that this seminal study raised have been answered; others continue to challenge and tantalize researchers. Both these sets of questions, in different ways, dominate the rest of this book.

I hope that in this volume I have captured the complexity of schools and the difficulties of researching them. As I noted in the opening section of this chapter, schools have been given multiple aims by society. They exist as expressions of that society. But they are also expected to create a better generation than that from which the parents and the policy makers have emerged. Whereas once they were given considerable freedom about how they went about their tasks, today they are more constrained. Exactly how the balance between how much freedom they should have and how much their work should be decided by the state—or at least by those outside of the teaching profession—is a matter for debate. Amongst the most critical right-wing commentators—and amongst some researchers—there is a view that teachers should exercise relatively little control over 'what' is taught. However, I judge that only a small minority in the profession believe teachers should be the sole arbiter on both these matters. My own preference—in line with most teachers—is for a position in which the state has the right to create a national curriculum but chooses to do so in conjunction *with* the profession. Whilst retaining powers to intervene if necessary, it should delegate the task to a body in which the profession can play a leading but not exclusive role. The alternative, that politicians—of whichever party—should determine the content of the curriculum, is far too dangerous and may result in pendulum swings in selected knowledge and skills.

Increasingly there is also an argument over the level of control which should be exercised by the state over 'how' the curriculum is taught. I have heard researchers argue that if a successful technology can be identified all teachers should be forced to use it. This is a tempting view but it is surely an erroneous one. It assumes too readily a direct and straightforward link between teaching and learning. As I will argue in chapter eleven, this link is neither direct nor straightforward. The accounts of 'my best teacher' which appear regularly in the *Times Educational Supplement* illustrate the range of skills and the enormous variety of personalities that distinguish the teachers chosen. One commonly identified characteristic is the sensitivity of the teacher to the needs and the problems of the learner. We should guard against the 'simple' view that any mechanical approach to teaching—no matter how precisely specified—can operate better than trusting teachers to work with their pupils in an atmosphere dedicated to learning. For me this remains the best solution and this is actually what the research evidence portrays—as the following chapters demonstrate.

The selected writings which follow are drawn from over twenty years of my research and it is apparent as one reads them that terminology has changed, methods of inquiry have advanced and statistical techniques have become ever more sophisticated. The development of the computer has radically improved the way researchers work. The scope for storing, processing and analysing data is now enormous. I have undertaken minor editing to avoid undue repetition and, where appropriate, reworded certain sections of the texts. The basic documents, however, remain substantively the same as when they were first published. Tempting though it is to take advantage of hindsight to indulge in some judicious rewriting, I have resisted the opportunity, since the main purpose of this book is to trace the development of a research idea and the changing perspectives on the effectiveness of schools.

The rationale for deciding which publications from my corpus of work to include in this collection was that the book should 'tell the story' of my research into school effectiveness in England over the past quarter of a century. Chapters have been selected because they represent staging posts along the research road which—in the company of many talented and committed researchers and practitioners—I have travelled.

The early chapters indicate the roots of my school effectiveness work (other researchers may well have arrived at the same kinds of questions from different beginnings). For me, my work as a secondary school teacher and then as a research officer in a primarily medical institution highlighted the similarities and contrasts within and between institutions. Chapter two looks at the variation between predominantly non-educational residential institutions in terms of their processes (how and in which ways the institutions work) and their outcomes (whether it makes a difference). Chapter three focuses on schools and draws from early studies which indicated school differences in order to construct a model for evaluating their potential effects on students.

The next four chapters draw on the two major studies of school effectiveness with which I have been involved. Chapter four is an overview of the seminal study on which I worked as a young research officer. Directed by Michael Rutter, the study was published in 1979 as *Fifteen Thousand Hours: Secondary Schools and Their Effects on Children*. The study of junior schools which I subsequently directed *(School Matters)* is summarized in chapter five and, in chapter six, is presented in more technical detail. Both studies occasioned considerable interest in the media and amongst members of the research community. The reactions—some positive, some hostile—and how they were dealt with, are the subject of chapter seven.

Chapter eight jumps forward a number of years and broadens the scope of the collection with a wide-ranging review of the research literature on the effects of schooling.

The next group of chapters illustrates how, during the early 1990s, the field of school effectiveness research was developing. Chapter nine looks at problematic issues, some of them methodological and others related to the sometimes unrealistic expectations of how school effectiveness research could lead to school improvement. Chapter ten represents a metaphorical 'pausing to draw breath and check the map' in order to consider various options under the question 'where next?'. Chapters eleven, twelve and thirteen then address specific and important issues within the field, focusing on, respectively, the relationship between effective teaching and effective learning, value-added analyses and differential effectiveness.

I used my inaugural lecture as Director of the Institute of Education (chapter fourteen) to review the achievements and limitations of school effectiveness and school improvement and to argue for a fundamental restructuring of the relationship between researchers and policy makers. Aware of the mutual suspicion and hostility which had characterized the last decade, I proposed a new model of collaboration in which policy makers would take more notice of empirical evidence, in return for which researchers would address some of the hard questions.

The wide-ranging review in chapter fifteen charts the progress from school effectiveness to school improvement and sets the scene for the next two chapters. Chapters sixteen and seventeen consist of two case studies of schools which, in their different contexts, appear to be achieving—or to be on the way to achieving—success 'against the odds' or a reaction to failing an inspection.

Chapter eighteen deals with a literature review of the challenges for—and the limits of—school effectiveness and improvement in the face of social disadvantage. As governments turn their welcome attention to lifting the educational achievements of the whole population rather than the favoured few, there is a danger that they could 'blame' the schools with the most challenging intakes. The chapter serves to remind policy makers that the correlation between disadvantage and low achievement is a feature of all competitive systems.

The advances in methodology, researchers' and practitioners' experience of assessing effectiveness and attempting improvements, the changing political climate and policies—and the wisdom of hindsight—have all contributed to the development of critiques of school effectiveness and school improvement. In chapter nineteen these various criticisms are addressed and answered. In the final chapter twenty the implications of what we have learned from this—by now extensive and significant—area of research and the possibilities for future studies are discussed. The book concludes with a brief personal acknowledgement of what I as an educationalist have gained from my twenty-year odyssey in this field of research.

2

The Study of Institutions

Introduction

This chapter comes from a 1978 journal article which I wrote whilst struggling as a part-time doctoral student whose full-time job was as a research officer on the Fifteen Thousand Hours *project, overseen by Michael Rutter and undertaken by Barbara Maughan, Janet Ouston and myself. In our hectic working schedule the research team grappled with the challenges of empirical research: collecting data in busy and very lively schools; analysing the results using the relatively primitive computing facilities of the early 1970s; clarifying our thoughts on these data and comparing them to other research findings and beginning to write up the results.*

In the evenings and early on Saturday and Sunday mornings, I worked on my thesis, seeking to relate studies of schools to those of other institutions and, through this comparison, to explore whether any of the models of institutional effects fitted with what we were learning about the effects of schools. My supervisors were confident that, if there were patterns to data and hence to relationships in complex organizations, careful scrutiny would reveal them. To me, at the time, it seemed a bit of a fog. I hoped that the supervisors would prove right and that a shape would eventually emerge.

One helpful aid to understanding at that time was reading the literature about research on similar institutions to schools. This illustrated that many of the patterns we were seeing were not peculiar to schools. They clearly represented something fundamental about the way people were likely to behave in certain circumstances—when, for instance, they were supported or rejected, treated with dignity or abused. It is the study of these other institutions—nurseries, hostels and homes—which forms the subject of this chapter.

Re-reading the original article today, a number of the terms appear quaint or anachronistic. We no longer talk about 'approved schools' or about the 'mentally handicapped'. The large district mental hospitals have been replaced with the 'Care in the Community' policy. Nonetheless, the arguments about the capability of either institutions or programmes of care to have long-term influence remain relevant and, in many cases, unresolved.

In recent years there has been an increase in public concern with education which, strengthened by the writings of the Black Paper authors (Cox & Dyson, 1969a, 1969b, 1970, 1975) and their opponents (Johnson & McAthlone, 1970; Rubenstein & Stoneman, 1970) has grown into a national debate. Educational research has also flourished, producing a variety of studies which stem from many disciplinary backgrounds. However, no researchers have as yet presented acceptable ways of comparing the achievements of schools which are sensitive enough to take account of differences in recruitment of pupils. There is little agreement as to what makes a good school.

In this article, research in a quite different field is to be reviewed, with the purpose of constructing a model, which could then be applied to the study of schools. The area of residential institutions has been chosen for three reasons:

- its researchers have been concerned with studying variation between regimes;
- much of it actually has to do with children;
- its utility has been recognized by practitioners (Grygier, 1975).

Although Goffman (1961) in his work on total institutions stressed the similarity of regimes, recent work has emphasized the diversity that exists among places with similar functions (Tizard et al., 1975). Four types of variation between residential institutions have been identified (Tizard et al., 1975): that of ideology, organization, staffing, and resident response. For simplification in this article, these types have been reduced to two main divisions. First, process, which will include aspects of the first three sources of variation. Second, outcome, which is equivalent to resident response, and which may further be subdivided into concurrent and long-term effects.

Concurrent outcome will be concerned with measures of difference between the inmates of institutions while they are still members. Long-term outcome will attempt to compare the results of institutions by following up past inmates and evaluating their progress. Thus, in Sinclair's study of probation hostels (see below), the absconding of a boy would be classed as a concurrent outcome, and the presence or absence of a conviction within two years of leaving, as a long-term one.

Six studies of different groups of residential institutions have been chosen for review and the combined findings will be used to suggest answers to the following questions:

- Are there differences in style between institutions dedicated to the same task?
- If there are, do these differences have any effect on the inmates?

The locations of the studies

Mental hospitals

Brown and Wing (1962) carried out a comprehensive study of three mental hospitals, each of which contained a large group of long-stay schizophrenic patients. The study sought to test whether the varying social conditions of the hospitals would be reflected in the clinical condition of the patients.

They used standardized procedures to classify the clinical condition of a sample of patients, together with two supplementary scales, one concerned with ward behaviour, and one which attempted to capture the self-reported attitude towards hospital discharge of the patients. For social characteristics they used two sets of measurements dealing with the possession of individual personal items, and with the daily management of the wards. The results of the study showed that there were real social differences between the three hospitals in their effects on both major and minor aspects of the patients' lives. There were also significant clinical differences, even when other variables (such as age, length of stay, and social class) were controlled. The study is important in that it demonstrates considerable differences between three separate hospitals ostensibly doing a similar task and drawing patients from a similar population. Most striking was the fact that the number of personal possessions in the different hospitals varied enormously (for example, in one hospital 60 per cent of patients did not even own their toothbrushes).

Residential care for children with special needs

The second study developed from the interest of the Child Development Research Unit of London University in the provision of residential care for retarded children (King et al., 1971). The questions the researchers sought to ask were: What is the effect of the organizational structure on the role of staff? Does staff behaviour influence the development and behaviour of the children? The methodology they used consisted of specially designed scales which sought to account for the differences in practice.[1] These two types of practice resulted in significantly different scores on the scale of child-management practices, even when differences in size of living unit and severity of handicap of the children were taken into account.

Second, in conjunction with this finding of differences in child management, they also found considerable differences in organization, with greater autonomy

---

1 After much pilot work we devised an objective and highly reliable, 30-item child management scale to enable us to measure certain commonly occurring child management practices and so permit comparisons among the units to be made (Tizard et al., 1975, p. 57).

and less role differentiation in the child-oriented units. The institution-oriented units also had less stability of staff and generally employed people who were trained in nursing, rather than childcare. In these units there was less positive staff interaction with the children. Finally, and perhaps most importantly, the children from the child-oriented units were significantly more advanced in feeding and dressing skills and in speech development. However, both of these studies have taken place in institutions where the residents were mentally handicapped, and it may be unwarranted to assume that such findings would apply to other settings; the remainder have been chosen from quite different types of residential institutions.

Residential care

One study which followed from the residential-care project was that of Barbara Tizard, who used similar methods to look at residential nurseries run by British voluntary societies catering mainly for illegitimate children (Tizard, 1975). Unlike the facilities for mentally handicapped children, the nurseries displayed no gross organizational differences; most of them used modern child-centred methods. There were, however, differences in social organization and in the accepted role of the staff. The researchers grouped the nurseries on the basis of these differences into three classes: those with a low amount of autonomy, where most decisions were referred to the matron; those with a much greater level of autonomy, which resulted in informal, self-contained family groups; and those that fell in between, with a mixture of autonomy in some matters and central control in others.

The outcome that was chosen by the researchers for study was language development, and predictions were made that the more informal class of nurseries, with high autonomy of staff, would be likely to provide more opportunities for verbal interactions between children and adults and so would result in a higher level of development.

When the children were tested by a psychologist who was unaware of the predictions, the mean language comprehension score of the second group of nurseries, those with high autonomy, was found to be one and a half standard deviations above the first group, where there was least autonomy. Similar differences were also found in the verbal intelligence tests, but not in the non-verbal ones. From their observations the researchers found that there were differences between these groups of nurseries, not in the actual amount of talk between staff and children, but in the quality of such talk. The researchers suggest that this was because there was more informative staff-talk which used longer sentences, fewer negative commands, and more reading to the children, in the nurseries with higher staff autonomy. This research programme is still continuing in both day and residential nurseries. Control groups of non-institutionalized children are being used to enable direct comparison of the effect of residential upbringing with ordinary home life to be made.

Probation hostels

The fourth study to be discussed was carried out by Ian Sinclair (Sinclair, 1971) and examined differences in the influence of wardens and matrons in probation hostels. At the time the study was carried out there were 23 hostels in England and Wales, usually catering for 19 or 20 men. These men, who were in their late teens, had been committed by the courts to the care of the hostel for one year. Sinclair was interested, first, in whether there were any differences in the regimes imposed by the wardens; and second, if there were, whether these would be reflected in any outcome measures.

Methodologically this study was similar to the others; data were collected about the different regimes and a scale of restrictiveness was constructed. Differences between the hostels included freedom to use television and radio, to go to the dormitory, and to have pin-up photographs on locker doors. This scale correlated with another scale measuring the warden's attitude to control.

As noted earlier, there were two different outcome measures: concurrent outcome, made up of the number of absconding and further offences committed by the men at each hostel and termed the failure rate; and long-term outcome, consisting of the number of offences committed within two years of the inmates leaving the hostel. Sinclair found that the failure rate was associated with the characteristics of the regime imposed by the warden, whereas the long-term outcome was not. In his report he stresses the problems experienced by the wardens and their families and underlines the daunting task that they have to face. Interestingly, he underlines the importance of agreement between the wardens and their wives, which was a feature of hostels with a low failure rate.

Approved schools

At the same time as Sinclair's study was being carried out, research interest was also focused on approved schools, or, as they were later to become, community homes. The Dartington Research Unit studied a number of these (Millham et al., 1975). Their methods were to visit each of the schools for a period of up to 3 weeks and to carry out an intensive research programme consisting of observations, interviews, and the completion of questionnaires. Their aim was to blend the rigour of positivist sociologists with the insights of a more interpretative approach. They found, first, that school regimes varied considerably in aims, in the amount of control exerted, in provision of facilities, and in atmosphere; and second, that these differences had a substantial effect upon the boys in their day-to-day experience, as measured by their responses to the questionnaires.

Like the other studies of institutions, certain outcome measures, chosen from three areas of the boys' lives, were used. These were criminal behaviour; work or further schooling; and family relationships. In their study of the school regimes, the researchers found that there were considerable intake differences between the schools in the form of very different backgrounds for the boys, and this made measurement of outcome difficult. As the authors point out, the factors that are likely to influence a boy after release are considerable and they report that the teasing out of the proportion of influence that the different regimes have contributed is very difficult. Their attempts to follow up the boys' careers consisted of two small-scale surveys carried out in co-operation with after-care officers and involving a group of families. They found that some schools, which had been more successful in promoting staff–pupil relationships and had offered better training facilities, had better outcomes than others when measured at both 1- and 2-year intervals.

Contrasting houses in one approved school
The final study to be reviewed in this article reached quite different conclusions. Interestingly, it was a study of two autonomous houses in an approved school in the same part of the country, and drawing boys from the same classifying school, as that of the Dartington Study. It was carried out by two research workers, who were at that time connected with the school, and has been fully reported by them (Clarke & Cornish, 1972; Cornish & Clarke, 1975). The authors used a variety of techniques to quantify considerable differences in the regimes of the two houses, one based on a traditional approved-school model and the other on the idea of a therapeutic community.

The design of the study was that of a controlled trial. Boys allocated to the school who were judged suitable for a therapeutic regime were randomly allocated to one of the two houses being studied, while those that were not were allocated to a third.

The findings demonstrated striking differences of process in the regimes of houses. Significant differences were found between staff from the two houses in their attitudes to intervention, to school goals and to training in the school. There were also differences in leadership patterns, in frequency of house meetings, in relations with staff, and in matters of personal autonomy.

The differences found in concurrent outcome between the regimes in respect of the boys' attitudes and behaviour is in some ways surprisingly low. Given such different ideological attitudes of the house masters and staff, one might have expected that there would be greater differences in the boys' behaviour. However, as the authors comment, it is difficult to decide whether the similarities in response to the two regimes were due to the fact that life was really very similar in the houses due to the teaching and trade programme being common to both houses, or to the use of inadequate measures.

The measure of long-term outcome was, as in Sinclair's study, the number of offences committed within two years by ex-inmates. Differences both between the two houses and between these and the third house, which had accepted the boys least suitable for a therapeutic regime, were minimal.

Clarke and Cornish then question the value of this type of treatment, based as it is on a 'disease model of delinquency' and a 'medical model of intervention'. In their latest writing on this subject (Clarke & Cornish, 1977), they argue that this negative finding is supported by similar results both in England and in the United States and that it may be explained by the strength of the 'familiar pressures and inducements to delinquent conduct' after the boy has returned home.

Discussion

These six studies have been chosen because they represent good examples of recent work in the field of institutional research. They share a number of common features: all are based on a comparative methodology; all use similar techniques, such as the construction of special scales with which to compare features of the organization; all attempt to use at least one measure of outcome, and all endeavour to relate this to other measures of process.

Theoretical model
By combining these six studies, is it possible to say anything about institutions in general? Can the questions posed in the introduction now be answered?

First, there do appear to be major differences between institutions that are serving the same function and containing the same type of inmate. Brown and Wing reported quite different conditions in the three hospitals. Both the studies dealing with residential nurseries found considerable variation in the organization and deployment of staff. In Sinclair's probation hostels and in the approved schools studied by the Dartington Unit, different regimes were found, and Clarke and Cornish have described the quite different approaches taken by staff in a therapeutic community and in a traditional house. In contrast to the findings of Goffman, whose work largely dealt with such total institutions as prisons and mental hospitals, these studies stress that considerable variation exists between institutions.

The second question concerned the effect that such differences had on the inmates, and here the answer is not so easily provided. First, among researchers who have looked at concurrent outcome, there is considerable agreement that the differences in process do have an effect on the inmates. Brown and Wing found differences in the clinical judgements made of patients, and the Tizards showed that the capabilities of children were related to the organization of the units. The study of probation hostels revealed quite different failure rates, and the Dartington researchers found that there were considerable differences in academic achievement between approved schools, one with the lowest IQ entrants regularly obtaining some of the best results. Similarly there was wide variation in the amount of work training enjoyed by the boys, with some gaining skills that could be used on their release and others being provided with quite irrelevant techniques.

Finally, what the research team termed 'the boys' commitment to the schools', measured through the use of attitude scales, also varied considerably. Clarke and Cornish, however, while finding some difference in the boys' attitudes and behaviour, noted that there were surprisingly few, considering the ideological differences of staff and the practical differences of the regimes. Drawing conclusions from this study is difficult because the boys' lives were regimented through the organization of the school as well as through that of the houses, so that common experiences may therefore have stemmed from the school rather than from the different regimes. However, some differences have been shown to be directly related to regimes, as in the case of absconding behaviour reported by Clarke and Martin (1971).

The weight of the evidence reviewed here suggests that the different processes observed in institutions have an influence on the behaviour of the members of those institutions. Gauging the strength of this influence, however, is rather more difficult. Most researchers have claimed that this is likely to be a powerful influence, while Clarke and colleagues have argued that it is more likely to be fairly limited.

The answer to the next question, of whether this influence is of a lasting nature, depends on the evidence available from measures of long-term outcome. In their follow-up to the study of schizophrenic patients, Wing and Brown (1970) found that 40 patients had either died or been discharged and that 233 remained in the hospitals. In each of the three institutions there were significant changes in social environment, which for approximately a third of the patients were associated with an improvement in their clinical condition. For the purpose of this article, the reality of long-term outcome differences is unclear, because the greatest social improvements during 1960 to 1964 had taken place at the hospital with the worst measures of concurrent outcome.

The children who had been studied in residential nurseries were retested at 4½ years of age (Tizard & Rees, 1974). Because so many of the children had been adopted, however, the study was largely concerned with differences between those living in families and those remaining in institutions, rather than between the different groups of nurseries. Unfortunately, it is not therefore possible to see whether the long-term effect of the differences in language development had persisted.

As noted earlier, the study of probation hostels found that the differences in failure rate disappeared when reconviction within two years of leaving a hostel was used as a long-term outcome measure. Similarly, the study by the Home Office Research Unit found no difference in the reconviction rates of inmates of either of the two specially monitored houses, or between those and that of the third house, which had accepted the least suitable entrants. This conflicts with the findings of Millham et al. (1975), who have also studied approved schools and have found significant differences between two groups of schools at follow-up.

It is possible that no firm answer can yet be given to the question of the length of effect. Perhaps this is due to three of the studies being concerned with delinquency, where being sent to either an approved school or a probation hostel seems to be a good predictor of later offending. Clarke and Cornish have questioned the real value of such institutions in view of their inability to 'cure' delinquency, though they do see them as fulfilling other functions, such as acting as a deterrent to other children, and of providing the only placement available for certain children in desperate need of care and control.

The question of long-term outcome measurement is difficult for two other reasons: the time and location of the measure and the choice of which aspect of behaviour to study. By focusing on events separated in time and place from any former experience, researchers have to separate out complex interactions of different determinants of behaviour. In terms of delinquency, this may represent a criminal offence being explained by the present circumstances of a boy's life, including his home conditions, his relationship with his family, his work situation and his emotional state, or by the effect of the time (anything up to two years) spent in an approved school. It is probable that alternative single-cause factors are unduly simplistic and that any real explanation is likely to involve all of these components. This example, perhaps, emphasizes the difficulty of looking to past experiences in order to explain present behaviour.

The choice of which aspect of behaviour on which to focus is also difficult, for there are often alternatives available without clear criteria on which to base decisions. In the area of delinquency, possible choices might be: further offending—as chosen by Clarke and Cornish—work record, or personal relationships—as examined by Millham et al. The first of these seems to be the most appropriate, because it was initial offending that caused the boy to be sent to an approved school, yet the experiences he will have had there will surely have been much more concerned with the other aspects. Therefore, if the school has an effect, it is more likely to be seen in the boy's work record or in his relationships. Further, because approved schools are a controlled environment, there is not the opportunity for boys to be trained in actually resisting the opportunities of delinquency.

What then is the answer to this question? The evidence from these studies suggests that the long-term influence of institutions may be limited. Unfortunately, two of the groups of researchers were prevented from examining this question. Of the others, only one found clear evidence of lasting effect. A quite different answer may, however, be provided by researchers studying other kinds of institutions. In view of this possibility, perhaps this question should be left unanswered until empirical evidence is available.

What can be learned about the organization of residential institutions?

At this point, it may be useful to speculate on some of the factors which have not been seen as crucial. First, the buildings which house institutions and which often reflect something of their climate do not seem to have a large influence. The gaunt Victorian buildings which house mental hospitals on the outskirts of London certainly convey many of the attitudes of society towards the mentally ill at that time. However, some of the present hospitals have overcome this legacy more successfully than others. In contrast, modern functionally designed buildings provide an excellent start, but are not able to guarantee successful institutions.

Second, the question of size is often discussed in relation to many different areas, including mental hospitals, schools, and hostels. A fairly common view has developed that institutions have to be big enough to run economically, and to enjoy the benefits of staff specialization and added resources. Present thinking is often a reaction to this, and 'smallness' is seen as a main aim of reorganization. However, the research that is being carried out, although often reporting favourably on small units, certainly does not find that this alone is able to guarantee successful functioning. Similarly, large institutions are not always reported as being unsuccessful.

Third, with regard to staff provision it is certainly true that in the past some institutions have been chronically short-staffed, and that this has hindered them enormously. It seems, however, that a low staff–inmate ratio is not of itself beneficial. Tizard & Tizard (1975) report two types of practice in nurseries: one where staffing is flexible, with full resources being used at crucial times, such as early morning and evening when the children need most attention; the other with a lower ratio, where the number of staff on duty remains constant during the day, even at relatively slack periods.

If modern buildings, small numbers, and adequate staff are not in themselves guarantees of good practice, they are at least able to provide certain advantages. The intention of this comment is to emphasize that they are not in themselves sufficient and that, as comparative studies have demonstrated, other factors are also important. What, then, are these other factors?

Use of buildings

It does seem that the way a building is used and maintained is as important as its initial design. Thus, even old Victorian buildings can be adapted, and living conditions improved. Likewise, modern buildings can be neglected and abused, so that the impact upon residents is depressing. In hostels, for example, it seems that having a new building is often seen to be sufficient and that little effort is made to enhance it, while staff who have to work in old ill-adapted buildings are often so aware of their surroundings that a great deal of effort is invested in improvements and decorations.

Level of organization and autonomy

As has been noted, size alone is not crucial; rather it seems it is the level of organization that matters. In large organizations, genuine responsibility has to be delegated at realistic levels. The nursery units organized as part of hospitals had difficulties because all decisions, even routine ones, had to be taken by the matron.

One major feature of staff conditions to emerge from the research is the importance of autonomy. It does seem that people are likely to take more interest in their work if they are able to control the way in which they act. In the nurseries, the heads of units that enjoy autonomy provided richer experiences for the children than those that regarded themselves mainly as child-minders.

Use of staff

An example has already been given of poor use of staff resources in nurseries; the flexibility of arrangements does seem to be more important than the mere numbers involved. A further requirement of nurseries is for the arrangements to encompass the need of children for continuity of relationships. Although changes of staff are inevitable, some nurseries have been able to organize their resources so that the effect of this is minimized.

Respect for inmates

Historically, inmates of institutions have often been regarded as inferior and unable to take simple decisions about personal matters. The legacy of this patronizing view is still found in some institutions, as Goffman has illustrated. The reasons for such a view lie partly in the philosophy of the Victorians—who established so many institutions of different kinds—and partly in the logistic problems of managing a large group of inmates with a minimum of staff. Today there is no justification for such a view and, indeed, there is strong evidence that the conditions of inmates, both material and psychological, do have an effect on the clinical state of mental hospital patients and on the development of young children.

A different aspect of respect for inmates can be recognized in the provision, in some approved schools, for training in practical skills. Some schools teach skills which are likely to be of use to the boys in earning their living after their discharge; in others, the craft training is clearly inappropriate to the prevailing labour market.

The institutions that have been discussed here are very different, yet have certain similarities in that they are all made up of two classes of members: medical staff and patients, teachers and pupils, nurses and young children, or wardens and probationers. None of this second class of inmates is, in any real sense, voluntary; all are subject to the authority of the institution. The staff, in contrast, possess considerable power but are in highly demanding jobs, often in difficult conditions, and sometimes having to work unsocial hours.

The ideas that have been discussed in this section of the article apply to all of these types of institutions and perhaps illustrate that there are no simple reforms that may be executed in order to make all successful. Rather, it seems that a successful institution is one in which all the features discussed here are used flexibly to produce a climate that is both stimulating and productive for the inmates, and satisfying for the staff.

What can teachers learn from these studies?

By examining studies of different types of institutions teachers may increase their understanding of the complex interactions between pupils and schools. Schools are often seen as having uniform influence upon pupils. For instance, research in the United States has suggested that the impact of schooling is slight when compared with other factors such as racial or family characteristics (Coleman, 1966; Jencks, 1973).

The six studies that have been reviewed above would suggest that this view of schools should be re-examined. If such diverse institutions as day nurseries, mental hospitals, and approved schools exhibit striking differences between particular patterns of care and their effects on the members, then it is surely likely that schools would also show similar variation.

An empirical study would enable this question to be answered, and indeed the work of Power et al. (1967), Cannan (1970), and Reynolds et al. (1976) has already suggested that the answer is likely to be that schools, in common with other institutions, also have varied impacts on children. What must, however, be made quite clear in such a study is that the school differences, if they are found to exist, are not just reflections of intake difference; it is possible that in both ability and behaviour school intakes are not uniform. Therefore, school differences in outcome measures should only be regarded as important if they continue to exist once adjustments have been made for variation in intake.

If a school study were to show such differences, and researchers were able to relate them to factors such as school policy, methods of organization, styles of discipline, or teacher attitudes towards pupils, in fact to just the factors that have been described above as process measures, then considerable progress would have been made towards identifying which factors are correlated with pupil success.

Such a project needs to be carried out. Teachers and school administrators would benefit considerably from such a comparative study, as ultimately, perhaps, would students. Not only could a practical way of judging a good school be identified, but the factors that contribute to its success would also be open to exploration.

What can educational researchers learn from these studies?

The previous section of this chapter has argued that teachers could gain from these studies. Educational researchers could also learn from them, and indeed they need to do so in order to enable teachers to co-operate on a study of schools.

The process–outcome model is not one which has often been applied to schools, surprisingly perhaps in view of the number of educational studies that have been carried out (Mortimore, 1977). However, it may well be an appropriate model to use at a time when public interest in education is common. If outcome were to be defined as either academic performance in examinations or as behaviour measured in or out of school, then schools could be evaluated in a similar way to the other institutions described in this review.

As with the other institutions, it would be helpful to relate process factors to the outcome, having accounted for the effects of differences in intake. Such a study would then provide a good test of the ideas that have been discussed here. Some possible questions might be:

• Does the type of building appear important?
• Is autonomy of staff valuable?
• Does the attitude of teachers towards pupils affect their performance?

In addition the study might shed light on the unresolved question of the permanence of long-term outcomes. Because of the nature of schools, the possible variation between the members of schools entering the world of higher education and work is likely to be considerably greater than between the ex-inmates of approved schools. Educational qualifications may ensure that this variation, in the accredited status of school leavers, is not only maintained but increased. Thus it may be that the question of long-term outcome can be answered in a way that has not been possible within studies of other kinds of institutions.

In this chapter, six studies of residential institutions have been reviewed and their findings interpreted in a process–outcome model. An argument has been presented that such a model could profitably be applied to the study of schools and that such an application would be likely to be of value to both researchers and teachers. At a time of falling enrolment and increasing arguments over the value of parental choice, a way of systematically evaluating schools able to take account of intake differences is surely overdue.

Postscript

The focus on institutions other than schools, and on their effects, does appear to provide a reasonable basis for the study of schools. Terms such as 'intake, 'process' and 'outcome' can be used equally well with a variety of institutions. The point about intake differences is crucial. It was important for the institutions noted here and it is so for schools. Until appropriate ways of taking account of the stark differences between patients, entrants to residential care or school students are found, any potential comparisons of efficacy remain flawed. This is a theme which will surface time and time again over the twenty years in which the contributions to this book have been written.

3

Schools as Institutions

Introduction

In this chapter the focus of the book shifts onto schools. It was written in parallel with the previous chapter but, due to the publishing schedules of the different journals, actually appeared in print a few months before it, towards the end of 1977. This chapter, therefore, is based on my earliest published work, written over twenty years ago.

During the Fifteen Thousand Hours *study, the constant conversations within the research team were enormously helpful in developing my understanding of the effects of schools. Having worked intensively within two successive schools for the preceding nine years, I began both the research project and the thesis with what I now realize was a false confidence. I soon learned that working in an institution was very different from researching it. I needed to distance myself from my previous teaching experience and from my role (a head of department in a large inner-city comprehensive school) in order to comprehend the bigger picture. I also had to learn the difference between the conviction that one feels from personal experience and hard evidence culled systematically—the collected views of students and teachers. Like other practitioners before me, I had to come to terms with the reality that not everything is researchable; when comparing a number of schools there will be several factors in which the variation between the institutions is so small that it cannot sensibly be studied in depth.*

On the other hand, I also discovered the opportunities afforded by research to focus on specific aspects of schooling and, with this 'magnified' view, to understand the patterns of interactions and even, at times, to gain insights into the causal relations operating in particular circumstances. I recall, for example, the sequence of actions (in a swimming lesson observed by one of our team) which followed directly from an instructor striking a student. The ensuing débâcle involved several students hitting their fellows and ended with one very unhappy scapegoat. The incident provided an unusually clear illustration of the power of modelling!

In this article, six studies employing a variety of different research techniques are reviewed. By combining the different methods from these studies it is possible to construct a model of school evaluation which itself will enable key questions to be asked about the efficacy of schools: how different are they and do such differences have any effects on students?

Although, as has already been noted, differences have been reported in studies of schools, both Coleman (1966) and Jencks (1973) have argued that schools are unimportant in their effects. The question of whether differences in the ongoing behaviour of members of institutions are reflected in outcome measures was discussed in the last chapter, though no definite conclusion was reached for it appeared that the point at which outcome measures were collected was crucial to the answer. In any form of evaluative research this is a fundamental problem and members of the Home Office Research Unit have researched it in considerable detail (Clarke & Cornish, 1972, 1977; Cornish & Clarke, 1975). Their view is that any differences between institutions, though interesting, are unimportant unless they are also reflected in long- term outcomes. The work of the unit has been concerned with the treatment of delinquency in residential approved schools, and the outcome measure has been the number of inmates who have committed further offences within two years of discharge.

Many different types of measures have been used in the studies of schools and, in order to fit the theoretical model, these have been categorized into three groups. Organizational structures have been classified as process measures; outcomes consist of the behaviour of pupils, both social and academic. Outcomes have been further subdivided into concurrent outcomes, dealing with present behaviour and longer term outcomes, concerned with subsequent behaviour— which may or may not be measurable in the school career of students.

Because of this strategy, a large number of interesting school studies have inevitably been excluded from the discussion. Both individual case studies such as those by Hargreaves (1967) or Lacey (1970) and the broader comparative work of the National Foundation for Educational Research (Monks, 1968) have been omitted, though the former have been important in alerting practitioners to the unintended consequences of pupil grouping practices, and the latter in documenting some of the organizational details of schools.

The school studies

Delinquency in Tower Hamlets

The first study to be considered is concerned with juvenile delinquency in Tower Hamlets (Power et al., 1967). The research team gathered data on all young people who had court appearances between 1958 and 1964 and analysed the results into different enumeration districts (EDs) of about 600 people and also into the different schools attended by offenders. They uncovered large differences in the numbers of court appearances of young people living in these districts. In some, as many as 12 per cent of the boys of one age cohort made a first court appearance each year whilst, in others, the comparable figure was one per cent. The researchers also looked at the schools the boys attended and found that, for the twenty secondary modern schools which took over 85 per cent of the boys in the area, there were dramatic differences in delinquency rates. During the six years on which data were available, four schools had an average of between 1 and 2 per cent of boys making first appearances. For three other schools, the average figures were between 5 and 7 per cent. These school differences in court appearances were not explained away by differences in size, type of building, or status (i.e. whether the school was voluntary or run by the local authority), by the selection process, by the fact that some were mixed and some were for boys alone or by the ethnic mix of the pupils.

When the court data were examined for second and subsequent offences, differences between the high- and low-scoring schools were even greater. Thus the three schools that had averages of between 5 and 7 per cent first appearances now had between 13 and 19 per cent of total court appearances whilst the four schools with low proportions now only accounted for 2.6 per cent. What is interesting about these figures is that they remain consistent over time, with the schools at both extremes of the range altering their positions very little. Having tested to see if this school variation was independent of the district in which the boys lived, the researchers concluded that some schools were able to protect their boys from delinquency whilst others may well have put their pupils at risk.

Unfortunately this study was prevented by the local education authority from continuing, after pressure had been mounted by teachers' associations. It would have been very interesting to have carried out the type of organizational analysis pioneered by Hargreaves and Lacey within schools with both high and low delinquency rates.

The study has been criticized by Baldwin (1972) on the grounds that the procedure of separating school from area influences was inadequate. He argues that precise information concerning the catchment area, the amount of parental choice and the reputations of the schools was needed before the claim of school difference could be made with confidence. His criticisms highlight the difficulty of separating out influences on outcome measures and, unfortunately, Power et al. did not have any measures of the boys before they entered secondary schools and the research team were thus unable to answer these points.

Delinquency in another London borough

Another study of delinquency in London is that of Cannan (1970). She was able to collect information about 400 court appearances over a period of six months. When the cases were analysed on an area basis only vague overlapping stress factors emerged, but when data were broken down between schools it was found that 53 per cent attended only 5 of the 66 possible schools. When the data were further analysed into categories of offence, and mean age of offender, clear differences between schools emerged. Some schools had an early onset of delinquency giving a mean age of 14.1 years whilst the mean of the others was, 12 months later, at 15.1 years. The type of offence also varied between schools, with students from some schools 'specializing' in theft or driving and taking away cars whilst others appeared to focus on vandalism or the possession of dangerous weapons.

Cannan argues that these findings support the view put forward by Power et al. that school factors are independent of other considerations in the 'genesis of an individual's delinquent career'. The fact that differences in the patterns of delinquency emerged between schools suggests that some schools are able to protect children from the risk of delinquency even when they live in a area of high risk. However, what Cannan is not able to answer is which aspects of the school are involved in these processes. Is it something about the organization of the schools or is it simply the influence of so many peers with delinquent backgrounds? As with the Power study, this is a key question that needs answering.

South Wales study

David Reynolds (1974, 1975; Reynolds et al., 1976) has been studying nine schools in a homogenous, economically deprived, working-class community. The schools involved are all secondary moderns, taking the lower two-thirds of the ability range, and data have been gathered on three outcome measures: delinquency, attendance and attainment over six years. The figures show that there are large differences in the types of pupils that the schools have been producing over this period. Delinquency, as defined by a court conviction or an official caution, ranged amongst the schools from 3.8 to 10.5 per cent of all boys. Attendance figures varied from 77.2 per cent to 89.4 per cent and attainment (which in this case has been measured by entry into the local technical college) ranges from 8.6 to 50 per cent. Even more interesting is the fact that Reynolds found remarkable consistency in these results. Schools that were high on truancy, one year, remained high. Similarly, those that sent their pupils into the technical college repeated this regularly. What substantiates the author's claim that schools do make a difference is the fact that the school measures are consistent with each other. In other words, schools which are high on delinquency are low on attainment and also low on attendance. Such variation could of course be explained by inconsistencies in the collection of data, by the schools' entry policy rather than attainment and by the differential response by the police, although these have all been investigated by the author. Crucially, the findings could reflect differences of intake, with some schools, owing to their reputations, attracting 'better pupils' while others have to accept 'worse' ones. However, this does not seem to be the case, as each of the schools draws its population from geographically separate areas of the community and there is, as a result, no parental choice.

Reynolds has used extensive outcome measures. He is fortunate in enjoying good relations with the local education authority and the teachers involved and so is in a position to attempt to unravel what it is about the schools that may be responsible for the differences found. Preliminary findings suggest that certain of the schools have unofficially 'negotiated agreements' between staff and pupils whilst others have been unable to reach any such consensus so that rebellion and delinquency may well result. The work is continuing. The author has summarized the outcome measures to produce an overall school performance rate and then compared this to the number of unemployed school leavers for each school for the four months following the official leaving date in 1972 (Reynolds et al., 1976). This report showed clearly that the most successful schools also had the best employment rate and that those with the lowest overall ranking had the worst.

Isle of Wight/Inner London comparative study

This study of a comparison between the Isle of Wight (IOW) and an inner London borough (ILB) by a team from the Institute of Psychiatry has been well reported (Berger et al., 1975; Rutter, 1973; Rutter et al., 1974, 1975a, 1975b). It was concerned with measuring the prevalence of psychiatric disorders and of specific reading retardation in these two areas. Many of the details of research methodology are not relevant to the subject of this book and will not be repeated here; only the relevant educational findings will be given. Three separate measures on which the two areas could be compared were created. These were: the incidence of psychiatric disorder; the rate of deviance—as assessed by a teacher questionnaire; and the amount of specific reading retardation. The measure of deviance[1] was also used as a screening instrument with children selected for further study if they had deviant scores on this or if they formed part of a randomly selected control group. Further measures consisted of standardized parental interviews and an individual diagnosis. As the first area studied (IOW) contained no children whose parents were immigrant, all such children in the London area were excluded and formed another distinct sample, the results of which are published separately (see Rutter et al., 1974).

The main conclusions of the study were that children from ILB scored considerably higher than those from IOW on all measures. Thus the teacher-rated scale of behavioural dysfunction was 19.1 per cent of ILB children compared to 10.6 for IOW. The rate of psychiatric disorder, as assessed by psychiatric interview, was lower, but still in similar proportion: 12 per cent ILB and 6 per cent IOW. Finally, the reading retardation rate was 6.6 per cent ILB and 3.8 per cent IOW.

---

1 For a fuller explanation of the construction and use of the teacher rating scale see Rutter et al. (1970).

In relating these findings to features of both family life and school conditions, the authors found that London families were more often discordant and disrupted and schools had a higher rate of turnover of both staff and pupils. Rutter et al., like Power et al. and Reynolds suggest that some schools may be more successful than others in reducing children's problems. However, London schools are likely to have a far higher proportion of such problems than one would expect in a rural, less crowded area. Certain gross features of school organization have been related to these outcome measures but a much more detailed analysis of what happens in the schools that are associated with either less or more problems is needed.

The Northern study

One study that has attempted to look at differences in the perception of pupils in both schools with high and low delinquency figures has been carried out in a northern city. Finlayson and Loughran (1976) used a similar strategy to Power, Cannan and Reynolds for gaining outcome measures. Data were collected from juvenile court records during a five-month period and the number of court cases per school was calculated. The authors selected four schools, of which two were voluntary aided and two were maintained by the local authority. Each pair consisted of one school with a high, and one with a low, rate of delinquency. These pairs were matched on other factors such as buildings, organization and type of catchment area. All the boys in the fourth years of the four schools were given confidential questionnaires to complete, which consisted of four scales. These have been described in full[2] and were also used in the NFER study mentioned earlier. Two of the scales refer to pupil behaviour and two to teacher behaviour. Using these data the researchers then looked at three sets of perceptions: between delinquent and non-delinquent pupils in the same school; between upper- and lower-stream pupils also in the same school; and between pupils in the high and low delinquency schools. The results showed that in all four schools boys in the top streams were more accepting of work tasks, and saw their teachers as less authoritarian, than boys in lower streams, who felt themselves to be working in a less supportive atmosphere. Secondly, in the high delinquency schools the boys were seen to be less work oriented and to be deriving less social and emotional satisfaction from school.

This is an interesting study, but is open to several criticisms. First, the sample size is small, only 166 boys divided between eight classrooms. Second, the delinquency rate is very different for the two pairs of schools: the rate for the voluntary school with low delinquency being only just less than the rate for the controlled school with high delinquency. Third, although indices for 'social decay' are given, no effort seems to have been made to control for social conditions of individual boys or for the catchment area boundaries. Hence, the same criticisms as were made by Baldwin about the Power study apply here. Fourth, all the data are self-report measures and—as stated by the authors—may lack

---

2   See the administrative manual for Pupils' Perception Questionnaire II (Finlayson, D.S. (1970). Slough: NFER.)

'objective assessment'. Nevertheless, they argue that perceptions may in some cases be more real than objective observations, although it is difficult to accept that observations would not have aided the analysis. The study is valuable, however, in that it uses outcome measures collected from court data and attempts to relate these to the process measures gathered in the schools. The problem is that with only four schools it is very difficult to identify any patterns of causality in such complex organizations.

Teaching styles

The final study is a report of a research programme undertaken in primary schools (Bennett, 1976). This was a project which attempted to relate teaching style to pupil performance as measured by special tests in reading, English and mathematics in 37 classrooms. The style of the teacher was designated as the result of a survey of 468 questionnaire replies to detailed questions concerning teaching methods, classroom organization, curriculum, discipline, assessment of work, allocation of teaching time and opinions about educational issues. On the basis of these replies, 12 distinct teacher types were constructed. These ranged from very informal to very formal. Owing to limitations of resources, only seven of these types were validated by observation methods and were used in the study.

The findings suggest that children's attainment increased in the formal classrooms more than in either the mixed or the informal ones in tests of English and mathematics. However, in reading, the mixed classrooms achieved the most progress. Bennett also observed, within a sample of classrooms, interaction between the pupils and the teacher and related the test results to these observations, in order to see if certain children responded differentially to teaching styles because of personality traits. He found that formal classrooms again seemed to be better for all pupils, thus claiming that teaching style had a more powerful effect than personality of the pupils on achievement.

This research has stimulated much discussion on the educational issues involved and, in particular, on whether a 'child-centred' approach is justifiable in view of these results. It is as yet too early to report what any eventual consensus may be, but a number of criticisms may be made about the study. First, despite the existence of the 12 teacher types, in fact only three groups were used and, of these, the mixed group covered a very large range of teacher behaviour. Second, there was no control for the children's history of schooling—this applies to the previous year as well as to the length of time spent in the infants' school. Thirdly, there may have been a confounding effect of the 11-plus examination which was taken in some but not all of the schools.

Of the total sample, 13 schools took the 11-plus and 24 did not, but this turned out to mean that 42 per cent of the formal schools and of the mixed schools were involved in the selection process, in comparison to only 23 per cent of the informal ones. In view of the fact that the study found overall gains in the 11-plus schools in all areas of assessment, this is of crucial importance and one wonders why schools were not chosen from either an area which had abolished the exam, or one that still maintained it, or why this factor was controlled not for with an equal number from each. Fourth, there have been numerous criticisms of the statistical treatment involving the unit of analysis and the actual calculations.[3] Whether these are crucial is not yet clear. The ultimate value of the study may well rest on its combination of outcome and process measures and on its seeking to make possible an evaluation of teaching style.

Discussion of issues arising from these studies

Use of a model

Six different studies of schools have been reviewed and their findings briefly noted. A variety of methods have been used by the researchers, who have concentrated on several aspects of school-functioning. The basic aim, however, has been similar: to compare certain schools and to show that some appear to be more successful than others. Each researcher has presented evidence concerning some measure of performance, such as social behaviour, personal adjustment or academic skill. This chapter has sought to combine these partial answers in order to say something about schools in general, taking as a sample the 100 or so schools used in the different studies. By using the terms 'process' and 'outcome', both concurrent and long term, an effort has also been made to provide a methodological framework for further research.

The strategy of combining six different studies has obvious weaknesses yet also has strengths. If similar answers can be obtained from quite different studies, the argument gains in credibility. The questions posed earlier were: are schools different, and, if so, do such differences have any effect on the students? Tentative answers to these questions will be offered through an examination of both the methods and findings of these studies.

Use of process measures

Unlike the residential studies reported in the last chapter, not all the school research was able to measure process or the current features of life in the schools. Both Power's and Cannan's data were restricted to external measures of delinquency, though in the case of the former the plan to include detailed observations within the schools was frustrated by the withdrawal of support by both the education authority and the teachers' associations. However, each of the four remaining studies was able to include data on some of the features of the school. In the Rutter study, this consisted only of statistical information supplied by the education authority. But Bennett carried out observations of actual teaching and also had self-reported questionnaires of teachers. The recorded perceptions of the pupils were used for this purpose by Finlayson and Loughran and the most detailed study has so far been carried out by Reynolds.

---

3 See article by Rogers and Barron in *The Times Educational Supplement,* 30 April 1976, and also letter from H. Goldstein in *The Times Educational Supplement*, 7 May 1976.

Use of outcome measures

What have been termed 'concurrent outcome measures' have been used by each of the researchers. In the work of Power, Cannan, Reynolds and Finlayson, these have consisted of measures of delinquency taken whilst the pupils were still attending the schools, even though they actually occurred outside of school life. The deviance rating used by Rutter was, in contrast, completed in school by the teachers. These measures have been concerned with behaviour rather than academic success, but the latter has also been used as a concurrent outcome, by Bennett in the form of attainment tests; by Rutter, through a measure of reading retardation; and by Reynolds, in the form of the number of acceptances at a technical college.

The long-term outcome measure as used by the Home Office Research Unit is not easily available to school researchers, though it is certainly of great importance if the claim of long-term impotence of schools that is made by Coleman and Jencks is to be critically examined. In these six studies, only Reynolds has been able to incorporate such a measure, through the employment figures of the ex-pupils of his schools.

Findings

In answering the first question as to whether differences between schools exist, Bennett found differences in teachers' styles and in organization. Rutter found differences between schools and Finlayson found interesting patterns of variations in his student perceptions. Reynolds, although his study is not completed, has suggested that quite different attitudes exist between the students and teachers of different schools.

The second question asks whether these differences are likely to have any real influence upon the pupils. The various studies reviewed have demonstrated differential outcomes in delinquency, the numbers of children showing behaviour problems and in academic attainment. These differences have been found when the intake has been shown to be similar and also where there have been initial differences which have been taken into account. Therefore it seems reasonable to conclude that schools vary in these important respects.

On the basis of these findings, is it possible to define a 'good' school? First, in terms of behaviour outside the school, it seems clear that some schools are able to protect their students from participation in delinquent acts, even when they live in areas of high risk. Second, it appears that some schools are able to ensure considerably less misbehaviour than others. Whether the same processes within the schools affect both these outcomes is not clear. The same process may produce one result in class behaviour and another in corridors or playgrounds. There may also be differences in their effect due to the sex composition of the school or to size factors. It is possible, however, to speculate about the type of processes which are at work:

- *A large number of pupils having the opportunity of succeeding in some aspect of school life.* This obviously has implications for grouping practices, for the allocation of resources and for the means of conferring of status. Hargreaves' (1967) study portrays a school where only half the pupils had such opportunities and where, as a result, a distinctive anti-school subculture was maintained.

- *The existence of appropriate models of behaviour in staff and senior pupils.* The role of modelling as a powerful form of learning has been experimentally investigated by social learning theorists (Bandura et al., 1961). In school settings it provides a mechanism whereby the interaction between teachers and pupils becomes a model for that between different pupils, though as yet the precise mechanisms which underlie such imitation and learning are not clear (Danziger, 1971).

- *The use of a small number of 'explicit' rules acceptable to both staff and pupils.* Clegg and Megson (1968) have written of the dangers of having a large number of unenforceable rules which become devalued, and the importance of the fair implementation of discipline procedures has been stressed by a practising teacher discussing different school organizations (Giles, 1975). The particular kinds of atmosphere that are achieved by schools vary considerably, partly as a result of the amount of attention paid to such rules, and partly as a result of the prevailing philosophies of education amongst teachers. In some schools confrontation and challenge are seen as the means of maintaining control whilst in others, such a policy is viewed as highly detrimental to staff-pupil relations, to be avoided whenever possible.

- *The availability of help and support for pupils.* The range of problems that can be faced by some pupils is large (see Galloway, 1976). Some of these stem from home backgrounds whilst others are the direct result of schools; all need to be dealt with to prevent, not only the unhappiness of the individual, but possible disturbance to the class or school. Examples of such problems noted by an ex-school counsellor are: children who have found the change from primary to secondary school difficult; those experiencing difficulty in reading and writing, leading to feelings of frustration and aggression; those who have an excess of physical energy and not enough space to 'let off steam' and those who have had a weak teacher who failed to stimulate or stretch them (Jones, 1976).

With regard to attainment, it is undoubtedly true that some schools get better academic results than others. In view of the large amount of research which has shown that the pupils' first demand of a school is its ability to teach successfully (Musgrove and Taylor, 1972), this is obviously a point of major importance. Nash's (1973) research on attitudes of pupils has demonstrated that children are very good judges of teachers' views of their ability (which is one possible explanation of the means by which self-fulfilling prophecies are constructed and maintained). In an interesting theoretical reconstruction of streaming conditions, Lacey (1975) has shown that increased examination performance was more related to the school organization than to the designated ability of the pupils. Therefore, any school which is actively aiming to prevent pupils from 'giving up' academic subjects, and is going to encourage and sustain motivation, should be counted as 'good'; though having raised expectations of success in the pupils, naturally a school will have to provide competent teaching, suitable courses, and a degree of continuity for the students.

In terms of conditions, some schools are able to achieve both a pleasant physical environment, even in older accommodation, and a warm personal climate in which good staff–pupil relationships are valued highly by both parties. Without the academic success, these may not be appreciated by the pupils, yet if these conditions are compared to those in which no pride is taken in the buildings, where broken furniture and graffiti are allowed to remain for long periods, and where staff and students are engaged in power struggles then the contrast is striking.

These areas of school life are my choices; they have support from the research literature, though there are obviously many paths to achieving a 'good' school. Unlike studies of residential institutions, the existence of long-term outcomes is not in doubt, because of the role of schools in shaping the occupation of the ex-student.

What is now needed is a comparative study, which, whilst identifying and controlling for any intake differences that do exist, is able systematically to relate these to the outcomes in a predictable way. Thus poor outcome in attainment could possibly be shown to occur in schools where staff and pupil turnover is high. Even better than this would be a study which was able to identify the very complex factors within schools, which are associated with both low delinquency and high attainment outcomes. Such a study would of course need a high level of co-operation between researchers and the heads, staff and pupils of any schools concerned; yet if this were forthcoming it would be valuable in highlighting the processes that contribute to the different ways possible of making a 'good' school.

Postscript

When I wrote this article in 1977 I was trying to interpret the results of some of the most interesting school studies of the 1960s and 1970s. Re-reading it, I am struck by how the technique—crude though it was—generally worked. The same themes recur: the methodological importance of controlling for intake; the variations between schools; and the appearance of potential mechanisms of effectiveness such as modelling and high expectations.

The controversial Bennett study was subsequently reanalysed by the author and colleagues (Aitkin & Bennett, 1980). The result led to a substantial re-interpretation of the previous results.

It is worth reiterating the point made in my introductory remarks about the difference between 'knowing' a school as a participant and as a researcher. In a number of countries today, teachers are expected to draw on research techniques in order to enhance their teaching and understanding of school processes. This, in my judgement, is a positive move which, twenty years later, echoes the views of a highly distinguished English educationalist—Lawrence Stenhouse. Today's proponents sometimes forget, however, that it is extremely difficult for teachers to do this without adequate training and—preferably—some experience of the educational system outside their own school. The 'transitional' experience that I received, studying first for a master's degree and then for a doctorate at the beginning of my research career, enabled me to develop a more informed perspective. Contemporary teachers who wishes to make a similar transition now have many more opportunities to do so: they can take a master's degree which focuses on school effectiveness or enrol on a course which leads to a doctor of education. Such courses provide many experiences and opportunities to ease and support the transition between the role of practitioner and researcher.

4

Effective Schools for Secondary Students[1]

Introduction

This chapter is based on brief extracts from Fifteen Thousand Hours *(Rutter et al., 1979a) and an article which appeared in* Concern, *a regular journal of the National Children's Bureau. The article was written following a presentation made at the 1980 Annual Conference of the Bureau at the University of Bath. The Conference was quite a milestone in my research career. My fellow speakers included Jerome Bruner—who was returning to the United States after a few years at Oxford—and the distinguished American paediatrician T. Berry Brazleton. Outside of the conference we discussed Anglo-American differences in popular attitudes to schooling.*

The slow birth of British studies of school effectiveness has been described in chapters two and three. The publication of Fifteen Thousand Hours *dramatically upped the stakes. Its research methodology was quite different from previous studies of schools. The comparison of outcomes—having taken as much account as possible of differences in the backgrounds of the students—provided a much harder edge to the study. Given such data, it was possible to identify schools which promoted, to a greater extent, student achievement and a range of social outcomes. These results could have been used in a negative way to*

---

1 The original book on which this chapter is based was written by Michael Rutter, Barbara Maughan, Peter Mortimore and Janet Ouston.

attack teachers and to focus on unacceptable standards. In fact, the research team went out of its way to focus on the positive aspects of the study and on the achievements of the successful schools.

The publication of the study was nevertheless controversial. The most sustained attacks came from academics rather than practitioners and, as chapter seven makes clear, probably stemmed from a variety of reasons.

> For almost a dozen years during a formative period of their development children spend almost as much of their waking life at school as at home. Altogether this works out at some 15,000 hours (from the age of five until school leaving) during which schools and teachers may have an impact on the development of the children in their care. Do a child's experiences at school have any effect; does it matter which school he goes to; and which are the features of school that matter? These are the issues which gave rise to the study of twelve London secondary schools. The research findings provide a clear 'yes' in response to the first two questions. Schools do indeed have an important impact on children's development and it does matter which school a child attends. Moreover, the results provide strong indications of what are the particular features of school organisation and functioning which make for success. (Rutter et al., 1979a, p. 1).

Recent educational research has claimed that schools do not exert a powerful influence on children's development. Researchers have not argued that schools are ineffective in the teaching of skills but that the personal characteristics of children, such as their intelligence, their social class and their ethnic origin, are likely to be of much greater importance than any school effect on their subsequent lives (Jencks et al., 1972).

This view, however, is not always accepted by parents, who may consider that a particular school is likely to have a powerful influence on a child's learning. In both the maintained and the private sectors of schooling, parents frequently go to elaborate lengths to send their child to a particular school, in the belief that the educational outcome will be better for the child than at any alternative.

How then can these two views of schooling be reconciled? Have the researchers been measuring the wrong things, or are parents misguided in their enthusiasm for particular schools? Similar questions can also be posed in connection with other types of institutions such as children's homes and hospitals. Studies of these have been reviewed elsewhere (chapter two).

A study of secondary schools and their effects on children

Questions such as those posed above led to a longitudinal study of the progress of over 2,000 children through 12 similar secondary schools in London (Rutter et al., 1979a). Earlier work (noted in chapter three) had enabled a large group of ten-year-olds to be tested in their primary schools, and these children were followed through secondary schooling.

One difficulty, already well rehearsed, concerns the fact that the intake to schools varies considerably. Some schools accept a number of children who, at age 11, have a history of learning difficulties; others receive a proportion of students who have shown behaviour problems in primary school. Endeavouring to compare the performance of these schools with others taking fewer students with problems is unfair. As has been stressed, a technique has to be found of judging performance whilst, simultaneously, taking into account any initial differences in intake.

Overall research strategy

The following extract describes the strategy adopted in *Fifteen Thousand Hours*.

> Our principal concern throughout the research has been to investigate the reasons why there are differences between schools in terms of various measures of their students' behaviour and attainments; and to determine how schools influence children's progress. As we have seen in our discussion of other comparable studies, any evaluation of this kind must involve assessments of at least four rather different features.
>
> First, measures are needed on the characteristics of individual students at the time they enter secondary school. There are important individual differences between children with respect to their social background, cognitive abilities and behaviour which may be relevant to their later development and progress. These individual differences must be taken into account in any study of possible school influences on children's progress. We will refer to these measures of what the children were like at the time they were admitted to the twelve schools under the general heading of *intake*.
>
> Secondly, measures must be developed for the particular facets of the *process* of schooling which are to be studied. In our case, the focus here was on the social organisation of the schools and on the types of environments for learning which they provided for their pupils.
>
> Thirdly, the *outcomes* of schooling for these students must be examined to assess the extent to which they have met their relevant educational goals. In this way, the performance of a school is reflected in the attainments and behaviour of the children who went there. The basic strategy of the research involved an evaluation of the ways in which outcomes are affected by school processes, after making due allowance for the effects of individual intake characteristics.
>
> This approach to the analysis of our data provided an essential basis for the study of possible school influences on children's

development. However, as a model of schooling it greatly oversimplifies the many influences at work. What we have termed school processes are likely to be influenced not only by the policies of the school, but also by the pupils themselves. Schools are not self-contained institutions, and what happens within them will be affected by the communities they serve. Eggleston (1977) has described this set of interactions between the school and its environment under the title of 'The Ecology of the School'.

Our fourth set of measures concerns some of these ecological influences. In our analyses we were concerned to determine both how far these ecological factors were associated with variations in outcome, and also how far their effect was mediated through an influence on school processes. (Rutter et al., 1979a, pp. 43–4)

Outcomes

In order to investigate the extent of school influence, four measures of student outcomes were chosen. These were academic results, behaviour, attendance and delinquency. These are not the only goals of schooling, but they represent four areas which most parents and children regard as important and they provide a good basis on which the school can build other more expressive aims. A range of intake and outcome data was collected in the course of the three-year study.

We found significant differences between schools in the results for all four outcomes. Although, for example, students who appeared more academically able at age ten generally achieved better examination results than those who appeared average or below average, there were marked variations between schools. In some schools, all the students performed better than average; in others, all the students performed worse.

The examination scores were then adjusted to take account of the differences in the intake and, in addition, the differences in the occupational levels of parents. This last factor was introduced because, as with other studies (Fogelman et al., 1978), a strong relationship between parental occupation and academic performance was found. What emerged was that the school with the best results gained 70 per cent above the expected level, whilst the school with the worst results recorded results nearly 60 per cent below the expected level.

The other outcomes adopted in the study, concerned with attendance, behaviour and delinquency, were dealt with in a similar way so that, wherever possible, the relevant background factors could be taken into account. As with examination performance, stable differences were found even after allowing for initial differences in the student intake characteristics. In summary,

> Taking all the findings together, we have now seen that there were large and statistically significant differences between secondary schools with respect to levels of attendance, children's behaviour in

Comparison of Different Outcome Measures in 12 Schools.

Attendance	Academic	Behaviour
1	1	1
2	2	4
3	6	3
4	5	5
5	8	10
6	4	6
7	10	11
8	9	9
9	3	8
10	7	7
11	12	12
12	11	2

school, delinquency and academic attainment—differences which still remained even after controlling for the relevant intake variables. The last issue to consider in these connections is how far each of these separate outcomes produces a similar pattern of school variation. [The table] sets out the rank orders of the twelve schools on the attendance, behaviour and academic outcome measures. It can be seen that the picture which emerges is a rather consistent one, with the exception of the one school with a good behaviour score, but otherwise poor outcomes. On the whole, schools which have high levels of attendance and good behaviour tend also to have high levels of exam success. The delinquency rankings can only be considered between the different types of outcome (correlations for delinquency and attendance = 0.77; for delinquency and academic outcome = −0.68; for delinquency and behaviour = 0.72). We have shown that the marked school variations in each different type of outcome could not be accounted for in terms of individual intake characteristics on any of the measures available to us. As such measures included not only student behaviour and attainments at primary school, but also social background, it seems likely that the school variations in outcome are linked with characteristics of the schools themselves. In short, it appears that in a part of inner London known to be disadvantaged in numerous ways, some schools were better able than others to foster good behaviour and attainments.

However, it is necessary to appreciate that our analyses which 'control' for intake differences cannot by themselves show that the variations in outcome are due to school characteristics. All that they demonstrate is that the outcome differences were *not* due to differences in any of the intake measures, and that they were due to 'something else'. The inference that 'something else' concerned schools would be immensely strengthened if it could be shown that the school variations in outcome were consistently associated with mea- sured differences in school structure, organizations or functioning. Such evidence, of course, would also indicate *which* features of school life were most likely to influence children's development. (Rutter et al., 1979a, pp. 92–4)

The next question examined by the research team was whether the four mea- sures of school life used as outcomes were related or independent. In other words, whether schools could be seen as successful institutions or whether there was no clear pattern, with some schools being successful in one or two outcomes and not in the others.

When the individual schools' performance on these outcome measures were compared, it was found that, with one or two exceptions, schools appeared rea- sonably consistent, with those that had high levels of attendance and good behaviour also having high levels of examination success.

The question that immediately follows from these findings is simple. How does school influence operate? In other words—what processes were at work?

School process

Many of the administrative and physical features of school life did not appear important, in contrast to those factors which reflected the processes and quality of life of the students. An additional important finding was that the academic balance of the intake was more important than either the social or ethnic mix and was influential in making it easier to organize a good school.

The features of school life that appeared to be important were:

- *Academic influence.* This was measured by the amount of homework set and completed; the display of students' work; teacher expectations of stu- dents' success; and the extent of the use by students of library facilities. All these 'process factors' were related positively to the outcome measures.
- *Classroom strategies of teachers.* The strategies of teachers were recorded during week-long observations of classes. Broadly speaking, it was clear that using a style that effectively engaged the whole class was helpful, whilst spending a lot of time on equipment was unhelpful, as were fre- quent disciplinary interventions and ending lessons early.
- *Rewards and punishments.* The management of a large number of students always involves the use of rewards and punishments. In this study, con- siderably more punishment than rewards was observed, even though the latter appeared to be more effective in achieving the desired end of good behaviour.
- *Conditions of school life.* This indicator attempted to measure the quality of life for students and sampled the consideration shown to them in the

classroom and in the school in general. It correlated positively with good progress.

- *Opportunities for participation and responsibility.* The schools varied considerably in the opportunities they provided for students to take responsibility. The important factor seems to be allowing a large number of students this opportunity, rather than having a small number of official positions. It was also found that encouraging students to take responsibility for their own resources and active participation in assemblies and house meetings were important.

In addition, the results demonstrated the importance of a consistent approach within the school. Schools which had a common policy on behaviour and expected particular standards of work had better outcomes than those which were happy with a variety of approaches. On the crucial question of leadership, it was found that, in schools where there were better outcomes, there was also effective leadership by senior staff. Furthermore, ways had usually been found to ensure that all teachers—rather than a favoured few—could put forward their views.

School ethos

These particular characteristics of school life have been highlighted because they showed a statistically significant relationship with the outcome measures. There were, of course, many other features of school life which were examined, but which did not achieve the same level of statistical significance. Those which did, were grouped together and formed a general variable which was termed 'school ethos'. The individual items should be seen as indicators rather than as key items in their own rights with prescriptive implications. The items can best be thought of as indicating an underlying positive ethos. Certainly they were more common in schools with better outcomes.

Before discussing the implications of the findings, it may be helpful to summarize the ten main conclusions which emerged from the study.

First, secondary schools in inner London differed markedly in the behaviour and attainment shown by their students. This was evident in the children's behaviour whilst at school (as observed by us as well as reported by teachers and by the students themselves), the regularity of their attendance, the proportions staying on at school beyond the legally enforced period, their success in public examinations, and their delinquency rates.

Second, although schools differed in the proportion of behaviourally difficult or low achieving children they admitted, these differences did *not* wholly account for the variations between schools in their students' later behaviour and attainment. Even when comparisons between schools were restricted to children who were quite similar in family background and personal characteristics prior to secondary transfer, marked school variations remained. This meant that children were more likely to show good behaviour and good scholastic attainment if they attended some schools than if they attended others. The implication is that experiences during the secondary school years may influence children's progress.

Third, the variations between schools in different forms of 'outcome' for their pupils were reasonably stable over periods of at least four or five years.

Fourth, in general, schools performed fairly similarly on all the various measures of outcome. That is, schools which did better than average in terms of the children's behaviour in school tended also to do better than average in terms of examination success and delinquency. There were some exceptions to this pattern, but it appeared that in most schools the different forms of success were closely connected.

Fifth, these differences in outcome between schools were *not* due to such physical factors as the size of the school, the age of the buildings or the space available; nor were they due to broad differences in administrative status or organization. It was entirely possible for schools to obtain good outcomes in spite of initially rather unpromising and unprepossessing school premises, and within the context of somewhat differing administrative arrangements.

Sixth, the differences between schools in outcome *were* systematically related to their characteristics as social institutions. Factors as varied as the degree of academic emphasis, teacher actions in lessons, the availability of incentives and rewards, good conditions for pupils, and the extent to which children were able to take responsibility were all significantly associated with outcome differences between schools. All of these factors were open to modification by the staff, rather than fixed by external constraints.

Seventh, outcomes were also influenced by factors *outside* teachers' immediate control. The academic balance in the intake to the schools was particularly important in this connection. Examination success tended to be better in schools with a substantial nucleus of children of at least average intellectual ability, and delinquency rates were higher in those with a heavy preponderance of the least able. Interestingly, however, while the balance of intake was significantly associated with student outcome, it did not *appear* to have any comparable influence on school functioning, as reflected in our school process measures.

Eighth, this effect of balance in the intake was most marked with respect to delinquency, and least important in the case of the children's observed behaviour in the classroom and elsewhere about the school.

Ninth, the association between the *combined* measures of overall school process and each of the measures of outcome was much stronger than any of the associations with individual process variables. This suggests that the *cumulative* effect of these various social factors was considerably greater than the effect of any of the individual factors on their own. The implication is that the individual actions or measures may combine to create a particular *ethos*, or set of values, attitudes and behaviours, which will become characteristic of the school as a whole.

Tenth, the total pattern of findings indicates the strong probability that the associations between school process and outcome reflect in part a *causal* process. In other words, to an appreciable extent children's behaviour and attitudes are shaped and influenced by their experiences at school and, in particular, by the qualities of the school as a social institution. (Rutter et al., 1979a, pp. 177–9)

Implications

Because the bulk of the evidence drawn from the study was in the form of associations between different data sets, causal connections can only be inferred. What now needs to be undertaken is an experimental study which investigates ways of achieving a positive school ethos and which can contribute to the field of school improvement. In the meantime, the most obvious implications for those working in the education service will be identified.

School admissions
In view of the main findings of the study, that schools do make a difference to students' attainment and behaviour, many parents will be strengthened in their conviction that the choice of school for their child is important. However, given also the finding that it is important for each school to have a reasonable balance of academic ability, educational administrators are likely to have difficulties ensuring that schools have a balance and that parental choice is still accommodated.

The model of judging a good school by the use of indicators needs to be studied. Those responsible for school districts should consider carrying out similar appraisals of school performance. Following this appraisal, they may wish, through their inspectors, to work on strengthening the 'process' areas of the school performance. It may also be appropriate for schools to be encouraged to begin a programme of self-evaluation, as has been suggested by some local education authorities. Such a programme would enable teachers to become aware of any potential disappointing performance long before the effect of a downward spiral begins to be felt in the behaviour of the children and in the morale of staff.

Parents

In some ways, the implications of the study for parents are the converse of those for administrators. Parents, as well as local education authority officials, may be forced to compromise on their choice of school. Parents certainly need to be able to ask questions, use their parent governors to elicit information, and be permitted to visit the school during the daytime. Shipman (1978) has proposed that schools should present an annual report. Such a practice, if adopted, would enable more information to be made available to parents and this may cause the judgements of researchers and of parents to converge.

Teachers

The implications of the study for teachers are also considerable. First, the importance of schools has been confirmed and teachers will be pleased to see their role recognized as important, through its influence on the performance of students in so many different ways. Second, the creation of a positive ethos has been shown to be much more dependent on the actions of the teachers than on the administrative or physical features of a school. Third, the importance of an effective decision-making procedure within the school and the benefit of all staff using a common approach have been underlined. Fourth, rewards, rather than punishments, appear to be effective in changing behaviour. Unfortunately, punishments, rather than rewards, have often been used in school life and it may be difficult to find ways to provide rewards. As, however, the study demonstrated, even simple acts such as classroom praise can be effective. Finally, the importance of providing conditions which are pleasant and encourage students to feel that the school cares about them as individuals needs to be stressed. Interestingly, the results of the study suggest that at secondary level a low student–teacher ratio does not necessarily correlate with better performance. Of course, it may be argued that it means less teacher stress. However, in terms of student attainment, the reduction of class size may be less effective than the provision of very small tutorial groups, which are 'paid for' by slightly larger classes.

These are just a few of the many implications it is possible to draw from the findings of this study. However, one important group of people concerned with schooling has been ignored. The main implications of the findings of the research for *young people* deserve consideration, given that they spend approximately 15,000 hours in compulsory schooling. It is, perhaps, unrealistic to expect children—seen as the junior partners—to initiate change, particularly since most of them have only been to one secondary school and are therefore limited in their experience. Because of this, any changes to schooling need to be proposed by administrators, parents and teachers. These may argue that students should be more actively involved in their own learning than is at present the case in many schools. In this, perhaps secondary teachers may learn from their colleagues in primary schools. Certainly, the shock of moving from a junior school, which has encouraged independence and the use of initiative, into a secondary school which does not value that training, must be unhelpful to many young learners.

In this International Year of the Child (1979), the research that has been undertaken could play a part in encouraging the re-examination of schools and, if necessary, the modification of practice within them. Many children begin their 15,000 hours with a large number of disadvantages stemming from their social background (Wedge & Prosser, 1973). School cannot alter this background, but it can, perhaps, offer a positive influence which may help prevent, for some children, the transition from early social disadvantage into permanent educational disadvantage.

Conclusions

One of the common responses of practitioners to any piece of research is that it seems to be a tremendous amount of hard work just to demonstrate what we knew already on the basis of experience or common sense. Was the effort really worthwhile? It might be felt that the same applies to this study. After all, it is scarcely surprising that children benefit from attending schools which set good standards, where the teachers provide good models of behaviour, where they are praised and given responsibility, where the general conditions are good and where the lessons are well conducted.

Indeed this is obvious but, of course, it might have been equally obvious if we had found that the most important factors were attending a small school in modern purpose-built premises on one site, with a particularly favourable teacher–child ratio, a year-based system of pastoral care, continuity of individual teachers, and firm discipline in which unacceptable behaviours were severely punished. In fact *none* of these items was significantly associated with good outcomes, however measured.

Research into practical issues, such as schooling, rarely comes up with findings which are totally unexpected. On the other hand, it is helpful in showing which of the abundance of good ideas available are related to successful outcome. The present study of secondary schools has just such a contribution to make. In this final chapter, we have tried to go further in considering what mechanisms might be behind the statistical findings. Our discussion of school processes has been guided by knowledge stemming from previous research, informal observations of twelve schools over three years, and numerous helpful suggestions from the teaching staff in those twelve schools with whom we have discussed our findings. However, necessarily a certain amount of imagination has been involved in making the difficult step from tables, figures and graphs to suggestions of a kind likely to be appropriate and helpful in the everyday life of a school. Nevertheless, this more speculative account of possible practical implications is based on some rather firm research findings.

It is appropriate to end by summarizing some of the most important of these.

First, our investigation clearly showed that secondary schools varied markedly with respect to their pupils' behaviour, attendance, exam success and delinquency. This had been observed before, but the demonstration that these differences remained *even after taking into account differences in their intake* was new. This suggested that, contrary to many views, secondary schools *do* have an important influence on their pupils' behaviour and attainments.

Secondly, we found that these variations in outcome were systematically and strongly associated with the characteristics of schools as social institutions. The pattern of findings suggested that the association reflected a causal relationship. There were indications from previous studies that this might well be the case but it had not previously been systematically demonstrated by comparing different secondary schools.

Thirdly, the research showed *which* school variables were associated with good behaviour and attainments and which were not.

Fourth, the pattern of findings suggested that not only were pupils influenced by the way they were dealt with as individuals, but also there was a group influence resulting from the ethos of the school as a social institution.

We may conclude that the results carry the strong implication that schools can do much to foster good behaviour and attainments, and that even in a disadvantaged area, schools can be a force for the good. (Rutter et al., 1979a, pp. 204–5)

Postscript

Twenty years on it is clear that Fifteen Thousand Hours *has had an extraordinary influence on our understanding of schooling and Michael Rutter deserves considerable praise for leading the pioneering research approach and establishing a new paradigm. Nevertheless, at the time of publication the issues were hotly debated at education and research conferences. As noted in the introduction, the reaction of the educational community to the publication of the study was loud and quite divided. In general, policy makers tended to ignore it, practitioners—except for the English schoolteacher unions—were positive, and academics were divided. (See chapter seven for a fuller discussion of these issues.)*

I was much involved in the debates which occurred and was frequently called on to defend the approach we had taken. One issue in particular worried fellow researchers, even though it was hardly fair to blame the research team. This was the strength of interest in the study shown by the media. We were both flattered and concerned by it—and by the negative reaction of some academics. We had certainly not orchestrated the media attention nor employed any of the tactics now so commonly undertaken by 'news managers' and spin doctors. The findings reported in the book had simply struck a chord with the mood of the time. As noted in the introduction to this chapter, we authors had deliberately decided to express the findings as positively as possible. We stressed the positive effects of some schools rather than the negative impact of others. We could equally well have reversed this stance and made much of the inadequacy and the failings of teachers—the glass was either half full or half empty—but we believed in the psychological literature which shows that reward, rather than punishment, is the best method of changing behaviour. How different to some contemporary thinking!

Less dramatic criticisms were raised when I spoke at the British Educational Research Association Conference in 1979. These concerned the methodology used to control for differences in student intake to schools, the lack of detailed work on the curriculum and the absence of information from parents. These issues were addressed in detail in the planning for a primary school equivalent study which I was undertaking at that time and which is the subject of the next chapter.

Many of the policy issues raised by the study are still relevant to schooling today. In particular, the question of how to ensure a balance of pupils at any one school within a framework of parental choice has still not been resolved. The availability of relevant information on which parents can base their choice of school has been increased greatly since 1978, but whether the behaviour of parents has altered very much is still unclear. Annual reports have long since become a statutory requirement for schools but have often proved disappointing. The special meeting called by school governors for the purpose of presenting the report to parents is often attended by only a few parents. It is as if the formality of the occasion—introduced by a government convinced that schools should emulate the business model—has been rejected. Parents have not seen this model as appropriate and have made this clear by their behaviour. The proposal for a system of self-evaluation remains relevant and could form the basic strand in a revised system of school inspections.

5

Effective Schools for Primary Students[1]

Introduction

The School Matters *study was funded by the Inner London Education Authority and undertaken by its Research and Statistics Branch between 1980 and 1987. The research design was modelled on the* Fifteen Thousand Hours *study but contained numerous modifications to reflect not only the younger ages of the students but the suggestions for improvement which had emerged from the debates surrounding the publication of that study. I had been appointed Director of Research and Statistics in 1978 and part of my role was to plan and undertake research which was likely to prove beneficial to the ILEA's 1,000 schools. To the credit of the Authority, and particularly of its Schools' Sub-Committee, my plans for a large-scale study of primary schools were supported and the extra resources (needed to pay for four experienced teachers to work as field officers in the schools) were provided. The total costs of the study over its entire period were high as, in addition to the field officers, we employed a research co-ordinator, a dedicated computer programmer and some part-time assistance. These costs—and a proportion of my time— were met from our general budget. The total budget would certainly exceed the amount normally awarded today to a social science project. It is a tribute*

1 The original authors of *School Matters* and of most of the papers emanating from the study are Peter Mortimore, Pam Sammons, Louise Stoll, David Lewis and Russell Ecob.

to the ILEA that the Authority maintained its commitment to the project. It provided scope for the excellent research team which I was able to build around the field officers and the other experienced, energetic and talented members of the branch. This team included Pam Sammons, who acted as the research co-ordinator, and Louise Stoll, one of the four original field officers. I am privileged to be still working with these talented researchers, though now at the Institute of Education.

This chapter is based on work undertaken as part of the Inner London Education Authority's Junior School Project (JSP). A number of publications have already reported on detailed aspects of the study (Mortimore et al., 1985, 1986a, 1986b, 1988a, 1988b). This chapter, therefore, will provide background material, describe briefly the methodology of the research, describe some of the analyses that were employed, and present some of the major findings.

Background to the study

In recent years, researchers in a number of different countries, operating different systems of schooling, have been debating a series of questions concerned with the differential effectiveness of individual schools. Chapter three lists many of these questions and discusses their importance to educators. At its heart, the debate has been about the impact of an individual school on many of the structural factors operating within our societies—such as privilege, social class, race and gender. Can an individual primary or secondary school modify the influence of such factors? Not surprisingly, given the complexity of societal influences—and of the techniques required to tease them out—the answers have seldom been unambiguous. The implications of the debate, however, are crucially important at a time when—for whatever reasons—societies are demanding more from their schools. In Britain, in particular, where recognized success in schooling in the form of public examination credentials has been limited to a minority, the issue is of the utmost importance. For schools with students who are, in any way, disadvantaged, the anticipation of effectiveness can act as a powerful motivator to teaching and administrative staff. Likewise, the lack of effectiveness can be a destructive de-motivator.

The wide-ranging Education Reform Act of 1988 deals specifically with issues arising from the popularity of one school over its nearest neighbours. Open enrolment—up to the limitations of a school's buildings capacity—is to be enforced. Similarly, the individual school governing body (a group of trustees made up of parents, teachers, representatives of local business and community interests and the local education authority) is to have greatly increased executive powers over the financial and staffing aspects of the school. This body, therefore, will have the means to pursue greater effectiveness and the impetus to do so. The need for researchers to provide helpful advice as to what constitutes effectiveness is clear.

This legislation is new, yet research into school effectiveness frequently has to employ longitudinal designs. When we planned the Junior School study, nearly ten years ago, these developments could not have been foreseen. In our judgement, however, the consequences of the legislation make the quest for the key factors of effectiveness even more important than we could have anticipated.

The fieldwork for the study took place between 1980 and 1985. The data were analysed between 1985 and 1987. Publications dealing with different aspects of the study have been produced during the lifetime of the project.

The project was concerned with the study of just under 2,000 students who entered junior school at the age of seven in September 1980 and transferred to secondary schools in September 1984. The students attended a randomly chosen sample of 50 primary schools which reflected both the geographical distribution of schools and the balance of different types of schools within the Inner London Education Authority.[2]

Aims of the project

The first aim of the Junior School Project was to produce a detailed description of the students, the teachers, and the curriculum and organization of schools in an inner-city area. The second aim was to document the progress and development of nearly 2,000 students over four years of schooling. The third aim was to establish whether some schools were more effective than others in promoting students' learning and development, when account was taken of variations in the characteristics of students entering the schools. The fourth aim was to investigate average differences in the educational outcomes of different groups of students. Special attention was paid to variations in achievement related to race, sex, social class background and age within the school year.

In order to pursue these aims, three key questions were addressed by our research team:

(i)   Are some schools or classes more effective than others in terms of students' educational outcomes, when variations in the intakes of students are taken into account?
(ii) Are some schools or classes more effective for particular groups of children?
(iii) If some schools or classes are more effective than others, what factors contribute to these positive effects?

---

2 Two distinctions need to be borne in mind: between county (managed by the local education authority, LEA) and voluntary (financially supported mostly be the LEA); and between junior and infants' schools (age 5–11) and junior-only schools (age 7–11).

Methodology and analyses

The data

Our data can be divided into three categories, which reflect the questions addressed by the study. The categories are as follows:
(i)   Measures of the students' background characteristics in the intakes to schools and classes.
(ii)   Measures of students' progress and development.
(iii)   Measures of the classroom learning environment and school processes.

Measures of the background characteristics of the student intakes

In order to explore the effectiveness of schooling for different groups of children (according to age, social class, sex or race) and to explore the impact of background factors upon educational outcomes, we required detailed information about students' characteristics.

Previous studies of school effects have been criticized on the grounds of the paucity of their measures of intake and because they collected data at the level of the school, rather than the individual student (Gray, 1983; Gray & Jones, 1983). This point is crucial for studies of school effectiveness. Whereas some researchers have related average achievements of students in a particular school to the proportions of parents from particular social classes (this being better than ignoring background altogether), we were able to relate the achievement of particular students to their own characteristics, including their particular social class background. Unless comprehensive background data are obtained, research on school effects is unable adequately to compare 'like with like'.

The measures of intake we collected in the Junior School Project cover two areas: the social, ethnic, language and family background characteristics of the sample; and their level of attainment when they entered junior school. Data about each child's cognitive attainments in reading and mathematics and a class teacher's rating of behaviour were collected. This information enabled us to take account of differences in the *past* achievements of students (which may be related to their previous membership of particular infant classes and schools). It also provided us with the necessary baseline against which to assess the *later* progress and development of individuals during the junior school years.

Measures of students' progress and development

The result of studies of school effectiveness, to a certain extent, are dependent on the choice of measures of educational outcomes. Many studies have focused only on children's attainments in the basic skills. Basic skills are undeniably important, but other areas, including aspects of non-cognitive development such as attitudes, behaviour and attendance, also warrant attention. We feared that studies which used only one or two measures of outcomes may give an unbalanced and simplistic view of class and school effects. In the Junior School Project, therefore, we investigated a wide variety of cognitive and non-cognitive outcomes.

Cognitive outcomes
We found considerable variations in student's attainments in reading and mathematics skills at entry to junior school. Students, therefore, were assessed regularly in these areas to enable progress over time to be investigated. Only by studying *progress* could proper account be taken of the impact of the school on the very different levels of skills possessed by students at the start of their junior education. We employed standardized tests of reading and mathematics. The tests used were: the Edinburgh Reading Test (ERT) and the National Foundation for Educational Research Basic Mathematics Test (BMT). These tests have been shown to be reliable and to be reasonable predictors of academic success.

An individually-based assessment of practical mathematics was also conducted in each school year. In order to take account of the importance of writing in the junior curriculum, an assessment of creative writing was also made on an annual basis. To broaden the assessment of language development, the oral skills of a sample of children were assessed in the fourth year of junior schooling. For this assessment we used exercises developed specifically for the study by the Language Survey Team of the Assessment of Performance Unit (APU) of the Department of Education and Science (Gorman & Hargreaves, 1985).

In addition to these data, we collected the students' scores in the London Reading Test and in the ILEA's Verbal Reasoning Test when they were assessed in their fourth year.

Non-cognitive outcomes
Studies of school differences have tended to neglect many of the 'social' outputs of education (such as students' self-perception, attendance and attitudes). In order to do justice to the diverse aims and breadth of the curriculum of junior schools, we included a wide range of non-cognitive measures.

Information about the students' behaviour in school (as assessed by their class teachers) was collected using an instrument specially developed for use with the junior age group. This information was obtained for individuals in the autumn and summer terms of each school year. It was possible, therefore, for us to examine changes in behaviour during the three years, and to obtain an overall measure of behaviour.

We also drew, in each school year, on a self-report measure, of students' attitudes towards different types of school activities, curriculum areas and other aspects of school life. Measures of each child's perceptions of how they were seen by the teacher and by their peer group, as well as their views of themselves in the context of the school environment, were also collected at the end of the third year. Full attendance data were also collected for every student in the three terms of each school year.

Measures of the classroom learning environment and school processes
The third group of data relate to the teachers, the classrooms and the schools involved in the study. Because of our interest in identifying which factors make

some schools or classes more effective than others, we collected a wide variety of information under this heading.

School organization and policies
We obtained information about school organization and policies through interviews with heads, deputy heads and teachers. Questions concerning role, educational philosophy, qualifications and experience were included. We paid particular attention to the way students were initially grouped into classes, the allocation of teachers to classes, the allocation of staff responsibilities and teacher involvement in decision-making.

Class organization and policies
The class teachers of students in the sample were questioned about their qualifications, responsibilities, philosophies of education and involvement in decision making. Information was gathered about their methods of assigning work to pupils and their grouping strategies within the class. We also collected detailed information about special needs teaching, the curriculum and use of timetables.

Teacher behaviour
Classroom observations in each of the three years were undertaken by field officers (who were all experienced primary teachers). A systematic procedure, the 'Oracle' schedule (Galton & Simon, 1980), was adopted because of the necessity for examining comparability over time and between classes. Subjective ratings were also made of classroom behaviour and the activities of teachers and students. Additionally, we drew heavily on case studies and the verbatim accounts of field officers.

Views of parents
Parents of a large sub-sample were interviewed in their homes. Specially trained interviewers—fluent in the home language—were employed. Parents were able to validate information obtained about the students and to give their own views of their child's schooling.

School life
We used a variety of methods to collect information about the classes, teachers and school features of the sample. Methods included assessments of students, teachers' assessment of behaviour through the use of observation schedules and interviews.

The use of multiple sources of data enabled checks to be made on the validity of different instruments.

Methods of analysis

Analyses of our data were necessarily complex. Earlier research studies on school effectiveness had been criticized on methodological grounds (see, for example, Tizard et al., 1980; Goldstein, 1984). We wished to avoid these pit-falls, though, as with all empirical studies in the field of social science, we had to work within severe limitations. We used, therefore, a range of instruments and techniques. Whenever possible, we adjusted estimates for unreliability and took account of the effects of clustering.

We carried out analyses of students' outcomes in reading, mathematics, writing and speaking, and in attitudes, behaviour, attendance and self-concept. These analyses were all conducted at the level of the individual child. The influences of background factors and initial attainment were also explored in detail in the analyses of progress in the different cognitive areas. Only when we had taken full account of these relationships did we address the question of school effects on students' educational outcomes.

We looked in detail at three crucial aspects of the effects of junior schools on their students:

(i)   The size of the effects in terms of the proportion of the overall variation in students' progress or development which can be 'explained' (in a statistical sense) by different schools, in comparison to that explained by the students' background characteristics.
(ii)   The size of the effects of individual schools on their students' outcomes.
(iii) The processes which relate to the effects on their students' educational outcomes of individual schools and classes.

In examining the overall impact of school membership during the junior school period, it was possible for us to draw on data collected over three full years. When the size of the effects of school and class membership were compared, however, it was necessary to examine the data for each year separately (because of the frequency of changes of teacher and membership of classes between years). Multilevel models of analysis enabled us to do this.

In addition to analyses of the effects of schooling, we examined attainment, progress and non-cognitive development for all students, and for different groups. When investigating differences in outcomes due to age, social class, sex or race, our analyses controlled simultaneously for all other background factors. In reporting any differences, therefore, the figures we quote represent the *separate* effects of a given factor, only when the impact of all other background characteristics have been taken into account. The effect of sex, for example, was identified *net* of the effects of age, social class, race and other background factors.

As well as examining the *overall* relationships between progress and achievement in different cognitive and non-cognitive areas, we examined the relationships for children with different characteristics (according to age, social class, sex and race). The relationships between attainment and progress and teachers' ratings of students' abilities have also been investigated. Again, we conducted the analyses for all students and, separately, for children of different groups.

A large number of school variables were derived from the interviews, questionnaires, observations, ratings and notes collected by field officers during the study. We tested these variables to establish whether they were related to the effects of school and of class membership on each of the cognitive and non-cognitive outcomes. In conducting these analyses, both our educational and our research judgements were applied.

The significant variables were included in further analyses using multiple regression methods which explain (in a statistical sense) the variation between schools in their effects on each of the cognitive and non-cognitive outcomes. The aim of these analyses was to establish how much of the variation between schools in students' progress and development was accounted for by school and class-based factors and processes. Additionally, regression analyses were used to explore the relative importance of the different factors.

By relating information about these variables to school effects on different student outcomes, it was possible for us to account for much of the variation between schools in their effectiveness. Regression analyses identified several factors as being particularly important in the explanation of school and class effects upon progress and development. Many other significant relationships were identified in the analysis. Details of these are provided in the full report of the research, as is a list of *all* the significant factors used in the identification of the mechanisms of effectiveness.

Major findings

Differences between students at entry to junior schools

At entry to junior schools, there were marked variations in the reading, mathematics and writing skills, and in the behaviour of students, in the sample. In terms of the reading assessment, this represented a considerable difference in reading age, exceeding one year four months.

These differences indicate the importance of studying the progress and development of individual students. Only by taking account of attainment at entry was it possible for us to look at the long-term effects of schooling.

Progress and development over time

Analyses showed us that a student's performance in reading at the start of junior school was a good predictor of her or his performance four years later. Although initial performance in the written mathematics assessment gave a good idea of the child's likely performance in mathematics after three years of junior education, there was rather more possibility of change. Writing performance was more variable than either reading or mathematics over time.

In practical mathematics, we found that students who achieved high scores in the assessment in one year tended to achieve highly in later years. The relationships, however, were not as strong as those identified in reading or in written mathematics.

Oracy was assessed on only one occasion. It was not possible, therefore, to examine the relationships between oracy performance in different years. What we did find was considerable variation between students in their ability to communicate effectively.

For measures of behaviour, we assessed students at the beginning and end of each year on three possible types of behaviour disturbance—aggression, learning difficulties and anxiety. Learning difficulties (related to concentration, motivation and perseverance) were the most commonly reported problems.

Average attendance was very high in all three years: 91.8 per cent in the first year; 91.2 per cent in the second year; and 91.7 per cent in the third year. Even so, there were marked variations in the attendance of individual students.

In each year, we found that the students' attitudes to 'basic skills' curriculum areas (mathematics and language activities), though generally positive, were less favourable than attitudes to other curriculum areas (project or topic work, art and craft, music, physical education and games). There was a tendency for attitudes towards specific curriculum areas to be more positive than the *general* attitude to school. Overall, attitudes became slightly less positive in the later years of junior schooling. The only area to show a slight but consistent improvement over the years was attitude to project work.

In general, we found students' self-concepts were positive. However, students tended to believe that teachers viewed their behaviour less positively.

Relationships between outcomes

There were close relationships between students' attainments in different aspects of language activities (reading, writing and oracy). Performance in the written and practical mathematics assessments in each school year were also related. Furthermore, we found a strong relationship between attainment in the reading and the written mathematics assessments.

Results suggest that oracy skills and practical mathematics performance were also highly related. This indicates the value of assessments which do not require students to possess high levels of competence in reading and writing. Such assessments may reveal strengths in cognitive areas which may not be revealed in reading- and writing-based tasks.

In general, we found that relationships between the different non-cognitive areas were much weaker than those for the cognitive outcomes. However, students who were assessed by their teachers as having behaviour difficulties held significantly more negative attitudes to school than did others. They also rated their own behaviour less positively.

Results also indicate that behaviour and attainment were quite closely linked, especially amongst younger children. In particular, we found evidence that students with a higher rating in learning difficulties in one year tended to make less progress in reading in the next year. Similarly, those with lower reading scores in a given year tended to show an increase in behaviour difficulties (especially those concerned with learning difficulties) in the following year. These results show that the relationship between behaviour and cognitive attainment is complex; each influences the other.

Students with high absence rates also tended to have generally lower attainments in reading, mathematics and writing. These relationships, though significant, were nevertheless small.

Differences according to age, social class, sex and race
The students in our sample were drawn from a wide variety of backgrounds. Some lived in families which were advantaged in material terms, while others were living in very difficult circumstances. Such differences in circumstances can have a considerable impact upon educational outcomes, although the causes are seldom clear-cut. Although there is evidence that various factors (such as eligibility for free meals) are related to lower attainment, their relationship to *progress* has been less researched. Moreover, little attention has been paid to the impact of disadvantage on non-cognitive outcomes of education.

Age
Differences between summer-born and autumn-born members of the year group were identified in attitude to school; behaviour difficulties; and in reading, writing and mathematics attainment. The findings indicate that younger members of a year group attained less highly and were at risk of experiencing greater difficulties in adjustment to junior school. In part, this was due to the marked difference in length of infant schooling (an average difference of nine months between autumn- and summer-born children). The results of these analyses suggest that it is important to promote teachers' awareness of the impact of age differences, even within year-based classes.

Social class
We found that students from non-manual family backgrounds had higher attainment in the majority of cognitive areas. They also made greater progress than other groups in reading and writing. A small but significant difference was found in teachers' assessments of ability in favour of the non-manual group, even when the group's superior attainment was taken into account.
    Children whose fathers were in semi-skilled and unskilled manual work, and whose fathers were absent, were significantly more likely to exhibit behaviour difficulties in school. There were no consistent differences according to social class, however, in attendance or self-concept.

Sex
We identified marked differences between girls and boys in reading and writing attainment, with girls attaining more highly than boys in all years. However, there were no sex differences in progress in these areas. In mathematics, differences in attainment were slight, but girls made slightly more progress than boys over the junior years. There were no sex differences in the ability to communicate effectively (oracy).
    Girls tended to have more positive attitudes towards school and more favourable self-concept. Class teachers identified marked differences between

the two sexes in behaviour in school. Boys were more likely than girls to be assessed as having behaviour difficulties in all years.

Race

There were significant differences between students of different ethnic backgrounds in reading and mathematics, both at entry to junior school and in later years. For example, Caribbean, Greek, Turkish and the Punjabi-speaking Asian students had lower reading scores, while the small groups of Chinese and Gujerati-speaking Asians had higher reading scores at entry. In addition, there were small but significant differences in progress in reading, with the Caribbean and Asian groups making poorer progress than predicted by their initial attainment. No differences, however, were identified for progress in mathematics or writing. Moreover, there were no ethnic differences in oral skills. Those whose first language was not English were still able to communicate effectively.

The incidence of behaviour difficulties (as assessed by their class teacher) was higher amongst Caribbean students (although still recorded for only a minority). The relationship appeared to be due to differences in attainment (behaviour and attainment being closely linked). When the relationship between behaviour and attainment was taken into account, there was no further association between ethnic background and behaviour.

The Caribbean students had better attendance, and the Asian students poorer attendance than others, during the junior years. On the whole, attitudes varied little. There was no difference between black and white groups in their self-concept.

School effects

Our analyses of school effects have taken into account each of the background factors identified as influential (age, social class, sex, race and language background, and family circumstances). Membership of each individual school was included so that the separate impact of the school on the student's progress and development could be established.

We found that school membership made a significant contribution to the explanation of students' attainment and progress over three years in reading, writing and mathematics, and also to the development of attitudes, self-concept and behaviour in school. The school had rather less effect upon attendance.

These results indicate that the school to which a student belongs can have a beneficial or a negative effect upon that student's progress and development. A major finding of our study concerns the importance of school in explaining variations in progress over the junior years. We found that the school made a far larger contribution to the explanation of progress than was made by sex and age and other background characteristics. We found, for example, that of the 30 per cent of variance in students' progress in reading that could be 'explained'—in statistical terms—over 23 per cent was due to school factors and only 6 per cent was due to background.

The differences between the most and the least effective schools in each of the outcomes were considerable: 25 points, compared to an overall average score of 54 for reading; 12 points, compared to an overall average score of 28 points for mathematics. Other outcomes showed a similar range.

On the whole, we found that schools which promoted good progress in mathematics tended also to do so in reading. In addition, such schools fostered self-concept and, to a lesser extent, promoted positive attitudes to mathematics. There were weaker relationships between school effects on progress in writing and progress in other cognitive areas. However, schools with good effects on writing progress generally enhanced attitudes to reading, progress in mathematics and attendance.

Overall, the effects of school membership on non-cognitive outcomes were not highly related to those on cognitive areas. Analyses indicate that the two dimensions were largely independent of each other. However, some schools had strong positive effects on progress and development on both cognitive and non-cognitive areas. Others had a negative effect on both areas. For example, 14 schools had positive effects on three or more of the cognitive outcomes and four or more of the non-cognitive outcomes. In contrast, we found five schools which had positive effects on only one or none of the cognitive areas and on two or fewer of the non-cognitive areas. For each student, therefore, the school that she or he joins at age seven can have a highly significant impact upon future progress or development.

We found, for most of the cognitive outcomes, that both the school attended by the student and the class in which she or he was placed contributed to the explanation of variations in progress. Over a three-year period, the effects of school membership were somewhat larger than effects over only one school year. The impact of schools upon their students appears to be cumulative. This suggests to us that factors related both to school and to class processes have an influence upon the effectiveness or otherwise of schools in promoting outcomes.

In terms of answering our first question (*Do junior schools make a difference to students' educational outcomes?*), it is clear that schools do make a difference and that the difference is substantial.

The impact of school on different groups
The results of our analyses of the effects of individual schools on progress in cognitive outcomes indicate that, in general, there were few differences between students of different backgrounds in these effects. Overall, schools which were effective in promoting progress for one group (whether of a particular sex, social class or ethnic group) also tended to be effective for any other group. Similarly, those which were ineffective for one group tended to be ineffective for other groups. It appears, however, that in this sample Caribbean pupils were over-represented in schools which were generally ineffective in promoting the reading progress of all pupils, irrespective of their ethnic background. One of the explanations for the poorer reading progress of the Caribbean group overall may have been related to their over-representation in such schools.

Which school a student attends can have a significant impact upon progress. In terms of answering our second question (*Are some schools or classes more effective for particular groups of children?*), these data suggest that schools which are effective for girls tend to be effective for boys. Similarly, school effects for different social classes are related, as are those for different ethnic groups.

Key factors

We collected a great deal of information about school and class policies during our four years of fieldwork. Data were also collected about those aspects of school life over which the school and the class teacher can exercise little direct control. These latter aspects we termed 'givens'. The two sets of information, about policies and givens, included many factors which related to the school as a whole and others which related specifically to the classes within schools. Examples of some of the 'given' factors are the status of schools (junior and infant or junior-only; county or voluntary) and their staffing. Examples of 'policy' variables at the school level (matters under the control of the school) are the methods of allocating pupils and teachers to classes, and the frequency and functions of staff meetings.

Our third major question was *If some schools or classes are more effective than others, what factors contribute to these positive effects?* We found that similar factors and processes appeared to help increase schools' effectiveness in promoting progress and development. By examining the ways in which these significant factors were interrelated, it was possible for us to gain a greater understanding of the *mechanisms* of effectiveness. From this analysis, we identified a series of key factors related to the differential effectiveness of schools.

In the same way, school and classroom processes were frequently related to each other. Thus, through a detailed investigation of these links, we evolved a picture of what constitutes effective schooling. This picture is not intended to be an exact recipe for success. Inevitably, many subtle aspects of schooling could not be examined in detail. Furthermore, schools are not static institutions. Many changes have taken place since the fieldwork for the study was completed. More changes are planned as a result of recent legislation. Nevertheless, we believe the key factors that we have identified are important and provide a sound basis for effective schooling.

We found that certain of the 'given' features made it easier to create an effective school. For example, schools that cover the entire primary age range, where students do not have to transfer at age seven, appeared to be at an advantage, as did voluntary-aided schools. Smaller schools, with a junior roll of under 160 children, also appeared to benefit their students. Class size is particularly relevant: smaller classes, with less than 24 students, had a positive impact upon students' progress and development, especially in the early years.

Not surprisingly, we found that a good physical environment, as reflected in the school's amenities, its decorative order and its immediate surroundings, created a positive situation in which progress and development could be fostered. Extended periods of disruption, due to building work and redecoration, had a negative impact on progress. The stability of the school's teaching force was also an important factor. Changes of head and deputy head teacher, though inevitable, have an unsettling effect upon the students. It seems to us, therefore, that every effort should be made to reduce the potentially negative impact of such changes. Similarly, where there is an unavoidable change of class teacher during the school year, careful planning will be needed to ensure an easy transition, and to minimize disruption. Where students experience continuity through the whole year, with one class teacher, progress is more likely to occur.

It is not only continuity of staff, however, that is important. Although major or frequent changes tend to have negative effects, change can be used positively. Thus, where there had been no change of head for a long period of time, schools tended to be less effective. In the more effective schools, heads had usually been in post for between three and seven years.

It was clear to us, therefore, that some schools were more advantaged in terms of their size, status, environment and stability of teaching staff. Nonetheless, although these favourable 'given' characteristics contributed to effectiveness, we do not believe that, by themselves, they can ensure it. They provide a supporting framework within which the head and teachers can work to promote progress and development. The size of a school, for example, may facilitate certain modes of organization which benefit students. However, it is the factors *within* the control of the head and teachers that are crucial. These are the factors that can be changed and improved.

We identified twelve key factors of effectiveness:

1 Purposeful leadership

'Purposeful leadership' occurred where the head teacher understood the needs of the school and was actively involved in the school's work, without adopting a negative autocratic style. In effective schools, head teachers were involved in curriculum discussions and influenced the content of guidelines drawn up within the school, without taking total control. They also influenced the teaching style of teachers, but only selectively, where they judged it necessary. This leadership was demonstrated by an emphasis on monitoring students' progress through the keeping of individual records. Approaches varied—some schools kept written records; others passed on folders of students' work to their next teacher; some did both—but a systematic policy of record keeping was regarded as important.

Heads exhibiting purposeful leadership did not allow teachers total freedom to attend any in-service course: attendance was allowed for a good reason. Nonetheless, most teachers in these schools had attended courses.

2 The involvement of the deputy head

We found that the deputy head played a major role in the effectiveness of schools. Where the deputy was frequently absent, or absent for a prolonged period (due to illness, attendance on long courses, or other commitments), this was detrimental to students' progress and development. Moreover, a change of deputy head tended to have negative effects. The responsibilities undertaken by deputy heads were also important. Where the head generally involved the deputy in policy decisions, it was beneficial to the students. This was particularly true in terms of allocating teachers to classes, delegation by the head teacher and a sharing of responsibilities, all of which promoted effectiveness.

3 The involvement of teachers

In successful schools, we found that teachers were involved in curriculum planning and played a major role in developing their own curriculum guidelines. As with the deputy head, teacher involvement in decisions concerning which classes they were to teach was important. Similarly, consultation with teachers about decisions on spending was important. Schools in which teachers were consulted on issues affecting school policy were more likely to be successful.

4 Consistency amongst teachers

We have already shown that continuity of staffing had positive effects. It also appears that stability, or consistency, in teacher approach is important. For example, in schools where all teachers followed guidelines in the same way, the impact on progress was positive. Variation between teachers in their use of guidelines had a negative effect.

5 Structured sessions

Students benefited when their school day was structured in some way. In effective schools, students' work was organized by the teacher, who ensured that there was always plenty for them to do. Positive effects were also noted when students were not given unlimited responsibility for planning their own programme of work or for choosing work activities. In general, teachers who organized a framework within which students could work, and yet allowed them some freedom within this structure, were more likely to be successful.

6 Intellectually challenging teaching

Unsurprisingly, we found that the quality of teaching was very important in promoting student progress and development. The findings clearly show that, in classes where students were stimulated and challenged, progress was greater.

The content of teachers' communications was vitally important. Positive effects occurred where teachers used more 'higher-order' questions and statements; that is, where their communications encouraged students to use their creative imagination and powers of problem-solving. In classes where the teaching situation was challenging and stimulating, and where teachers communicated interest and enthusiasm to the children, greater progress occurred. It appeared that teachers who more frequently directed students' work, without discussing it or explaining its purpose, had a negative impact. Frequent monitoring and maintenance of work, in terms of asking students about their progress, was no more successful. What was crucial was the level of the communications between teacher and students.

Creating a challenge for students demonstrates that the teacher believes they are capable of responding to it. It was evident that such teachers had high expectations. This was further demonstrated in the effectiveness of teachers who, having agreed with students what work was to be done, encouraged them to take independent control over it. Some teachers gave instructions only infrequently, yet everyone in the class knew exactly what they were supposed to be doing and continued working without close supervision.

7 Work-centred environment
In schools where teachers spent more of their time discussing the *content* of work and less time on routine matters and the maintenance of work activity, the impact was positive. We also found some indication that time devoted to giving feedback about work was beneficial. The work-centred environment was characterized by a high level of industry in the classroom. Students appeared to enjoy their work and were eager to commence new tasks. The noise level was also low, although this is not to say that there was silence in the classroom. Furthermore, student movement around the classroom was not excessive and was generally work-related.

8 Limited focus within sessions
It appeared to us that learning was facilitated when teachers devoted their energies to one particular curriculum area within a session. At times, work could be undertaken in two areas and also produce positive effects. However, where many sessions were organized such that three or more curriculum areas were concurrent, students' progress was marred. It is likely that this finding is related to other factors. For example, student industry was lower in classrooms where mixed activities occurred. Moreover, noise and movement were greater and teachers spent less time discussing work and more time on routine issues. More importantly, in mixed-activity sessions the opportunities for communication between teachers and students were reduced (as we will describe later).

A focus on one curriculum area did not imply that all the students were doing exactly the same work. There was some variation, both in terms of choice of topic and level of difficulty. We found positive effects occurred where the teacher geared the level of work to students' needs.

9 Maximum communication between teachers and pupils
It was evident to us that students gained from having more rather than less communication with the teacher. Thus, those teachers who spent higher proportions of their time not interacting with their students were *less* successful in promoting progress and development.

The time teachers spent on communicating with the whole class was also important. Most teachers devoted the majority of their attention to speaking with individuals. Each student, therefore, could only expect to receive a fairly small number of individual contacts with their teacher. When teachers spoke to the *whole class*, they increased the overall number of contacts. In particular, this enabled a greater number of 'higher-order' communications to be received by all students. Therefore, a balance of teacher contacts between individuals and the whole class was more beneficial than a total emphasis on communicating with individuals (or groups) alone. Furthermore, where students worked in a single curriculum area within sessions (even if they were engaged in individual or group tasks), it was easier for teachers to raise an intellectually challenging point with all students.

10 Record keeping
We have already noted the value of record keeping in relation to the purposeful leadership of the head teacher. However, it was also an important aspect of teachers' planning and assessment. Where teachers reported that they kept written records of work progress, in addition to the official record, the effect on the students was positive. The keeping of records concerning personal and social development was also found to be generally beneficial.

11 Parental involvement
We found parental involvement to be a positive influence upon students' progress and development. Such involvement included help in classrooms and on educational visits and attendance at meetings to discuss progress. The head teacher's accessibility to parents was also important. Schools with an informal, open-door policy were more effective. Parental involvement in educational development within the home was also beneficial. Parents who read to their children, heard them read and provided them with access to books at home had a positive effect upon their children's learning. One aspect of parental involvement was, however, not successful. Somewhat curiously, formal Parent–Teacher Associations (PTAs) were not found to be related to effective schooling. We believe that some parents found the formal structure of such a body to be intimidating, even excluding.

12 Positive climate
Our study provides confirmation that an effective school has a positive ethos: overall, the atmosphere was more pleasant in the effective schools, for a variety of reasons. Both around the school and within the classroom less emphasis on punishment and critical control, and a greater emphasis on praise and rewards, had a positive impact. Where teachers actively encouraged self-control on the part of students, rather than emphasizing the negative aspects of their behaviour, progress and development increased. What appeared to be important was firm but fair classroom management.

The teachers' attitude to their students was also important. Good effects resulted where teachers obviously enjoyed teaching their classes and communicated this fact. Their interest in the children as individuals, and not just as students in a group, was also valuable. Teachers who, when appropriate, devoted more time to non-school chat or 'small talk' fostered progress and development. Outside the classroom, evidence of a positive climate included: the organization of lunchtime and after-school clubs; teachers eating their lunch at the same tables as the children; organization of trips and visits; and the use of the local environment as a learning resource.

We found that the working conditions of teachers contributed to the creation of a positive school climate. Where teachers had preparation periods, the impact on student progress and development was positive. Thus, the climate created by the teachers for the students, and by the head for the teachers, was an important aspect of the school's effectiveness. This climate was reflected in effective schools by happy, well-behaved students who were friendly towards each other and to outsiders, and by the absence of graffiti around the school.

Conclusion

Of the 12 key factors identified in our study, some had a stronger effect than others on the cognitive and non-cognitive areas investigated, but all were positive. Unlike the 'given' characteristics, these factors depend on specific behaviours and strategies employed by the head teacher and staff. We believe that the school and the classroom are interlocked: what the teacher can or cannot do depends, to a certain extent, on what is happening in the school as a whole.

These 12 factors cannot guarantee success. What they can do is provide all those involved with schools with a set of examples based on empirical evidence collected over a long period of time. We hope this information will inform debate and that the dissemination of our findings will lead to the development of more effective schools.

Postscript

Thus ended one of the longest—and probably one of the most expensive—studies of schooling undertaken in the United Kingdom. The funding of such a study by a local education authority is a remarkable tribute to the members and officers of the ILEA. By broadly replicating the methodology of the earlier study and by incorporating new measures and new methods, we were able to develop the field of school differences. The reaction to publication, interestingly, was much less hostile than that accorded to Fifteen Thousand Hours. *Looking back, I suspect this was due to three separate reasons: the novelty of a research design which focused on outcomes had already been accepted by other researchers; most of the findings had already been published in peer-reviewed journals and had been discussed in a number of seminars; and the changes we had made in methodology were recognized as sensible. In terms of scientific progress in this field of research, the paradigm had been tested and found to be workable.*

Our study had highlighted, for the first time, the strength of the school differences and had suggested that these could be more important for younger students than for those of secondary age—and had identified the importance of measures of progress over those of attainment. It had also brought out the dif-

ferences between the 'given' and the 'policy' factors associated with the measures of progress. The 12 factors, including several to do with classroom practice, added to those identified as important at secondary level. One of the factors—'limited focus within sessions'—placed a clear question mark over hitherto common primary practice of simultaneously teaching separate groups of students different areas of the curriculum. Its identification by us led, in due course, to its inclusion in a government-commissioned report on primary practice by the 'Three Wise Men', Alexander, Rose & Woodhead (1992). A 'limited focus' is now held—probably too rigidly—to be an article of faith and has become part of an equally dogmatic approach to the one we were challenging. Another factor—'intellectually challenging teaching'—served to remind all those involved with the education of young children that this was the prime purpose of work in the classroom. Other worthwhile activities complement but should not supersede it.

We published—in one form or another—much information about the junior school study. Some of the information was technical; other pieces were specially written for lay audiences. The members of the research team also invested much time disseminating the findings in the United Kingdom and abroad. The highlights of the study were published in a commissioned article for the educational magazine with one of the largest circulations in the United States (Mortimore and Sammons, 1987).

The next chapter also deals with this study but in a much more technical manner. It discusses the advantages and disadvantages of particular methods of analysis.

6

The Effects of School Membership on Students' Educational Outcomes

Introduction

This chapter reports some of the more complex technical details of the School Matters *study described in the last chapter. Since many of the other publications emanating from the study were targeted at lay readers or at educationalists less interested in the methodological details, we thought it only fair to produce a substantial publication for those who were working in the field. The original article was written to inform researchers and is likely to be of interest primarily to those concerned with the technical aspects of analysis and interpretation. This chapter complements the Technical Appendices which we made available as we completed the study.*

The focus of the paper is an investigation of the existence and size of the effects of school membership upon these pupils' progress in a variety of cognitive outcomes (reading, writing and mathematics), attainment in oracy (which was measured only on one occasion) and upon several non-cognitive outcomes (attendance, attitudes, behaviour and self-concept). Particular attention is paid to the identification and separation of the effects of school membership from those attributable to background factors, sex and age. For the analysis of the effects of school upon pupils' progress in cognitive areas, initial attainment in the relevant area is controlled and acts as the baseline against which later progress is measured.

The study demonstrates the existence of substantial school effects for a wide range of outcomes, both cognitive and non-cognitive, and permits the discussion of whether junior schools are equally effective across all outcomes. It is shown that some schools are more effective in promoting pupils' progress and development in a broad range of outcomes than are others. Moreover, the results confirm that in determining pupils' progress during the junior years (taking account of initial attainment), school membership is far more influential than background factors, sex and age. (This is not to deny that the latter are strongly related to levels of initial attainment at entry to junior school.) For individual pupils, therefore, the particular school attended can make a considerable difference to future progress and development during the junior years.

Background

A longitudinal study of junior education has taken place within the ILEA during the last five years. The Junior School Project has focused attention upon an age group of nearly 2,000 pupils who entered junior school in September 1980, and transferred to secondary school in September 1984. These children attended a randomly chosen, representative sample of 50 primary schools which reflected the geographical distribution of schools within the Authority, and the balance of county and voluntary, and of junior only and junior and infant schools. Full details of the study have been given in an introductory paper (Mortimore et al., 1985).

In this paper, attention is focused on the methodology of the study. The methods of analysis are described which were used to establish whether schools had an impact upon their pupils' progress and development during the junior years. Results are presented which indicate the relative importance of school effects as compared with those due to pupils' background characteristics (including sex and age). Full details of the findings in the study are given in Mortimore et al. (1986a, 1986b, 1988a).

The need to take account of school intakes

There is evidence that schools vary considerably in the areas they serve and in the background characteristics of their pupils. This is especially true at the primary level.[1] The sample of junior schools included in the ILEA's Junior School Project was no exception. Marked variations in the initial attainments, behaviour and background characteristics of pupils forming the intakes to the sample schools have been identified (ibid.).

---

1 See Plowden, 1967; Little and Mabey, 1972, 1973; and Sammons et al., 1983 for details of variation in schools' intakes initiating (in the case of the Plowden Report) and contributing to educational priority research.

Analyses of the relationships between individual pupils' characteristics (sex, age, social and family background) and both cognitive attainment and non-cognitive development have demonstrated clearly the strength of relationships between pupils' backgrounds and their educational outcomes. These findings are in line with those of other studies of primary pupils (Marjoribanks, 1979; Mortimore & Blackstone, 1982; Rutter & Madge, 1976). These findings point to the need to take full account of differences in intakes when comparing the effects of individual schools on the progress and development of their pupils. Past studies of school differences, however, have been criticized on the ground of the paucity of their intake measures, or the crudity of the measures used (see, for instance, the criticisms of measures used to control the characteristics of school intakes by Gray, 1981).

Recent research by Marks (1983; Marks et al., 1986) illustrates the dangers of neglecting to measure differences in intakes adequately. This can lead to very misleading results in studies of school and LEA differences in examination results (see criticisms of Marks' research by Fogelman, 1984; Goldstein, 1984; Gray, 1983; Gray et al., 1984; Gray & Jones, 1983). As Gray and Jones (1985) have argued, the 'major weakness of many of these studies has been their failure to control adequately for differences in the prior attainments and home backgrounds of pupils at different schools'. In addition, Gray and Hannon (1985) have indicated that Her Majesty's Inspectorate's (HMI) interpretation of schools' examination results is seriously flawed because of the failure to consider the effects of differences between schools in their intakes.

How the effects have been studied

In the Junior School Project, because of the importance of age, sex, social class, race and language background, and family circumstances, the analyses of school effects have taken each of the background factors identified as influential into account (Mortimore et al., 1986a, 1986b). Membership of an individual school has been included as an additional characteristic for each 11-year-old, because this may well have had an impact upon the child's progress and on various other non-cognitive educational outcomes.[2]

---

2 The school was recoded into a 'dummy' variable for inclusion in the regression programme (SUPERCARP). The analyses took into account the effects of clustering in the sample (the 'design effect') and of unreliability. In addition, these analyses have been replicated using an adapted revision of a multilevel programme developed by Goldstein (1986). Using these methods the effects of background characteristics and of school membership can be identified and separated, whilst controlling for the affects of other factors simultaneously. Thus, the influence of school membership is estimated while account is taken of children's background. All analyses have been conducted at the level of the individual pupil. (Full details of the methods used in the analyses are provided in Ecob [1985] and Ecob et al. [1986].) Analyses are based on 49 schools unless otherwise indicated, because one school withdrew from the project during the third year.

The results of our analyses of the effects of school membership on progress in the various cognitive areas (reading, mathematics and writing) and upon attainment in oracy will be discussed first. It was not possible to investigate progress in oracy because only one assessment of pupils' oral skills was made. The effects of school membership are described in terms of the amount of variation in pupil progress explained (in a statistical sense) by the school. This method allows a comparison of the strength of school effects in general with those effects due to background factors. Also described are the variations in the effect of being a member of a particular school. Here, the sample schools are compared in terms of their influence upon pupils' progress in the different cognitive areas—for example, reading progress. Finally, the effects of particular schools on different cognitive areas are examined to see whether schools which have a positive effect on certain outcomes also have a positive effect on other areas of pupil progress. Such a strategy enables the identification of schools which appear to be more effective than others in promoting good progress over the junior years.

School effects upon non-cognitive outcomes (attitudes, attendance, behaviour and self-concept) are then explored. Clearly, a simple concept of progress cannot apply to some of the non-cognitive outcomes (attendance and behaviour, unlike reading, are not expected to improve automatically over time), although it is possible to investigate whether change has occurred. Likewise, behaviour difficulties may either disappear or develop further during the junior years.

For the behaviour measure, information was combined over three years to give an overall measure of adjustment to school. This will be used to indicate whether a high proportion of pupils in particular schools have consistently shown behaviour difficulties.[3]

As with the cognitive outcomes, the size of the influence of school (in terms of the proportion of variance explained) is compared with the amount due to different background factors for each non-cognitive area. In addition, the effects of particular schools have been investigated to see whether some schools were more effective than others in promoting good non-cognitive outcomes, once account has been taken of pupils' backgrounds.

School effects on cognitive and on non-cognitive areas are also compared. Here the intention is to answer the question—are some schools more effective than others in different areas?

Effects of school membership on cognitive outcomes

Reading attainment and progress
Children's reading performance was regularly assessed during the project using the most appropriate Edinburgh Reading Test for their age range. Four assessments were made, one early in the autumn term of each year (autumn 1980–2),

---

3 This approach reduces the effect of the assessment of a particular teacher in a particular year. To score highly a pupil must have been rated as having difficulties on several occasions.

Table 6.1.   The percentage of variance in third-year reading attainment explained by different factors in 1,101 children.

Factors	% of variance explained
Initial (first-year) attainment, age, sex and background factors only	64.04
Initial (first-year) attainment, age, sex, background factors and school	73.08
Unique contribution of initial (first-year) attainment alone	61.72
Unique contribution of the school after control for initial attainment, age, sex and background factors	9.04
Unique contribution of background factors, sex and age, after controlling for initial attainment	2.32

and one in the summer term of the third year (summer 1983). Reading progress was examined over three school years (autumn 1980 to summer 1983), whilst controlling for initial attainment, sex, age and background factors. In the discussion of school effects over three years, effects due to the school have not been separated from those due to membership of particular classes during the three years. Thus, the results describe the impact upon a child's progress over three years of being a member of one particular school, rather than of any of the other schools in the sample.

The results indicate that school membership has a highly significant impact upon reading attainment. In all, 9 per cent of the variation in children's reading attainment at the end of the third year was accounted for by the school as a factor. This figure is higher than that identified in previous studies of school effects where, in general, the estimates of the size of school effects ranged from between 3 and 6 per cent of the variation in pupils' cognitive outcomes.[4]

As shown in Table 6.1, the size of the independent school effect on third-year reading attainment is much greater than that due to background after taking account of initial (first-year) attainment. This is not to deny that background factors, sex and age are important in determining initial levels of attainment (for details of the links between background factors, sex and age and pupils' attainment at entry to junior school see Mortimore et al., 1986b, Part A). In these analyses the effects of initial attainment were calculated first. This provides a conservative estimate of the size of the effects of school membership and of background factors (including sex and age). All analyses were conducted at the level of the individual pupil using a fixed effects model. If relative progress over the three junior years is considered, it can be found that nearly 30 per cent of

4   Gray (1981), Reynolds (1982) and Rutter(1983) have described the possible range in the size of school effects in published studies. As Rutter noted, 'Jencks et al. (1972) concluded that school variables accounted for a mere 2–3 per cent of the variance, a figure far below the estimated 50 per cent attributable to family background'. Rutter concluded that, 'other studies have varied somewhat in the precise figures . . . but with one exception . . . all have agreed in finding that far more of the variance in pupils' attainment is attributable to family variables than to school variables' (p. 3).

the variation in children's progress can be explained by school membership and background factors taken together. But, the school has much the larger effect. The school attended explains nearly 24 per cent of the variation in reading progress between the first and the third year of junior education (see Appendix 1). It should be remembered that, in these analyses (which were conducted at the more statistically sensitive level of the individual child), the impact of a much wider variety of background factors than have appeared in many previous studies of school effects has been taken into account.[5] Because of thorough control for background influences, it seems unlikely that the variation due to school membership found in this study would be accounted for by the inclusion of still further background factors.[6]

Thus, for the sample, the analysis confirms that school membership is of considerable importance in determining the level of reading performance reached after three years of junior education, and by far the most important factor we could identify in determining the progress pupils made between the first and third years of junior school education. In comparison, therefore, the continuing influences of background factors, age and sex were relatively minor.

In particular schools, children made greater progress in reading than expected, given their initial attainment and background characteristics. In other schools, children made less progress than expected. For these pupils, therefore, it is clear that the school which they entered aged seven made a considerable difference to their progress in reading over the next three years.

The size of the effects of individual schools upon children's reading progress in terms of raw score points was calculated and compared. Estimates of the size of the effects of individual schools from the fixed effects analysis tend to be slightly larger than those from the multilevel analysis, because the latter were adjusted to take into account random fluctuations related to school size (as measured by the number of pupils of the relevant age group included in the particular analysis). The estimates are, however, very similar (the correlation between the two estimates obtained for each of the 49 sample schools was 0.98 for the analysis of school effects on reading progress). Figures presented in Table 6.2 show that the difference between the school with the most positive and that with the most negative effect was striking—between 25 and 31 raw

---

5   The background factors taken into account include eligibility for free school meals, ethnic background, fluency in English, father's social class, one-parent family status and family size. These were selected following extensive analyses of the impact of background factors upon both attainment and progress separately for each of the measures of pupils' educational outcomes included in the project (see Mortimore et al. [1986b] for details).

6   Most studies of school effects (such as that by Coleman et al. [1966] and by Jencks et al. [1972]) have examined attainment. But, as has been argued earlier, because of differences between schools in pupils' initial attainments, it is necessary to take into account initial attainments and examine effects upon progress in cognitive areas. The effect of background characteristics upon progress is lower than that on attainment, because such characteristics are strongly related to initial attainment.

Table 6.2.   The size of school effects on reading progress expressed in terms of raw score points (year 1 to year 3).*

	Difference in raw score points*	
School	Fixed effects analysis	Random effects analysis
Most effective school	+19.0	+15.0
Least effective school	+12.0	−10.0
SD school effects	7.4	5.9

* Maximum possible score on the third-year reading assessment = 100
Average raw score on third-year reading assessment = 54

score points compared with an overall average for all children of just under 54 points on the third-year summer reading test, and a range of possible scores of 0–100 points.[7]

Mathematics attainment and progress

The children's mathematics performance was regularly assessed using the NFER Basic Mathematics Test. Four assessments were made, one early in each of the autumn terms (1980–2) and one in the summer term of the third year (summer 1983). School effects upon pupils' attainment and their progress in mathematics over the three years were investigated in the same way as for reading. Again, the school was found to account for a sizeable proportion of the variation in children's third-year mathematics attainment when sex, age, background factors and initial attainment were taken into account. In all, 11 per cent of the variation was explained, in a statistical sense, by school membership (see Table 6.3).[8] As with reading, therefore, the school a child entered aged seven had an effect upon mathematics attainment over the next three years.

The size of the school effect upon third-year mathematics attainment is slightly larger than that found for attainment in reading over the same period. Again, the effect of school membership is much greater than that due to background variables. If relative progress in mathematics over the three years is considered (by taking out the effects of initial attainment), 26 per cent of the variation in children's mathematics progress can be explained by age, sex, background factors and school membership. The school uniquely accounted for 26 per cent of the variation in relative progress, while all the background factors combined explained less than an additional 3 per cent.

Turning to the size of the effects of individual schools upon their pupils' mathematics progress, striking differences between the sample schools were

---

7   A further indication of the range of attainment in the third-year (summer) assessment is given by the following figures: a quarter of the sample obtained scores of 69 raw points and above, while a quarter obtained scores of 33 and below.

8   A table comparing the relative size of school effects upon attainment and progress for all outcomes is presented in Appendix 2. This is derived from the fixed effects analysis.

Table 6.3.   The percentage of variance in third-year mathematics attainment explained by different factors in 1,101 children.

Factors	% of variance explained
Initial (first-year) attainment, age, sex and background factors only	53.96
Initial (first-year) attainment, age, sex, background factors and school	64.88
Unique contribution of initial (first-year) attainment alone	52.81
Unique contribution of the school, after control for initial attainment, age, sex and background factors	10.92
Unique contribution of background factors, sex and age, after control for initial attainment	11.15

identified. As Table 6.4 shows, the difference between the most and the least effective school reached a total of 12 raw score points (16 in the fixed effects analysis). This compared with an overall mean of just under 28 on the third-year mathematics test and a range of possible scores from 0–50 raw points.[9]

The relationship between school effects on progress in reading and mathematics

It is also of interest to establish whether schools which had a positive effect on one cognitive area were also effective in other areas. In other words, were the schools which were more effective in promoting reading progress also more effective in promoting mathematics progress? A measure of this relationship shows that there was a significant association—though not an overwhelmingly strong one—between the two areas of learning ($r = 0.41$, $p < 0.001$). Schools which were more effective in promoting progress in mathematics tended also to have a good effect upon reading progress. Thus, it is clear that success in one of the basic skills was associated with success in the other. However, some schools

Table 6.4.   The size of school effects on mathematics progress expressed in terms of raw score points (year 1 to year 3).*

School	Fixed effects analysis	Random effects analysis
Most effective schools	18.2	16.3
Least effective school	−7.7	−6.2
SD school effects	3.8	2.9

* Maximum possible score on the third-year reading assessment = 100
Average raw score on third-year reading assessment = 54

---

9 A further indication of the range of attainment in the third-year (summer) assessment is given by the following figures: a quarter of the sample obtained scores of 35 raw points and above, while a quarter obtained scores of 18 and below.

appeared to be more successful at teaching—or to have put more emphasis on— some areas rather than others.

Writing attainment and progress

In order to broaden the measures of language performance included in the study, regular assessments of the children's creative writing were conducted (these were made on three occasions in the summer term of the first, second and third years). A variety of measures were used in the writing assessments, including assessments of the quality of language and quality of ideas in the work, as well as more technical aspects such as legibility, length and punctuation. In this section the results are presented of analyses of school effects for an overall measure of writing quality (a combination of the assessments of quality of language and of ideas which were found to be closely related). As with reading and mathematics, results are adjusted for reliability. Experienced primary teachers were used as the writing assessors. They were not aware of the background characteristics of the individual pupils whose work they marked (for details, see Strachan and Sammons, 1986).

To investigate progress in writing, similar analyses to those used for reading and mathematics were adopted. The results show that nearly half of the variation in the quality (in language and ideas) of children's third-year writing can be explained by sex, age, background factors and first-year writing performance. As would be expected, initial attainment is important (see Table 6.5), but the school accounts for over 13 per cent of the variation in the third-year assessment.

As with reading and mathematics, when initial attainment was included in the analyses, the influence of children's background characteristics (including sex and age) is much reduced. School membership also makes a significant contribution to the explanation of variance in relative progress in quality of writing over three years. If the size of the effect of school membership upon relative progress is considered, nearly 20 per cent of the variation in children's writing progress was accounted for by the school and only 3 per cent was due to background.

Table 6.5.   The percentage of variance in the quality of third-year writing explained by different factors in 1,183 children.

Factors	% of variance explained
Initial (first-year) attainment, age, sex and background factors only	33.99
Initial (first-year) attainment, age, sex, background factors and school	47.41
Unique contribution of initial (first-year) attainment alone	31.98
Unique contribution of the school, after control for initial (first-year) attainment, age, sex and background factors	13.42
Unique contribution of background factors, sex and age, after control for initial (first-year) attainment	2.01

Quality of writing was measured on a ten-point scale ranging from 2 to 10 points.[10] The most effective school added 1.7 points to children's writing performance over the three years, whereas, in the least effective school, scores were depressed by 1.3 points over the same period. (The standard deviation for school effects on this outcome was 0.61 raw points.) Again, these results confirm that school membership had a significant impact upon pupils' progress.

Relationships between school effects on writing progress and those on reading and mathematics

In contrast to the significant relationships between school effects in reading and in mathematics, the associations between school effects on progress in these areas and progress in writing quality were weak. Thus, those schools which had a positive effect upon pupils' progress in reading did not necessarily have a positive effect upon progress in quality of writing ($r = 0.15$).

Schools with good effects on mathematics progress, however, showed a weak, but statistically significant, effect on progress in the quality of writing ($r = 0.28$, $p < 0.05$).

These results suggest that, in some schools, there was a special emphasis on particular curriculum areas. None the less, schools which had a negative effect upon progress in one cognitive area did not usually have a positive effect upon other areas (all the correlations, though weak, were in a positive direction). It is interesting to note that school effects on mathematics were more closely related to effects on both reading and writing than were reading and writing to each other.

Oracy attainment

Many primary schools place an emphasis upon the development of pupils' speaking skills. To take into account children's achievements in this area of language, a study of oracy was conducted during the pupils' fourth year of junior education. Measures specially developed by the NFER's Assessment of Performance Unit's (APU) language team were adopted (see Gorman & Hargreaves [1985] for details of the assessments used). These were designed to measure communicative effectiveness and children were not penalized for using non-standard English. Performance in different kinds of speaking activities (e.g. narrative, explanatory or descriptive) was examined. The children worked in pairs during the oracy assessment, to avoid any possible inhibition of their responses which might be caused by talking to an adult. Their performance was assessed 'on the spot' by the project field officers, and was also rated by mem-

---

10   As an indication of the range of attainment in the third-year assessment, nearly 28 per cent of children obtained scores of 5 points or below, while 23 per cent scored 8 points or more. The average score for pupils was 6.2. In this assessment, a higher score indicated a poorer performance.

bers of the APU language team using tapes. This enabled assessments to be adjusted for reliability.

Because oracy was assessed on only one occasion, it was not possible to look at school effects upon progress in this area. However, school effects upon oral attainment were analysed in the same way as other cognitive outcomes. In all, five separate assessments of oral performance were examined. A total of 10 per cent of the variance in children's attainment in the general assessment was attributable to background factors, sex and age, and 27 per cent was due to school membership. Thus, the school which a pupil attended had a significant impact upon the ability to communicate effectively through speech. This impact was greater than that due to individual children's characteristics of background, sex and age.

A similar pattern of results was identified for the specific and the verbal performance assessments, and the non-verbal and lexico-grammatical assessments. In all cases, the school explained (in a statistical sense) a much higher percentage of the variance in attainment than did background factors, sex and age (see Table 6.6). The individual school attended can promote—or have an adverse effect upon—pupils' abilities to communicate effectively in speech. Some schools apparently paid greater attention than others to oral work in the junior curriculum.

Turning to the size of the effects of particular schools on the two oracy assessments for which school membership had the largest effects (the general and the verbal assessments), marked differences between the most and the least effective schools were identified (see Table 6.7). Thus, for the general assessment, the most effective school added nearly 6 raw points to children's performance, whilst, in the least effective school, scores were nearly 5 points lower than predicted, compared with a mean of 21.5 points on this scale.[11] For the verbal performance assessment (where the average score was 10 points) scores were raised

Table 6.6. The percentage of variance in fourth-year oracy assessments explained by different factors in 374 children.

Factors	General	Specific	Verbal	Lexico-grammatic	Non-verbal
Percentage of variance in assessments explained					
Age, sex, background	10.24	7.91	6.95	6.83	2.68
Age, sex, background and school	36.93	21.19	30.92	22.10	17.30
Unique contribution of the school, after control for age, sex and background	26.69	13.28	23.97	15.27	14.62

11 The range of scores possible on the general oracy assessment was between 6 and 35 points. A quarter of the children obtained scores of 25 points or more, whereas 24 per cent obtained scores of 18 points or below.

Table 6.7.   The size of school effects on oracy attainment expressed in terms of raw score points (fixed effects analysis).

School	General assessment	Verbal assessment
Most effective	+5.7	+3.50
Least effective	−4.9	−1.60
SD school effects	2.7	0.83

Maximum possible score on the general assessment = 35
Average score on the general assessment = 21.5
Maximum possible score on the verbal assessment = 15
Average score on the verbal assessment = 10.0

by 3.5 points in the most effective school, but were 1.6 points lower in the least effective school.

The size of school effects upon pupils' performances in the specific and the general assessments of oracy were highly correlated ($r = 0.70, p < 0.001$). There were also strong positive relationships between school effects on the general, and on the task specific and the verbal performance assessments. Effects on other assessments were less closely related (see Table 6.8).

Relationships between school effects on oracy and progress in other cognitive areas

The effects of school membership on the various oracy assessments were only very weakly, though positively, related to school effects on progress in reading and quality of writing, and were not related to school effects on progress in mathematics. None of the correlations was statistically significant ($r = 0.15$ for oracy and reading; $r = 0.1 5$ for oracy and quality of writing; $r = 0.07$ for oracy and mathematics).

Thus, school effects on oracy are not generally related to effects on progress in other areas of the curriculum. Some schools have a good effect on progress in cognitive areas and a good effect on oracy; other schools appear to have had a good effect on other cognitive areas but not on oral communication.

Numbers of schools with good effects on cognitive outcomes

There were clear differences between the sample schools in the number of cognitive areas on which they had a positive effect. Giving each school a score of 'one' if it had a positive effect on any area and 'zero' if it had a negative effect, a scale was constructed to record the total number of areas on which each school had a good effect. The maximum possible score was 4 (good effects on progress in reading, mathematics, writing quality, and on oracy attainment [the general measure]) and the minimum zero—poor effects on all areas.

Table 6.8.   Correlations between school effects upon pupil performance in five assessments of oracy in 48 schools.*

	Assessment				
	General	Specific	Verbal	Non-verbal	Lexico-grammatic
General	1.00	0.70	0.57	0.44	0.27
Specific	–	1.00	0.55	0.26	0.42
Verbal	–	–	1.00	0.07 (ns)	0.59
Non-verbal	–	–	–	1.00	−0.10 (ns)
Lexico-grammatic	–	–	–	–	1.00

* Oracy was not assessed in one of the schools
ns = not statistically significant

The figures in Table 6.9 show that, in all, four schools scored zero; they recorded negative scores on all four cognitive areas. Nine schools had a positive effect on only one of the areas. In contrast, five schools had a positive effect on all areas, and fifteen had a positive effect on three of the four areas considered.[12]

In some cases schools had a very strong positive effect on the majority of cognitive areas. Thus, for example, one school increased its children's third-year reading performance by 24 per cent, or 13 raw points above that predicted by first-year attainment (compared with an average score for all pupils of 54 raw points), mathematics performance by 21 per cent or 6 raw points (compared with an average score for all pupils of 28 raw points), and writing quality by 14.5 per cent (or nearly 1 raw point compared with an average for all pupils of 6.2 raw points). In this school, therefore, taking into account initial attainment and background factors, children had made exceptionally good progress in reading, writing and mathematics during three years of junior education. Another school recorded equally striking progress in reading and

Table 6.9.   Numbers of cognitive outcomes on which the schools had a positive effect.

Number of cognitive outcomes on which school had a positive effect	Number of schools
None	4
One	9
Two	16
Three	15
Four	5
Total	49

12 Due to the crude nature of the 'cut off' employed (positive/negative), some schools may have had only a marginally positive or marginally negative effect.

mathematics, above average progress in quality of writing and above average positive effects on oracy. This school was effective in all four cognitive areas considered.

The school which had the most positive effect on general performance in oracy (raising pupils' performances by nearly 6 raw points compared with 21.5, the average for all pupils) also had good effects on progress in reading and in mathematics (increasing performance over three years by 8 raw points for reading, and 5 raw points for mathematics). However, school effects on writing were only average (neither positive or negative) in this school.

In contrast, in one school, effects on progress in reading, mathematics, writing quality and on oracy attainment were markedly negative. Children made less progress than predicted over the three years. Here, third-year reading scores were depressed by 10 raw points, mathematics scores depressed by 6 raw points, and writing quality by nearly 1 raw point. For oracy (general assessment), attainment was almost 3 raw points poorer than predicted. In all these cognitive areas, therefore, the performance of children attending this school was much poorer than expected over the junior years.

It is possible, therefore, for schools to be very effective in several cognitive areas and, equally, for schools to be ineffective in a number of areas. School membership over three years of junior education can make a very substantial difference to pupils' progress in different areas of learning. These differences in reading, mathematics and writing gains and in ability to communicate effectively through speech are likely to have an important effect on children's secondary-school careers.

Effects of school membership on non-cognitive outcomes

Behaviour in school
Information about each child's behaviour in school was collected from his or her class teacher on a regular basis (twice a year at the beginning of the autumn and end of the summer term) using the 'Child at School' form. Because of the difficulties involved in using teacher-based assessments, an overall measure of the child's behaviour (the sum of assessments made in the autumn terms of the first, second and third years) was used.[13] This overall measure helped to 'smooth out' any aberrant ratings because, to score highly, a child would have to be rated by different class teachers as having difficulties in more than one year.

To assess the impact of school membership, similar methods were used to those employed in analysing the cognitive outcomes. Thus, the same range of background factors, sex and age were taken into account.

---

13 Questions of the reliability of data arise because some children react in different ways with different teachers, and some teachers hold different views about what constitutes 'acceptable' or 'difficult' behaviour. Full details of the behaviour measures used in this project are given in Kysel et al. (1983).

Table 6.10. The percentage of variance in the overall measure of behaviour explained by different factors in 1,285 children.

Factors	% variance explained
Age, sex and background only	12.94
Age, sex, background and school	22.71
Unique contribution of school after control for age, sex and background	9.77

The results indicate that school membership made a significant contribution in explaining differences in behaviour over the junior years (see Table 6.10). Taking the overall measure of behaviour, it was found that background factors, sex and age uniquely accounted for nearly 13 per cent of the variance, while school membership uniquely accounted for (in a statistical sense) nearly 10 per cent of the variance.[14]

The size of the effects of some individual schools was substantial. In the most effective school, behaviour scores were reduced by an average of 19 raw points (a lower score signifying better behaviour in school). In the least effective school, scores were raised by an average of nearly 9 raw points. The difference (around 28 points) compares with an average rating for all pupils of 59.9 on the combined behaviour measure. (The standard deviation of school effects on the combined behaviour measure was 5.9 raw points.)[15]

Attendance

For most pupils, school attendance was very high during the junior years (an average of over 90 per cent was recorded in each year). Two measures were used to calculate the effects of school membership on this outcome. One was based on attendance in the third year, and one on change over the three years.

Overall, children's background characteristics, sex and age uniquely accounted for only a small proportion of the variance in third-year attendance (less than 4 per cent). These relationships are much weaker than those identified for analyses of cognitive outcomes in the third year (when no controls are included for initial attainment). The school made a slightly larger contribution at 5.6 per cent. Even so, only a small proportion of the variance in third-year attendance was accounted for by these factors (age, sex and background factors, and school), less than 10 per cent.

The results suggested that the school to which a child belonged could have some effect, even if this was small. The size of such an effect ranged from a decrease in absence of nearly 5 per cent below that predicted in the most effective school (a reduction in absence of roughly nine days), to an increase in

---

14 The level of explanation is lower for overall measure of behaviour than for the analyses of progress in cognitive areas, because no control was made for initial behaviour scores.

15 The range of possible scores was between 27 and 135. A quarter of children received ratings of 45 points and below, and a quarter 73 or more.

absence of over 4 per cent above that predicted (an increase in absence of rough-ly seven days) in the least effective school. (The standard deviation for school effects on attendance was 2.2 per cent, roughly 4.5 school days.) For junior age pupils, therefore, there is some evidence that membership of particular schools may help to promote regular attendance, whereas, in others, the reverse is the case.

When changes in attendance were examined, by taking into account child-ren's first-year attendance, the importance of school membership was reduced (in these analyses school membership accounted uniquely for only 4 per cent of variance in third-year attendance when first-year attendance was controlled). The size of the effects of particular schools (which were highly correlated on the two attendance measures: $r = 0.89$) were reduced, ranging from 3 per cent less absence for children in the most effective, to 4 per cent more time absent in the least effective school.

These results suggest that the impact of the school upon attendance during the junior years is of less importance than for behaviour and for cognitive out-comes. This finding is in marked contrast to those reported in studies of sec-ondary schools (Reynolds, 1982; Rutter et al., 1979a), and may reflect the fact that junior age pupils, because of their age and dependence on parents, are able to exercise much less choice about attending school than are secondary school pupils.

Self-concept

The children's assessments of themselves in school (a measure of one aspect of self-concept) were obtained on only one occasion, at the end of the third year. The 'Me at School' measure (based on the 'Child at School' schedule used in the teachers' assessments of behaviour) was adopted. This is a self-report measure consisting of eleven items which measure four aspects of self-concept—aggres-sion, anxiety, learning difficulties and naughtiness. The total score on the sched-ule gives an overall measure of self-concept in school (see Sammons and Stoll [1988] for details of the measure used). Because of this, it was not possible to examine any changes in self-concept over the junior years.

As with attendance, it was found that the background characteristics, sex and age of individual children did not account for much of the variance in children's ratings of themselves (a mere 3.2 per cent). The school uniquely accounted for a higher percentage of the variance (8.4 per cent), indicating that school mem-bership can have an impact upon the development of children's self-concepts in relation to school. The range between the school with the largest positive effect upon self-concept and that with the largest negative effect was over 7 points. This compared with an overall mean of 27.7 points and a range of possible scores from 11–55 points. The standard deviation of school effects on this out-come was 1.8 raw points. The analysis of school effects on self-concept was based on a total of 1,451 pupils.[16]

---

16 In all, 23 per cent of children's self-ratings were 23 points or below, while 24 per cent were above 32 points. As with behaviour, a higher score signified a poorer self-image in school.

None the less, under 12 per cent of the variance in self-concept scores was accounted for, suggesting that other factors must also have an important impact (peer groups and parental relationships may well have had a major influence).

Attitudes

Information was collected on a regular basis (in the summer term of the first, second and third years) about children's attitudes towards a variety of curriculum areas, and towards school, using a self-report measure consisting of 29 items (see Stoll and Sammons [1988] for a description of the Smiley attitude scale). It was not appropriate to draw up a composite measure of attitudes, as earlier analyses had shown that children had very specific attitudes towards different activities, and that relationships between attitudes to school and to school activities were not strong (see Mortimore et al., 1986a, 1986b). The concept of progress or change in attitudes was also not considered appropriate in this study. Instead, school effects upon attitudes were examined for the third-year assessment. This, it was hoped, would give the most accurate information about the cumulative effects of school membership. There is evidence to suggest that measurement problems in assessing children's attitudes are reduced for older age groups (Piers & Harris, 1964).

Information about the children's attitudes towards school and towards mathematics, reading and writing (the three curriculum areas for which progress data were available) was analysed. The results showed that, as with self-concept and attendance, the overall level of explanation of variance for the attitude measures was low. Again, children's background characteristics, sex and age made only a small contribution (see Table 6.11).

Background factors, age and sex, were slightly more important in accounting for differences in attitudes to school than in explaining attitudes towards the three curriculum areas, suggesting that school was especially important for this area. In all cases, however, school membership uniquely accounted for a larger proportion of the variation than background factors, sex and age (between 7.5 per cent and 12.2 per cent). School effects were largest for attitude to mathematics (12.2 per cent) and smallest for attitude to reading (7.5 per cent). It is possible that attitudes to reading are more subject to influences from the home than are attitudes towards mathematics.

Nonetheless, children's attitudes are affected by school membership. In particular schools, children's attitudes towards school and towards curriculum areas are more positive than in others, even when account is taken of the influence of age, sex and background factors. For example, looking at attitude to school—which was measured on a 5-point scale—for the school with the most positive impact, the average effect was an improvement of attitudes by over 1 point, whereas in the school with the least favourable, impact, scores were depressed by over 1 raw point. (The standard deviation for school effects on attitude to school was 0.49 raw points.)

Table 6.11. The percentage of variance in third-year attitudes explained by different factors in 1,463 children.

Factors	% variance in attitude			
	to school	to mathematics	to reading	to writing
Age, sex and background factors only	5.00	2.29	3.12	1.81
Age, sex, background factors and school	13.74	14.5	10.57	9.88
Unique contribution of the school, after control for age, sex and background factors	8.74	12.21	7.45	8.07

Relationships between school effects on non-cognitive outcomes

Information about each school's effects on the various non-cognitive measures were correlated. This was done to establish whether there were any consistent relationships, such that schools which had a 'good' effect on one area tended to have a 'good' effect on other areas also. The results revealed some statistically significant associations, although, on the whole, correlations were not strong. Overall, schools which had a 'good' effect upon pupils' attitudes to one area tended to have a 'good' effect upon attitudes to other areas. In particular, attitude to 'school' and attitude to 'mathematics' were significantly correlated (see Table 6.12).

In addition, school effects upon self-concept (a self-report measure) were also significantly and positively related to effects on attitude to school and on attitude to mathematics ($p < 0.01$).

Thus, there is a general tendency for schools with a favourable impact upon pupils' attitudes to school and to mathematics to have a favourable impact upon self-concepts. Those with a negative impact upon attitudes to school and to mathematics tended also to have a negative impact upon pupils' self-concepts.

The measures of behaviour were significantly, though weakly, related to two of the measures of attitudes (see Table 6.13). Schools with a positive effect upon

Table 6.12. Correlations between school effects on attitudes and self-concept in 48 schools.

Attitude to school and attitude to mathematics	0.38**
Attitude to school and attitude to reading	0.30*
Attitude to reading and attitude to mathematics	0.28*
Attitude to reading and attitude to writing	0.33**
Self-concept and attitude to school	0.36**
Self-concept and attitude to mathematics	0.36**

Only significant correlations are presented; * $p < 0.05$; ** $p < 0.01$

Table 6.13. Correlations between school effects on behaviour, attitudes and self-concept in 47 schools.

Behaviour and attitude to mathematics	0.35**
Behaviour and attitude to school	0.30*

Only significant correlations reported; *$p < 0.05$, **$p < 0.01$

behaviour tended to have a positive effect on attitude to school, and on attitude to mathematics.

School effects upon attendance were generally uncorrelated with the other measures of non-cognitive outcomes. The only statistically significant relationship was with the effects on self-concept ($r = -0.25, p < 0.5$). Interestingly, this was a negative correlation, indicating that schools with good effects on attendance tended to have a slightly unfavourable impact upon pupils' self-concepts.

Numbers of schools with positive effects on non-cognitive outcomes

A total score was calculated for each school to record the number of non-cognitive outcomes on which it showed a positive effect. The maximum score possible was 7—representing positive effects on behaviour, self-concept, attendance, attitude to school, attitude to mathematics, attitude to reading and attitude to writing—and the minimum zero—representing poor effects on all areas.

Five schools had a positive effect on only one of the seven non-cognitive areas considered, and a further eight a positive effect on only two of the seven areas (see Table 6.14).

In contrast, two schools recorded a positive effect on all seven areas, and four schools had a positive effect upon six. There is strong evidence, therefore, of variation between schools in their effects upon pupils' non-cognitive outcomes. From

Table 6.14. Numbers of non-cognitive outcomes on which schools had a positive effect in 47 schools.*

Number of non-cognitive areas with a positive effect	Number of schools
none	0
one	5
two	8
three	9
four	10
five	8
six	5
seven	2

*One of the sample schools did not assess behaviour in the third year and attitudes were not assessed in another. These two schools, therefore, are not included in this table.

these results it appears that some schools apparently paid more attention to promoting the social aspects of education than did others. Some differences were
striking. For example, in one school the effect on pupil behaviour over three years
was markedly positive (scores were 19 raw points better than predicted—compared with an overall mean for the pupil sample of 59.9 on this combined assessment). This school also had a weak positive effect on self-concept, improving
scores by 1.4 raw points better than predicted (compared with an overall mean
for the pupil sample of 27.7), a substantial positive effect on attitude to school
(improving attitudes by 1.2 raw points compared with an overall mean for all
pupils of 2.9 on this 5-point scale) and moderately positive effects on attitudes
to the curriculum areas of reading, mathematics and writing.

At the other extreme, one school had a negative effect upon behaviour (children's scores were 8 raw points poorer than predicted), a poor effect on attitude
to school (scores were depressed by 0.74 of a raw point for this measure) and
weak negative effects on self-concept and on attitudes to reading, mathematics
and writing.

From these results it would appear that particular schools had placed a
greater emphasis on the non-cognitive aspects of education than others.
Children's attitudes to school and to different curriculum areas, self-concepts
and behaviour are improved by attending some schools and schooling is enjoyable. In others, however, attitudes, self-concepts and behaviour are depressed.
For children in these schools, junior education appears to have been considerably less enjoyable than it might have been.

Relationships between school effects on cognitive and non-cognitive outcomes

Correlation techniques were used to examine the links between school effects
upon cognitive and non-cognitive outcomes. The results indicated that effects on
attitude to mathematics were significantly, though weakly, related to school
effects on progress in mathematics over the junior years ($r = 0.24$, $p < 0.05$).
Moreover, good effects upon progress in the quality of writing were associated
with positive effects on attitude to reading ($r = 0.33$, $p < 0.01$). However,
school effects on reading progress were not related to effects on attitude to reading. These results provide, therefore, limited support for the view that schools
which are effective in promoting progress in a particular area will tend to promote good attitudes towards that area (see Table 6.15).

School effects upon progress in the quality of writing were related significantly to both the measures of attendance. Thus, in schools which had a positive effect on attendance, children tended to make more progress in writing
during the junior years. Poor attendance was associated with poorer progress in
writing. However, attendance was not related to school effects on progress in
reading or in mathematics.

There was a strong and highly significant correlation between school effects
upon self-concept and those on progress in mathematics ($r = 0.58$, $p < 0.0001$).

Table 6.15. Correlations between school effects on cognitive and on non-cognitive outcomes.

	r
Absence (change year 1–3) and quality of writing	0.31 *
Absence (effect year 3) and quality of writing	0.33**
Mathematics and attitude to mathematics	0.24* (n = 48)
Quality of writing and attitude to reading	0.33* (n = 48)

n = 49 unless otherwise indicated; $p < 0.05, p < 0.01$

Schools with positive effects on the measure of self-concept were very likely to have good effects on children's mathematics progress. Negative effects on mathematics progress were likely to be related to negative effects on children's self-concepts. The relationship between school effects upon self-concept and upon reading progress, although in the same direction as that identified for mathematics, was much weaker ($r = 0.25, p < 0.05$).

Using methods of confirmatory factor analysis, it was possible to establish whether, in general, school effects upon cognitive areas were independent of those upon non-cognitive areas. The results of these analyses showed that these two dimensions were separate. Thus, 'positive' effects upon cognitive outcomes are not necessarily related to 'positive' effects on non-cognitive areas. Neither are 'negative' effects upon one area necessarily related to 'negative' effects on other areas (though, as will be discussed below, some schools do have 'good' or 'poor' effects on both of these areas).

Confirmatory factor analysis indicated that, within the various cognitive areas considered, school effects upon progress in reading, in mathematics and in writing quality and length formed one dimension. Effects in these (the more formal aspects of the curriculum) were more closely related and can be seen as a separate dimension from those on the general oracy assessment.[17]

Amongst the non-cognitive areas, it appeared that school effects on behaviour, attitude to reading, attitude to mathematics and attitude to school formed another separate dimension. Effects on attendance, self-concept and attitude to writing were not generally related to the school effects on behaviour and the other attitude measures. The two dimensions of cognitive effects (on progress in the two aspects of writing and on reading and mathematics) and of non-cognitive effects (on behaviour, attitude to mathematics, attitude to reading and attitude to school) formed independent factors. The correlation between the two

---

17 A variety of Lisrel models were used to test the relationships amongst school effects upon the various cognitive and non-cognitive outcomes. One, two, three and four factor solutions were tested for all, and for sub-sets of the outcomes. The adjusted goodness of fit index and the reduction in chi-square values were examined to establish the model giving the best fit to the data. School effects on writing length were included in these analyses.

dimensions was 0.14 and the 't' value for this relationship was 0.62, which was not statistically significant.

The interpretation of the result that school effects upon pupils' cognitive and non-cognitive outcomes are independent suggests that the sorts of processes which are responsible for schools exerting 'positive' or 'negative' effects upon these two dimensions may be different. However, it is encouraging to note that school effects upon cognitive outcomes are not negatively related to effects on non-cognitive outcomes. It is not necessary, therefore, to sacrifice good effects on the non-cognitive or social aspects of junior education in order to promote pupils' progress in cognitive outcomes. Nor is it the case that, in promoting non-cognitive outcomes, progress in cognitive areas will be adversely affected.

Numbers of schools with positive effects on cognitive and non-cognitive areas

Although the two dimensions of school effects on cognitive and non-cognitive outcomes were found to be independent, it is of importance to establish whether schools can be effective in promoting good outcomes both for cognitive and for non-cognitive areas. This is because the majority of teachers and parents are keen to promote children's progress and development in both areas. Few would support a narrow focus on only one or other of the two dimensions.

To establish the extent to which schools were effective on a variety of the cognitive and non-cognitive outcomes, the total scores recorded on each area (ranging from 0–4 for the cognitive and 0–7 for the non-cognitive) were cross-related. The figures in Table 6.16 show that a number of schools in the sample recorded positive effects on several cognitive and several non-cognitive areas. For example, 14 schools had positive effects on three or more of the cognitive and four or more of the non-cognitive outcomes. In contrast, 5 schools had positive effects on only one of the cognitive areas, and on only three or fewer of the non-cognitive areas.

A very few schools, however, scored highly on one dimension but not on the other. Thus, two schools recorded positive effects on all four of the cognitive areas but only two of the seven non-cognitive areas. In contrast, six schools had a poor effect on nearly all cognitive areas (one or none) but positive effects on four or more non-cognitive areas.

Conclusions

School membership made a significant contribution to the explanation of differences between pupils in attainment and progress over three years in reading, writing and mathematics, and also to the development of attitudes, self-concept and behaviour in school. The school for junior pupils had rather less effect upon attendance than upon other outcomes. These results indicate that the school a

Table 6.16. Relationship between schools' scores on the total of positive effects on cognitive and the total of positive effects on non-cognitive outcomes.

Number of positive cognitive outcomes	Number of positive non-cognitive outcomes							
	One	Two	Three	Four	Five	Six	Seven	
None	–	1	–	2	–	–	1	4
One	2	2	1	1	1	1	–	8
Two	2	3	6		5			16
Three	1	–	2	5	1	4	1	14
Four	–	2	–	2	1	–	–	5
Number of schools	5	8	9	10	8	5	2	47

child attends during the junior years can have a beneficial or a negative effect upon his or her progress and development. The importance of school membership in explaining variations in pupils' progress over the junior years is a major finding of this study. It has been shown that the school makes a far greater contribution to the explanation of progress than is made by pupils' background characteristics, sex and age. This result is of significance for teachers, pupils and parents.

Some schools were particularly effective at promoting progress in specific cognitive areas, and others were especially effective at promoting behaviour or attitudes or self-concept. The relationships, though complex, indicate that, on the whole, schools which promoted progress in mathematics, tended also to do so in reading. In addition, such schools tended to foster self-concept and, to a lesser extent, positive attitudes to mathematics. There were weaker relationships between school effects on progress in writing, and progress in other cognitive areas. However, schools with positive effects on writing progress tended to have similar effects on attitude to reading, good progress in mathematics and good effects on attendance.

In general, effects of school membership on non-cognitive outcomes were not highly related to those on cognitive areas. Analyses indicated that the two dimensions were largely independent of each other. None the less, amongst the sample of schools included in the study, there were striking differences in effectiveness. Some schools had strong positive effects on progress and development for several areas. Others had a negative effect on several areas. For the pupil, therefore, which school he or she joined at seven years of age can have a highly significant impact upon future progress or development in several different areas. These effects of junior schooling are likely to be carried forward with the child at secondary transfer and may have a long-term influence on future progress and achievement.

One of the central questions addressed by the Junior School Project was '*Do junior schools make a difference to pupils' educational outcomes?*' It is clear not only that schools do make a difference, and that the difference is substantial, but also that school effects on cognitive outcomes are generally independent of those on non-cognitive areas. However, some schools are effective in many different areas. These results confirm the value of including assessments of a variety of educational outcomes in a study of school effects. By using information about the broad range of outcomes, a much fairer picture of the general effectiveness of schools is obtained.[18]

Postscript

This chapter illustrates the technical advances made in the early 1980s in the analysis of complex data sets. The increased sophistication of the techniques permit more penetrating questions to be asked of the data. When the constraints within which research has to work can be broadened, the value of the work to policy makers and to practitioners increases. The identification of robust methods of measuring progress, for instance, underpins many later developments in statistical analyses in this field of school effectiveness. I think our School Matters *research team had cause to be proud of this paper.*

---

18 The factors and processes responsible for these differences in the effectiveness of junior schools are reported in Mortimore et al., 1986b.

Appendix 1

Calculating the size of school effects on pupils' progress

Method for results from fixed effects model
In order to calculate progress, it was necessary first to separate out the effects upon attainment in year three due to, i) initial attainment, ii) school, iii) background factors, age and sex.[19]

Calculating the effects of school on attainment[20]
R_2 due to school = Adjusted R_2 (model 2) − Adjusted R_2 (model 1), where: model 1 includes background factors, sex, age and initial attainment with third year attainment dependent; model 2 includes school, background factors, sex, age and initial attainment with third year attainment dependent; and model 3 includes attainment with third-year attainment dependent.

Calculating progress over three years

The overall amount of variance in pupils' progress which could be accounted for was calculated as follows:

$$\frac{\text{Adjusted } R_2 \text{ (model 2)} - \text{Adjusted } R_2 \text{ (model 3)}}{1 - \text{Adjusted } R_2 \text{ (model 3)}}$$

Cognitive progress

Percentage of variance due to initial attainment (model 3)

Writing quality	31.98
Mathematics	52.81
Reading	61.72

Percentage of variance due to school, initial attainment, background factors, sex, age (model 2)

Writing quality	47.41
Mathematics	64.88
Reading	73.08

Table continues

---

19 All calculations adjusted for reliability where applicable.

20 The method of calculating school effects on progress adopted was that described by Plewis, I; Progress in Language and Mathematics in the Reception Year of Infant School: A Preliminary Analysis, February 1985 (confidential report).

(Table *cont.*)

Percentage of variance due to initial attainment, background factors, sex, age (model 1)	
Writing quality	33.99
Mathematics	53.96
Reading	64.04

Total percentage of variance in progress explained

Writing quality
$$\frac{(47.41 - 31.98)}{100 - 31.98} = 22.08\%$$

Reading
$$\frac{(73.08 - 61.72)}{(100 - 61.72)} = 29.68\%$$

Method for Results from the Multilevel Model
In order to confirm findings derived from the fixed effect model on the importance of school membership in determining pupil progress, the results of multilevel analyses were examined.

Here, the school effect was calculated as the percentage of the error variance attributable to the level of the school (school effects being treated as random). The results also indicated that the school made a substantial contribution in accounting for pupils' progress in cognitive outcomes.

Cognitive outcomes	% error variance due to school
Reading	19.93
Mathematics	16.60
Writing quality	11.66

Appendix 2

The relative size of school effects for each outcome*

Cognitive outcomes	% variance in attainment	% variance in progress
Reading	9.0	23.6
Mathematics	10.9	23.1
Writing quality	13.4	19.7
Practical Mathematics		
Length	20.9	–
Number	12.3	–
Weight	11.9	–
Volume	3.4	–
Oracy		
General	26.6	–
Specific	13.3	–
Verbal	24.0	
Non-verbal	14.6	–
Lexico-grammatical	15.3	

Non-cognitive	% variance	
Behaviour	9.8	–
Self-concept	8.4	–
Attitude to school	8.7	–
Attitude to mathematics	12.2	–
Attitude to writing	8.1	–
Attitude to reading	7.5	–
Attendance	5.6	–

* Estimates derived from analyses using fixed effects model

7

The Reception of Educational Research

Introduction

This chapter was written for a book edited by Geoffrey Walford, at that time a lecturer at the University of Aston. Walford wanted to produce a collection of accounts written by practising researchers about what it was really like to work in the field of educational research. I based my contribution on the impact of the publication of the two major studies of school effectiveness with which I had been involved. I enjoyed the 'research on the research'—going through the various press cuttings, re-reading the reviews, reflecting on what had happened and speculating as to why people had reacted as they did.

Publicity for researchers is a double-edged sword. If we get it we are frequently unhappy with the results, which are never accurate enough for our tastes. Yet if our work is ignored we feel affronted. Because we know our work so well, we often consider that journalists give it the wrong emphases or totally distort its meaning. We are aware, however, that if the research findings are ever to influence public policy we need the press coverage. It was for these reasons that I drew up the list of recommendations with which I end the chapter.

British educational researchers are a relatively new breed. Although there is a rich tradition of writers, like Arnold of Rugby, addressing educational ideas, it is only in the last thirty or so years that educational research—as distinct from psychological, sociological or even psychiatric studies—has been funded from public sources and that the results of studies have begun to influence what goes on in schools. (A lucid account of developments through this time can be read in Shipman, 1985). Even so, it is sometimes difficult to identify clearly what makes up an 'educational research study' and to distinguish this from similar studies carried out in the general area of the social sciences. This is because educational researchers usually have taken their degrees in other subjects and have frequently worked in different traditions. It is a strength of education, in my view, that it can draw on the methods and concepts of other disciplines and that it can adopt—as appropriate—their perspectives, paradigms and theories.

This flexibility of approach and youthful vigour are helpful. But perhaps less helpful is the lack of collective experience of publishing work and disseminating findings. Furthermore, because education is such an important aspect of our society—especially in current times—publishing results and disseminating findings can take place in a highly charged political atmosphere. Alternatively, findings can be ignored—hence the title of the original article—*The Front Page or Yesterday's News*.

In this chapter, I will examine the publication of research results. I will draw on my experience as co-author of two major studies of school effectiveness—*Fifteen Thousand Hours*, a study of secondary schools by Rutter, Maughan, Mortimore and Ouston (1979a), and *School Matters*, a study of primary schools by Mortimore, Sammons, Stoll, Lewis and Ecob (1988a)—rather than from the general repertoire of recent educational studies.

I have chosen to focus on these studies because, as someone closely involved in them, I was aware of the issues raised by their publication and kept records of the newspaper coverage. Authors of other studies might have different or more interesting stories to tell. For example, the first researcher into school effectiveness in the United Kingdom was Michael Power. He analysed delinquency data and endeavoured to relate these to school and area influences. The work was highly controversial and a premature letter to *The Times*, appearing to lay blame for differential delinquency rates on teachers, virtually ended the study (Power et al., 1967).

Likewise, the media reports that followed the publication of *Teaching Styles and Pupil Progress* (Bennett, 1976), were extensive—including a prime-time television programme—and contributed to a controversy over styles of teaching. The re-analysis of the data collected for this study using more sophisticated analytical techniques led to the subsequent reinterpretation of the findings.

The reinterpretation of this work (Aitkin & Bennett, 1980), in contrast, never appeared to elicit the same media response. More recently, the publication of *The School Effect*, a research study exploring the relative strengths of the influence of individual secondary schools and of the race of secondary pupils (Smith and Tomlinson, 1989), received an enormous amount of attention in the press. The scope for exploring the role of the media in relation to these studies, therefore, is considerable, but will not be dealt with here.

I should also make clear that, whilst Rutter et al. (1979a) and Mortimore et al. (1988a) received a great deal of attention, a number of other pieces of work with which I have been involved have not. In some cases this may have been because the work was smaller in scale or inherently less interesting. In other cases, however, it is likely that the work was less politically appealing to newspaper journalists. Thus, the work evaluating support centres for disruptive pupils (Mortimore et al., 1983) received only academic book reviews and no coverage in the daily press. Curiously, I also received considerable publicity for a study which, though planned, was never undertaken. The proposed study, of high-achieving minority pupils, was abandoned because of a fear by some communities that the results might be used as an excuse for a lack of positive action (see discussion in Swann, 1985).

This chapter will end by listing a set of recommendations for researchers. These will include precautions to be taken before a study is planned, as well as during its active life and at the crucial time of publication.

The *Fifteen Thousand Hours* research

The idea for a study which investigated how much individual secondary schools were able to influence the achievement and development of their pupils can be traced to earlier work carried out by Michael Rutter and various associates—in particular, the seminal Isle of Wight epidemiological study (Rutter et al., 1970) and the subsequent Inner London Borough comparison (Rutter et al., 1975a, 1975b). Having explored the influence of the neighbourhood on the lives of children and their parents, it seemed natural to explore in more detail the impact of the school—an idea enthusiastically sponsored by a group of local head teachers. The initial investment in research on a cohort of 10-year-olds could be exploited by a carefully planned follow-up study of those same young people as they progressed through secondary education.

The Department of Education and Science grant was agreed and the research team appointed by January 1975. By this stage, Rutter and colleagues had already collected a range of follow-up measures on the (by then) 14-year-olds who made up the original 10-year-old sample and who had progressed to twenty secondary schools. The measures collected included tests of reading and non-verbal intelligence, teacher ratings of behaviour, and up-dated background information.

Data collection
Between January 1975 and June 1978, the research team, of which I was a member, collected a great deal more information on twelve of the schools selected to form a representative sample. Schools were given assurances of complete confidentiality. Using a variety of research techniques (including classroom observations, interviews with head teachers and teachers and researcher-administered questionnaires to pupils, we established a large pool of pupil and school measures. These data were enhanced by supplementary material from the census (using the Office of Population and Census Surveys/Centre for Environmental

Studies classifications), records of official delinquency (we were given access to data by the Metropolitan Police Juvenile Bureau) and the public examination results of the cohort's fifth year.

The co-operation extended by the head teachers and their colleagues to the research team was quite remarkable. No school dropped out. No teacher refused us access to the classroom. Considering the difficulties—mainly through teacher turnover—experienced by secondary schools during the 1970s, this was very impressive. Equally impressive was the interest shown by the twelve schools in the preliminary results presented to each school staff by the research team at the end of the study. The findings of the study, as with most large-scale empirical work, were complex (for a full account see Rutter et al., 1979a), but our four major conclusions were as follows:

1   Secondary schools varied in respect of their pupils' behaviour, attendance, examination success and delinquency . . . even after taking into account differences in intake.
2   Variations in outcome were systematically and strongly associated with the characteristics of schools and social institutions.
3   The research showed *which* school variables were associated with good behaviour and attainments.
4   The pattern of findings suggested that not only were pupils influenced by the way they were dealt with as individuals, but also there was a group influence resulting from the ethos of the school as a social institution. (p. 205)

Impact of publication

The results of the study were made available to all those involved in the study in the summer of 1978 and, in 1979, a book aimed at wider readership was published by Open Books. Accompanying its launch, at a press conference on 22 March, were a series of accounts and commentaries—notably by Rick Rogers in the *New Statesman* (Rogers, 1979) and Caroline St John Brooks in *New Society* (St John Brooks, 1979) and a more varied batch of newspaper articles. The newspaper comments were led by the *Observer*, which broke the publisher's embargo as early as January in an article headlined 'When Potted Plants Are Better Than Discipline' (Stevens, 1979). This was followed by an article on 18 March by Rhodes Boyson in the *News of the World* complete with a photograph of an urban school (Boyson, 1979). Whereas Boyson had focused on the negative findings, Alan Whitehouse, writing in the *Yorkshire Post* on 21 March, highlighted more positive aspects in an article headlined 'Lessons for a Perfect School' (Whitehouse, 1979). *The Nottingham Evening Post* (22 March) chose the headline 'Education Myths Are Exploded' (Bailey, 1979). In the *Daily Express* of 22 March, Bruce Kemble provided a seven-point practical check-list entitled 'Your Good School Guide' (Kemble, 1979).

The *Evening News* of the same day carried a series of articles by their staff reporter, Tony Doran, with a headline 'Do as I Do—Not as I Say' (Doran, 1979).

Christopher Rowlands of the *Daily Mail* chose to widen the scope of the discussion with the headline of 'Schools that Harm the Gifted' and an opening paragraph that stated: 'Gifted children do not achieve their potential in badly organized comprehensive schools' (Rowlands, 1979). Another (local) paper—the *Southend Evening Echo*—picked up the story on 27 March with a curious and somewhat inaccurate headline 'Less Caning Does Not Spoil the Child' (Oswick, 1979).

The review in the *Teacher*—the weekly paper of the National Union of Teachers—was supportive of the research in a somewhat lukewarm way, as illustrated by the headline 'Secondary Findings Stress the Obvious' (National Union of Teachers, 1979). Finally, the *Economist* for the week ending 31 March devoted three columns to a positive review entitled, simply, 'Schools Count' (*Economist*, 1979). The *Times Educational Supplement* was unable to report the study, since, like all *Times* publications at that time, industrial action meant it was not being produced.

Most of the press commentary on the study dealt only with the central finding—that individual schools varied in their effects—even though, as has been noted, the interpretations of these findings and their implications for schools varied widely.

The extent of the coverage was surprising—at least to the research team. In retrospect, it may not have been as helpful as initially it appeared. To have so much space in the daily newspapers devoted to research findings means that the work will be taken seriously. It also means that critics will focus on the study and, to some extent, search for any weaknesses which can be exposed!

Critiques by researchers
The second wave of commentary on the study consisted of a series of critical articles by fellow researchers. Acton (1980), Tizard (1980), Goldstein (1980) and Heath and Clifford (1980) published major critical articles on the study. The research team felt bound to respond and, accordingly, a reply to Acton was printed in the same edition of *Educational Research* (Rutter et al., 1980a). Likewise, rejoinders to the comments by Tizard and by Goldstein were included in the same edition of the *Journal of Child Psychology and Psychiatry* (Rutter et al., 1980b). The reply to Heath and Clifford's critique in the *Oxford Review* appeared in a later edition (Maughan et al., 1980) and was followed by a further rejoinder (Heath & Clifford, 1981).

Two collections of discussion papers were produced as a result of symposia devoted to debate on the study: one at the Thomas Coram Research Unit of the Institute of Education (Tizard et al., 1980) and one at Exeter University (Dancy, 1979). Both provided space for our responses (Mortimore, 1979; Rutter et al., 1979b).

The British Journal of the Sociology of Education devoted twelve pages to a review symposium on the study. Comments were invited from three sociologists: Reynolds, whose evaluation was mixed; Hargreaves, who was rather critical; and Blackstone, who, on the whole, was positive (Reynolds et al., 1980).

Academics, however, were not the only reviewers of the work. Practitioners—especially from inner London—also expressed views. Peter Newsam, then the Education Officer of the ILEA, provided a positive half-page review in the *Observer* (Newsam, 1979); Trevor Jagger, then the Staff Inspector for secondary education in the ILEA, published a long and highly supportive review in *Education* (Jagger, 1979); Marten Shipman, the ex-Director of Research and Statistics in the ILEA, wrote a positive review in *Research in Education* (Shipman, 1980).

As if all this was not enough, during 1980, *Education*, the *Times Educational Supplement* (by now back in print) and the *Education Guardian* each decided to give space to a second look at the study. *Education* published an article by Ted Wragg in which he summarized the arguments expressed at the Exeter symposium (Wragg, 1980). In an article entitled 'Second Thoughts on the Rutter Ethos' in the *Times Educational Supplement*, Bob Doe also drew on the Exeter publication to summarize criticisms and replies (Doe, 1980). In the *Education Guardian*, Maureen O'Connor, in a delightfully headlined article—'Fifteen Thousand Hours That Shook the Academics'—drew on Goldstein's, Heath and Clifford's, Thomas Coram's and Acton's critiques and the responses to these (O'Connor, 1980).

Constraints of length in this chapter lead me to exclude the equally numerous reviews and articles that appeared in American papers and journals. Suffice it to say that for a British book to receive so much attention in the United States is unusual. On the whole, comment by academics was more uniformly positive than in the United Kingdom. The most critical review, carried in the organ of the American Educational Research Association—*The Educational Researcher* (Armento, 1980)—was itself severely criticized by two other academics for its negative tone in a subsequent edition (Gideanse, 1981; Owens, 1981).

Conclusions about the publication of *Fifteen Thousand Hours*

My aim in documenting all this material is certainly not to re-open these debates, but to illustrate what researchers can provoke when they publish their work! My personal view is that while some of the technical criticisms were justified (is there any research study which, with hindsight, could not be improved?) the enthusiasm with which such criticism was levelled was possibly a reaction to the positive press comments and was probably fuelled by a variety of motivations, from the political to the personal. Looking back, more than ten years after publication, I consider that the book—and the study and reports—have stood up well to the test of time. It was an ambitious study—probably attempting to solve statistical problems before appropriate methods and computer software had been developed—but certainly a worthwhile endeavour. *Fifteen Thousand Hours* has been cited a great deal in both the British and the North American educational literature and has been widely adopted by practitioners—at home and abroad—anxious to participate in school improvement work.

What was the effect of the press coverage? In retrospect, I think there were two main effects: one negative and one positive. The negative effect was that the complex findings of the study were trivialized and some journalists and other commentators seized the opportunity to claim support for their particular hobby horses—regardless of whether, in fact, the data lent any support to their cause. The positive effect was that a number of head teachers, teachers and inspectors/advisers were alerted to the study. The sales figures for the period indicate that many readers purchased copies. In a country where there was not a strong tradition of practitioners studying the results of educational research, this was very encouraging to us.

The *School Matters* research

The study reported in *School Matters*—the Inner London Education Authority Junior School Project—stemmed directly from the research debates resulting from the publication of *Fifteen Thousand Hours*. The attraction of planning a study that could take advantage of the results of the methodological debate and emerging new methods of statistical analysis (such as probabilistic cluster analysis and multilevel modelling) was considerable and was discussed at the 1980 British Educational Research Association. The opportunity arose within the ILEA when, as the recently-appointed Director of Research and Statistics, I was able to plan the future research programme for the Authority. With support from the ILEA inspectors and senior officers, and from the then Education Officer and Chair of the Schools Sub-Committees, a longitudinal study—of two years in the first instance—was funded and undertaken.

The formal aims of the study were to:

- Produce a detailed description of pupils and teachers and of the organization and curriculum of schools
- Document the progress and development of 2000 pupils
- Establish whether some schools were more effective than others in providing learning and development, once account had been taken of variations in the characteristics of pupils
- Investigate differences in the progress of different groups of pupils

The study, in the event, ran for four years and was thus able to follow the cohort through the whole of their junior schooling. A related project—the Secondary Transfer Study—exploited the data and studied the same cohort as they transferred from primary to secondary schools. (The opportunity to carry out a prospective study was too good to miss. Pupils, teachers and parents were interviewed *before* and *after* transfer and comparisons drawn—see Alston, 1988, for full details).

Like the earlier study, confidentiality was assured to participants and a variety of research techniques were drawn upon: classroom observations—using the methodology created for Leicester University's Oracle Study—were undertaken; interviews and questionnaires were used for teachers and pupils; with the help of a special grant from the Leverhulme Foundation, home interviews with parents were carried out with interviewers speaking the language of the family.

Despite the difficulties facing schools in the early 1980s, the demands of the fieldwork were tolerated by the heads and teachers in the 50 schools of the sample. In the whole of the four-year time span the research team was involved with fieldwork, only one head teacher found the demands so great that the school was withdrawn from the study. There were probably many reasons for the goodwill extended towards the research but three, especially, seem important.

First, the heads and teachers accepted that the aims of the study were worthwhile (we had invested a great deal of time briefing heads with information about the proposed study and had visited each school prior to its start). Second, the project team was very fortunate in its staffing. We had been allocated four field officer posts for seconded teachers by the Authority and, without exception, over the four years we had attracted excellent, experienced primary teachers to work in these roles. In fact, only one field officer stayed with the project for its duration. Others moved on and needed to be replaced. This change of personnel during a project could have been disruptive but, in the event, proved beneficial, by ensuring that our links to current classroom practice remained active.

The third possible reason for the schools' co-operation was the research team's policy of keeping heads and teachers informed about the progress of the study and about any new demands that we were likely to make. Thus, we provided a regular bulletin which summarized all the research activity that had taken place that term and laid out our plans for the next term's data collection.

Nevertheless, despite the co-operation given to the research team, the period 1980–84 was an eventful one for the sample schools. In fact, we maintained a register of interruptions to each of the schools over this time. The result was a daunting list ranging from temporary closure due to emergency building work to—in some cases—an almost complete change of staff. It was during this time that the Brixton street disturbances took place, though, as was noted at the time, the amount of damage inflicted on schools was minimal. Much more serious interruptions to the school life were caused by staff, especially head teacher, changes. The following extract from *School Matters* reports an extreme case that illustrates the lack of stability that can occur in some schools:

> The Deputy Head went on maternity leave and an acting Deputy was appointed during the first year of the study. In the second year, in this school, the Head Teacher left and was replaced, in an acting capacity by the original Deputy who later became Head Teacher. An acting Deputy Head was appointed during this period but was replaced in the third year by a permanent Deputy. Therefore, two Heads and three Deputies or acting Deputies were in place over two and a half years! (Mortimore et al., 1988a)

The progress of the study was also reported to the research community in a symposium at the 1983 conference of the British Educational Research Association (BERA) and in an introductory publication (Mortimore et al., 1985). Further progress reports were presented at subsequent BERA conferences and at the first meeting of the International Congress of School Effectiveness and School Improvement held in London in 1988. A final progress report was presented at a series of local meetings for the head teachers and the staff of the sample schools.

The main findings

As with the earlier case study, the findings of the research were complex. Our interpretations of those findings are reported in various places: in the summary report (Mortimore et al., 1986a) and in the four project reports—including the technical appendices—published by the ILEA (Mortimore et al., 1986b), as well as in the book *School Matters* (Mortimore et al., 1988a), which was produced for more general readership. In addition, some of the statistical issues are discussed in more detail in a journal article in *Research Papers in Education* (Mortimore et al., 1988b). In terms of the four principal aims listed earlier:

- We endeavoured to produce a detailed account of the life of the urban primary school, focusing, in turn, on the head teachers and deputies, and on the teachers and pupils, and we attempted to describe the organization of schools and of the curriculum, not only as it was planned but also as it was experienced by pupils.
- We documented the progress of the targeted cohort through the four years of junior schools (and into secondary schools).
- We showed that schools varied considerably in their effectiveness, with some appearing to enhance pupils' cognitive and non-cognitive progress and development far more than others, even when initial intake differences to the schools had been taken into account.
- Finally, we found that schools that were more effective benefited all groups of pupils, though not necessarily to the same degree.

Reactions to the study

The research findings were written up in a formal report to the April 1986 meeting of the Schools Sub-Committee of the ILEA. Prior to this, a press conference was called by the leader of the Authority on 14 April and journalists were briefed on the overall findings. Due to the recent industrial action, and the general newsworthiness of the Authority, the press reaction to the research was partly overshadowed by the political context in which the study was presented.

On the day following the press conference, John Izbicki of the *Daily Telegraph* published an article in which he claimed our findings were 'contrary to the claims of so-called progressive educationalists' (Izbicki, 1986). Water Ellis, in the *Financial Times*, provided a short summary which included several quotations from the leader of the Authority (Ellis, 1986). Sarah Boseley of the *Guardian* picked out several of the key findings of the study, but the headline carried was 'Traditional Teaching Values Vindicated by ILEA Study into Pupils' Achievement' (Boseley, 1986).

The *Evening Standard* carried two separate pieces by its education reporter, David Shaw. One listed the twelve key factors identified by the research. The other carried a story that 'education chiefs are planning a purge to improve primary school students in the wake of a 4-year research study' (Shaw, 1986). A similar story—reacting to a comment made at the press conference—was carried in the *Daily Express*, with a punchy opening statement: 'The one-time trendy lefty leader of Britain's biggest schools' authority yesterday called for a return to basic 'three Rs' teaching for primary pupils' (Wood, 1986). The same sentiment was echoed in its leader column. Similarly, the *Daily Mail* assured readers that the Authority 'is moving to ensure that youngsters in its primary schools once more get a grounding in basic learning' (Rowlands, 1986). The *Sun* was content with two paragraphs under the heading 'Poor Schools Get a Caning'. *The Times*, too, focused mostly on the comments of the leader of the Authority but added a brief comment on two of the twelve key factors included in the study's report.

More considered comment was provided by the *Times Educational Supplement*. This devoted a page to a summary of the report, with only one column on press conference matters. The leading article related the findings of the study to American research and to those of *Fifteen Thousand Hours* (Times Educational Supplement, 1986). *Education* made the study its 'document of the week' and provided a helpful brief summary (*Education*, 1986). *New Society* carried a two-column article relating the findings to discussion of *Fifteen Thousand Hours* and commenting on the statistical methodology (*New Society*, 1986).

The danger of misleading headlines was well illustrated by a follow-up article by John Marks in the *Daily Mail* on 22 March entitled 'I Explore the Alibi of Our Failing Schools'. In a wide-ranging, whole-page article, Marks cited two of the findings and added—with no relevance to the citations—'many schools—both primary and comprehensive—are also failing their pupils through politically motivated teaching' (Marks, 1986).

The March edition of *Good Housekeeping* contained a more factual article by Angela Neustatter. This discussed in some detail the findings of the study and sought to relate these to a particular London school (Neustatter, 1986). The July edition of *Junior Education* also carried a one-page summary of the study (Junior Education, 1986).

However, controversy returned with an article by John Clare published in the *Listener* of 31 July 1986. In this article, Clare argued that 'progressive ideas' hindered the teaching of working-class pupils. He also used it to mount a personal attack on an educational statistician. Support for these somewhat different points was ostensibly culled from the findings of the Junior School Project and from the recently published Brent Enquiry (Clare, 1986). The succeeding edition of the *Listener* carried criticisms of Clare's arguments in the form of letters from a current and an ex-head teacher.

Finally, the third report from the Education, Science and Arts Select Committee referred on a number of occasions to findings from the Junior School Project and related these to other published work concerned with primary education (House of Commons, 1986).

The report of the project was thus cited by journalists in support of a number of different arguments. There was very little serious analysis of its findings or even of its implications for schools. Whilst it is unrealistic, perhaps, to expect journalists writing for lay audiences to question the validity or reliability of findings, it is regrettable that only superficial accounts of a detailed study should be disseminated. However, it is only fair to point out that the summaries in *Education, Junior Education* and the *Times Educational Supplement* were accurate and provided basic information about the study. In this particular case, the press conference was probably unhelpful to the study, focusing attention more on political than on educational concerns.

Translation to book form
The work of the project had thus been reported to its funding body (the ILEA) and details had been made available to the research community and to the media. There remained the task of converting a lengthy, and necessarily technical, report into a book suitable for a wider readership of practitioners. In particular, we were hoping to write something which would be of interest to teachers, head teachers, advisers and inspectors, as well as to education officers. As so often happens in such cases, however, all the research team had by this time moved on to other jobs and the task of re-writing and editing had to be undertaken in evening and weekend slots. Saturday morning breakfast meetings were used by the team to reach agreement on points of interpretation. Because of the pressure of other commitments, the manuscript was not ready until the autumn of 1987 and the book finally appeared in March 1988.

Reaction to the publication of the book
Because of the earlier exposure of the study's findings in 1986, the book was launched towards the end of March without a press conference and with relatively little expectation of media interest. Nevertheless, a number of comments about the book did appear in the media.

Curiously, the first comment preceded publication day and was not directly about the book but referred to a forthcoming article by the research team (Gow, 1988). This article (Mortimore et al., 1988b) was mainly technical and dealt with different methods of analysis adopted in the study. (See also the subsequent criticisms of this in Preece, 1988, and our riposte, Mortimore et al., 1988c.) However, because of the sensational and misleading headline in the *Guardian* piece by Gow, 'ILEA Survey Downgrades Social Factors in Pupil Attainment', a letter of response which attempted to sort out differences between attainment and progress was immediately despatched to that newspaper (Mortimore & Sammons, 1988).

The next comment—also prior to publication day—appeared in the *Evening Standard*. Bruce Kemble (who had reported on *Fifteen Thousand Hours* for the *Daily Express*) provided a two-page, detailed summary complete with suitable quotations. With this article, Kemble included a checklist for a 'good junior school'. This had a scale of 1–15 and, according to Kemble, a score of 9–12 indicated 'a good school' (Kemble, 1988).

The *Sunday Times* carried a thoughtful comment with quotations from eminent educationalists on the Sunday before publication day. This was written by

Caroline St John Brooks, who had earlier provided a very clear summary of *Fifteen Thousand Hours* for *New Society* (St John Brooks, 1988a).

Before publication day the *Daily Mail* had six paragraphs on the study. These paragraphs were embedded in the text of an article about the pressure being brought to bear on the Secretary of State from right-wing educationalists. The paper's reporting of our findings was reasonably accurate though the context many have been puzzling for some readers (Bates, 1988). On the same day, the *Evening Standard* also ran a short leader on 'Social Classes', in which the study was cited as supporting the notion of independent assessment throughout pupils' schooling (a point specifically discussed and rejected in the final chapter of *School Matters*) (*Evening Standard*, 1988).

Perhaps the most thoughtful commentary on the book was published in the *Independent* on the day of publication—24 March. In this article, the education editor, Peter Wilby, located the central findings of the study within the context of the educational debate on the influence of homes and schools. He also used the book's comments on progress to advise the Prime Minister on how testing for progress would be far more sensible than testing for attainment (Wilby, 1988).

The *Times Educational Supplement* provided extensive coverage of the book on the day following publication. Three full pages were devoted to the study. The first page contained articles which both described and criticized the research, by the head of a Birmingham junior school (Winkley, 1988) and the Professor of Primary Education at Exeter University (Bennett, 1988b). The second and third pages were devoted to an investigation, by one of the paper's reporters, of schools chosen to illustrate the project's findings. This included a description of two London primary schools chosen by the reporter because one appeared to possess the factors identified by *School Matters*, while the other did not (Hagedorn, 1988). In addition, the *TES* carried an article on the study which noted that plans to abolish the ILEA would prevent a longer term follow-up of the pupils at the end of their secondary schooling (Bayliss, 1988), plus a personal column by Anne Sofer recalling that she had agreed the funding for the study when she was the ILEA chair of the Schools Sub-committee in 1979 (Sofer, 1988).

Education devoted its Document of the Week to the study on the day after publication (*Education*, 1988).

A follow-up to publication appeared in the *Sunday Times* of 27 March in the form of an interview with me in which I tried to relate the findings to previous research and to the current situation facing teachers (St John Brooks, 1988b). A postscript to that interview came in the form of a letter from Jakarta published in the paper two weeks later (10 April) in which I was firmly taken to task for my comments that the research had found no support for rote learning and streaming. According to the letter, 'such views were not in line with employers, parents or even children' (Ishewood, 1988).

Further interviews were reported in two Ontario papers—the *Toronto Star* and the *Burlington Spectator* (Contenta, 1988; Porter, 1988). In both cases, these were stimulated by local conferences and sought to relate the research findings to the situation in Canadian schools.

In the May edition of the *Teacher*, the NUT's principal officer with a research brief provided a detailed commentary on the research and discussed it in relation to the reporting of the tabloid press. In comparison to the review of *Fifteen Thousand Hours* ten years before, the union review was far more supportive of research (Barber, 1988). Similarly, the largest American teacher union, the National Educational Association (NEA), published a positive review of the study in the February edition of its paper (Needham, 1988). A two-page article also appeared in the June edition of the *School Governor* (Taylor, 1988). From slightly further afield, in November the *New Zealand Herald* published an article on schools and the issue of parental choice. Embedded in it was a summary of *School Matters*, with a discussion of its implications for the New Zealand situation (Guy, 1988).

Critiques by fellow researchers

As may be expected, the more detailed and, in some cases, more critical comments came in the form of book reviews in academic journals. These included the review in the *Oxford Review* (Galton, 1988), the *British Educational Research Journal* (Davies, 1988), *Forum* (Simon, 1988), *Educational Research* (Boydell, 1988), and the *British Journal of Educational Psychology* (McNamara, 1988).

The most critical of these reviews was McNamara's. This was the only review that the research team felt deserved a riposte—mainly because the critic appeared to be unaware of the many related publications of the study and accused us of producing something that was data-free! Unfortunately, the *British Journal of Educational Psychology* policy was not to permit dialogue and therefore would not publish our carefully drafted response, thus cutting off what might have developed into a fruitful debate (Mortimore et al., 1989). Shortly after this, a long and critical review—not of *School Matters, per se,* but of almost all research studies about school effectiveness—appeared in *Research Studies in Education* (Preece, 1989).

Issues arising from press and journal comment

For research teams, interest in published work is always double edged. On the one hand, it is gratifying to have notice taken of one's work by the media. If findings make a contribution to the public discussion of educational issues, this can be very satisfying. On the other hand, however carefully writers present their data, if they are accorded sensational or politically-biased interpretation, this is very distressing. Such coverage in the media can influence the way academics respond to the study and, as was seen with *Fifteen Thousand Hours*, can encourage some reviewers to blame the research team for the biased reporting.

A problem for researchers concerns the audience to be targeted and the choice of the most appropriate publishing channel to be adopted. Fellow researchers will expect to hear of results through scientific journals; practitioners will look for useful summaries in the trade press; students, teachers updating their qualifications, interested parents and other lay people will require a book. *Fifteen*

Thousand Hours was reported through seminars for those involved, in the ILEA's in-house journal, and in the book form.

Nearly ten years later, the *School Matters* research was reported through seminars, in the range of newly established ILEA in-house papers for teachers, parents and governors, and through a series of journal articles (Mortimore et al., 1987a, 1987b, 1987c), as well as through the ILEA reports (including a separate technical publication) and, finally, the book. Thus we attempted to write in the appropriate style, with the correct level of technical detail, for the various audiences. As noted earlier, this policy can fail if a reviewer in a *general* publication criticizes the lack of *technical* details.

A more fundamental problem is how best to present research data. Thankfully, the International Statistical Institute (ISI) has produced a code of ethics which has been widely discussed by statisticians and others with an interest in ethical aspects of research (Sammons, 1989a). This code and publications by the Radical Statistics Education Group (RSEG, 1982) provide guidance to researchers on how best to present and process data and on the principles which need to be followed if statistics are to clarify, rather than obscure, relationships between variables.

It is obvious that criticism of published work is essential. It is only through criticism that work is improved. There is a danger, however, that well-publicized disagreements may reduce public confidence in the value of research. Whether this risk can be reduced is doubtful—given the situation in this country of a high quality educational press. In other countries, where there is a sharper distinction than in the UK between the popular press and academic journals, academic disputes may be carried out in a private, rather than the public, domain. In the UK, where publications such as the *Times Educational Supplement* and *Education* flourish, and where so many practitioners and academic researchers read these publications, there is likely to be a blurring of this distinction.

While the existence of this 'trade press' is a cause for celebration, it also increases the likelihood of researchers being involved in controversy when they publish their work. Such an experience can be very off-putting. Press conferences can be daunting and radio or television interviews frightening. What steps can be taken to maximize the chance of getting a fair hearing?

One obvious step is for the research team to build in regular meetings with a support group which can be used as a sounding board. Paradoxically, it is within such a supportive context that strong criticisms can best be made. If the research team acquires the experience of having to respond to challenges in this way, then they gain the opportunity to build up the skills necessary to defend their work in the more public arenas occupied by the mass media.

In both the studies discussed in this chapter, such support was available. In the case of the *Fifteen Thousand Hours* study, the support consisted of a group of primary and secondary head teachers, together with the local education officer and inspector. For the *School Matters* study, the necessary support and criticisms were provided by the School Differences Research Group that had been established and supported under the auspices of the Association for Child Psychology and Psychiatry.

What lessons can be learned from these case studies? The general lessons for good research, perhaps, are obvious: sound preparation, methodical work, statistical caution, careful interpretation and simple, jargon-free writing! Some of the specific lessons of how best to deal with media attention to research findings are also obvious; others less so.

The following list of recommendations has been compiled after my experience of 'publications' in order to assist researchers to deal with these issues. There are probably many other ways in which researchers could prepare for publication, but this list identifies a number of actions that are possible and may be helpful.

As will be clear, the actions suggested in the list cannot all be dealt with in the weeks before publication: some need to be considered even before the start of the study, and others are best dealt with during the course of the work.

Recommendations

1   Before committing oneself to a study, invest time in thinking about the area and its key issues. Try to gauge how sensitive an area it is and how strongly people feel about the issues.

2   Think through possible results for your study. Is it likely that clear answers will emerge? If clear answers were to emerge, would they be likely to cause a furore? Would they be likely to offend a particular group in society?

3   If your planned study is likely to lead to controversy, decide if you have the temperament to cope with it. Seeing one's name in the papers can be stressful, especially when it is the subject of a vitriolic or personalized attack.

4   During the planning of the study, set out clear aims and provide a simple statement of how these are to be achieved. Have copies available to give to people who show an interest in the study.

5   During the course of your work, consult with those who believe they have a right to be involved. You clearly cannot see everyone and will need to choose carefully those who are representative and, sometimes, those who are powerful. Use an advisory group to sound out ideas and to give you warnings of potential problems. If possible, consult with other researchers at the key stages of your work and, especially, when crucial decisions over fieldwork or methods of analysis are about to be taken. For this reason, it is very helpful to provide progress reports at conferences or in preliminary papers. These can provide a vehicle for discussion with others working in similar fields and also serve to advise the research community as to your future findings.

6   Always take criticisms of the study received through these mechanisms seriously. Use your advisory group to discuss whether you need to modify your programme, or whether you should hold your nerve and continue. Pay adequate attention to the validity and reliability of any measures collected and of any statistics being used. Refer to the ISI code.

7   Keep all those participating in the study informed of what you are going to do next. Never trick or deceive your respondents. Recognize their privacy and their rights.

8   At the time of publication, write as clearly as possible and use data and statistics only to clarify your findings. Try out drafts on your advisory group and remember you will have to write for different audiences who will need different formats and styles. Be prepared to stand by what you claim.

9   Brief journalists *before* publication. It has to be realized, however, that it is difficult to accommodate their different publication deadlines. If you go for the *Times Educational Supplement* your press conference will have to be on a Monday or Tuesday; if you go for the Sunday papers—and their circulations are large—then you have to choose a different day.

10   Prepare for possible controversy ahead of time (although you may still be surprised at what does turn out to be controversial). Make sure your arguments are marshalled and rehearsed—again use your advisory group to play the devil's advocate. In any arguments in the public forum always remain polite—whatever you are feeling. Nothing dispels an aggressive question as much as a polite answer. Always be sensitive and considerate to any parties who come out of the study badly. Whenever possible, accentuate the positive and thank your respondents for their time and trouble.

These ten points might not prevent your work from being misinterpreted in the press. They might not protect you from the experience of controversy. But they may aid your work by ensuring that you are better prepared to deal with the misinterpretation and controversy if they do occur.

Postscript

The issues to do with the presentation and publication of research have not gone away. In fact, interest in educational debates has increased greatly over the last decade. In England, for instance, education was the main issue promoted by both the major parties in the 1997 general election. At the same time, the power and influence of the media has grown, so that how well studies are or are not reported seems—in many ways—to be more important than the quality of the actual work. Obviously, luck also plays a part. If the publication of a research study coincides with a major item of news, reporting of it is likely to be skimpy. If, however, it occurs at a lean time, it may well receive an inordinate amount of attention. For researchers—untrained in the ways of the media—there are tricky decisions to be made: how far should publicity be courted or avoided? How do you cope if your report becomes the focus of political debate?

8

The Positive Effects of Schooling

Introduction

This chapter was commissioned by Michael Rutter in preparation for a three-day seminar on psycho-social disturbances in young people. The seminar was sponsored by the Johann Jacobs foundation at its Communication Centre at Marbach Castle on Lake Constance. The main theme of the seminar was how young people were coping with the extensive social, demographic, economic, technological and cultural changes taking place around them. It also reviewed potential preventative strategies—of which the school was deemed one of the most powerful. Writing the paper for this seminar caused me to undertake a review of the literature on school effectiveness as it had developed since the publication of Fifteen Thousand Hours.

In almost all societies, attendance at school is considered essential for children between the ages of six and sixteen. In some countries, high proportions of students start school earlier and finish later. There is a widespread presumption that schooling must have a positive effect (see, for example, the six ideal types of schools recently specified by European educationalists Husen, Tuijnman and Halls, 1992), although, for some children and young people, there is evidence that schooling has had a negative impact on their development. This question of the impact of school has been explored over the last twenty or so years by a series of specialist research studies. These studies have shown that the effects of schooling are differential: some schools promote positive effects, others negative ones. Furthermore, some researchers have found evidence that the same school can impact differentially on groups of students according to their gender, social class, or perceived ability.

Although the circumstances and contexts of schooling differ widely across the world, there is a fairly common view—held by governments at least—that schooling, in general, is increasing in cost and decreasing in quality. Although it is often difficult to investigate empirically the truth of these claims, they are constantly stressed by the popular media, with the result that reforms are introduced based more on ideological commitment than on research evidence. Findings from scientifically sound studies (especially where these are replicated) about the power of individual schools to promote or reduce their positive impacts are, therefore, of critical importance.

This chapter will present some of the available evidence on variations between schools with regard to four sets of outcomes: attendance, student attitudes, student behaviour and scholastic attainment. The mechanisms identified by researchers as being implicated in the differential impacts of schools will also be discussed and differences between schools in terms of their effectiveness for different groups will be considered. Knowing what makes one school more effective than another (for all or some of its students), however, is not the same as knowing how to change a less effective school into a more effective one. For this reason, we will comment on the efficacy of various interventions undertaken in a number of different countries. Finally, we will consider the implications for policy makers and practitioners of the evidence that has emerged from studies of school effectiveness and school improvement.

A major difficulty of writing a chapter like this is deciding what should and should not be included. Given the extent of the relevant literature, it will be impossible to be exhaustive. Studies have been selected, therefore, on the basis of their relevance to the argument being undertaken. Inevitably, both relevant individual works and whole categories of studies have been omitted. One example of this general omission is the category of social policy research, thus excluding from the United States the study of 'High School Achievement', focusing on public and private differences, by Coleman, Hoffer and Kilgore (1982); from the United Kingdom, 'The Comprehensive Experiment' by Reynolds, Sullivan and Murgatroyd (1987); and from Germany, the study of 'The Management of Individual Differences in Single Classrooms' by Roeder and Sang (1991).

A model of school effectiveness

Studies of variations between schools exist in both simple and more sophisticated forms. The simpler studies take little or no account of differences in the characteristics of students entering and attending the schools. They also tend to focus on only one outcome measure: student scholastic achievement. The difficulties of this simple approach, as experienced teachers will recognize, is that schools do not receive uniform intakes of students. Some take high proportions of relatively advantaged students likely to do well in examinations; others (on the whole) receive high proportions of disadvantaged students who, all things considered, are less likely to do well. To compare the results of scholastic achievement tests or examinations, without taking into account these differences in the students when they enter the school, and to attribute good results to the influence of the school may, therefore, be quite misleading.

The more sophisticated form of research endeavours to overcome the problem of differential student intake by using a statistical technique to equate, as far as possible, for these differences. Ideally, the statistical technique would be replaced by a random allocation of students to schools but, in most countries, this would be considered to be an unacceptable infringement of the parental right to choose schools. Accordingly, various definitions of effectiveness have been formulated. One definition of an 'effective' school that has been used is 'one in which students progress further than might be expected from consideration of its intake' (Mortimore, 1991a, p. 9).

Note that this definition does not assume that all students from disadvantaged backgrounds are likely to do badly in tests of scholastic attainment. Some individual students from disadvantaged backgrounds will undoubtedly do well; they will buck the trend. What the definition implies is that, all things being equal, disadvantaged students are less likely to do as well, in any assessment which is highly competitive, as those from advantaged backgrounds. Accordingly, measures of progress are needed that can take account of the students' initial starting points.

Various methods have been developed by researchers to deal with the problem of intake differences, and various statistical methods, ranging from simple standardization, to multiple regression techniques, to the latest multilevel modelling, have been employed to equate for the initial differences. Regardless of the technique used, however, most approaches have been based on an underlying model of school effectiveness. In this model, a series of outcomes suitable for the type of school must be identified. For an elementary school, these might include basic skills of literacy and numeracy, as well as other measures to do with the students' personal and social development. For a secondary school, the outcomes are likely to be based on achievement but may also include attendance, attitudes and behaviour.

The second stage of the usual procedure is to relate these chosen outcomes to available data on the characteristics of the students as they entered the school. Such characteristics can include earlier reading levels, former attendance rates, behaviour ratings completed by teachers in the previous phase of schooling and any available information on home background, including the occupation of the parents. Using the most sophisticated mathematical techniques available, researchers attempt to take account of this intake variation and to adjust the outcome measures accordingly to provide what is increasingly known as a value-added component. An attempt is thus made to see how the outcomes would look if all schools had received a similar intake. To use the research terminology: like is being compared with like.

At the third stage, researchers usually seek to relate the adjusted outcomes to whatever information has been collected about the life and functioning of the school. Researchers sometimes call this 'backward mapping' of outcomes to process measures. To avoid a mismatch, these previous measures must have been collected as the particular students were passing through the school. In essence, this is the model that school effectiveness researchers have been refining over the last twenty or so years as they investigated the differential effects of schools.

Methodological issues

Studies of the effects of schooling, like so many other research topics, vary a great deal in the scope of their designs and in their chosen methodologies. Some of the problems of interpretation of a number of the earlier studies have already been discussed by Rutter (1983) and by Purkey and Smith (1983). More recently, a number of articles in a special edition of the *International Journal of Educational Research* addressed this topic (Bosker & Scheerens, 1989; Raudenbush, 1989; Scheerens & Creemers, 1989), as does a series of papers in Reynolds and Cuttance (1992). The types of issues that have been raised include:

- The need for clearer conceptualization and theory development
- The use of more sophisticated statistical techniques (such as multilevel modelling) and the inadequacy of current sampling techniques
- The choice of appropriate outcome measures
- The methods of relating outcome to process data

On the whole, the later studies have used more sophisticated methods than the earlier ones. The improvement in methodology, however, has not been matched by similar advances in the development of theory. The need for better theory has been recognized and a number of research teams working in this area are addressing the issue.

The findings of studies into variations between schools

As noted earlier, the most common outcomes chosen by researchers have been the attendance patterns of students, their attitudes towards schooling, their behaviour, and their scholastic attainment. We will discuss each of these in turn and refer to a selection of the research studies that have been carried out.

Attendance
Attendance data have been collected by many researchers. Attendance can be defined as an outcome of schooling as well as being used as a measure of students' attitudes towards school. It can also be seen as a process variable: all

things being equal, schools with high attendance rates are better able to secure scholastic achievement for their pupils than those with poorer attendance rates. Various measures of attendance have been used in studies, including one-day surveys and whole-year individual student data sets. A number of studies of the elementary years of schooling have also used this measure. In Mortimore and colleagues (1988a), for instance, attendance data were collected for each student. When these were aggregated, it was found that there were systematic differences between schools. When the proportion of variance between students in their attendance was divided, however, it was found that the contribution of the school was relatively small, possibly because the overall level was so high (92 per cent), thus leaving little scope for school variation.

At secondary level, measures of attendance were used by Reynolds et al. (1976) in a study of nine schools in a mining community of South Wales. The researchers found that attendance data varied from a school average of 77.2 per cent to 89.1 per cent. In a study by Rutter and colleagues (1979a) data on individual students in three separate age groups were collected in each of the twelve schools in the sample. The whole-school figures revealed considerable differences. For example, out of a possible maximum of twenty attendances over two school weeks, the average for sixteen-year-old students varied from 12.8 in one school to 17.3 in another. Furthermore, the proportion of poor attenders in each school varied between 6 and 26 per cent.

Attendance was also addressed by Galloway et al. (1985) in a study of schools in the Sheffield area of England. They found clear evidence of school effects on the attendance rates. Smith and Tomlinson (1989) collected statistics of attendance in research which followed the careers of students transferring to twenty multi-ethnic secondary schools at the age of eleven, through to the end of compulsory schooling. Using a measure of the number of half-days a pupil was absent from school, they drew up a series of outcomes for each school. This measure was repeated in each of four years. On average, researchers found students to be absent about 7 per cent of the time. They found no differences between boys and girls but they did find some between students from different ethnic groups. In general, those from Caribbean ethnic backgrounds had better attendance than their British counterparts, whereas those from Asia had poorer attendance records.

Attitudes towards school
Only a few studies have used systematic measurements of attitudes to school. This is partly because the measurement of attitudes is complex and partly because the attitudes of young people tend to be less stable than those of their older counterparts. Measures have been used, however, in three studies. Mortimore and colleagues (1988a) developed a set of measures to capture the feelings of young students towards their schools. A series of 'smiley' faces was used so that members of the sample were able to indicate their overall approval or disapproval of particular aspects of school life. The results showed considerable variation between schools on a range of activities. Overall, the most effective school had

an average of 4 points and the least effective had an average of 2.7, out of a scale of 5. The school appeared to be a more important influence on attitudes than were the student background factors.

The same measure was adopted by Tizard and colleagues (1988) in their study of infant schools. The researchers interviewed their sample of elementary school children at the age of seven and also used the 'smiley' method to elicit feelings about mathematics, reading to the teacher, reading to themselves, writing, and going to school.

Pupil attitudes were examined in relation to secondary school students by Smith and Tomlinson (1989). They sought to investigate pupils' enthusiasm for school, as well as participation in activities within the school or organized by it. A different approach towards student attitudes was adopted by Ainley and Sheret (1992) in their Australian study of twenty-two secondary schools. These researchers sought to investigate the effectiveness of schools' 'holding power' over students. They found that some schools retained a higher percentage of students in the senior year than others, even after they had allowed for differences in the social background of students, but retention was not necessarily linked to achievement.

Behaviour of students

Like attendance and attitudes, behaviour can be viewed as an outcome of school. The rationale for such a view is that specific experiences at school, or the particular group of pupils attending it, lead to a collective style of behaviour, both within and beyond the school. Like the other variables, however, behaviour can also be viewed as part of the school processes. Other outcome measures can be influenced by the behaviour experienced within the school.

Overall, seven studies using behaviour as an outcome will be noted here. The study of student behaviour is problematic. Taking account of the impact of different teachers on different sets of students, and *vice versa*, is difficult. Bennett (1976) studied the relationship between teaching style and pupil progress. As part of his study, he sought to measure the on- and off-task behaviour in a sample of over one hundred students. He also collected measures of the level of student and teacher interactions for the same sample. In the second study, Mortimore and colleagues (1988a) developed a behaviour scale which was completed by teachers. One advantage of this scale was that good as well as bad behaviour could be recorded. The results showed that the average behaviour score for a school ranged from 48 to 76 on a scale with a maximum of 135 points.

Heal (1978) studied a random sample of pupils in both elementary and secondary schools. Data from the elementary schools were used to assess their influence on subsequent behaviour of students. The measure included petty misdemeanours and more serious activities, both in and outside of school. Rutter and colleagues (1979a) used a scale compiled from items from a self-report student survey, teachers' interviews, and researchers' in-school observations. In all, twenty-five items were aggregated together. Some were minor (not having a pen or pencil with which to write), but others were more important and included the serious interruption of the lesson by aggressive behaviour. The twenty-five items revealed a highly significant pattern of intercorrelations. Overall, some schools had up to five times as much good (or bad) behaviour as others. Intake differences were taken into account using the results of the 'Rutter B' behaviour scale, collected on a sample of the students during their elementary schooling.

Although the study of Reynolds et al. (1976) did not deal directly with in-school behaviour, it included a measure of delinquency. This showed that the school average ranged between 4 and 10 per cent. Delinquency data have also been used by Power and colleagues (1967) and by Cannan (1970). They used police data to examine school differences and reported considerable differences in the average delinquency rates of schools. In a study carried out in Scotland (Gray et al., 1983), over 20,000 students were tracked through the secondary school system and clear evidence of school differences were revealed.

Scholastic attainment

A great number of studies have been carried out in the United States focusing on the scholastic attainments of students (witness the 750 references in the register of the Northwest Regional Educational Laboratory synthesis [NREL, 1990]). One of the first major studies was conducted in the late 1960s by Weber (1971). Four schools, considered to be 'institutionally effective', were selected for study. It was found that scholastic attainment (measured by reading levels) was markedly above the average for the school neighbourhood. A second study was carried out in 1974 by the New York Department of Education. Two schools, with contrasting levels of average attainment but with similar intake characteristics, were identified and studied (Edmonds, 1979).

Further studies focusing on student scholastic attainment by Madden (1976), Brookover and Lezotte (1977) and Edmonds and Frederiksen (1979) reinforced the conclusion that some schools were more effective in promoting achievement than others. As a result of these pioneering studies, a number of intervention projects were inaugurated (Clark & McCarthy, 1983; McCormack-Larkin & Kritek, 1982; Murphy et al., 1982).

A long-term empirical investigation has been started and its early results reported (Teddlie et al., 1984, 1989). A relatively new strand of work concerns what is known as 'self-efficacy' (Wood & Bandura, 1989). In this work the learners' beliefs in themselves are reinforced or reduced and the effects on achievement noted. In general, the stronger the feeling of 'self-efficacy' the better the level of achievement. Moreover, the individual's feeling is affected by the school attended. If the teachers hold positive views about ability and about their teaching skills, they are more likely to produce academic learning in their classrooms (Bandura, 1992).

Bennett (1976) studied reading, writing and mathematics progress and attainment in elementary schools in the United Kingdom. Galton and Simon (1980) also studied reading attainment and progress. In addition to reading and mathematics, Mortimore and colleagues (1988a) studied writing and speaking skills and, where possible, included measures of progress as well as attainment in their study of school differences. Tizard and colleagues (1988) included measures of reading, writing, mathematics attainment and progress in their study of early student attainment.

In a study of Welsh secondary schools, Reynolds et al. (1976) found a range of over 40 percentage points between the school with the highest and that with the lowest academic attainment. Brimer and colleagues (1978) worked with a sample of 44 secondary schools and used information on parental background to control for differences in intake in their study of examination results. Rutter and colleagues (1979a) found systematic large-scale differences between school averages when examination results were collated.

Gray, Jesson, and Sime (1990), drawing on a sample of over 20,000 Scottish students' records, found evidence of both social class and school influence on academic attainment. In their study—again focusing on examination results— Smith and Tomlinson (1989) found that school differences were stronger than differences in the ethnic background of students. Daly (1991) studied examination results in a sample of thirty secondary schools in Northern Ireland and found a complicated pattern of school differences, made more difficult to interpret by the selective school system.

Nuttall and colleagues (1989) studied the examination performance of over 30,000 students taking British school examinations over several years. They found clear evidence of school differences, as well as differences related to family background and ethnic group. Blakey and Heath (1992) have recently released preliminary findings from the Oxford University School Effectiveness Project. These findings show that, in their schools, the proportion of students obtaining high levels in five subjects in public examinations varies from 1 to 19 per cent.

Attention so far has focused on a selection of research studies carried out in the United States or in the United Kingdom. Similar studies, however, have also been undertaken in many other parts of the world. See, for instance, Fraser (1989) in Australia; Brandsma and Knuver (1989) and Creemers and Lugthart (1989) in the Netherlands; Dalin (1989) in Norway; and Bashi and colleagues (1990) in Israel.

Although the studies cited vary considerably in rigour, scope and methodologies, their findings are fairly uniform: that individual schools can promote positive or negative student outcomes; that those outcomes can include both cognitive and social behaviours; and they are not dependent on the school receiving a favoured student intake. The fact that the studies have taken place in different phases of students' schooling and in different parts of the developed world adds considerable strength to the interpretation that schools can make a difference to the lives of their students. Although in some cases the range of attainment outcomes that can be traced directly to the influence of the school might be relatively small, it can be the difference between academic success and failure, and so can have a long-term effect on students' life chances.

It has also become apparent from these studies that there are likely to be differences in the average progress achieved by students from different schools, and that this variation is less susceptible to factors of home background than are the more usual measures of attainment at any time.

Because there have been more studies of scholastic attainment than of attendance, attitudes, or behaviour (largely been confined to the UK), measures and instruments are more likely to be available for this first outcome than for the others. As a result, differential effectiveness in cognitive areas is more widely understood. The scope, however, for further development of sensitive measures of behaviour and attitudes and the opportunities for studies to use non-cognitive measures is considerable. This is especially important in view of the lack of perfect agreement between outcomes reported by Reynolds et al. (1976), Rutter and colleagues (1979a), and Mortimore and colleagues (1988a).

The studies cited here have been criticized and their methodologies dissected. (See reviews by Clark et al., 1984; Good & Brophy, 1986; Purkey & Smith, 1983; Rutter, 1983.) For a detailed description of the processes involved in the public discussion of two British studies, see Mortimore (1990).

Do the positive effects of schooling vary according to time?

The evidence on whether positive effects of schooling vary over time is mixed. The earliest British studies (Reynolds et al., 1976; Rutter et al., 1979a) drew on student outcomes for different years and found that, in general, there was consistency over time. Two large-scale analyses, one from the Scottish data set (Willms & Raudenbush, 1989) and one from the work carried out in inner London (Nuttall et al., 1989), revealed, however, large-scale differences in student academic outcomes over time. Unfortunately, the other large-scale London-based study, by Mortimore and colleagues (1988a), studied only one cohort of students over a four-year period and thus cannot contribute to this interesting debate.

The possibility of change over time should not be surprising. After all, schools take in different groups of students each year and, in some cases, change staff regularly. The question is whether the ethos of a school, once it has been established, is strong enough to resist that change. There is also the question of how rapid any change is likely to be. Gradual change in outcomes is likely if the particular ethos changes and staff are replaced. A faster rate of change would be likely if, for instance, the intake to the school varied considerably from one year to another, in terms of its social class background or its earlier performance in other phases of schooling. The school is also likely to change more rapidly as a result of some outside intervention (if a new principal is appointed or an inspection by outside experts takes place). Finally, and not surprisingly, rapid change can be expected as a result of a particular crisis in the life of the school, such as the threat of closure due to lack of students. Schools can also be conservative places, however, which seek to resist change (as the later section on interventions will demonstrate). Further work is needed to identify the most potent mechanisms for change and to investigate under what conditions they are likely to be most successfully introduced.

Do the positive effects of schooling vary according to school membership?

To answer this question, it is necessary to ask a series of related questions. First, do students with different levels of ability or with different gender, class and ethnic characteristics achieve different outcomes from the same school processes? The British evidence on this question is mixed. A large number of publications emanating from the Scottish study (Cuttance, 1985; Gray et al., 1990; MacPherson & Willms, 1987; Willms & Cuttance, 1985) all suggest that schools can have differential effects according to the characteristics of their students. This actuarial approach suggests that, given the students' gender, age and social class, the likely academic outcomes can be predicted for particular schools. Further supporting evidence comes from a methodological study by Aitken and Longford (1986), which found that schools did have differential effects on the progress made by particular groups.

Against this view of differential student effect can be set the evidence from the early studies (Reynolds et al., 1976; Rutter et al., 1979a) that schools that were positive were likely to have a consistent effect on all groups of students. Furthermore, Gray et al. (1990) reported little evidence of varied outcomes for different kinds of students.

The findings from Mortimore and colleagues (1988a), were also positive on this question. In general, they found that schools that had positive effects for one group were likely to have similar positive effects for others, although these could be more or less pronounced. For example, some schools had positive effects in promoting reading progress for girls but not for boys. It is interesting, however, that in their sample of fifty schools the research team found no case where students whose parents had manual occupations performed markedly better, on average, than those from non-manual groups. Schools were not able to overcome these powerful social class effects. Students from manual groups in the most effective schools, however, sometimes outperformed those from non-manual groups in the least effective schools. The school was the unit of change rather than the class group within it. A re-analysis of the data of the London School Study shows that the regression line slopes are similar for all groups of students (Sammons & Nuttall, 1992). The data collected by Smith and Tomlinson (1989) showed that, although differences between ethnic groups varied between schools, much greater variations could be found in general school differences: 'The ones that are good for white people tend to be about equally good for black people' (p. 305).

Studies in the USA (Hallinger & Murphy, 1987; Teddlie et al., 1989) have investigated this problem in a different way. By focusing on schools which, by chance, attracted different intakes and could be classified as serving low-, middle-

or upper-middle-income communities, the researchers were able to investigate whether schools that were unusually effective were similar or different in how they related to their students. They report that, in general, schools had similar characteristics regardless of the intake of students. Commonly cited correlates include a safe and orderly environment; a clear mission; capable instructional leadership; high expectations; a well co-ordinated curriculum; monitoring of student progress; and structured staff development (Hallinger & Murphy, 1986, cited in Levine & Lezotte, 1990, p. 65).

The researchers also found some differences. In the low socio-economic status (SES) schools, there was a tendency for the curriculum to focus on basic skills, and principals in low SES schools tended to be more forceful in asserting themselves and in intervening in classes. The researchers found that, in the high SES schools, principals tended to use a more collaborative style of decision-making (Hallinger & Murphy, 1986).

The second related question concerns whether, if schools have different outcomes for different groups of students, this is due to policy differences in the way the students have been treated, or to differences in the reactions they have elicited from those who work in the schools. It is quite possible that a school, or an individual teacher, may have a policy of treating students equitably in terms of adult time and encouragement and yet may end up responding to some groups of students differentially. In the London study (Mortimore et al., 1988a), for example, classroom observations showed no evidence of inequitable attention or any obvious signs of bias. Yet the same study produced evidence of lower expectations for certain groups of students—in the main, those from Caribbean family backgrounds, or those who were chronologically young for the school year. It was not possible to explain these differences satisfactorily, but it can be speculated that a mixture of unconscious prejudice—against groups of students from a different cultural background or against children who appeared immature—and of successful student strategies, involving the elicitation of positive responses by other groups, was responsible. Those students with advantaged backgrounds, perhaps, used their advantages to get more out of their schooling experience.

In other cases, it is likely that schools will target those groups that teachers believe most likely to benefit. Evidence shows that, in 'tracked' selective schools, the premier group of students received a greater share of attention and resources than others and that this had a deleterious effect on all but this group (Lacey, 1975). At the other extreme, Athey (1990) has shown how pre-school programmes can be targeted at the most disadvantaged students in order to lessen the gap between their achievements and those of other children. This evidence is in line with a series of studies based on other kinds of institutions, such as the work in mental hospitals which shows that differential efforts can be targeted to considerable effect (Brown & Wing, 1962).

The answer to the key question of whether the positive effects of schooling vary according to school membership is, therefore, complex. The evidence suggests that, at the secondary stage at least, different subgroups of students may or may not benefit and, furthermore, that schools can choose to target certain groups. At the elementary stage, the evidence points to a more uniform effect. Schools that are effective are likely to be positive for all subgroups of students, although some groups may benefit to a greater extent than others. There is no evidence in either sector of schools, however, to suggest that different factors are responsible for differential effects. It is a question of which subgroup is affected, for which group are high expectations held, who is likely to be rewarded, and so forth.

Do the positive effects of schooling vary according to the particular strengths and weaknesses of schools?

It appears that, even though schools that are generally effective in one area are usually reasonably effective in others, some variation is possible. In the London study of fifty primary schools, fourteen were uniformly effective, seven were uniformly ineffective, and the rest had mixed profiles (Mortimore et al., 1988a). The extent of this within-school variation is important and will be further investigated in a new British study of secondary schools (Nuttall et al. [1993], personal communication).

What are the mechanisms associated with differential school effectiveness?

It is seldom possible for educational researchers to impose experimental conditions on their subjects. They are generally welcomed into schools and classes, but they usually have to observe things as they are. This helps them to gain a realistic picture of school life but means that they are rarely able directly to trace causal relationships. All too frequently, researchers are limited to tracing patterns of association and the use of correlations. Nevertheless, even with such methodological limitations, researchers from different countries have reached a number of conclusions about the variables commonly associated with the functioning of more effective schools. The plausibility of these variables operating as mechanisms of school effectiveness has been increased by the frequency with which they have been replicated.

The following list of mechanisms is not intended to be comprehensive or exhaustive. It has been culled from a sample of ten reviews or studies drawn from different countries, selected because of their use of different methodologies. Because of different wording and a lack of scientifically precise language, it is not possible to compare in a highly accurate way findings from so many different studies, many of which are composite reviews of a number of individual research projects. It is possible, however, broadly to collate variables to ascertain the most common mechanisms found by researchers to be associated with effectiveness. The following list is the result of this exercise.

Strong positive leadership

Although a few studies (notably, Van de Grift, 1990) have claimed that the principal has little impact or that the leadership of the school can be provided by somebody else, almost universally this mechanism was found to be important.

Different studies have drawn attention to different aspects of principals' roles, but Levine and Lezotte (1990) have provided a clear analysis of how strong leadership can provide mechanisms to aid effectiveness. In their view, this occurs through the rigorous selection and replacement of teachers; 'buffering' the school from unhelpful external agents; frequent personal monitoring of school achievements; high expenditure of time and energy for school improvement actions; supporting teachers; and acquiring extra resources for their schools.

The British studies support this analysis but add a further, rather subtle task: that of understanding when—and when not—to involve other staff in decision-making. The British studies have found evidence that both autocratic and over-democratic styles of leadership are less effective than a balanced style which depends on the crucial judgement of when, and when not, to act as decision-maker. Fullan (1992a) has argued that strong leadership, by itself, is not sufficient in a complex, postmodern society. Instead, he argued that heads (principals) have to find appropriate leadership roles for teachers.

High expectations: an appropriate challenge for students' thinking

This mechanism was commonly cited by researchers. Despite the limitations of the original experimental work (Rosenthal & Jacobson, 1968), the concept of expectations and the way these can affect the behaviour of both teachers and students have been well assimilated. Dorr-Bremme (1990), for instance, drew attention to the differing mind-sets of two groups of teachers from more, and less, effective schools. Members of the less effective group see their work one way:

> We are educators who work hard to take our students' needs into account. This means considering their total life situations and not expecting more of them than they can do.

In contrast, those in the more effective group saw their similar task in a quite different way:

> We are people who take our students' needs into account as we teach. This means that we challenge our students, make them work hard and do the very best that they can. (Levine & Lezotte, 1990, p. 35)

The one group chose a passive role, affected by forces (the students' problems) over which they could have little control. The other group, although recognizing that problems existed, adopted a more active stance and sought to challenge the difficulties through challenging the students' thinking.

Mortimore and colleagues (1988a) looked at ways in which expectations could be transmitted in the classroom. The researchers found that teachers had lower expectations for students who, for instance, were young in their year group (those with summer birthdays) or who came from lower social classes. They found that low expectations were not held in any simple way for either girls or boys *per se*, despite the fact that boys received more critical comments and girls more praise. These data were difficult to interpret and the research team drew on the findings of Dweck and Repucci (1973) to help explain them. (Dweck and Repucci found that greater praise from male teachers to female students for less adequate work was linked to stereotyped views of female performance.)

Monitoring student progress
Although monitoring, by itself, changes little, the majority of the studies found it to be a vital procedure—as a prelude to planning instructional tactics, altering pedagogy, or increasing or decreasing workloads. They also saw it as a key message to students that the teacher was interested in their progress. Whether it is more effective for the monitoring to be carried out formally or informally cannot yet be answered and further work on the way this mechanism operates may be worthwhile.

Student responsibilities and involvement in the life of the school
The mechanism—in its various forms—of ensuring that students adopt an active role in the life of the school was also commonly found to be important. By seeking to involve students in school-oriented activities, or by allocating responsibilities to elicit a positive response from them, teachers have endeavoured to provide a sense of ownership in the school and in the students' own learning.

Although examples of talented, but alienated, students can frequently be found in literature, the general rule appears to be that learning is most likely when the students hold a positive view of the school and of their own role within it. The attitudes of students towards themselves as learners was used as a school outcome by Mortimore and colleagues (1988a). The outcome consisted of a specially designed measure of self-concept. This was the mirror image of the behaviour scale completed by teachers and by students themselves. The measure revealed clear school differences. Some schools produced students who—regardless of their actual ability—felt reasonably positive about themselves; other schools produced students who were negative about themselves even when, in the judgement of the research team and according to their progress, they were performing well.

Rewards and incentives
Unlike punishments, rewards and incentives appear to act as mechanisms for eliciting positive behaviour and, in some cases, for changing students' (and at times teachers') behaviour. Thus, Purkey and Smith (1983) noted that a key cultural characteristic of effective schools is a school-wide recognition of academic success: 'publicly honouring academic achievement and stressing its importance encourages students to adopt similar norms and values' (p. 183).

Levine and Lezotte (1990) made two further points. First, that the use of rewards extends beyond academic outcomes and applies to other aspects of school life—a point supported by the British research. Second, that school-wide recognition of positive performance may be more important in urban schools, and especially those in inner cities where, because of the correlation with disadvantage, there are low achieving students. Levine and Lezotte cited Hallinger and Murphy's (1985) study to support this argument. Hallinger and Murphy argued that one of the roles of principals in advantaged schools was to sustain existing norms, rather than create new ones:

> In low SES (disadvantaged) schools the principal must ensure that the school overcomes societal and school norms that communicate low expectations to the students . . . (whereas in higher SES schools) school disciplinary and academic reward systems need not focus as much on short-term accomplishments, rely heavily on tangible reinforcers or develop elaborate linkages between the classroom and the school. (p. 3)

Finally, in one of the British studies, Mortimore and colleagues (1988a) found that rewards could be given in a variety of ways, if the policy of the school was positive. In some schools, the policy was to reward individuals for good work or behaviour, whereas in others it was to focus on sport and social factors. Schools experienced the problem of trying to create a common system of incentives. This was a particular problem for schools where the age range was wide: rewards that appealed to younger pupils sometimes lost their enchantment for older students.

Parental involvement in the life of the school

Parental involvement is possibly one of the most important issues in the current educational debate. The idea is not new and has been pioneered by a number of educational researchers in the United Kingdom and in the United States. There is also a large and rapidly growing literature on the topic. In the United Kingdom, much of the debate has been about the gains to be made from developing contact between homes and schools with regard to children's learning, as well as about ways to increase the accountability of schools to parents.

The vital role that parents can play in the intellectual development of their children has long been known, but experiments to use this resource more effectively have met with varied success. One pioneering British study (Tizard et al., 1982), however, demonstrated that parental involvement in reading more than equalled the benefits from the use of an extra teacher in schools.

The Head Start programmes in the United States (Lazar & Darlington, 1982) have also provided evidence that the involvement of parents is an important aspect of the programmes' success. Similar programmes in England show that the gap between the achievement levels of advantaged and disadvantaged can be reduced (Athey, 1990). In another British study, Mortimore and colleagues (1988a) found that schools varied a great deal in their attitudes towards parents. Some schools kept parents out; others used parents as cheap labour. A few schools involved parents in school planning and sought to use their talents and abilities in both the classroom and at home. The researchers found, however, that some principals appeared to be insufficiently confident in their relationships with parents, especially in more socially advantaged areas. They found, though, that when the energy and talents of parents were harnessed, the rewards for the school were high. It is interesting that they also found Parent–Teacher Associations were not necessarily positive, in that they could form a 'clique' for particular groups of parents and thus present a barrier to the involvement of others. The range of parental involvement programmes in both elementary and secondary schooling in the United Kingdom has been summarized by Jowett and Baginsky (1991).

The ways in which parents act as a mechanism for effectiveness are not well understood. It is possible to speculate that, where both long-term and short-term objectives are shared by teachers and parents, where parents are able to offer considerable help through coaching, and where ideas generated in one area of a child's life can be rehearsed and expanded in another, learning will be helped. Stevenson and Shin-Ying's (1990) study of three cities (Taipei in Taiwan; Sendai in Japan; Minneapolis in the United States) illustrates the lengths to which oriental families will go to involve not just parents, but other relations, in coaching their children. Stevenson and Shin-Ying showed that a belief in the supremacy of hard work over natural ability and the willingness to be critical, when combined with high expectations, can provide powerful support for learning. Parental involvement, however, is not without difficulties and those responsible for school programmes need to have clear policies in place before embarking on this potentially valuable strategy (Mortimore & Mortimore, 1984).

Joint planning and consistent approaches towards students

The efficacy of joint planning and consistent approaches have been clearly recognized by many research studies. Levine and Lezotte (1990) argued that, almost by definition, faculty members committed to a school-wide mission focusing on academic improvement for all students tend to exemplify greater cohesiveness and consensus regarding central organizational goals than do faculty members at less effective schools (p. 12).

Levine and Lezotte maintained that cohesion and consensus are especially important to schools (rather than other institutions), because schools set teachers a number of difficult and sometimes conflicting goals. Teachers must respond to the individual needs of students while emphasizing the requirements of the whole class. They have to be fair to the group but take account of individual circumstances. It is thus easy for what Levine and Lezotte call 'goal clarity' to be reduced and for improvement efforts to be fragmented. Where students are subject to conflicting expectations and demands and, as a result, become less confident, they often take time to learn the ways of each new teacher. This exercise may provide a helpful pointer to the ways of adults, but it is clearly not a useful mechanism for a school.

The involvement of faculty members in joint decisions relates to the strength of leadership of the institution. There is clear evidence that when teachers and others in authority (including the assistant principal) are given a role to play, they—in the best management tradition—will be far more likely to feel owner-ship of the institution and, as a result, offer greater commitment to it.

Academic emphasis and a focus on learning

There has been much research on this topic. Some of it has been concerned with the question of time-on-task (see, for example, Sizemore, 1987). A number of research studies have drawn attention to the waste of time in the school day, particularly at the start of classes, through poor administration and lack of preparation (Blum, 1984). Rutter and colleagues (1979a) found evidence of time wasted at the end of classes. The researchers described the chaotic situation that could develop when a high proportion of classes in the school finished before the scheduled time. The problem, therefore, is not simply about time: it is about the use of time. Mortimore and colleagues (1988a) noted that, although some schools in their sample programmemed extra time (some twenty minutes per day) for classes, a straightforward correlation with effectiveness was not found. The value of time appeared to depend greatly on how it was used.

Emphasizing the learning of core skills has also been cited as an important aspect of this mechanism. In the United States, this has sometimes been associ-ated with experiments in mastery learning (Gregory & Mueller, 1980). Levine and Lezotte (1990) argued, however, that in some cases the original concept of Bloom-type mastery learning has been mis-implemented and cannot fairly be judged. In Britain, a Department of Education and Science (DES) discussion paper (Alexander et al., 1992) has drawn attention to the danger that elemen-tary schools can lose sight of the central focus on student learning and dissipate the energies of teachers in an unproductive way.

These were the most commonly cited mechanisms arising from the research literature. As noted earlier, however, other factors have frequently been studied and may also be of considerable importance for particular schools at particular times. Thus, if schools receive students of a certain background, if the commu-nity is subject to particular experiences, or if the school authorities invoke a spe-cific series of reforms, other mechanisms for coping with change will come into play. These may act as mediating influences and, as a result, distract the atten-tion of teachers and principals. They should never supplant the prime focus of school—the learning of pupils.

How successful have preventative interventions been?

This question is difficult to answer. It requires a clear definition of preventative interventions and in view of the most recent history of schooling in many parts of the world such a definition is not easy to formulate. Straightforward applica-tion of the knowledge and understanding of, for instance, school effectiveness, by those involved in school improvement programmes, represents one kind of intervention. Complex governmental initiatives, for what have previously been considered fairly autonomous school systems, is another. Both may be found in some school systems.

In reality, school effectiveness and school improvement are very different phenomena. As Clark et al. (1984) have argued so clearly, researchers pursuing these two lines of enquiry pursue different questions (about what affects student outcomes and about how schools change) and use different outcome measures (student achievement and the level of innovation). What the two approaches share is their interest in schools. The contrast between school effectiveness and school improvement is illustrated by a comparison of the work of Rutter and colleagues (1979a), seeking explanations for poor student outcomes in one geographical area, with the International School Improvement Study's (ISIS) endeavours, operating in fourteen countries to describe and, where appropriate, to change various school processes (Bollen & Hopkins, 1987).

A different kind of initiative is a government-sponsored project, such as that on the school development plans of the (then) English Department of Education and Science (now the Department for Education). This project was designed to promote concepts, culled from research, on the necessity of systematic planning (Hargreaves & Hopkins, 1989; DES, 1991).

Different again are the programmes of school restructuring and school reforms that have been introduced in the United States and the United Kingdom. In the case of school restructuring, a variety of different interest groups have expressed their fears about aspects of American schooling and, in line with political policy, have been encouraged to put thinking into practice (Murphy, 1991). In Chicago, for instance, a parents' collective alliance has been established to oversee the restructuring of the city's education system (Hess, 1992). In New York, critics such as Domanico and Cenn (1992) have argued that curtailment of the city's power over education is essential to enable parents and others— using public money—to run their own schools.

In the United Kingdom, a series of legislative changes have dominated recent educational events. Among other actions, the 1988 Education Reform Act established a national curriculum and its associated testing at the ages of seven, eleven, fourteen, and sixteen; it introduced a system of parental choice based on open enrolment; and it delegated financial decision-making to the school principal and the governors (a small group representing the interests of teachers, the local education authority and—where appropriate—the wider community).

The 1992 Education Act created a new form of privatized school inspections, whereby appropriately qualified and trained inspectors can compete for contracts to inspect schools as part of a four-year cycle. Among the proposals of recent British legislation are the establishment of 'education associations' to take over the management of failing schools and a further loosening of local government powers over schooling.

These developments in the United States and the United Kingdom have led to different kinds of interventions, designed by researchers and practitioners, with different patterns of outcomes. The American situation has been summarized in a briefing report to the House of Representatives by the United States

General Accounting Office (GAO, 1989). This shows that, in the last year for which full data were available, approximately 41 per cent (6,500) of US districts representing over 38,000 schools were involved in various forms of interventions and that a further 17 per cent of districts were planning to implement such programmes during the next couple of years. Based on published accounts, Levine and Lezotte (1990) have drawn up a list of the most promising interventions. Practices studied by researchers include the following 14 types of intervention:

- Establishment and facilitation of an informal group of participating principals who regularly meet and work together
- Provision of parallel and co-ordinated training for administrators
- Sponsorship of individual schools' audits
- Establishment of principals' academies
- Redesign and utilization of personnel evaluation instruments
- Assignment of new principals to a programme of shadowing
- Selection of faculty at poorly functioning schools for a tailored programme of improvement
- Training of future administrators
- Establishment of a central office intervention team to work with schools
- Establishment of paid link teachers between individual schools and central office
- Assignment of former principals to serve as mentors
- Accelerated learning programmes for students
- Development of auditing and other technical assistance teams
- Establishment of mentor teachers to staff other than the principal

The United Kingdom has had fewer interventions by researchers and practitioners, but more government-generated initiatives. Reynolds (1992) has summarized those that have taken place. In particular, he has drawn attention to the following developments:

- Teacher–researcher movement's focus on improvement in the 1970s
- Self-evaluation and review programmes of the 1980s
- Local Education Authorities' own initiatives (such as the Hargreaves and the Thomas Reports, Inner London Education Authority [ILEA], 1984 and 1985 respectively)
- Schools' Council's Guidelines for Review and Institutional Development (GRIDS) scheme

To this list should be added the recent work on school development planning (Beresford et al., 1992) and government-sponsored activities. The work on school planning shows that almost all LEAs have encouraged their schools to adopt school development plans and that many authorities are now using these as a basis for their own support and interventions in schools.

By seeking to create a market in which parents can choose schools to suit their children, the UK government has striven to induce competitive conditions which, it hopes, will improve the effectiveness of schools. In particular, by enabling school communities to opt out of their school districts and to manage themselves, it has sought to encourage principals to take initiatives otherwise denied them. It is as yet too early to report systematically on the outcome of this experiment, but it is already possible to see both encouraging and worrying signs in those schools that have taken advantage of opting out. Encouraging signs can be detected in the increasing self-confidence of staff and in the benefits of local, rather than area-based, decision-making mechanisms. (The schools have also benefited from increased funding.) The worrying signs are that, rather than parents choosing schools, the schools appear to be choosing the students, and, because of a leg-islative requirement to publish examination results, pupils with special needs, or those who are likely to be low-achieving, are less likely to be chosen than are their more able, less problematic, peers. If this trend develops, the low achievers will be clustered in those schools (with less resources) that have not opted out and the vital ingredient of effectiveness—a balanced intake—identified by Rutter and colleagues (1979a) will be stymied. This situation needs to be monitored closely.

Table 8.1 shows the range of interventions that take place. This list is not intended to be exhaustive. Interventions have been included simply to illustrate the available range of activities. Two dimensions have been identified, focus and scope. The *focus* varies from specific to general. The *scope* includes single schools, groups of schools, the local system, and national categories.

In terms of success, most of the preventative interventions cited have achieved something. None, however, has been hailed as a panacea for all the ills of school-ing. Each will have a range of costs and benefits. Some initiatives, such as the Reading Recovery Project (Clay, 1985), are still the subject of critical evaluation (for example, Glyn et al., 1989) but have been hailed as being of direct value in other countries and other systems. Others, such as the Comer Programme (Comer, 1991) and the Olweus (1991) project, have been recognized nationally as being capable of supporting young people and their schools, particularly in urban areas. The London study (Maughan et al., 1990; Ouston et al., 1991) revealed much information about whether—and how—schools can change their practices and their outcomes, although the changes were not brought about as a direct result of the intervention. More work needs to be done in order to exploit fully the knowledge that now exists about the potential positive effects of schools.

The Olweus intervention (one of the 'national systems') is interesting in view of its long time-scale and its complex research design. Its major goals were to limit, as much as possible, the number of incidents of bullying and to prevent development of new bully and victim problems. The intervention programme included the development of better information for teachers and school admin-istrators about bullying and what they could do to counteract it. Information about bullying was also provided to parents of all children in the Norwegian school system. A cassette showing episodes of bullying was produced and made available for schools to rent or borrow. Finally, a questionnaire was designed to elicit information about all aspects of the bully and victim problem in schools. This was completed anonymously by individual students in school time.

Table 8.1. Interventions classified according to their focus and scope.

Focus	Single school
Specific	US High School Academies of enriched schooling (Archer & Montesano, 1990)
	Changing an English Disruptive School (Badger, 1992)
General	The Baz Attack–Canada (Toews & Murray-Barker, 1985)
	Enrichment for preschool students (Athey, 1990)
	Group of schools
Specific	The Comer New Haven Programme (Comer, 1991)
	Cognitive Interactions in Primary Schooling in Germany (Einsiedler, 1992)
General	The London Study (Maughan et al., 1990)
	The Israeli Study (Bashi et al., 1990)
	Local systems
Specific	Sheffield Early Literacy Programme (Hannon et al., 1991)
	Academic Feedback in Northern Ireland (FitzGibbon, 1991a)
General	The Halton Growth Plan (Stoll & Fink, 1989)
	The Calgary Plan (Waldron, 1983)
	National systems
Specific	Norwegian Ministry of Education anti Bullying Program (Olweus, 1991)
	Reading Recovery in New Zealand, US and the UK (Clay, 1985)
General	What Works? (US Dept. of Education, 1987)
	The Australian Project (McGaw et al., 1991)

About 2,500 students drawn from 42 schools in Bergen were followed up over a period of two-and-a-half years. This student sample was divided into four cohorts and a series of measurements were collected from before the initiation of the anti-bullying programme until several years after it had been completed. The research team used time-lagged contrasts between different cohorts to investigate whether there were genuine changes in behaviour over this period. A series of outcome variables based on the reported accounts of being bullied or of taking part in bullying incidents were developed from a questionnaire completed by the students. The research team concluded that reductions in bully and victim problems had taken place and that these were likely to be the result of the intervention programme rather than other factors.

What are the implications of this work for policy and practice?

There are numerous possible implications stemming from the work carried out over the last twenty or so years on the positive effects of schooling. Perhaps the most important is an implication for those involved closely with schools—the confirmation of the potential power of schools to affect the life chances of their students. Although the difference in scholastic attainment likely to be achieved by the same student in contrasting schools is unlikely to be great, in many instances it represents the difference between success and failure and operates as a facilitating or inhibiting factor in higher education. When coupled with the promotion of other pro-social attitudes and behaviours, and the inculcation of a positive self-image, the potential of the school to improve the life chances of students is considerable.

The second major implication of this work relates to governments. Legislation can provide a helpful framework for achieving an education system of high quality, but this can only be guaranteed by the conscious strategies of teachers and administrators, and the purposeful commitment of students. Excellence cannot be mandated by politicians or bureaucrats. Governments, central or local, would do well to realize this and ensure that any legislative framework that is created is likely to stimulate and elicit from those most involved ownership, commitment and dedication—rather than learned help-lessness and resentment.

The third major implication relates to practitioners. A critical body of knowl-edge—replicated, in many cases, over time and in many different settings—has been established. This knowledge needs to be drawn upon more frequently in the quest for better schools. Some practitioners complain that information drawn from research studies is seldom made accessible or disseminated widely. This criticism undoubtedly has some validity: research journals seldom make compulsive reading for busy practitioners. It is not true, however, that efforts to disseminate widely the findings reported here have been half-hearted. Many con-ferences and meetings of principals' associations in many different countries have featured presentations on this topic. The work needs to continue. All those involved in trying to improve schools need to recognize the potential—not just in terms of specific actions by principals or teachers that may or may not be related to the rest of their way of working—for describing, analysing, and eval-uating effectiveness.

The fourth and final implication concerns the work of researchers. The liter-ature on school effectiveness is now enormous. There are vast numbers of books, journal articles, chapters in edited collections, and conference papers on this topic. There are, however, relatively fewer detailed empirical studies than there are critiques and commentaries. If the field is to flourish, more empirical work is needed. Further studies extending the focus from schools to other edu-cational institutions would help to broaden still further the knowledge base. Possibly even more important is the need for careful experimental work that tests the mainly correlational findings of the early studies. This, coupled with a compilation of an adequate theory both of what makes schools effective and of how to make them more so, would be of great value to the educational com-munity. Some work on the theoretical underpinning of the topic has been under-taken, as the very careful synthesis of research on educational change illustrates (Fullan, 1991), but more is needed.

In conclusion, therefore, it can be stated that the positive effects of schooling have been well documented by a number of research studies carried out in different countries at different times. The mechanisms associated with these effects are also well known and are, to a large extent, common to the studies. The effects vary, however, according to a number of different variables and more work is needed to disentangle the influence of student characteristics from school effects. Justified by the groundbreaking early research, a number of intervention studies have been carried out, but the outcomes of such work have, in general, proved less than hoped for. The difficulties of integrating such interventions—based on sound research findings—with those dictated by the political concerns of governments remain. Finally, a number of implications for different groups, stemming from this work, still need to be addressed.

Postscript

So schools can be positive but they cannot—by themselves—put right all the other problems affecting students' lives. In Bernstein's words: 'Schools cannot compensate for society'. This is a theme to which I will return in chapter eighteen.

9

Technical Issues in School Effectiveness Research

Introduction

The subject of this chapter stems from a presentation I made at the 1990 meeting of the school effectiveness Special Interest Group (SIG) at the American Educational Research Association in Boston. My brief was to identify some of the key issues that needed resolution if school effectiveness research was to flourish. With the experience of both the Fifteen Thousand Hours *and the* School Matters *studies still fresh in my mind, this was an opportunity to identify some longstanding but unresolved weaknesses and to feel our way towards solutions. As the SIG was a meeting of professional researchers, I tried to focus on matters with practical significance for American and British colleagues. It was an opportunity for all of us to learn from the totality of our research experience.*

It is important that researchers in any field pause periodically in their investigations and reflect on the worth of all this endeavour. As part of this process it is highly appropriate to attempt to identify the key issues of that field. In a field in which—despite its youth—one of the most striking characteristics is its international nature (with committed researchers in the United States and Canada, Australia, the United Kingdom, the Netherlands and an increasing number of other European countries), it may well be right to call these 'universal issues', despite the somewhat grandiose nature of the term.

My intention, in this chapter, is to select nine issues and to identify at least some of the debates that surround them. The number nine has no significance other than its manageability; it could have been twenty or thirty. These issues are those that seem to me—at this stage of the development of our chosen field— to be important. In some cases the issues I have chosen are to do with method- ological problems and are amenable to solutions. In others, they concern the context in which we work, and are related to societal problems which simple solutions are unlikely to solve.

In some ways, it is an idiosyncratic list: four issues are concerned with research matters and deal with technical questions of investigations; one is what I have termed a pivotal issue and deals with the interface between research on school effectiveness and school improvement projects; two are about improve- ment programmemes; one deals with the question of international co-operation; and the final issue, naturally, is focused on future developments. (I have tried to structure this collection into a model but with little success. The first four research issues could be defined as basic building blocks and the three issues concerned with school improvement could be described [in the Fullan et al., 1990, idiom] as 'cogs', but there remain one pivot and two antennae, pointing somewhat vaguely at the international community and the future!)

Sampling

Sampling is a very obvious issue with which to begin. It is discussed at the start of most academic courses devoted to research methods. Its importance should never be underestimated. If, as a community of researchers, we aim to produce work which deserves to be taken seriously by policy makers—in the United States, the work of Congressman Gus Hawkins is a prime example of such attention (House of Representatives, 1986)—the sample used in our research must be large enough and suitable enough to permit reasonable generalization.

Drawing on some of the work with which I have been associated, the sample of secondary schools chosen for *Fifteen Thousand Hours* (Rutter et al., 1979a) was small because it had been determined by earlier work. It served its purpose well but was far from ideal and, in the Harvard University Press edition of the book, an appendix has been added to explain its use. In the later *School Matters* study (Mortimore et al., 1988a), the sample of primary schools was both ran- dom and, when checked, representative: 50 junior schools drawn from a popu- lation of over 650.

Size of sample, however, is not the only criterion. Reynolds (1990b) has drawn attention to the fact that many of the major studies of school effectiveness have used samples from populations of disadvantaged schools. We also need to inves- tigate the mechanisms of effective schooling in *advantaged* areas, as well as, I suggest, in schools that serve a wholly minority community. To obtain similar findings in groups of schools with such different student bodies would add con- siderable weight to the strength of our arguments. To obtain different findings would be an interesting challenge to those arguments. Between the various research studies we need to cover the range of possible samples, not only so that we can indulge in meta-analysis techniques (which, in the field of school effectiveness research, present difficulties) but so that our school improvement follow-up work can be built on more secure foundations.

Measuring outcomes

The school outcomes studied in many of the school effectiveness investigations have been restricted to pencil and paper tests of cognitive skills. In the American studies, this has meant an almost exclusive focus on tests of English and mathematics. In the United Kingdom, the focus has been broader and, in fact, some of the pioneering work was devoted to the study of measures of delinquency (see Mortimore, 1991c, for a discussion of the methods and findings of British research). The details of the British work, however, are not well known in the United States and claims are sometimes made that the non-cognitive and the affective outcomes have been neglected in studies of school effectiveness.

Fifteen Thousand Hours used four outcomes of which only one—public examination results across the range of the curriculum—was cognitive. The other three—attendance, behaviour and delinquency—focused on the non-cognitive development of students. In *School Matters* the list of outcomes is longer: reading, mathematics (written), mathematics (practical), writing, speaking, attendance, behaviour, self-image and a range of students' attitudes to school. Such a list enabled us to chart the progress and development of students with a reasonable degree of confidence that we were tapping their all-round capabilities. Even so, we were not monitoring the full range of the school curriculum. We were unable to measure the humanities, social studies, aesthetic subjects and physical and religious education (the latter included by law in the United Kingdom). In these areas we found the variation between schools to be so great that there was little basis for valid comparison. Interestingly, the introduction, from 1989, of an English and Welsh national curriculum will enable future studies to make up this deficiency.

In my view, the adoption of a broad range of outcome measures is essential if studies are to address adequately the all-round development of students and if they are to be used to judge the effectiveness of schools. In *School Matters*, for example, we found considerable variation in effectiveness, with some schools appearing particularly effective on cognitive outcomes, others seemingly effective on non-cognitive outcomes, and a group of fourteen schools straddling both dimensions. A replication of this approach with a sample of secondary schools might generate some interesting data.

Methods of analysis

Over the past ten years, developments in statistical techniques and in computer programmes to handle data sets have been impressive. In England, for example, the work of Murray Aitkin (Aitkin et al., 1981) and Harvey Goldstein (1984, 1987) has expanded considerably the range of available techniques. In particular, the development of multilevel analysis and of associated programmes enables the data to be treated in an appropriate manner, rather than being reduced to a single level. Thus, differences between classes, year groups and schools can be recognized separately, rather than being aggregated together arbitrarily.

These developments are welcome. They represent a considerable improvement from standard multiple regression techniques (Preece, 1989) and go some way towards solving the difficulties identified by Purkey and Smith (1983) and Gray (1989). But, as all researchers should be aware, sophisticated techniques of analysis cannot compensate for inadequate measures and the best analysis depends on a matching of appropriate techniques with correctly specified, high-quality data.

The relationship of outcome to process techniques

My final 'research' issue poses as a problem something that often passes as unproblematic: the way different sorts of measures are linked, both conceptually and in terms of data relationships.

Conceptually, the division of variables into inputs, processes and outcomes, although subject to criticism on grounds of an over-mechanistic approach, has proved helpful in clarifying the question of how to study schools. Using this model, student outcomes (measured, as I have noted, in various ways and on a number of dimensions) can be adjusted to take account of the level reached by the student on a number of dimensions on arrival at the school (intake measures). These adjusted outcomes, by a process of 'backward mapping' (Murphy, 1990), can be related to a series of process measures, provided they have been collected contemporaneously and so are related to the conditions that the target students would have experienced.

The statistical techniques used for backward mapping have usually been based on some form of correlation. Whilst this technique is easy to use in order to clarify relationships, the difficulty with correlations—as is widely recognized—lies in determining the direction of influence. Thus, distinguishing whether higher achievement is influenced by higher expectations or *vice versa* is impossible unless other information is available. Occasionally, it is possible to use a cross-lagged technique to investigate such a question. This was the case in *School Matters*, when my colleagues and I were able to investigate the relationship between reading problems and behaviour difficulties. Interestingly, our use of this technique illustrated that *each could be an antecedent condition for the other*. For some students, reading difficulties preceded any signs of behaviour difficulties, while for others early behavioural difficulties were followed by the identification of reading problems. In my judgement, the linkage between the outcome and the process variables in empirical work is often weak. In view of the use that is made of the findings of research, it is obviously of the utmost importance that techniques of backward mapping be improved and the experience of such techniques be increased, perhaps through the further development and extension of multilevel methods.

These are the four issues I have selected concerning research on school effectiveness. As I noted in my introduction, however, there are a number of others that could equally well have been addressed. I turn now to my 'pivotal' issue, which stands between the research on school effectiveness and the developmental work on school improvement.

Models for school improvement

The issue here is simple: are the processes identified by the various research studies in effectiveness necessarily the best models for school improvement work? Factors such as sensitive headship, the careful management of students and teachers, the care of students, the quality of the environment and the positive climate of the school have been identified as important in a number of different studies (Mortimore, 1991c). These factors have been shown to be associated with greater student progress; they have emerged from studies of good practice but there is a question as to whether they are necessarily appropriate for schools which do not *yet* have good student outcomes. Are these appropriate for a school that is not yet effective? Furthermore do such factors rest on other conditions that have had to be secured at an earlier stage? This possibility of the necessity for *antecedent* variables is difficult to explore, since, by their nature, such variables are likely to be unobtrusive or, in some cases, transient conditions. A concrete example may clarify the issue:

> *A new head teacher is appointed to a run-down school where students' outcomes are very poor and teachers are demoralized. Parents are extremely vocal in their criticisms and the community is hostile to students and staff.*

Is this a situation in which sensitive leadership and careful management are needed or, before these can be employed, are more dramatic gestures necessary? The answer to this question will depend on different philosophies of management adopted by the new head teacher, but it seems likely that a variety of strategies could be adopted (and some may not have emanated from effective schools research), *provided they were suited to the style and skills of the new head teacher*. My personal view, however, is that the factors that *have* been identified in the research provide an excellent starting-point. This example illustrates the complexity of the issue. Satisfactory resolution may emerge from a study of the burgeoning literature on school change.

This issue, which I have termed pivotal, leads away from studies of school effectiveness to the area of *school improvement*. The next two issues to be considered arise from attempts to improve schools.

The impetus for change

In the section above, an example of a run-down school was cited. The unsatisfactory state of such a school provided an impetus for change. Unfortunately, most educational jurisdictions will have responsibility for some schools in a similar state because of a variety of circumstances to do with the history of the management of the school or its environment, funding or political circumstances. There are, however, other sources from which the impetus for change may spring. Governments in a number of countries—most notably in the United States, New Zealand and the United Kingdom—are currently seeking reforms of different aspects of schooling. This pressure for change does not stem directly from particular examples of schools that are failing—although it may be strengthened by public discussion of such schools—but rather from a general criticism that *all schools are inadequate for the needs of our changing societies.*

While different governments will put different glosses on this argument, it is clear that this attitude is not restricted to particular countries or to governments or particular political hues. Whilst—having worked in the education service for over twenty-five years—I feel a defensive loyalty to schools as they are now, I also acknowledge that as the needs of societies change, schools, which tend to be highly conservative institutions, also need to be modified. Where I dissent from the actions of some governments is that I do not accept that the most effective way to secure change is to heap blame on schools and opprobrium on teachers, often for outcomes beyond their control. I also believe that change cannot be achieved overnight by hostile legislation but, rather, by co-operation over a suitable time period.

The reality for many teachers, however, is that governments in many parts of the world, ably assisted by a teacher-unfriendly media, are endeavouring to force change on schools. In the phrase adopted from Shaw by Fullan, they are attempting to change schools by 'brute sanity' (Fullan, 1982). In the United Kingdom, for example, schools are being expected to:

- Introduce a national curriculum with an associated programme of individual student assessment
- Operate a system of delegated site-management on the basis of formula-funding
- Compete with each other for students under an open enrolment scheme

In the United States and in some Canadian provinces, programmes of school restructuring are being introduced for similar reasons to the British reforms. Australia and New Zealand, too, are involved in programmes of school reform.

The impetus for system-wide change has been strengthened by the demands of higher education. In the United States, for instance, Bloom (1987) and Burton Clark (1985)—both university professors—have criticized the quality of current applicants for higher education (and, in the case of Bloom, the quality of higher education itself) and have predicted dire consequences at societal level. Such arguments have lent considerable weight to the pressure for reform.

What must not be overlooked in any consideration of system-wide change, however, is the willingness of individual schools and their supporting bodies (local education authorities in the United Kingdom; school boards in North America) to embrace change in their search for greater effectiveness. Many schools have grasped the school effectiveness literature and used this to assist and support their own development. For a variety of reasons, there has been more activity of this sort in North America than in the United Kingdom (Mortimore, 1991c), but in places as far apart as San Diego in southern California (Chrispeels & Pollack, 1989) and Halton County in Greater Toronto (Stoll & Fink, 1989) school improvement work is flourishing.

Where a support team—funded by a school board or state department—can work sensitively to support an individual school's request for greater effectiveness, the conditions are conducive to positive change. Having provided a reasonable legislative framework, governments—in my opinion—would do well to encourage this type of co-operative endeavour rather than the bullying and deriding tactics that are more commonly employed.

In summary, then, the impetus for change can stem from a number of different sources. System-wide change emanates from governments; individual school change can be stimulated by the local education authority (school board) or by the school itself, either because a crisis has developed or because it is searching for greater effectiveness.

The limits of change

In many ways this is the most difficult issue that I have chosen to discuss. In much that has been written about school effectiveness and improvement, it is tacitly assumed that all schools have an equal chance of improvement. The reality is that schools in all countries vary enormously in their conditions and in the nature of their student intakes. The acceptance of this reality is not to condone a defeatist attitude by teachers of disadvantaged students but merely to note that judgements of school effectiveness have to be made sensitively, using sophisticated methodology and avoiding over-simplistic generalizations.

Such judgements of schools frequently involve comparisons of one with another. To ensure that like is compared with like, however, is difficult. In terms of cognitive development, any examinations or tests that are norm-based and that have high failure rates (or criteria-based assessments that are pitched too high) will demonstrate that—in general—schools serving disadvantaged populations are likely to achieve less than their more advantaged peers. Of course, some individual students will 'buck the system': some of the disadvantaged will be academically successful just as some of the advantaged will fail to achieve. The odds of academic success, however, remain firmly in favour of the advantaged.

In the United Kingdom, where for historical reasons standards in public examinations have been pitched high (five higher-level grades in the General Certificate of Secondary Education for entry into the advanced study which is a prerequisite for most of the more prestigious occupations), this is a particular problem. Average students, having achieved at an average level, drop out of school at age sixteen feeling that their schooling has been a failure. From the point of view of the functioning of society, this assessment system performs the task of sorting individuals into particular sets of aspirations and expectations about future life styles. It is efficient, in that, on the whole, young people believe this judgement and accept their role in society, but, in my view, is totally unacceptable on the grounds of equity or of the national interest. Although it might have served the country well in earlier times, the waste of the potential 'cooled out' by the system is far too serious to be tolerated by a modern country competing for trade and industry and needing highly trained and motivated workers.

For schools, which have to operate this system of role-selection, the price is considerable alienation on the part of many students. Given the strong relationship between academic success and social advantage, it is clear that, for schools serving disadvantaged populations, the proportion of alienated students is likely to be much higher (Mortimore and Blackstone, 1982). Yet such schools are powerless to alter the examination framework of the system in which they have to operate. The limits of change for such schools are, therefore, clearly defined: no matter how efficient they might be in enabling *individual* disadvantaged students to make progress, the odds against their students, as a group, achieving acknowledged levels of success will remain stacked against them.

In the United States, with a history of lower drop-out at the end of the statutory school years and greater opportunity for higher education, the situation is less clear cut. From the point of view of school improvement studies, it is still possible to follow the advice of the late Ron Edmonds, that 'if you want to change a school you need to start at the bottom with the least successful students; the rest will automatically improve' (Edmonds, 1982).

The capacity of the advantaged (whether students or adults) to get more out of any situation, however, poses a serious problem for school improvement. If a school's overall achievement is improved, yet there remains a large differential between advantaged and disadvantaged students within the school, has much been gained? In my judgement the answer is 'yes'—but with reservations. *School Matters* found that *disadvantaged* students in the most effective schools could perform better than advantaged students in the least effective schools. My reservations exist because of the failure to maximize the chances of *all* students. There is no obvious solution to this problem. Restricting coaching classes to the disadvantaged, though logical, would be likely to generate enormous resentment among groups of students. While it is possible to discriminate positively with resources between schools (Sammons et al., 1983), doing so between students is likely to be divisive.

International co-operation

The issues arising from school effectiveness and school improvement are after all common to a number of countries but, all too frequently, both researchers and policy makers are relatively ignorant of other situations. My own knowledge, for example, of developments in the Netherlands has increased considerably since the inception of the International Congress of Effective Schools and its journal *School Effectiveness and School Improvement*. I am still disappointed, however, when I discover that American scholars are unaware of much British and Canadian work.

This prompts me to pose the question of whether an international study would be an appropriate way of bringing together teachers from different countries. Clearly, such a study would need a great deal of planning so that a number of alternative strategies could be considered and the maximum value extracted from it. My own view is that such a study would be worthwhile and, if it took the form of a series of replications, could add considerably to our understanding of many practical concerns, as well as to the theoretical underpinnings of the work.

I am uncertain, however, as to whether such an international study would best be directed towards a further investigation of school effectiveness, or whether it would be more useful to focus on school improvement. As always, there are costs and benefits to either choice. A large-scale study of, say, secondary schools drawing on established research instruments and analytical techniques would strengthen the repertoire of studies and, undoubtedly, would strengthen our understanding of the characteristics of effective schools. Yet it would take time and would not necessarily further our knowledge of how to *change* schools. On the other hand, a study of school improvement could address more immediately the questions concerning change, but it would have to be built upon a foundation of various *national* rather than *international* studies.

On balance, I think my own preference is for a study of school improvement, on the grounds that governments are already engaged in school reform and the time-scale for work which could inform (and in some cases rescue) these government initiatives is short. Such a study would, hopefully, avoid the successive bureaucracy and government interference that so often characterizes international projects. It is likely, in my view, that a number of researchers in different countries would welcome the opportunity to participate in such a study if funding could be procured. Who the appropriate body to co-ordinate the work would be is, however, an open question. Perhaps this chapter, reflecting the mood of the Special Interest Group on school effectiveness, will act as a stimulus to funding bodies. At a time of such world change, few investments in the future could be more worthwhile than the improvement of schools.

The future

The final issue to be presented in this chapter presents the risk that both researchers and policy makers may be restricted to an outmoded model of schooling. Such a model has a number of features:

- Large groups of children and adolescents are controlled by adults
- A considerable proportion of their time is spent in passive roles
- Knowledge, and the school day, are compartmentalized by bells or sirens
- Assessment is mainly carried out using expensive, formal techniques of testing

My own position is that, while schools have to work to this model, I want to help them to be as effective as possible, but that I also believe other—perhaps more appropriate—models should be developed. Who is better equipped to share in this task than those who have studied school effectiveness? Such people, whether researchers or practitioners, should be aware of the difficulties of change and of the need for cogs that fit rather than grate (Fullan et al., 1990). A new model of schooling dedicated to producing effective learners, who are also caring and responsible people, is surely a worthwhile ambition?

Postscript

The discussion between practising researchers in Boston was helpful. Looking back, I believe that we addressed issues of considerable importance. The points about the need for a representative sample and for appropriate methods of analysis, able correctly to link data on outcomes with data stemming from the management of processes, still apply to empirical research. The points about school improvement and change in education are even more relevant today than when the original paper was delivered. These issues will recur throughout the remaining chapters of this book.

10

Which Way at the Crossroads?

Introduction

This paper was prepared for a keynote speech at the 1991 International Congress of School Effectiveness and Improvement (ICSEI) held in Cardiff. I had been asked to use the occasion to look both forwards and backwards: to reflect on the achievements of past research and to spell out the need for future studies. The congress had been established at a London conference in 1988 in order to bring together those interested in research into schools. Over the years, the numbers attending its annual meeting have grown steadily. The international journal associated with the congress, in which this keynote was subsequently published, has established itself as a high-quality instrument of dissemination.

> Two roads diverged in a wood, and I—
> I took the one less travelled by,
> And that has made all the difference.
> *The Road Not Taken*, Robert Frost

This article is about factors that make a difference. In this case we look at schools rather than roads, but Frost's words also provide a metaphor for the journey that researchers of school effectiveness have been making over the last twenty or so years. Like Frost, many of us would choose the less travelled route if we were confident it would lead us to where we want to go. The problem is that we are not always sure where that is! This paper will explore what might be a reasonable goal and then consider the different routes available—to keep to the metaphor: to decide which way at the crossroads.

The search for quality

The purpose of this article is to consider the options open to researchers after twenty years' work in school effectiveness. First, however, a basic question— *What is the intellectual core of the work on school effectiveness?*

Quite simply, it is the search for ways—both adequate and reliable—to measure the quality of the school. The term 'quality' itself, of course, is not unproblematic. When used in connection with schools, it is bound up with fundamental questions about the nature of education itself. Should schooling be discussed in Aristotelian terms, whereby it is seen as an essentially ethical activity guided by values open to continual debate and refinement (Carr, 1986). Alternatively, is it sufficient to think of it simply in instrumental terms—designed to bring about the achievement of specifiable and, generally, uncontroversial goals—a view increasingly being adopted, according to Hartnett and Naish (1986).

This fundamental debate over the different conceptions of schooling underpins many of the controversies that surround educational practice in different societies. For the purpose of this article, however, it will be accepted that in the education system of England and Wales, at least, both conceptions of schooling are necessary. Accepting, at face value, the general aims of the 1988 Educational Reform Act that the national curriculum 'promotes the spiritual, moral, cultural, mental and physical development of pupils at the school and of society; and prepares such pupils for the opportunities, responsibilities and experiences of adult life' (HMSO, 1988), the methods of measuring the quality of schooling must be sufficiently complex to deal with both moral and practical attributes (Mortimore & Stone, 1991).

The measurement of the quality of a school, of course, is of critical importance at a time when so much school reform is being undertaken in so many different parts of the world. For this reason, the OECD has funded a project designed to clarify the use of the term. A related OECD publication lists a number of definitions adopted by different countries. Amongst these, the comments put forward by the Australian government are noteworthy:

> There is no simple uni-dimensional measure of quality. In the same way as the definition of what constitutes high quality education is multi-dimensional, so there is no simple prescription of the ingredients necessary to achieve high quality education: many factors interact—students in their backgrounds; staff in their schools; schools in their structure and ethos; curricula; and societal explanations. (OECD, 1989)

Many practitioners will be relieved to hear that at least one national government accepts that the task is far from simple! However, just because it is difficult does not mean that it should not be attempted nor that researchers should not be seeking continually to refine their methods. As Caroline Stone and I have argued

> As a way of identifying components of educational quality, research is superior to other methods. This is because its methods should be public and can be examined for bias and its scope is very broad. Whilst the idea of perfectly value-free research is now recognized as something of a myth, there are well tried methods of limiting bias and of guarding against systematic distortion of evidence-gathering techniques. Perhaps the most potent aspect of research, as opposed to other ways of gathering information, is that its methods are stated publicly and are open to critical scrutiny. This, at least, ensures that where bias is detected its strength can be estimated and recognized. (Mortimore & Stone, 1991)

Research, because of its costs, cannot be a practical way of evaluating the quality of individual schools. But it can provide instruments, methods and models which may be more generally applicable and which can enable the debate about quality adequately to be conceptualized.

One critical feature of such a conceptualization must be an explanation of the relationship of the term 'effectiveness' to the issue of quality. The interpretations of effectiveness used by researchers have varied slightly, although there is some underlying agreement. For instance, the editors of the journal *School Effectiveness and School Improvement*, in their mission statement for the first edition of the journal, argue that:

> In certain countries the school effectiveness movement has already become associated with a narrow, back-to-basics orientation to the teaching of basic skills . . . (Reynolds & Creemers, 1990).

This narrow focus is unfortunate. In my view, 'quality schooling' needs also to be judged on broader criteria even where these are less tangible and, as a result, less easy to measure.

Rutter et al. (1979a) in their pioneering study noted that: 'schools can do much to foster good behaviour and attainment, and that even in a disadvantaged area, schools can be a force for the good'. The Rutter interpretation recognizes the importance of outcomes other than the solely academic ones and deals implicitly with the question of intake. Similarly, Smith and Tomlinson (1989), in a more recent contribution to the subject, argued:

> The central objective was to measure differences between schools and the outcomes they achieve, in academic and other terms, after taking full account of differences in the attainment and background of children at the point of entry.

The simplest definition, perhaps, is that drawn from a Scottish publication on effective schools: 'an effective school is one in which pupils progress further than might be expected from consideration of its intake' (Mortimore, 1992). Implied in such a definition is an acceptance that the progress of pupils (in any aspect of development, non-cognitive as well as cognitive) is usually strongly related to the student intake of the school. This somewhat deterministic relationship, of course, can only be found at the level of whole groups; individual students will vary in their progress according to their talents and motivation. Nevertheless, when the progress of all the individual students of an age-group is aggregated, the advantage is likely to be both powerful and positive. In like manner, the relationship with disadvantage (poverty, low social class occupations of parents, etc.) is also likely to be strong and, in this case, negative. Thus, in a DES analysis, the correlation between high socio-economic grouping and the proportion of pupils gaining at least one A level was 0.7 and that between low socio-economic grouping and the same factor was 0.56 (DES, 1983).

Against this background of overall relationships, individual schools—like individual pupils—vary. Effective schools may foster greater progress than might be expected (on the basis of the overall relationships) and non-effective schools will foster less. It must also be borne in mind, however, that schools can be classified as effective whatever the absolute level of advantage/disadvantage of their intake. Those serving severely disadvantaged areas can equally well be found to be highly effective. In the same way, those schools that serve very advantaged populations can fail to be effective and can result in underachievement amongst their pupils.

Moreover, no school—even one that is on all counts highly effective—can guarantee, without reservation, progress for all its students. Many teachers will have encountered pupils with a great deal of talent who lack the motivation to achieve and who fail, despite all the advantages that they bring to their schooling. Finally, it is clear that, whilst effectiveness and efficiency in some ways overlap, they do not necessarily represent the same facets. It is possible to run what appears to be an efficient school that is not effective and *vice versa*.

It is the consideration of such matters and how to overcome the conceptual and methodological problems of the topic that has formed the intellectual core of the work on school effectiveness (see, for example, Gray, 1990) carried out by a number of different researchers over the last twenty years or so years.

This article, therefore, will review—albeit rather briefly—some of the studies of school effectiveness that have been carried out in the United Kingdom and in the United States over two decades, as a prelude to a discussion of the main directions open to researchers in school effectiveness at this moment. These 'directions'—in my judgement—represent the most significant choices that researchers need to make at this time in order to determine the best way to move forwards in relation to the quality of schooling debate. They can be seen as a series of signs at crossroads: there is a choice of direction to be determined. As with the real thing, however, the choice of direction is sometimes determined more by luck than judgement and, sometimes, steps have to be retraced!

There are a number of directions that researchers could follow. Those that I wish to consider in this article are whether:

- The main emphasis of research work should now be directed towards the application of the concepts and methodology to other aspects of the education service
- The energy and resources of the research community should now be directed mainly towards projects of school improvement
- The main emphasis of researchers' work should now be placed on the formulation of theory
- The 'restructuring' programmes being undertaken (mainly but not exclusively in the US) should be used as vehicles for furthering the school effectiveness work
- School improvement work should always include an economic analysis so that the costs and benefits of such interventions can be taken into account
- Equity should be reinstated as a primary goal of school improvement programmes

Studies of school effectiveness

The United States

There have been a great number of important studies of effectiveness carried out in the United States, as illustrated by the excellent review by Clark et al. (1984) and most recently the revised register compiled by the Northwest Regional Educational Laboratory (NREL, 1984, 1990). Here attention will be drawn, for illustrative purposes, to only a small selection, mainly of the early studies.

The first major American study was carried out in the late 1960s by Weber (1971). In this project, Weber studied four inner-city schools, chosen because they appeared to Weber to be 'instructionally effective'. The levels of reading achievement in the schools were well above the average for the neighbourhood, which was considerably disadvantaged. The researcher identified leadership and resource distributions as being key factors, as well as the high expectations and relative orderliness of the schools. A second study followed in 1974 and emanated from the New York Department of Education's Office of Educational Improvement. In this study, two inner-city schools serving poor populations were identified, one which was considered to be high achieving and the other low achieving. The researchers identified a number of factors which appeared to discriminate between the two schools. These factors included the administrative role of the principal as well as the school-wide reading strategy used by teachers (see Edmonds, 1979).

Edmonds referred to another study, carried out by Madden (1976) in California. Madden matched twenty-one pairs of elementary schools on the basis of the student intakes. He found differences between the schools in terms of the attitudes of the principals and the attitudes and actions of the teachers, as well as in the way that time was used within the different schools. Brookover and Lezotte (1977) carried out a study of effective schools in Michigan. Using data from a standardized testing programme, they studied six schools of which four appeared to be improving and two declining. Using interviewers to visit the schools and elicit responses from both teachers and students, the authors identified differences in the behaviour of staff, in their expectations and in the way the principal carried out his/her job. In 1979, Edmonds and Frederiksen published a summary of their research, which had focused on the relationship of pupil background and school effectiveness. In it they included a reanalysis of data from the 1966 Coleman Equal Opportunity Survey and they identified a number of effective schools which, they argued, had not been found in the original analysis (Coleman et al., 1966) The Coleman study, however, had at least recognized that schools were likely to make a positive difference for the most disadvantaged students. The findings of the Rand Corporation Study (Averch et al., 1972) were even less enthusiastic, arguing that there was little research evidence to support the view that schools could make a difference!

In contrast to those earlier conclusions of Coleman et al. and of Averch et al., the impact of positive findings was considerable. Spurred on by the rather optimistic outcomes, a number of research agencies endeavoured to institute school improvement studies based on the methodology of the school effectiveness research teams. For instance, in New York between 1978 and 1981, Edmonds (who had become special assistant to the chancellor of the New York school system) inaugurated a school improvement project. A similar project was also started in Milwaukee (McCormack-Larkin, 1982) and in California (Murphy et al., 1982). Other important work in this field has been carried out by Huberman and Miles (1984), Miles and Ekholm (1985) and Joyce (1986).

According to Lezotte (1989), many of the early school improvement pioneers were naïve. They first tried to 'mandate' change, then attempted to pin the blame for the lack of success on the principals of the schools and, finally, resorted to exhortations for both principals and teachers to work harder. In Lezotte's view, none of these techniques was likely to be successful and it is a wonder that the 'effective schools movement' survived this period.

In fact, a number of American researchers used the eighties to take stock of developments and make methodological improvements (Good & Brophy, 1986; Purkey & Smith, 1985; Robinson, 1983). Many of their lessons have generally been heeded by contemporary researchers (for example, Miles et al., 1988; Stringfield & Teddlie, 1988).

The switch from studies of effectiveness to programmes of improvement that took place in the United States during the 1980s received a considerable boost by the amendment to federal legislation introduced by the Hawkins/Stafford 1988 Amendment to the 1965 Elementary and Secondary Education Act. This amendment has enabled school districts to spend public money on a range of school improvement projects.

Work has since continued in a number of different States—much of it co-ordinated by agencies such as the National Center for Effective Schools Research and Development in Michigan or the Center for Effective Schools at the University of Washington, Seattle.

The relationship between the studies of school effectiveness and those of school improvement, however, is not simple. Even though—as Clark et al. (1984) argue—the two approaches share the same intake and process data, they differ in their focus (individual student achievement and school change). The United States experience, therefore, is particularly significant because it enables questions about both types of studies to be framed. Drawing on both sets of data, Clark et al., influenced by the management approach of Peters and Waterman (1984), list seven attributes of effective schooling—with appropriate indications of the limitations of such an exercise. Recent progress in both fields has been drawn upon in a collection of papers 'rethinking effective schools research' by Bliss et al. (1991).

Elsewhere

Considerable work on improving schools has also, of course, been undertaken in other parts of the world. For instance, Bashi et al. (1990) have reported on developments in effective schools in Israel. Creemers and Lugthart (1989) have written about a number of studies in the Netherlands and Dalin (1989) has reported on research in Scandinavia. In Canada, work has been undertaken in Alberta and in a number of school boards in Vancouver and in Ontario (Stoll and Fink, 1989). The writings of Fullan (1982, 1991) have made an important contribution in this connection. Most recently, school effectiveness research—including work from Australia—has been noted by Chapman and Stevens (1989). The pioneering work of the International School Improvement Project (ISIP) must also be noted. This project has been in operation since 1982. It is co-ordinated by the OECD and involves 14 separate countries in conferences, seminars and workshops. The project has been written up in a number of books and papers and its work was described in one of the symposia of the 1991 ICSEI Conference (Hopkins, 1987).

The United Kingdom

In the United Kingdom, a considerable number of research studies have addressed—directly or indirectly—the question of school effectiveness but few, as yet, have systematically been concerned with the progress of school improvement programmes. As with the US studies, the following selection has been compiled for illustrative purposes. (See Reynolds, 1990a, for a more exhaustive account.)

Among the earliest researchers into school effectiveness in the United Kingdom were Power et al. (1967). The researchers attempted to investigate the delinquency rate of students in a number of schools. Having used a somewhat crude attempt to control for intelligence, the research team identified stable differences over a six-year period. They showed these differences to be relatively independent of the catchment area of the schools. Unfortunately, due to disagreements with one of the teacher unions over the publication of results, the study was never completed. Its chief benefit, therefore, was in the way it opened up the research question to subsequent researchers.

Brimer et al. (1978), unlike Power, chose to focus on the academic achievement of students. The research team collected information on the prior achievements of a sample of students drawn from 44 schools. It used measures of parental occupations and educational levels to control for differences in home background. The researchers found differences between schools, even when these intake factors had been taken into account. Both delinquency and academic achievement, together with attendance and student behaviour, were included in the outcomes adopted by the *Fifteen Thousand Hours* research team (Rutter et al., 1979a). The sample for this study was small (12 schools), but a wide range of data enabled the question of whether there were differences between schools, once the intake had been taken into account, to be addressed. The controls for intake factors, such as socio-economic background data, students' prior scores, their attendance records and behaviour questionnaires, were more comprehensive than those used by Power et al. or Brimer et al. Working in a totally different environment, Reynolds (1982) examined the impact of schools on attendance, attainment and delinquency in a Welsh community over six years. Although this team did not have individual data on students, they were able to collect evidence about the catchments of the schools and to show that schools had received roughly comparable intakes. They identified systematic differences in attainment, delinquency and attendance and, furthermore, in student unemployment rates after leaving school.

Gray, McPherson and Raffe (1983) used a sample of Scottish schools to examine the effects of school organization on student achievement. Drawing on a survey of over 20,000 school leavers, they found some evidence of school differences, over and above those influenced by the social class of the students. Another Scottish study (Willms and Cuttance, 1985) also used data from the Scottish leavers' survey. Working with a sample of 15 secondary schools, the researchers used sophisticated statistical techniques, including multi-level modelling, to examine differences in attainment whilst controlling for intake.

The work of my colleagues and I on the *School Matters* study transferred some of the focus of British research from secondary to primary schools (Mortimore et al., 1988a). We followed a cohort of nearly 2,000 students through four years of schooling from age 7 to age 11. We adopted a series of outcomes, including reading, mathematics, writing, attendance, behaviour and attitude to schooling. We were also able to collect data on speaking skills and on students' attitudes towards themselves as learners. With rich measures of the students' backgrounds (including their language and ethnic group, the occupations of their parents, whether they received any welfare benefits, family size, health records and early educational experience), we were also able to gather data on prior attainment in reading, mathematics and writing and to seek a behaviour rating for each student.

In our analysis we sought to use the more sophisticated techniques that had been developing in recent years; in particular, multilevel modelling. We found considerable differences between schools. Interestingly, some schools appeared better able to foster progress in some aspects of student development than in others. Overall, however, of the 49 schools that remained in the sample at the end of the study, 14 appeared to foster progress across the board. (See

Mortimore et al., 1988b, for discussion of some of the technical issues arising from this work.)

Tizard et al. (1988) switched the focus to infant schools. Tizard and her colleagues focused on the first two years of compulsory schooling with a sample chosen to contain high proportions of children from ethnic minority groups. The researchers paid careful attention to the collection of information on home background. In addition to the more usual measures, they collected data on the mothers' educational activities. Other measures included teachers' judgements about children's prospects and the children's own views on behaviour.

In an interesting variation on school effectiveness, Smith and Tomlinson (1989) studied whether schools were differentially effective for students of minority ethnic groups. Their data included information about the ethnic backgrounds of students, their religion, and the employment status of their parents, as well as progress in schools. Using a sample of 20 multi-ethnic schools drawn on a national basis, Smith and Tomlinson used a variety of instruments to collect data. In their statistical analysis they made use of the methods of variance component analysis which took account of the multilevel data. Smith and Tomlinson concluded that school differences were more important than those caused by the ethnic background of students.

Finally, using data collected by the Inner London Education Authority, Nuttall et al. (1989) studied the examination performance of over 30,000 students drawn from 140 schools. Using intake measures which included a verbal reasoning score, ethnic details, gender and a measure of family income, the research team investigated differences between ethnic groups. The team found that school performance varied along several dimensions, with school having powerful effects on some groups of students. Nuttall and colleagues also found evidence of variation over time, with some schools being more effective in one year than in others.

Signposts at the crossroads

This brief account of some of the major studies in the field of school effectiveness illustrates the range of activity of educational researchers. By focusing on 'real-world' problems, these researchers have left the shelter of the university and the laboratory and sought to chart the complexity of individual, social and institutional influences. Some researchers (especially those from the US who have been encouraged by the support of their Federal Government) have tried to go further and to change the ways that schools operate. Generally, they have found this difficult to achieve. Fullan's (1991) work helps explain why this is likely to be so. Nevertheless, the researchers have demonstrated models of intervention that—in a world anxious for successful school reforms—need to be evaluated, improved and, if shown to work, replicated.

In the next section of this article, I will discuss the directions that can be taken by researchers as they focus on the names written on the signposts at the crossroads.

Directions

The directions outlined earlier represent different routes available to researchers today. The first direction concerns the application of the concepts and methods of work on school effectiveness to other aspects of the educational service. This option envisages the study of, for example, special schools or units for students with any form of disability; further education or tertiary colleges; or, indeed, universities, polytechnics and colleges of higher education. It could be argued that such parts of the education service are in greater need of investigation than are schools which, on the whole, are more likely to be involved in research. Yet, to take each sector in turn, the problems facing those who work in special education are considerable: how best to integrate these with special educational needs whilst continuing to provide necessary support, for instance? In many different systems there is concern over how to link, in the post-statutory years, academic and vocational education and how to exploit the motivational benefits of schemes such as 'compacts' between employers and educational institutions. The issues facing higher education are also considerable, ranging from selection and access, to models of assessment and financial support for students.

Most of these types of institutions would benefit from the application of school effectiveness research designs to their own fields of inquiry. In each case, the details of the type of institution would need to be incorporated into the general model. But the underpinning approach—taking account of any differences in student intakes, identifying appropriate outcomes, and backward mapping to contemporaneously collected institutional processes—would be the same. This approach has two benefits: knowledge would be gained about what constituted high quality provision in the chosen field; and the empirical investigation would provide a further testing of the concepts and methodology of school effectiveness. (In a paper presented to the third International Congress in Jerusalem in 1990, I proposed initial teacher education as a focus of inquiry [Mortimore, 1992].)

The second direction envisages transferring the energy, knowledge and skills of school effectiveness research to the study of school improvement. As has been noted, this field of activity is more usual in North America than in the United Kingdom, although there have been a small number of such studies carried out here (Maughan et al., 1990; Reynolds et al., 1989b). In contrast, however, according to Cross (1990), of the 16,000 school districts in the United States, more than half 'have implemented some form of effective schools programme'. These programmes seek to use the findings of school effectiveness studies in order to stimulate change and to incorporate elements of proven good practice in other schools.

As has been argued elsewhere, the systems of assessment in the United States and in the United Kingdom are imbued with different cultural values. Thus, in Britain the formal public examinations are constructed to have high failure rates. Even though there have been recent changes in the organization of the examinations, the reality in Britain is that three out of four students still do not reach a level of generally accepted academic success. In these circumstances it is perhaps not surprising that one out of every two students opts to drop out of full-time education at the age of sixteen.

In contrast, it is argued that 'average' students in America usually leave school feeling successful and the school drop-out rate is far lower than in Britain. Despite the criticisms of American schooling (Clark, 1985) and the need for such interventions as Project Equality (Redman, 1982) in order to ensure that college students are sufficiently prepared for advanced study, the system appears (at least to a non-American) to be more efficient, in that a far greater proportion of each age group enter higher education (approximately 60 per cent compared to approximately 14 per cent) in the US than in the UK.

The third direction is whether researchers should now focus on the generation of theory rather than engaging in further, possibly repetitive, empirical work. The role of theory is, of course, a controversial matter. For some it is worse than irrelevant; it is a distraction. According to an article in a recent educational publication (Daly, 1990), 'ordinary people' are uneasy about what they see as excessive theorizing about learning. 'They rightly suspect that the more abstract a discussion, the more it is likely to create "unreal cities" in T.S. Eliot's phrase: metaphorical topographies of children's minds which may go on, as they filter down through practice, to be taken literally'.

Such criticisms about theories of child development are not new. Goethe, in the apprentice scene in *Faust* (1832) comments, 'Theory is all grey and the golden tree of life is green'. Nevertheless, it can be argued that it is important that the findings of school effectiveness should now be incorporated into some kind of theoretical framework in order to gain the maximum value from all the empirical work and to seek to identify underlying patterns. The problem is that the nature of the theoretical framework itself is the subject of a further set of options: whether to focus on individual learning and child development, or on institutional concerns, such as school management or change? My own view is that the most productive use of theory would be to begin to construct a set of postulates to be treated empirically and focused on the mechanisms of school improvement. In the Scottish paper cited earlier (Mortimore, 1992), I proposed a particular set of postulates generated from studies of interventions. They are as follows.

Schools are likely to improve if:

- Most staff and the head teacher can agree on a clear mission for the institution
- A systematic audit of current strengths and weaknesses is carried out
- A change-plan is thoroughly thought through
- An outside agent is involved
- The implementation of the change-plan is supported by all appropriate external authorities
- An evaluation of progress is used formatively to support the implementation

Research is now taking place in the United Kingdom to test out under which conditions these postulates can be shown to be true and, if appropriate, to formulate alternatives to, and developments of them. Barbara MacGilchrist and I are currently undertaking a research study into the use of School Development Plans in improving primary schools and hope to test these postulates in the field.

The fourth direction concerns the relationship of school effectiveness research to government-inspired reform programmes, such as the implementation (in England and Wales) of the 1988 Education Reform Act or some of the Restructuring Programmes being implemented in the United States or Australasia. Although different in many ways, a number of restructuring programmes share the 'market' philosophy inherent in the 1988 Act. Shifting power and authority down to lower levels (and to the school itself) in order to make heads and principals more receptive to the views of their 'clients' (parents and students) is likely to alter the traditional ways in which some have operated (see, for instance, Caldwell & Spinks, 1988).

School effectiveness researchers need both to be aware of these changes and to be able to accommodate them in their own approaches. The basic question of whether the reforms affect students' progress also needs to be asked. Interestingly, in a review of a set of case studies dealing with school restructuring, the reviewer (a school-effectiveness researcher) notes how this vital question was neglected (Chrispeels, 1990). Moreover, restructuring may make some interventions by some agencies (local authorities, for example) less likely. Their role in helping schools to become more effective may become unsustainable, given the restrictions in their funding, and, in England at least, the need for them to pass down—on the basis of a formula—80 per cent of the funds available for schools. Furthermore, the role being given to governing bodies (managing groups of members of the community) may itself cause school effectiveness researchers to modify their habits. Instead of working exclusively with the head teachers and staff of the school, they may need to devote a much higher proportion of their time to working with governing bodies.

The fifth direction concerns the importance increasingly accorded to the cost-benefit analysis of any school intervention. Given the financial constraints currently imposed on the education services of most countries (Taiwan, with its law that the education budget has to keep pace with the development of the national economy, is an exception), 'value for money' is bound to be an important consideration. Yet, up to now, educational researchers have too often ignored the financial implications of school effectiveness work (Hough, 1991). It is likely that the value for money of an 'effective' school is considerably greater than of less-effective schools, but—to the best of my knowledge—no systematic analysis exists to prove it. The only respectable cost-benefit analyses that are regularly cited concern the 'High Scope' Pre-school Programme. This is a situation that must change and it is a tempting direction in which researchers may like to move.

The sixth and—in this article—the final direction available to researchers involves the reinstatement of equity as a primary goal of school improvement programmes. This was one of Ron Edmonds' main themes: 'inequity in American education derives . . . from our failure to educate the children of the poor. . .' (Edmonds, 1979). Yet this aim is, in some ways, under challenge in our brave new world! The evidence about the power of schools to modify—at a group level—the influence of social class or race is hard to find.

At a seminar held in London in 1981, I presented data on the achievement in the capital of black students, girls and those from working-class (low socioeconomic status) families. The evidence about girls was interesting: they outperformed boys in all aspects of the curriculum except mathematics, the physical sciences and technology, where they were under-represented. The evidence about the other two groups was depressing: in both cases, successive research studies showed that—in comparison to their peers—they underachieved (ILEA, 1983). Yet a number of the schools which those students attended were probably effective! What was wrong? The answer to this enigma only became apparent when the analysis of the *School Matters* data was being carried out. My co-workers and I found that in no school were the students of (say) working-class families, on average, out-performing those from more middle-class backgrounds. What we did find was that, in the most effective primary schools, those from working-class backgrounds made considerably *greater progress* than those from middle-class families in the less-effective schools.

We found no evidence of what is sometimes called the 'within school slope effect'—of schools that, by putting efforts into helping one group, actually hinder the progress of others (Mortimore et al., 1988a). This finding, however, is not universal: three studies of secondary schools (Cuttance, 1985; Gray et al., 1983; Nuttall et al., 1989) show that some schools are more effective with some groups of students than with others. It may be that there is a crucial difference between the phases of schooling, but it is a direction that needs further exploration.

Which direction to follow?

Which direction to follow? Can a single choice be made? My answer is 'no'. Rather, I believe we should divide our forces and explore all routes, as they are each important. In this way—and if we keep in touch *via* associations like the International Congress for School Effectiveness and School Improvement—we stand a greater chance of reaching our goal: the improvement of the quality of schooling for all pupils. Edmonds (1979) argued that: 'all children can learn'. If we believe him, we now need to demonstrate how. The task may prove difficult, but good maps are at hand (Bliss et al., 1991; Fullan, 1991; Reynolds and Cuttance, forthcoming) and the possible rewards—both in terms of the clarification of the concepts and methodology of school effectiveness and of the illumination and improvement of practice in other aspects of the education service—are considerable. The phrase 'education cannot compensate for society' (Bernstein, 1970) is undoubtedly true. What may also be true, however, is that schools can enhance the ability of their students. What must be desirable is that children of each generation should be able to compete on the basis of their talents and motivation, rather than on the basis of their parents' wealth, class or race. Researchers have an opportunity to explore ways of making these ideas not only possible, but commonly acceptable.

As researchers in school effectiveness, perhaps we have all been tempted to take Frost's 'less-travelled road'. Let us continue to do so in the hope that it will, indeed, make all the difference.

Postscript

This conference paper provided the opportunity for me to review the direction of my research interests and to take stock. Such an opportunity is a crucially important juncture in a researcher's life. Academic and practitioner conferences provide fora in which preliminary results can be tested out, new methodologies considered and the potential implications of particular findings aired. The Cardiff conference gave me a platform to speculate on the possible routes forward. Some roads—school improvement projects, for instance—have been enthusiastically trodden by researchers, practitioners and policy makers. Other journeys—involving, for example, the application of the research approach to special higher or further education—have yet to be undertaken.

11

The Management of Effective Learning and Teaching

Introduction

The 1993 ICSEI conference in Norrkoping, Sweden, is the source of this chapter. My task was to outline existing knowledge about teaching and learning. I set out to discover what was known about these two crucial school activities and to consider how these twin pillars of schooling related to the work of school effectiveness.

The article on which this chapter is based attempts to get to the heart of school effectiveness. It addresses issues concerned with *effective* learning and *effective* teaching, and the role of the school in promoting these processes. Whilst there is a lack of experimental evidence that could point to *causal* connections, research—carried out in a variety of countries over the last twenty or so years—has identified a number of characteristics that are associated with schools which appear to be particularly effective. Some of these characteristics concern the *ends* of schooling—the promotion of effective learning and the attainment and progress of students. Others relate to the *means* of effective schools, such as effective teaching, planning, use of resources and staffing policies.

The specific questions to be addressed are:

- What do we know about effective learning?
- What do we know about effective teaching?

- How does the effective schools research contribute to this debate?
- What are the relevant factors?
- What are the lessons for school improvers?

What do we know about effective learning?

Unlike the technical meaning which is often attributed to the term in connection with the effective schools research (see later), I shall use the word *effective to* indicate the acquisition of knowledge, understanding or skill in a way which:

- Has taken as little time and effort as possible
- Can easily be assimilated and accommodated with other learning
- Will endure for as long as it is deemed to be relevant by the learner

Theories about learning

Many different theories about learning have been proposed by psychologists but, because learning is a covert process not amenable to direct observation even at a physiological level, these have had to be postulated on the basis of inferences about the prior and the subsequent behaviour of the learner. One obvious limitation of such a methodology is that the observer can never be certain as to quite *what* has been learned: a specific item of information, a clearer understanding of its characteristics and of how it relates to previously held knowledge, a better notion of how to learn more effectively or, indeed, a mixture of all three.

Theories of learning, in general, do not appear to have influenced to any great extent the daily work of teachers. There have been, however, some exceptions, such as the work of Piaget, Vygotsky and a number of North American psychologists.

Piaget's (1955) theories are based on the notion that children proceed through increasingly complex stages of learning. According to Piaget, each stage has to be worked through and each child needs to come to terms with the world in which they live through the twin processes of assimilation—whereby they take in information about the external environment—and accommodation—whereby they *rearrange* their knowledge and understanding in order to come to terms with and exploit that new information. Gipps (1992) reports that Piaget's model is now widely criticized on the grounds that he underestimated the influence of language and, furthermore, that the dependence of his theory upon the existence of rigid stages has led to a legacy of low expectations being held for young children.

In contrast, Vygotsky (1978)—whose work is currently receiving renewed attention—developed a theory in which language and thought were seen as twin processes: the one helping the other. As Gipps notes, Vygotsky's notion of *proximal* development—whereby it is believed that children, with the help of an adult, can perform tasks normally beyond them—can be used as a basis for maintaining high expectations.

American research on learning theory has long been influenced by behaviourism. Work by psychologists such as Thorndike (1898), Skinner (1938) and Hull (1952) and social learning theorists such as Bandura (1974) has contributed to the view that learning can occur simply as a result of a response to a particular stimulus. Critics, however, argue that behaviourism treats the learner as passive, only able to respond when stimulated.

Other theories place learners in a more active role, seeking to build up their knowledge and skills through experience. Carroll (1963), for instance, proposed a model of school learning in which three factors to do with the learner (aptitude, ability to understand instructions and perseverance) were brought together with two teaching factors (clarity of instruction and matching the task to the student) in the context of the opportunity to learn. The Carroll model forms the basis of a number of other theories including that of Bruner (1966), Bloom (1976), and Glaser (1976). All these models stress the importance of individual differences amongst the learners.

A relatively new strand of work on learning theory concerns what is known as 'self-efficacy' (Wood and Bandura, 1989). According to this theory, the learners' beliefs in themselves are reinforced or reduced, with concomitant effects on achievement. In general, the stronger the feeling of self-efficacy the higher the level of achievement. Moreover, how people feel about themselves is influenced by the schools they attend—and their perceptions of how teachers view them/their abilities. If the teachers hold positive views about students' abilities and about their own teaching skills, they are more likely to promote academic learning in their classrooms (Bandura, 1992).

A further development of models of learning came with the introduction of the theory of adaptive instruction (Wang et al., 1990). This theory positioned the learning of the individual within the learning environment of the school and hypothesized that the better match between the two would lead to optimum learning.

In the mainstream of cognitive psychology, there is now widespread acceptance that learning is likely to be affected by the intellectual, linguistic and social context in which it is attempted. Researchers such as Light and Butterworth (1992) have stressed the importance of context in relation to what they term as *domain-specific* thinking skills. Interestingly, a different view—that there are *general* thinking skills that can be taught—has been put forward by Adey and Shayer (1990) on the basis of their work in a cognitive acceleration in science programme. In this pioneering study, they found that learners could be taught to *think* about thinking, through the use of experimental strategies. They report that the benefits of this approach were apparent not only in the results of subsequent science tests but also in other areas of the curriculum, including English.

There is thus no shortage of interesting theories and models of learning. There is a danger, however, in assuming that *school learning* is the same as *learning in general*. Resnick (1987) has suggested that there can be differences between the two and that school learning, in particular, is often aimed at *pure* rather than *applied* thought, and that it is *individual* rather than *collaborative*.

Attempts to relate school and life learning draw on the adaptation of attribution theory and achievement motivation to the school setting.

Attribution theory is concerned with how we perceive causality and the consequences of our perceptions. Ichheiser (1943), writing half a century ago about success and failure, discussed 'the misinterpretations which consist in underestimating the importance of situational and in overestimating the importance of personal factors' (p. 152). In relation to learning, attribution theory illuminates how we understand and react to our achievement, whether we judge it to be the result of internal factors—(lack of) ability or (lack of) effort, or external factors—poor teaching or scarcity of books. The attributional model of achievement motivation theory is described by Atkinson (1957). The model stresses 'the degree of perceived personal responsibility for success or failure' (Eiser & Van der Pligt, 1988, p. 68). Dweck and Repucci (1973) argue that girls and boys attribute failure to quite different causes: girls, to lack of ability (internal); boys, to their lack of effort (internal); or bad luck (external) and that their teachers, often unwittingly, provide differential feedback to them. The researchers suggest that, as a result, *learned helplessness* can be induced. The poor performance of boys in language-based subjects and of girls in technology-based subjects may be the outcomes of this process.

So, what do we *know* about effective learning? We know, or can reasonably infer, that it is:

- Active rather than passive
- Overt rather than covert
- Complex rather than simple
- Affected by individual differences amongst learners
- Influenced by a variety of contexts

It is this last point that, perhaps, is most relevant to those interested in school effectiveness and improvement.

The second question to be addressed concerns effective teaching.

What do we know about effective teaching?

As with the earlier discussion about learning, this question will only be examined at a general level. Those seeking detailed information should consult specialist sources such as Wittrock (1986). Unlike learning, teaching is an *overt* activity and should, therefore, be easier to describe and evaluate. Disappointingly, however, the many descriptions and evaluations that have been recorded since the days of Plato and Aristotle, and the resulting theories and models, tend not to do justice to the complexity and sophistication of the activity.

The problem with models such as those put forward by, for example, Scheffler (1967) is that they are not sufficiently different. The effective teacher is likely to range across models, trying aspects of each, as and when deemed necessary. It is for this reason that energy has gone into attempts to classify, more specifically, theories of teaching styles. Since the work of Dunkin and Biddle (1974), researchers have sought to categorize the different aspects of practice observed in classrooms. In the UK the work of Bennett (1976) is probably the best known, though his initial conclusion (that particular styles of formal teaching made a significant difference to the performance of learners was subsequently considerably qualified (Bennett, 1987). His latest work in this area presents classrooms as much more complex environments, for both teaching and learning activities, than was previously believed (Bennett, 1988a).

In our work on a large sample of London's primary schools (Mortimore et al., 1988a), my colleagues and I endeavoured to classify teachers' styles into particular categories, on the basis of detailed classroom observations. Whilst traditional methods of cluster analysis delivered as many groups as we needed, when we used more sophisticated analyses—with the technique pioneered by Aitken et al. (1981) known as 'probabilistic cluster analysis'—we found that we were unable to identify stable groups. The activities of the teachers in our sample appeared to be too complex; depending on the task, they switched across between styles too frequently for us to be able to classify these with any degree of certainty.

The greatest interest in research on effective teaching has been in the United States. Research in this area includes the work of Light and Smith (1971), Bloom (1976), Glass (1977), and Gage (1978). According to Walberg (1986), who carried out a synthesis of much of this research, large-scale meta-analysis identified a number of common factors across a range of studies. The functions that he has identified as being most important were: social and psychological environments; home factors; the influence of the media and television; the influence of peer groups; the aptitude of students; the scope of homework; and the availability of extra-curricular tuition. This list demonstrates a number of the problems and limitations of using the meta-analysis technique: it contains many different variables reflecting the different kinds of studies. It is, though, a useful amalgam of the work of researchers over a period.

In Britain a quite different approach has developed from the work of Her Majesty's Inspectors (HMI, 1982; HMI, 1988). In its 1982 Survey, HMI focused on eight factors:

- Relationships with pupils
- Classroom management
- Planning and preparation
- Aims, objectives and their achievement
- Choice of materials
- Marking
- The match of work to pupils
- Question and answer techniques

The list of factors appears quite plausible but, again, incorporates different kinds of activities: some relate to the preparation of materials; some to interactions with pupils; and some to the application of educational judgement.

In their second survey, HMI focused on a slightly different collection of factors: classroom organization; planning and preparation; match of work to pupils; classroom interaction; mastery of subject; competence in teaching skills.

It is interesting to compare the contents of the two lists and to note the addition, in the second, of the term *competence*. In an overall assessment of the sample, HMI found that 43 per cent of the primary teachers and 57 per cent of the secondary teachers displayed a *high* or *relatively high* degree of competence. Twenty per cent of primary and 11 per cent of secondary teachers 'lacked some or many of the basic teaching skills. . .' (p. 24).

The term 'competence' has been used fairly frequently in the United States (Pearson, 1984) but is less common in the United Kingdom. More recently, however, it has been used by the British government in its review of teacher education. In a 1992 speech, the then Secretary of State referred to the term ('. . .providing that students do achieve the required competences. . .' [Clarke, 1992, p. 16]). As a result of this speech, the criteria for the approval of teachers' courses have been re-written in order for them to be based on the use of competences rather than the number of hours devoted to particular aspects of training.

There is certainly more to teaching than having basic competence, however. Two psychological mechanisms that have proved helpful to our thinking about how teaching actually operates are *expectations* and *modelling*. The first is the notion of a self-fulfilling prophecy which could either be of negative or positive expectations (Merton, 1968). Experimental evidence for such a phenomenon came from Rosenthal and Jacobson (1968). In a cleverly contrived study, they provided selective (but untrue) information about certain pupils. Teachers were told that some pupils were likely to 'bloom'. The researchers claimed that these predictions were subsequently achieved and they explained this by recourse to the self-fulfilling prophecy. Although the original experiment by Rosenthal and Jacobson has not been replicated, large-scale reviews of the area (Brophy and Good, 1974; Pilling and Pringle, 1978) provide considerable evidence about the potential power of such expectations. It is not hard to understand how extreme expectations, of either a positive or a negative nature, can prove a powerful factor in teaching. We all, surely, try to live up to high expectations others may hold about us. Similarly, obvious low expectations of our performance can trigger a mechanism whereby we sink to a performance level in line with the negative expectations being transmitted. For a pupil who is regularly taught by a teacher with low expectations, the experience can be demoralizing and, too often, leads to underachievement.

Second is the concept of modelling, which works on the premise that we are influenced strongly by role models (Mowrer, 1960). We like to do what others—especially those in authority or those we (rightly or wrongly) admire—also do. For teachers, this mechanism is important, since there are few neutral stances—they are either good models or bad models! In many schools the power of modelling is eloquently demonstrated in the way that particular classes take on the characteristics of their form teacher or personal tutor.

These two psychological phenomena have influenced our views of teaching, but new studies are needed in order to clarify the issues further and to identify how teachers can use such mechanisms positively in their daily work.

At the 1990 ICSEI conference, I presented a paper on Teacher Training for Effective Schools (Mortimore, 1992). In this paper, I drew attention to some of the knowledge and skills that are needed for the task of teaching. Briefly, I argued that curriculum knowledge needed to be sound in principle and detailed in scope. I argued that pedagogical knowledge—though sometimes described in somewhat derisory terms as *theory*—was frequently neglected. I suggested that an understanding of how learners learn and how subject knowledge can be transformed and presented (see below) in a manner appropriate for pupils of different ages was crucial. Psychological knowledge—in my judgement—is also essential, so that teachers can understand how young minds operate and how young people cope with different cultural patterns and family traditions. I argued that sociological knowledge of the way factors such as race, gender, class or religion operate to help or hinder successful teaching was also important. Finally, I suggested that school and classroom process knowledge—the meat and drink of school effectiveness work—can provide teachers with ways of planning and monitoring their own work.

In terms of the necessary skills, I argued that modern teachers need *organizational skills* to sort out materials and sources of information; *analytical skills to* enable them to break down complex bodies of knowledge into coherent components; *synthesizing skills* so that ideas can be built into arguments, propositions and *theories; presentational skills* so as to clarify complex information for varying ages and abilities without harming its integrity; *assessment skills* so that the work of pupils can be judged and appropriate feedback given; *management skills* so that the dynamics of individual learners, groups and classes can be effectively co-ordinated; and, finally, I stressed that teachers needed *self-evaluative skills* so that teaching, itself, can be improved continually.

In creating such a long list concerning both knowledge and skills, however, I was conscious that I was still failing to do justice to the complexity of effective teaching. Effective teachers, in my judgement, weave together their skills and knowledge (not just pedagogy but knowledge of the power of expectations and modelling), along with their imagination, creativity and sensitivity, in order to stimulate, support and encourage learning. We know that even this impressive battery of competences is not enough to guarantee *learning*. Determined pupils can, and do, resist. Somewhat frustratingly, we also know that effective learning can take place in the absence of effective teaching. However, optimum results are likely to occur when there is a good match between the two.

How does the effective schools research contribute to the debate?

Many readers of *School Effectiveness and School Improvement* are likely to be familiar with the approaches used over the last twenty or so years to identify the characteristics of effective schools, and with the respective strengths and weaknesses of this paradigm. Those unfamiliar with this area may wish to consult

Reynolds et al. (1989a); Creemers et al. (1989); Bashi and Sass (1992) or any of the issues of the journal, for more detailed information.

The single, most researched factor in the work of school effectiveness concerns the area of *variation* between schools. There have been both simple and sophisticated studies of variation. The simpler studies take little or no account of differences in the characteristics of students entering and attending schools. They also tend to focus on only one measure of outcome: that of scholastic achievement. The limitations of such an approach—as experienced teachers will know—is that schools do not receive a uniform intake of students: some take high proportions of advantaged young people, likely to do well in examinations; others receive high proportions of disadvantaged students who, all things considered, are less likely to do well. Therefore, to compare the results of achievement tests or examinations without taking into account these differences in the student intake, and to attribute good results to the influence of the school, may be quite misleading. Accordingly, various definitions of effective schools have been formulated. One simple definition that I have used is: 'one in which students progress further than might be expected from a consideration of intake' (Mortimore, 1991a, p. 9).

It must be noted, however, that this definition does not assume that *all* students from disadvantaged backgrounds are likely to do badly in tests or examinations. Some of these individual students will do very well; they will buck the trend. What the definition implies is that, all other things being equal, disadvantaged students as a group are less likely to do well than are those from advantaged backgrounds, in any kind of competitive assessment. Accordingly, measures of progress are needed which can take account of the students' initial starting points.

Various methods have been developed by researchers to deal with this problem. The methods range from simple standardization, through multiple progression techniques, to the latest multilevel modelling. Regardless of the specific technique used, however, most approaches have been based on a common model of school effectiveness in which outcome measures, suited to the type of school, are identified. At the elementary level, this might include basic skills of literacy and numeracy. At the secondary school level, the outcomes are likely to be based on achievement but may also include measures of attitudes and behaviour. The second stage of this procedure is to relate these chosen outcomes to the available data on the student characteristics upon their intake. Such characteristics can include earlier reading levels, former attendance or behaviour ratings and any available information on home background. Using the most sophisticated statistical techniques available, researchers then attempt to take account of the intake in variation and to adjust the outcome measures accordingly, to provide what has come to be known as a *value added* component. In this way an attempt is made to see how the outcomes would look if all schools had received a similar intake. To use the research terminology: to compare like with like. Finally, at the third stage, researchers have usually sought to relate the adjusted outcomes to whatever information has been collected about the life and functioning of the school—the school processes. Researchers call this technique *back-ward mapping* of outcomes to process measures (Murphy, 1991).

Methodological issues

Like many other research topics, studies of effects of schooling vary a great deal in the scope of their designs and their chosen methodologies. Some of the problems of earlier studies have been discussed in detail by Rutter (1983) and by Purkey and Smith (1983). A number of articles in the *International Journal of Educational Research* also addressed this topic (Bosker & Scheerens, 1989; Raudenbush, 1989; Scheerens, 1992; Scheerens & Creemers, 1989), as does a series of papers in Reynolds and Cuttance (1992). The types of issues that have been raised include:

- The need for clearer conceptualization and theory
- The use of more sophisticated statistical techniques
- The inadequacy of current sampling methods
- The choice of appropriate outcomes
- The methods of relating outcome to process data

On the whole, the later empirical studies have used more sophisticated methods than have the earlier ones. The improvement in methodology, however, has not been matched by similar advances in the development of theory. The need for better theory is well recognized and a number of publications have addressed this issue (Mortimore, 1991a; Reynolds & Packer, 1992; Scheerens, 1992, 1993).

Contribution of research findings about effective schools

School-effectiveness studies have generated considerable amounts of information about the management of learning and teaching. In the United States, for instance, early studies by Weber (1971), Brookover and Lezotte (1977) and Edmonds and Frederickson (1979), although focusing almost exclusively on academic attainment in elementary schools, produced important findings. Since the publication of Weber's groundbreaking study, there has been a flood of critiques, replications and evaluations. One review and analysis of the field contains over 400 references (Levine and Lezotte, 1990), whilst the synthesis carried out by the Northwest Regional Educational Laboratory (NREL, 1990) traced over 700 publications on this topic.

In the United Kingdom, Reynolds (1985) and Reynolds and Cuttance (1992) have charted the field. Work on school effectiveness is no longer restricted to the UK and the US but, largely under the auspices of the International Congress on School Effectiveness and Improvement, has spread to several countries. The findings of many studies have focused on measures such as attendance, attitudes towards schooling, classroom behaviour and scholastic attainment. Although studies vary considerably in terms of their rigour, scope and methodologies, their findings have been fairly uniform: that individual schools can promote positive, or negative, student outcomes; that those outcomes can include both cognitive and social behaviours; and that they are *not* dependent on the school receiving a favoured student intake. The fact that the studies have taken place in different phases of students' schooling and in different parts of the world adds strength to the interpretation that schools can make a difference to the lives of their students. Whilst, in some cases, the range of attainment outcomes that can be traced directly to the influence of the school might be relatively small, they can make the difference between academic success and failure, and so can have a long-term effect on students' life chances. What has also become apparent from these studies is that there are also likely to be differences in the average *progress* achieved by students from different schools, and that this variation is less susceptible to factors related to home background than are the more usual measures of attainment. Thus the findings have clarified considerably our understanding of the potency of schooling.

There are still, however, a number of outstanding issues concerning, for instance, the question of whether the positive effects of schooling vary according to time; whether they vary according to school memberships; and whether they vary according to the particular strengths and weaknesses of individual schools. Such questions need answers and whilst—to a certain extent—these can be resolved by meta-analysis and by interpretation of existing studies (Chrispeels, 1992; Scheerens, 1992; Mortimore, 1995b), they also need to be addressed in new or ongoing empirical work. Recent reports emerging from the Louisiana Study (Teddlie et al., 1984; 1989), the new programme of research established by Creemers et al. (personal communication), and new British studies at the Institute of Education on the variation within secondary schools (to be carried out by Nuttall, Sammons, Thomas and myself) and on School Development Planning (being carried out by MacGilchrist, Savage, Beresford and myself), will attempt to take forward our knowledge of these difficult issues.

What are the relevant factors?

It is seldom possible for educational researchers to impose experimental conditions on their subjects. Whilst they are generally welcomed into schools and classes, they usually have to observe situations as they are. This helps them to gain a more realistic picture of school life but means that they are rarely able, directly, to trace *causal* relationships. All too frequently, therefore, researchers are limited to the tracing of patterns of association and the use of correlations. Nevertheless, even with such methodological limitations, researchers from different countries have reached a number of conclusions about the variables commonly associated with the functioning of more effective schools. The plausibility of these factors has been increased by the frequency with which they have been replicated.

The following list of eight factors is not intended to be comprehensive or exhaustive. It has been culled from a sample of reviews and studies drawn from different countries and selected because of their use of different methodologies. Because of a lack of scientifically precise language, it is seldom possible to compare accurately findings from so many different studies, many of which are composite reviews of a number of individual research projects. It is possible, however, broadly to collate variables in order to ascertain the most common factors found by researchers to be associated with effectiveness. The following selection is the result of this exercise.

Strong positive leadership of schools

Although a few studies (notably Van de Grift, 1990) claim that the principal has little impact or that leadership of the school can be provided by somebody else, most studies found strong, positive leadership to be important. Different studies have drawn attention to different aspects of principals' roles but Levine and Lezotte (1990) have provided a clear analysis of how strong leadership can aid effectiveness. In their view, this occurs through the rigorous selection and replacement of teachers, 'buffering' the school from unhelpful external agents, frequent personal monitoring of school achievements, high expenditure of time and energy for school improvement actions, supporting teachers, and acquiring extra resources for their schools.

The British empirical studies support this analysis and have identified another, rather subtle, task: that of understanding when—and when not—to involve other staff in decision-making. The British studies found evidence that both autocratic and over-democratic styles of leadership are less effective than a balanced style which depends on the crucial judgement of when, and when not, to act as decision-maker. Fullan (1992a) has argued that strong leadership, by itself, is not sufficient in a complex modern society. Instead, he argues that heads (principals) have to find appropriate leadership roles for teachers. Mortimore et al. (1992) have investigated the effectiveness, and the cost-effectiveness, of different approaches to staffing. This research has revealed that associate staff (non-teaching colleagues) can undertake a variety of roles within the school which enable their teaching colleagues to focus more directly on pedagogic matters. The study also revealed a number of 'grey areas' between the roles of teaching and associate staff but, overall, identified a number of benefits in an innovative approach to staffing issues. One of the key findings of the research, however, was that management of staffing matters by the head teachers (principals) needed to be handled sensitively if the effectiveness of the school was to be enhanced.

High expectations—an appropriate challenge for students' thinking

As noted earlier, this factor has been commonly cited by researchers. Mortimore et al. (1988a), for instance, looked at ways in which expectations could be transmitted in the classroom. The researchers found that teachers tended to have lower expectations for students who, for instance, were young in their year group (those with summer birthdays) or who came from lower socio-economic groups. However, they found that low expectations, as such, were not held in any simple way for either girls or boys *per se*, despite the fact that boys received more critical comments and girls more praise. These data were difficult to interpret and the research team drew on the findings of Dweck and Repucchi (1973) to help explain the data. (Dweck and Repucci found that greater praise from male teachers to female students for less adequate work was linked to stereotyped views of female performance.)

Monitoring student progress

Whilst recognizing that monitoring, by itself, changes little, the majority of studies have found it to be a vital procedure, as a prelude to planning instructional tactics, altering pedagogy or increasing/decreasing workloads. The researchers have also seen it as transmitting a key message to students—that the teacher was interested in their progress. Whether it is more effective for the monitoring to be carried out formally or informally cannot yet be answered and further work on the way monitoring operates is essential in view of the increase in formal testing taking place in many school systems.

Student responsibilities and involvement in the life of the school

Ensuring that students adopt an active role in the life of the school has also been found to be important. By seeking to involve students in school-oriented activities, or by allocating responsibilities so as so elicit a positive response from them, teachers have endeavoured to provide a sense of ownership in the school and in the students' own learning. Whilst examples of talented, but alienated, students can frequently be found in literature, the general rule appears to be that learning is most likely when the students hold a positive view of the school and of their own role within it. The attitudes of students towards themselves as learners was used as a school outcome in Mortimore et al. (1988a). The outcome consisted of a specially designed measure of self-concept. This was the mirror image of the behaviour scale completed by teachers but was also completed by students themselves. The measure revealed clear school differences: some schools produced students who—regardless of their actual ability—felt reasonably positive about themselves; others produced students who were negative about themselves even when—in the judgement of the research team and according to their progress—they were performing well.

Rewards and incentives

Unlike punishments, rewards and incentives appear to enlist positive behaviours and, in some cases, change students' (and at times teachers') behaviour. Thus, Purkey and Smith (1983) note that a key cultural characteristic of effective schools is a 'school-wide recognition of academic success: publicly honouring academic achievement and stressing its importance encourages students to adopt similar norms and values' (p. 183).

Levine and Lezotte (1990) make two further points. First, that the use of rewards extends beyond academic outcomes and applies to other aspects of school life—a point supported by the British research. Second, that school-wide recognition of positive performance may be more important in urban schools—

and especially those in inner cities where, because of the correlation with disadvantage, there are low achieving students. Levine and Lezotte cite Hallinger and Murphy's (1987) study to support this argument. Hallinger and Murphy argue that one of the roles of principals in advantaged schools was to:

> sustain existing norms, rather than create new ones . . . in low SES [disadvantaged] schools the principal must ensure that the school overcomes societal and school norms that communicate low expectations to the students . . . [whereas in higher SES schools] school disciplinary and academic reward systems need not focus as much on short-term accomplishments, rely heavily on tangible reinforcers or develop elaborate linkages between the classroom and the school (p. 3).

Finally, in one of the British studies, Mortimore et al. (1988a) found that rewards could be given in a variety of ways, if the policy of the school was positive. In some schools, the policy was to reward individuals for good work or behaviour, whilst in others it was to focus on sport and social factors. Schools experienced the problem of trying to create a common system of incentives. This was a particular problem for schools where the age range was wide: rewards that appealed to younger pupils sometimes lost their enchantment for older students.

Parental involvement in the life of the school
The nature of parental involvement in schooling is possibly one of the most important issues being discussed in current educational debates. The idea is not new and has been pioneered by a number of educational researchers in Canada, the United Kingdom and in the United States. There is also a large and rapidly increasing literature on the topic. In the United Kingdom, much of the debate has been about the gains to be made from developing contact between homes and schools with regard to children's learning, as well as about ways to increase the accountability of schools to parents.

   The vital role that parents can play in the intellectual development of their children has long been known, but experiments to use this resource more effectively have met with varied success. One pioneering British study (Tizard et al., 1982), however, demonstrated that parental involvement in reading more than compensated for the use of an extra teacher in schools. Evidence from the headstart programmes in the United States (Lazar and Darlington, 1982) has also provided evidence that the involvement of parents was an important aspect of the programmes' success, and evidence from England shows that the gap between the achievement levels of advantaged and disadvantaged can be reduced (Athey, 1990). In another British study, Mortimore et al. (1988a) found that schools varied a great deal in their attitudes towards parents. Some schools kept parents out; others used parents as unpaid labour. A few schools involved parents in the school planning and sought to use their talents and abilities in both the classroom and at home. The researchers found that some principals appeared to be insufficiently confident in their relationships with parents, especially in more socially advantaged areas. When the energy and talents of parents were harnessed, however, the rewards for the school were high. Interestingly, Mortimore et al. (1988a) also found that parent–teacher associations were not necessarily positive, in that particular groups of parents could form a 'clique' and thus present a barrier to the involvement of others. The range of parental involvement programmes in both elementary and secondary schooling in the United Kingdom has been summarized by Jowett et al. (1991).

The ways in which parent involvement contributes to effectiveness are not, however, well understood. It is possible to speculate that where both long-term goals and short-term objectives are shared by teachers and parents, where parents are able to offer considerable help through coaching, and where ideas generated in one area of a child's life can be rehearsed and expanded in another, learning will be helped. Interestingly, Stevenson and Shin-Ying's (1990) study of three cities, Taipei (Taiwan), Sendai (Japan) and Minneapolis (US), illustrates the length to which oriental families will go to involve not just parents, but other relations, in the coaching of children. The authors show that a belief in the supremacy of hard work over natural ability and the willingness to be critical, when combined with high expectations, can provide powerful support for learning. Parental involvement, however, is not without difficulties and those responsible for school programmes need to have clear policies in place *before* embarking on this potentially valuable strategy (Mortimore & Mortimore, 1984).

Joint planning and consistent approaches towards students

This mechanism has been clearly recognized in many research studies. Levine and Lezotte (1990) argue that:

> almost by definition, faculty members committed to a school-wide mission focusing on academic improvement for all students tend to exemplify greater cohesiveness and consensus regarding central organizational goals than do faculty at less effective schools. (p. 12)

They argue that cohesion and consensus are especially important for schools (rather than other institutions) because schools set teachers difficult and sometimes conflicting goals. Thus, teachers have to respond to the individual needs of students whilst emphasizing the requirements of the whole class. They have to be fair to the group whilst taking account of individual circumstances. These conflicts are sometimes difficult for teachers to resolve to their own—and to their students'—satisfaction. In such circumstances it is easy for what Levine and Lezotte call 'goal clarity' to be reduced and for improvement efforts to be fragmented. Where students are subject to conflicting expectations and demands and, as a result, become less confident, they often take time to learn the ways of each new teacher. Whilst this exercise may provide a helpful pointer to the ways of adults, it is clearly not useful for effective learning in a school.

The involvement of faculty members in joint decisions relates, of course, to the strength of leadership of the institution. There is some evidence that when teachers and others in authority (including the assistant principal) are given a role to play, they—in the best management tradition—will be far more likely to feel some 'ownership' of the institution and, as a result, offer greater commitment to it. The complexities of planning have been explored (Goddard & Leask, 1992; Hargreaves & Hopkins, 1991), but the question of how much school-wide planning influences the daily lives of individual teachers remains to be answered.

Academic press and learning

There has been much research in this area; some of it on the question of time-on-task (Sizemore, 1987), some on class size (Mortimore & Blatchford, 1993). A number of research studies have also drawn attention to the amount of time wasted during the school day, particularly at the start of classes, through poor administration and lack of preparation (Blum, 1984). Rutter et al. (1979a) also found evidence of time wasted at the end of classes and described the chaotic situation that could develop where a high proportion of classes in the school finished before the scheduled time. The issue, therefore, is not simply time: it is also the *use* of time. Mortimore et al. (1988a) noted that, whilst some of the schools in their sample programmed extra time (some, 20 minutes per day) for classes, a straightforward correlation with effectiveness was not found. The value of time appeared to depend greatly on how it was used.

An emphasis on the learning of core skills has also been cited as important. In the United States this has sometimes been associated with experiments in mastery learning (Gregory and Mueller, 1980). Levine and Lezotte (1990), however, argue that in some cases the original concept of Bloom-type mastery learning has been mis-implemented and cannot fairly be judged in these circumstances. In Britain, a DES discussion paper (Alexander et al., 1992) has warned that elementary schools can lose sight of the central focus on student learning and dissipate teachers' energies in an unproductive way.

These are eight commonly cited factors arising from the research literature. As noted earlier, however, other factors have frequently been studied and may also be of considerable importance for particular schools at particular times. Thus, if schools receive students of a certain background, if the community is subject to particular experiences, or if the school authorities invoke a specific series of reforms, other factors associated with coping with change will come into play. Whilst these should never supplant the prime focus of school—the learning of pupils—they may act as mediating influences and, as a result, distract the attention of teachers and principals.

Lessons for school improvers

There are a number of lessons concerned with effective learning and teaching that those involved with school improvement can draw from the corpus of school effectiveness work. Many of these have been discussed elsewhere (Fullan,

1991, 1992a; Reynolds, 1993; Reynolds & Packer, 1992; Reynolds et al., 1993; Stoll, 1992). I wish to comment on just two issues.

Need for planning
Studies of school effectiveness have shown that the effective management of learning and teaching relies upon systematic planning both at the school and the classroom level. Hargreaves and Hopkins (1991) have drawn together the lessons from a government-funded project on School Development Planning. The researchers found that effective planning was a continuous process rather than a one-off activity. They also drew attention to the difference between maintaining the state of the school and developing it in a new direction. Goddard and Leask (1992) have also drawn attention to the need for a national plan that is not dominated by the search for short-term solutions. Our own work at the Institute of Education on School Development Planning is still in process. We are investigating—in a sample of contrasting schools—the forms which planning takes and, most importantly, the impact that it has on the effective learning of pupils. This is unlikely to be an easy task but is an extremely important one (Beresford et al., 1992; Mortimore et al., 1994a).

A focus on ends not means
A critical feature of the school effectiveness model is its focus on student outcomes. Whilst high levels of attendance, good behaviour, high levels of self-efficacy and positive attitudes to schooling might be seen as means towards the end of effective learning (shown by a high level of progress), they can also be seen—to a certain extent—as legitimate ends which result in the development of positive, well-adjusted and self-disciplined, young learners. There is thus no potential conflict between the energy and resources devoted to means and ends. There might well be a difference between those related outcomes and a number of the other school processes which are perfectly legitimate as means towards the end of effective learning, but which, divorced from such an end, might not represent sensible effort. The key lesson from school-effectiveness research is that the ends must constantly be kept in sight in order to prevent any of the means from assuming importance *in their own right* and, thereby, distracting energy from the main task.

Conclusion

As noted, the processes listed here are simply means towards the end of effective learning. None, by themselves, are likely to guarantee successful outcomes. Taken together, however, they represent a reasonable picture, based on the state of our current knowledge and understanding, of how effective schools function.

Future schools, of course, may be different. It is important, therefore, that the characteristics (positive though they are) of today's effective schools are not allowed to become reified and maintained beyond their proper usefulness. The schools of tomorrow may need to be very different, if, for instance, a recent

report from the OECD (1992) is to be believed. According to this, the availability of cheap and efficient information technology will lead to:

- A move away from class-based teaching towards individual learning
- The exploitation of 'smart card' monitoring and record keeping capabili-
  ties
- Increased contact between learners (and teachers) in different institutions
  and from outside of any formal bodies
- The erosion of the school as a geographical entity

The implications of such possibilities for all involved in managing, and teaching in, schools would be considerable. So also would be the scope for new ways
of working. The next generation of school-effectiveness researchers and school
improvers is unlikely to be short of challenges.

Postscript

*In writing this paper I had discovered that, despite the well-known theories of
Piaget and Vigotsky, our knowledge of how children learn is still very limited.
I also realized how easily commentators on learning could slip into a discussion
of teaching. Because the learning is—as I noted—covert rather than open, people equate it with the more observable teaching. However, as experienced practitioners will know only too well, the two do not always correspond.*

In the course of fieldwork for the Fifteen Thousand Hours *study, I had spent
some time observing classes of new students in their first few days at secondary
school. It was possible to see the parallel activities of the teacher and the class
of learners as well as their interactions. I was struck, in one case, by how a
rather 'show-offy' teacher took advantage of the new students' excellent behaviour and failed to establish appropriate classroom procedures and parameters of
behaviour. I was aware that he seemed to be wasting this opportunity, but I did
not foresee quite how much he would regret his confident oversight. Three
months later I observed the same teacher with the same class. By then the behaviour of the class was very poor and the teacher's attempts to gain control were
clumsy and inept. I doubted if that teacher would ever succeed with that particular class. In contrast, teachers in other classes used the initial period of grace
to establish the ground rules that would underpin their relations with the students. Three months later, I observed orderly classes in which there were many
opportunities for learning.*

*I was pleasantly surprised to find how well the school effectiveness factors fit-
ted with our knowledge of learning and teaching. They provided a classroom
and a school context in which the transmission of knowledge, understanding
and skills could be undertaken. As I noted at the end of the piece, however, it is
important for school effectiveness researchers to keep up with the changes in
information and communications technology so as to avoid 'freezing' the characteristics of effectiveness.*

12

Value-Added Measures and School Effectiveness[1]

Introduction

This chapter is based on an article which, in turn, was based on a conference paper written for the Desmond Nuttall Memorial Conference. Professor Nuttall was an Institute colleague who suffered an untimely death in 1993. His death distressed us all. He had been involved in educational research for most of his career and had worked for the National Foundation for Educational Research and the Open University, as well as being Secretary of an Examinations Board. In 1985, Desmond Nuttall had succeeded me as Director of Research and Statistics for the ILEA. Shortly before his death, he, Pam Sammons, Sally Thomas (who had both worked with him in previous jobs) and I had been awarded a grant by the United Kingdom's Economic and Social Research Council (ESRC) to investigate the phenomenon of 'differential effectiveness'. The conference paper we wrote was both a tribute to our former colleague and our attempt to integrate the concept of 'value added' into our existing work on school effectiveness.

The theory that schools can promote the progress of pupils so as to overcome the influence of family, community and individual attributes underpins British studies of school effectiveness. Measures of *value added* have been developed as

---

1 Based on an article by Peter Mortimore, Pam Sammons and Sally Thomas.

sophisticated ways of analysing potential school effects. The late Desmond Nuttall played a key role in adapting the statistical technique of multilevel modelling to the issue of value added. The original paper on which this chapter is based was written for a memorial conference in which researchers paid tribute to the work of our former colleague. In writing this paper, we are conscious that we represent a large group of researchers, not only from the International School Effectiveness and Improvement Centre (ISEIC) at the Institute of Education but also from the London School of Economics' (LSE) Centre for Educational Research, the former Inner London Education Authority (ILEA) Research and Statistics Branch, the Open University (OU) and the National Foundation for Educational Research (NFER). All our paths crossed Desmond Nuttall's at some point in his distinguished career.

In the paper we will endeavour to summarize some of the main issues relating to studies of school effectiveness and measures of value added. We will draw on the published papers of the teams in which Nuttall worked to illustrate his crucial role in the conceptual development of these areas of work. We will include a brief discussion of three of the most important unresolved issues:

- The level of stability of results over time
- The differential effects of schooling
- The effects of context on student performance

The United Kingdom context

Over the last six years, the British government has undertaken a major legislative programme of new Education Acts. The 1988 Education Reform Act introduced a series of changes to the system of schooling. The legislation was intended to raise standards and improve the quality of teaching and learning. It also had the explicit aim of encouraging the operation of market forces by increasing both parental choice and the emphasis on value for money.

The main changes are: the introduction of a national curriculum and an associated programme of student tests; a newly designed school inspectorate system working to a four-year cycle; delegation of financial responsibility to the level of the individual school; an increase in the powers of school governors (local community groups with parent and teacher representation); and allowing school governing bodies to ballot parents over their school 'opting out' of local authority control and receiving enhanced funding direct from central government.

Not surprisingly, the various changes introduced by the legislation have had different outcomes. The national curriculum—broadly accepted, in principle, by teachers and parents—has had to be revised and reduced in scale. The testing programme, after initial success with the 7-year-old age group, has run into difficulties and been resisted by a teachers' boycott on grounds of the excessive workload. At the time of writing this has yet to be resolved. The new style school inspections have been introduced for secondary schools and, from the summer of 1994, will be introduced at primary level. The delegation of financial responsibilities to the school level has proved popular, despite the considerable workloads being carried by the governing bodies. So far only a minority of schools have elected to opt out of the local jurisdiction and it remains to be seen whether the government will continue to seek actively to increase this proportion.

Attempts to emphasize the importance of market forces appear to have been partially successful—certainly schools are much more concerned about how they promote themselves to parents. For some parents there is a much greater awareness of choice, though this depends to a certain extent on where they live and the availability of alternative schools from which to choose. The introduction of the national publication of league tables of test and examination results, however, remains a contentious issue.

It is against this backcloth of change that the work on school effectiveness and value-added analysis of student outcomes needs to be viewed and its benefit to schooling judged.

Studies of school effectiveness

Over the last thirty years, there have been a number of empirical investigations of the theory that individual schools exert an influence above and beyond the talents and motivations of individual pupils, the nature of their families and communities and even of the social determinants of achievement: gender, social class and race. These investigations have been carried out in this country, in North America, in mainland Europe, Australia and, increasingly, in Asia.

The theory of the school effect is good for heads and teachers; it recognizes an important, even a crucial, role for schools. It is also good for educational policy makers who are relieved that the vital ingredients for effectiveness are not simply more resources. Not surprisingly, however, the theory is not popular with all governments and is frequently attacked on political grounds (Sirotnik, 1985). Like so many theories, that of school effectiveness emerged as a reaction to a counter-theory: that schools had uniform effects and that, in the view of some of the American sociologists, luck was probably more important than the choice of the school to a child's progress (see, for instance, Coleman et al., 1966, or Jencks et al., 1972).

The methodologies of studies of school effectiveness generally involve the sampling of populations of schools; the identification and collection of appropriate pupil outcomes and of information about the backgrounds of pupil intakes; and the mapping of patterns of results to life in schools, in order to identify particular school processes or mechanisms associated with good practice. British studies have been at the forefront of this work both in terms of their scope and their sophistication. Thus, British studies have: addressed issues concerned with primary and secondary schooling and the transition from one to the other; pioneered a broader range of outcomes to include non-cognitive as well as cognitive measures; and developed increasingly sophisticated statistical methods for analysing pupils' progress (Mortimore et al., 1988a, 1998b; Reynolds, 1985; Rutter et al., 1979a; Sammons, 1989b; Smith & Tomlinson, 1989).

Nuttall (1990), with his background in psychometrics and his work on school examinations, was drawn increasingly towards this field of study. He fully recognized the importance, in studies of school effectiveness, of having adequate controls for differences between schools in their student intakes and the need to use sophisticated methods to ensure that such factors are taken into account. Moreover, he was acutely concerned that any comparisons of schools' results should be conducted fairly to ensure that 'like' is compared with 'like'. As he so cogently argued, 'natural justice demands that schools are held accountable only for those things that they can influence (for good or ill) and not for all the pre-existing differences between their intakes. The investigation of differential school effectiveness, concentrating on the progress students make while at that school, therefore has a major role to play in the future, p. 25).

Nuttall's first interest in school effectiveness arose out of his involvement in the analysis of examination results of secondary schools during his time as Director of Research and Statistics for the ILEA. After the abolition of the ILEA, this work was continued in collaboration with the Association of Metropolitan Authorities (Nuttall et al., 1992b; Thomas et al., 1993a, 1994). In all, Nuttall worked with twenty different Local Education Authorities (LEAs) on value-added projects, drawing on the Key Stage 1 (KS1) national curriculum assessment results for seven-year-olds, General Certificate of Secondary Education (GCSE) results or both (see, for example, Thomas & Nuttall, 1992). Further value added analyses were also carried out at the post 16 level, in collaboration with the *Guardian* (a British national daily paper), and provided a high-profile alternative to the 'raw' league tables of school examination results published by the government in the local and national press (Thomas & Nuttall, 1992; Thomas et al., 1993b).

Whilst he was the director of the Centre for Educational Research at the LSE, Nuttall became increasingly interested in primary school effectiveness, in particular the continuity of such effects in the long term—in other words, did the primary school attended have an impact on later performance at secondary school? Indeed, one of Nuttall's last major presentations was at the 1993 meeting of the International Congress of School Effectiveness and Improvement in Sweden. At that Conference he delivered a paper based on a detailed follow-up study of the *School Matters*' (Mortimore et al., 1988a) primary cohort into secondary schooling. This analysis revealed the sustained influence of their junior school experience on students' subsequent performance in the GCSE examinations. It also suggested that primary school effects may be more powerful than those of secondary schools and pointed to the importance of this earlier stage of schooling (Sammons et al., l993a).

In 1992, Nuttall became the Professor of Curriculum and Assessment Studies at the Institute of Education. He also became involved in planning the creation of a new International School Effectiveness and Improvement Centre (ISEIC), which was intended to forge better links between these two fields and of which he was to have been the first director. Since joining the Institute of Education,

Nuttall had also been involved, with colleagues, in the preparation of an application to the Economic and Social Research Council (ESRC) for funds to study two of the most intriguing questions to do with studies of schools: how much stability can be found in the school effects of the GCSE results of successive cohorts of pupils; and whether there are differences at the subject/departmental level in secondary schools (Nuttall et al., 1992a). This application was successful and work on these questions is currently under way, based in the ISEIC.

The last research application with which Desmond Nuttall was involved was for the Scottish Office Education Department. He was attracted by the opportunity provided by this department to design a study able to bring together a methodology of school effectiveness studies and the techniques of school improvement. Tragically, he died before the bid was submitted. Involvement in such a study would have drawn on his knowledge of assessment techniques, his understanding of the issues of school effectiveness, his extensive grasp of methodological matters and his commitment to channel these resources to the improvement of schooling.

Value added

'For nearly thirty years research on school effectiveness has used the *progress* made by students from their level of performance on entry to their level of performance at the time they leave, rather than just their *raw* results at the time of leaving. This approach, well illuminated by the metaphor 'value added', makes intuitive sense and is readily comprehensible', wrote Desmond Nuttall in the *Times Educational Supplement* (TES) of 13 September 1991. This metaphor remains a figure of speech. Value-added tables are not included in the statutory duties of head teachers and governing bodies to publish public examination results. Only a few local educational authorities have collected sufficiently sensitive pupil intake data to enable raw results at age 11 or 16 to be interpreted in terms of the progress made by pupils.

Raw results tell parents the grades their children have obtained, but they can say nothing about how well the school attended has performed. In contrast, value-added results tell parents how effective their children's school is in promoting achievement.

Desmond Nuttall clearly understood the problems of how *comprehensible* the value-added work might be. In his address to the 1993 London Centre for Policy Studies Conference—a year after his TES article—he concluded his paper thus:

> Don't be frightened by a bit of complexity. We've learnt to live with seasonally adjusted unemployment figures, a Retail Price Index that includes both rent and mortgages . . . and incredibly complicated Rate Support Grant Settlements . . . I believe we can learn to live with appropriate complexity in 'value added'. (Nuttall, 1993, p. 31)

One of the origins of value-added work lies in the early studies of school effectiveness, such as *Fifteen Thousand Hours* (Rutter et al., 1979a), which used Verbal Reasoning (VR) data as a baseline measure of prior attainment and public examination results (the GCSEs). This study was limited, however, by the less sophisticated statistical techniques available in the 1970s. In particular, it was difficult to take full account of prior attainment, pupil background factors and contextual information, such as the neighbourhood characteristics of where pupils lived. Moreover, the research team had a small sample of just 12 schools.

The ILEA's Research and Statistics Branch (R & S), because of the number of schools it served, was able to take forward the work on value added. Between 1976 and 1990, R & S produced increasingly sophisticated analyses of the results of some 30,000 pupils, drawn from over 180 secondary schools. Most of the analyses were descriptive. They were of importance in illustrating, for the first time, the range of examination results achieved by successive year groups of 15/16 years olds. Unlike the then Department of Education and Science analyses, which treated all 15- to 19-year-olds as school leavers and pooled the results, the R & S data were of whole age-cohorts. The Research and Statistics team, moreover, created better ways to take account of academic performance at age 11 and to use proxy measures of disadvantage, such as eligibility for free school meals. The team produced the first complete LEA comparisons of the 'raw' and the adjusted rankings of schools.

At the primary school stage, the Research and Statistics team pioneered the collection and analysis of individual progress measures and carried out the first large-scale trial in the United Kingdom (UK) of the multilevel modelling procedures designed by Goldstein and colleagues at the Institute of Education. In *School Matters*, Mortimore et al. (1988a) reported the results of these analyses and, in related publications (Mortimore et al., 1988b; Sammons, 1989b), compared the results with those of more conventional techniques. The data from this project have been re-analysed using the latest versions of multilevel modelling techniques by a team which included Desmond Nuttall (Sammons et al., 1993a, 1993b). A number of areas, not covered in the original research, were also investigated as part of the *School Matters* re-analysis. The continuity of effects in the longer term has already been noted but, in addition, the research addressed ways of comparing school results in terms of value-added and 'raw' results. The authors noted that, 'this is a matter of increasing public and policy interest given the government's decision requiring the publication of "league tables' of schools" raw examination and national curriculum assessment results' (Sammons et al., 1993b, p. 399), and went on to point out the limitations of this approach.

Nuttall made many valuable contributions to the league table debate. He made it clear in his contribution to the discussion of the presentation of examination results and other information about schools (as part of the ILEA's Freedom of Information Inquiry; see ILEA, 1987, and Tomlinson et al., 1988) that he was in favour of providing more and better information about schools to parents and other appropriate parties. In an article on the publication of A-level results, he argued that value-added information 'is much more valuable than the "raw" A-level results to parents considering their own child's future', but added, 'I am not arguing that the raw results should not be published, as they tell one something about the emphasis that the school places on academic success and, indeed, its selectivity both academically and socially'. We think that Nuttall's conclusion still stands: 'With both "raw" results and "added value", parents are in a much better position to judge the effectiveness with which the school prepares students for examinations' (Nuttall, 1992, p. 14). Of course, he also added that parents 'will want a whole range of other information but that needs a separate article'.

Nuttall was also instrumental in developing further the Research and Statistics' annual analyses of examination results. By recognizing the complex nature of some of the variables, for instance, he was able to gain a more precise specification of the relationship between inputs and outcomes. A key article entitled *Differential School Effectiveness* (Nuttall et al., 1989) took account of sex, prior achievement, ethnic background and school contextual variables on the progress of cohorts of pupils. The study used multilevel modelling to show, for example, the *compositional* effects on achievement of schools having an over-concentration of under-performing groups. It also showed once again that: 'some schools narrow the gap between boys and girls or between students of high and low attainment on entry . . .' (Nuttall et al., 1989). Most interestingly, the results drew attention to the remarkable progress made by some of the ethnic groups during their years of secondary schooling.

These results have recently been replicated and extended by the re-analysis of the *School Matters* data. In a detailed multilevel study of gender, socio-economic and ethnic differences in attainment and progress, Sammons (1994a) illustrated that it is possible to identify and separate the impact of different background characteristics, taking account of school membership. This longitudinal analysis of data spanning nine years compared differences in absolute attainment and relative progress over time. Whilst the impact of gender and socio-economic factors (low income and social class) remained consistent and differences between groups increased as pupils grew older, the results for ethnic groups altered significantly between primary and secondary schooling. 'Although ethnic minority groups attained less highly during their junior education (both in absolute and in relative terms) these patterns altered markedly during secondary education. By the end of compulsory schooling (age 16) it was clear that those of ethnic minority backgrounds had made considerable achievement gains' (Sammons, 1994a, p. 14). Caribbean students' progress was no longer significantly lower than that of English, Scottish, Welsh or Irish students, whilst pupils of Asian backgrounds had made significantly better progress.

One of the most detailed longitudinal LEA-sponsored programmes of research on the use of value-added measures was begun by Nuttall. It involved working in collaboration with a large local education authority on parallel studies of 7-year-olds and 16-year-olds. The main aim of the study of 7-year-olds was to take account of factors outside the control of the school and to provide

LEA officers and head teachers with adjusted[2] scores to compare with the test results (Thomas & Nuttall, 1993).

The study of 16-year-olds, based on nearly 12,000 students drawn from nearly 90 secondary schools, collected detailed information about examination candidates (Thomas & Mortimore, 1994). This information included data from the 1991 census about the home neighbourhood and the catchment area of the schools that students attended. Much of this work is still continuing but we can report that—in order to explore the data as thoroughly as possible—we have created five separate models. The relationships of the models is interesting, as the correlations between the value-added scores for each model, shown in Table 12.1, demonstrate. Some models show remarkable agreement, whilst the model based on proxy rather than precise measures has the least agreement.

Using the basic model, it can be seen that raw and value-added results are similar for some schools but rather different for others. Figure 12.1 indicates the overall average of the sample (33.1 GCSE points). It also shows (for a sample of 40 schools) each school's raw results (shown by a horizontal bar [–]) and the 95 per cent confidence limits for the value-added results (shown by a vertical bar) with the value-added score at its centre-point. Particularly interesting are school 32—which has a high raw score but below average value-added result—and school 24—which has a similar raw score to school 32 but has

Table 12.1. Correlations between alternative models.

		Basic	Refined	Differential Band			Prior
				1	2	3	Achievement
Basic model*		–					
Refined model**		0.98	–				
Differential model**	} Band 1	0.81	0.82				
	} Band 2	0.96	0.97	0.83	–		
	} Band 3	0.83	0.85	0.44	0.79	–	
Prior achievement only model*		0.94	0.92	0.79	0.92	0.74	–
All schools model***		0.79	0.80	0.69	0.81	0.65	0.77

*sample 1:   8,566 pupils; 79 schools (excludes pupils with missing National Foundation for Educational Research [NFER] Cognitive Abilities Test [CAT] scores)
**sample 2:   8,052 pupils; 79 schools (excludes pupils with missing NFER CAT scores and postcode/census data)
***sample 3:   1,068 pupils; 87 schools (excludes pupils with missing postcode/census data)
Note that the correlations are based on the 79 schools common to all three samples.

---

2   Adjustments were made on the basis of the statistical relationship between KS1 attainment and a variety of *significant* pupil intake factors (gender, age, entitlement to free school meals, English as a second language, special educational needs) and one school context factor (% of pupils entitled to educational benefits).

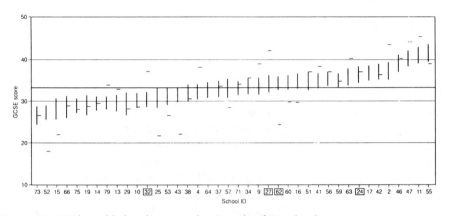

Figure 12.1. Value-added and raw results. Sample of 40 schools.

above average value-added. Another pair of interesting schools are 27 and 62. These have similar value-added scores but have very different raw figures.

These examples identify schools with different raw and value-added scores in students' performance in the GCSE examinations. They also show how important it is to have a technique which provides confidence intervals so that the statistical significance of the results can be considered. That noted, it is clear that, for many schools in this particular local authority, raw and value-added results are similar, although, for some schools, marked differences are found.

The use of the multilevel models also enables the impact of group differences to be estimated—net of other effects. Thus, Table 12.2 shows that girls, on average, have a lead of 4.1 GCSE points over boys; that for every 10 points above average on the verbal Cognitive Abilities Tests (CATs, a test taken at age 11) score a student is likely to have a 5.4 point lead over his or her peers in the GCSE examinations (taken at age 16); and that Chinese ethnic groups are likely to have a 16.8 lead over their white peers. As a consequence of the GCSE point scoring system, a mere 4 points can make the difference between a student being awarded four C grades, rather than four D grades, and 16 points is the equivalent of the difference between eight B grades and eight D grades. In the British system, such differences represent the gap between being seen as a middle-of-the-road performer or a potential academic high-flyer.

These analyses are continuing and expanding. The work that Nuttall carried out, and the developments that he pioneered, are proving to be of both practical use to those who are responsible for schools and of considerable interest to scholars.

The last major application in which Nuttall was involved was a response to an invitation to tender from the Office for Standards in Education (Ofsted). This

Table 12.2. Results (1) (Basic Model)

Group Differences			GCSE Points
Girls	compared with	Boys	+ 4.1
No FSM	compared with	FSM	+ 5.2
Verbal CAT 10 points (+)	compared with	10 points (−)	+ 5.4
Quantitative CAT 10 points (+)	compared with	10 points (−)	+ 4.1
Non-verbal CAT 10 points (+)	compared with	10 points (−)	+ 1.9
Age per month (+)	compared with	Per month (−)	+ 0.2
No previous school	compared with	Previous school	+ 3.6
5 years' education in UK	compared with	Less than 5 years	+ 10.2
Indian	compared with	White	+ 8.8
Pakistani	compared with	White	+ 8.4
Bangladeshi	compared with	White	+ 9.8
Chinese	compared with	White	+ 16.8
Black African	compared with	White	NS
Black Caribbean	compared with	White	NS
Black Other	compared with	White	NS
White	compared with	Other ethnic	+ 2.5

Note Benchmarks: 4 points = difference between 4 D grades and 4 C grades
16 points = difference between 8 D grades and 8 B grades
FSM = entitlement to free school meals
CAT = Cognitive Abilities Test (NFER, 1986)

invited us to establish the utility of using nationally available data sources to create indicators of secondary schools' intakes, in order to group them into 'broadly similar categories for the purpose of assessing schools' performance, so that in any comparison "like" is compared with "like"'. The Ofsted specification recognized that a 'value-added' approach, which employed baseline measures of pupils' prior attainment, would provide the most appropriate basis for evaluating school performance. In the absence of nationally available prior attainment data, however, the project was intended to investigate the usefulness of developing other, less sophisticated, ways of contextualizing performance. It was explicitly recognized that any grouping method developed would mainly be of use in the short to mid-term, until value-added methods could be employed.

ISEIC was successful in this application and we have recently submitted our report to Ofsted (Sammons et al., 1994c). We hope the analyses we have carried out will influence the way examination results and the academic effectiveness of schools are interpreted by future Ofsted inspection teams. We also hope that the results of this research will be of practical value to schools and will assist them in the processes of self-evaluation and internal monitoring of performance in a more realistic context.

Unresolved issues

We wish to draw attention to three issues emerging from Nuttall's work which continue to fascinate his colleagues at the Institute of Education and other researchers in many universities throughout the world.

Stability of results over time

The evidence on whether the effects of schools vary over time is mixed. Early British secondary studies examined students' overall examination results for different outcomes and found general consistency over time (Reynolds, 1976; Rutter et al., 1979a). Work by Willms (1987) and Goldstein (1987) reveals correlations ranging between 0.80 to 0.60. However, Nuttall et al.'s 1989 research in inner London points to the lack of stability in secondary schools' effects on student total examination scores, over a three-year period. These authors note that, 'the lack of stability may also be partly to do with the unreliability and lack of comparability of the examination scores'. They also report that statistical adjustment for prior attainment in their analysis is limited because the only measure available at that time was a crude three-category variable (VR band). Nuttall et al. conclude: 'this analysis nevertheless gives rise to a note of caution about any study of school effectiveness that relies on measures of outcome in just a single year, or of just a single cohort of students. Long time series are essential for a proper study of stability over time' (p. 775).

Like Nuttall et al., Raudenbush (1989) has also drawn attention to the importance of adopting a longitudinal model for estimating school effects and their stability. He concluded that school effects on overall attainment (at the secondary level) are fairly stable ($r = 0.87$) but that 'school effects on examination results in specific subjects were less stable' (p. 733). In the Netherlands, Luyten (1994a) has also recently pointed out that year effects are very modest, but likewise demonstrates that subject results can vary significantly, indicating the importance of departmental effects at secondary school.

Less attention has been paid to the stability of school effects at the primary than at the secondary level, although in the United States Mandeville (1987) reports correlations ranging from 0.34 to 0.66. However, Stringfield et al. (1992) in the *Louisiana School Effectiveness Study* maintained that most schools appear to remain stable outliers, either positive or negative, for at least 16 years. Recent work by Crone et al. (1994) and by Yelton et al. (1994) suggest that school effects are fairly constant over time, particularly for composite measures of achievement.

Overall, these results suggest a fair degree of stability in secondary schools' effects on academic outcomes over time (the correlations are moderately strong and all are positive), particularly for overall examination results and, to a lesser extent, for basic skills in the primary sector. There is less evidence of stability of specific subject results or social/affective (non-cognitive) outcomes of education. There is a need for further research to examine the extent of stability in school/departmental effects for a wider range of outcomes and in different sectors.

The fact that measures of stability are not perfect over time should not be too surprising. It is important to recognize that change in outcomes is likely over time periods of more than one or two years due to changes in staff, in pupil intakes and in school ethos. Schools may also change rapidly as a result of outside intervention (e.g. a new head teacher or an Ofsted inspection). Therefore, a method of identifying—and separately measuring—temporal and school effects is required in order to evaluate schools more accurately. In addition, further work on school processes related to effectiveness is needed to investigate mechanisms for change and ways in which it may be most successfully introduced.

Differential effects within a school

The importance of differential within-school effects is a topic of increasing interest in school effectiveness research, especially in the UK field, and is one in which Nuttall was particularly involved. Differential school effects concern the existence of varying differences in attainment between schools *for different pupil groups* (those with different levels of prior attainment or different background characteristics).

Prior attainment

Although the study by Rutter et al. (1979a) did not use multilevel techniques, it did examine schools' examination results for the most and least able children and compared the results for children of different levels of prior ability (using a three-category measure at intake—the VR band). The researchers found that 'the pattern of results for each school was broadly similar in all three bands' (p. 86).

Smith and Tomlinson's (1989) study of multi-racial comprehensives investigated differences between schools in their effectiveness in promoting examination performance. They found some evidence of differential effectiveness for pupils with varying levels of prior attainment. However, Smith and Tomlinson found that 'a more able pupil gains a greater advantage than a less able one from going to a good school' (p. 273). In the Scottish context, Willms and Raudenbush (1989) also report some evidence of differential school effectiveness for pupils of different prior attainment levels (as assessed on a Verbal Reasoning Quotient).

Secondary school analyses by Nuttall et al. (1989) and Nuttall (1990) also report evidence that schools' performance varies differentially, with some schools narrowing the achievement gap between students of high and low attainment on entry. The results suggest that variability in the results of high ability pupils between schools is much larger than that of low ability students. Analyses of the English Association of Metropolitan Authorities data by Thomas et al. (1993a; 1994) also indicated the existence of differential effectiveness for pupils of different ability on entry to secondary school. The correlation of value-added scores for pupils in the highest and lowest prior attainment bands was between 0.73 and 0.77.

At the post-16 level, the 1993 *Guardian* survey (Thomas et al., 1993b) showed that 26 per cent of schools obtained mixed (including both better and worse than expected) scores across three different GCSE ability groups.

Jesson and Gray (1991) investigated the issue of differential school effectiveness for pupils with different levels of prior achievement at the secondary level. Their research provides evidence of modest differential slopes but they concluded that 'schools which were more effective for one group of pupils were generally speaking more effective for other groups as well' (p. 46). This conclusion is broadly in line with that of Smith and Tomlinson (1989). Jesson and Gray (1991) suggest a number of possible reasons for the difference between Nuttall et al.'s 1989 results and their own. They draw particular attention to the high degree of social differentiation in inner-city areas and to the crude measure of prior attainment (VR band) in the ILEA research. They conclude that the use of a crude grouped measure, rather than a finely differentiated measure of prior attainment, may affect findings about the nature and extent of differential school effectiveness. This is an area in which more research is needed. We hope that our ESRC study on Department Differences in Secondary School Effectiveness, currently underway in the ISEIC, will throw further light on this issue (Nuttall et al., 1992b; Sammons & Mortimore, 1993).

Most of the evidence concerning differential school effectiveness and prior attainment has been conducted at the secondary level. The original analyses for the *School Matters* study (Mortimore et al., 1988a) did not examine in detail differential effectiveness for pupils with different levels of prior attainment. The subsequent re-analysis by Sammons et al. (1993b) found some evidence of differential school effectiveness for pupils with different levels of prior attainment, although this was less notable for reading than for mathematics. In the Netherlands, Brandsma and Knuver (1989) also investigated this issue at the primary level. No evidence of 'equity differences' (as these authors term such effects) were found for mathematics, although small differences were noted for language.

Gender
A few secondary studies have pointed to the existence of differential school effects related to pupil gender. For example, Nuttall et al.'s 1989 study of examination results over three years in inner London indicates the existence of such differential effects in terms of total examination scores: 'some schools narrowing the gap between boys and girls . . . and some widening the gap, relatively speaking' (p.774). However, in the Scottish context Willms and Raudenbush (1989) did not identify any differential effects for gender.

At the primary level, Mortimore et al. (1988a) produced no evidence of differential school effectiveness related to gender for reading or mathematics progress and the more detailed re-analysis supports the earlier conclusions of *School Matters* (Sammons et al., 1993b). In the Netherlands, Brandsma and Knuver (1989) also found no evidence of differential school effects related to gender for mathematics and only very small equity differences for the Dutch language.

Ethnicity
Nuttall's work highlighted the existence of differential school effects for students of different ethnic backgrounds. Nuttall et al. (1989) reported 'within-school'

differences in effectiveness between Caribbean and English/Scottish/Welsh (ESW) students and comment that other ethnic differences vary across schools even more than the Caribbean–ESW differences. However, the authors drew attention to the lack of individual-level data about the socio-economic level of students' families which could confound ethnic differences with socio-economic differences. Elsewhere in the UK, Smith and Tomlinson (1989) produced evidence of differential school effectiveness for students of different ethnic groups, although these differences were found to be 'small compared with differences in overall performance between schools' (p. 268).

At the primary level, neither the original *School Matters* (Mortimore et al., 1988a) analyses nor the later re-analysis (Sammons et al., 1993b) found evidence of significant differential school effectiveness for specific ethnic groups. Brandsma & Knuver (1989) likewise found no indications of differential school effectiveness according to ethnic group in their study of Dutch primary schools.

To date, therefore, research on within-school differences suggest that gender, ethnicity and prior attainment are relevant to academic performance at secondary school. Less evidence for differential effects, however, exist at the primary stage. Further research on a wider range of outcomes is needed to distinguish whether this is likely to be the result of a measurement problem or whether this represents a fundamental difference between the effects of primary and of secondary schools.

Effects of context

In addition to controlling for effects related to individual background characteristics (age, gender, social class, ethnicity, etc.), some studies have addressed the issue of contextual effects. Willms (1992) notes that 'the composition of a school's intake can have a substantial effect on pupils' outcome over and above the effects associated with pupils' individual ability and social class' (p. 41; see also Willms, 1986, and Willms & Raudenbush, 1989). We believe it is important not to confuse contextual effects with differential within-school effects related to social class. Willms (1986) examined social class segregation and its relationship to pupils' examination results in Scotland. He noted that 'some of the observed differences between schools in their adjusted outcomes were associated with school composition' (p. 239). The author concluded that pupils at all levels of ability tend to benefit from attending high socio-economic status schools. Willms (1985) also found contextual effects related to the balance of high ability students within a school. Students of average ability in high ability schools scored more highly than comparable students in schools where the majority of pupils were of lower ability.

As we noted earlier, Nuttall's 1990 research into inner London secondary school effects over three consecutive years noted some evidence of positive compositional effects related to the concentration of high ability students (indicated by a large percentage being in VR band 1) and negative effects related to the concentration of students eligible for free school meals. Recent research conducted by us as part of the Ofsted project has also demonstrated the importance of the concentration of students taking free school meals in relation to GCSE results for a national sample of schools (Sammons et al., 1994b). However, recent research for a large county LEA at GCSE level has indicated that, when rich and wide-ranging data are available at the pupil level (for example, three finely graded prior achievement measures), school context factors were not identified (Thomas & Mortimore, 1994).

In contrast to most studies of secondary schools, *School Matters* (Mortimore et al., 1988a) found no evidence of contextual effects related to social-class composition—a finding supported by the later re-analysis. Similarly, Bondi's (1991) analysis of the reading attainment in Scottish primary schools noted 'no evidence that the mean socio-economic status of a school influences variations in outcomes between schools after adjusting for the background characteristics of the child' (p. 211). Bondi argues that the contrast between primary and secondary schools suggests that peer-group effects are more marked among adolescents than among young children. More recently, Thomas and Nuttall (1993) looked at a variety of contextual effects in relation to the attainment of 7-year-olds in the national curriculum, once a wide variety of pupil intake factors (with the notable exception of prior achievement) had been taken into account. It was found that the percentage of pupils entitled to education benefits and the mean age at year 2 were both systematically associated with attainment, over and above the effects of individual pupil characteristics. However, it is likely that such effects might be removed if adequate prior attainment data were available.

The evidence for the importance of contextual effects is most evident for studies of secondary school effects on cognitive outcomes, although it appears that contextual effects may be reduced when good (finely differentiated) measures of prior attainment and detailed pupil background data are available.

Further research at the primary level and for a broader range of outcomes is needed if these important issues are to be better understood. As with all scientific endeavours, this resolution is likely to happen through a mixture of hard work, collaboration and—at times—competition between colleagues drawn from a variety of academic disciplines and from practising schools, and from a certain amount of luck. The ability to ask the right questions and the knowledge of how to go about collecting data in order to answer them are crucial to the enterprise. Nuttall, as we know only too well, possessed both of these attributes.

The way forward

In writing this paper and in considering the directions in which future researchers and practitioners should proceed, we have drawn our inspiration from the career and work of Desmond Nuttall. Like him, we are committed to, and fascinated by, methodological advances. The development of statistical analyses which allow for the difficult but inevitable fact that schools do not receive uniform batches of equally *intelligent,* equally *motivated* pupils, from equally *supportive* homes, has been crucial to much of this work. As the techniques have been developed—from methods of standardization, to the use of multiple regression, to sophisticated multilevel modelling—studies of schools have become better able to tease out the varied and unpredictable impacts of schooling.

We and all our colleagues in the ISEIC are also committed to the value of networks of scholars and practitioners. Nuttall was, of course, a superb example of an accomplished networker. Networks can enable us to share problems, explore possible answers and, perhaps, be inspired in further efforts. Thus, meetings (funded by the Economic and Social Research Council) of the extensive network for this area of our work have motivated scholars to produce the syntheses that are so badly needed. Likewise, the International Congress for School Effectiveness and Improvement—of which Nuttall was a loyal member— and its journal, bring together those interested in this work from all over the world. At a more local level, our own School Improvement Network is meeting a national need to disseminate and, where appropriate, celebrate the work of those who—in a variety of roles—are working in this field.

All too frequently in many societies, schooling has become the preserve of those most involved in its day-to-day concerns. At a time when so many countries are having to re-appraise their education systems, we in the ISEIC are conscious of our duty to bring what we know and what we can do to the service of practitioners and policy makers. We must persuade and encourage practitioners to accept that their work is crucially important. We believe, as did Desmond Nuttall, that the ways in which schools contribute to, fit with and, in the longer term, help shape our society, is of central concern. It behoves us, therefore, as researchers in this field to act as advocates on behalf of practitioners and, where appropriate, to represent their case to policy maker's for we have seen—as have few others—many instances of the difficulty and the worth of their work.

Postscript

The issues identified in this chapter—the stability of results over time, differential effects within a school and the effects of context—have become major considerations in school-effectiveness work. The next chapter, which reports on a major empirical investigation, continues the discussion.

13

Differential Effectiveness[1]

Introduction

As noted in the last chapter, Desmond Nuttall, Pam Sammons, Sally Thomas and I had become increasingly interested in the question of differential school effectiveness. We had participated in a series of seminars on school effectiveness research funded by the Economic and Social Research Council (ESRC). Both the review prepared for the series (subsequently published in Sammons et al., 1996a) and the seminar discussions focused on the need to 'unpack' the notion of consistency of school effectiveness and to address, in particular, the three themes that were introduced in the last chapter: consistency in promoting different educational outcomes; stability over time; and differential effects. We had also applied for funds to carry out a large-scale study of secondary schools capable of providing data which could answer these questions. The need for such research had been highlighted by the debate over the British government's policy of encouraging 'league tables' of schools' raw examination results in order to provide indicators of performance and to aid the identification of so-called 'failing schools'. In 1993, therefore, we embarked upon an ESRC-funded 30-month study. Desmond Nuttall tragically died early in the project, but the work was continued by Pam Sammons, Sally Thomas and myself. The project was

---

1 The major work on which this chapter is based is *'Forging Links: Effective Schools and Effective Departments'*. The first author is Pam Sammons.

superbly led by Pam Sammons, who had worked with me on the School Matters *study some fifteen years earlier. Sally Thomas was responsible for the multilevel modelling analyses. The project resulted in a formal report to the ESRC, a series of journal papers and a book—Sammons, Thomas and Mortimore, 1997a). This chapter is drawn from all these sources.*

The 'Differential Secondary School Effectiveness' project had three major objectives:

- To extend current knowledge about the size, extent and stability over time of differences between secondary schools in their overall effectiveness in promoting students' GCSE attainments. The research investigated the applicability of the concept of overall school effectiveness to the secondary sector and whether schools could be divided validly into broadly effective or ineffective groups.

- To explore the extent of internal variations in school effectiveness at the departmental level and for different groups of students classified by gender, eligibility for free school meals, ethnic group and by prior attainment. Comparisons of departmental, group and school differences were made in order to establish the extent to which schools are differentially effective in certain subjects and for particular groups. The focus was thus on consistency in schools' effects on different outcomes and for different groups of students.

- To investigate the reasons for any differences in effectiveness. The extent of overall school differences in effectiveness and differences at the departmental level were explored in relation to school and departmental organization and other process characteristics. In particular, the study investigated whether variations in school and departmental processes are important in accounting for better overall GCSE performance and performance in specific subjects.

   These issues all have important implications for policy makers and practitioners concerned with evaluating school performance. They are also areas which have been identified from reviews of the academic literature as crucial to the further development of both theory and practice in the field. After a brief summary of the methodology and the results of the study, this chapter considers the implications of the research for school improvement work.

Methodology

The Differential Secondary School Effectiveness project involved the detailed multilevel analysis of examination results for a large sample covering 94 schools and nearly 18,000 students over three years (1990–1992). Academic effectiveness was explored using seven measures of GCSE outcomes: total GCSE performance score, and six subjects—English, English literature, French, history, mathematics and science. In each case we used the highest grade in any science subject. These analyses were used to develop models of school and departmental effectiveness and to allow the simultaneous examination of stability, consistency and differential effectiveness.

We also conducted qualitative case studies of 6 schools and 30 departments. The case study schools were chosen from three groups (*academically more effective, academically ineffective,* and *highly mixed effects* in different subjects). Schools in these groups had significant, stable and consistent effects on students' GCSE outcomes. Using the language of school effectiveness researchers these schools were the 'outliers'. We interviewed head teachers (HTs), deputy head teachers (DHTs) and heads of departments (HoDs) to obtain information about the past (5 years before) and the current school and departmental policies and practices. This retrospective focus enabled us to look at the links between the policies and practices and academic performance (as measured by GCSE results for previous student cohorts).

The case studies also provided valuable indications about differences between *more* and *less* effective schools and departments, as well as pointers about what might have caused the positive and negative results. They helped us in the development of questionnaires (for HTs and two subject HoDs) for all project schools to enable us to test systematically the relationships between what schools did and their GCSE results.

Results

Four of the five questions addressed by the research were the focus of Phase I of the study:

The questions—and our answers—are taken in turn.

- *Are differences between departments in their effects upon students' GCSE attainments in selected subjects greater or less than differences between secondary schools in their overall effects upon students' total GCSE examination scores?*

Examination data were analysed for each of three years (1990, 1991, 1992) individually and also over the three years. Just over six per cent of the total variance in total GCSE performance scores was found to be attributable to differences between schools in the three-year analysis (variance due to changes in results over time were estimated separately). The results indicated the existence of important (educationally and statistically significant) differences between schools in their relative effectiveness in promoting GCSE performance *after* taking account of students' prior attainment and background characteristics. The difference between the most and the least effective school was 12 GCSE points in the three-year model, the equivalent of more than two extra GCSE passes at grade C, or between six grade D and six grade B GCSEs. For 11 of the 94 schools, the difference exceeded 10 points.

Evidence of marked departmental differences for six GCSE subjects was also found (differences exceeding one GCSE grade in size). In some subjects (e.g. French, history, English literature), the variation attributable to schools (in the three-year analyses) was larger than the variation in total GCSE performance scores. Thus, the conclusion must be that the evidence of departmental differences is greater than school effects on an overall measure of performance for these three subjects, but less in the three core curriculum subjects (English [language], mathematics and science).

• *Is there any evidence that some schools are generally more effective in promoting students' attainment at GCSE and that others are less effective in most areas, or is the concept of overall effectiveness too simplistic for the secondary age group?*

The general tendency which we found was for schools which were effective in promoting one outcome to be effective in other outcomes. The associations, however, were much stronger for some subjects than others and they were by no means perfect (ranging from 0.20 to 0.72). This means that, in some schools, particular departments were markedly more (or less) effective than others.

Only a minority of schools (around 25–30%) were found to be significantly more or less effective in overall performance and subject results in any single year. Using the stringent criteria employed for categorizing schools for the selection of case studies over three years, however, the figure was much lower (only 9%). So, for most schools, we conclude that clear-cut distinctions were not possible, pointing to the complexity of judging performance. Therefore, in secondary school studies it may be more valid to qualify the term 'school effectiveness' to 'school and departmental effectiveness'.

• *Is there any evidence of differential effectiveness in terms of GCSE attainments for different groups of students (divided by eligibility for free school meals, ethnicity and prior attainment level)?*

Clear evidence of differential effects was identified both for the total GCSE score and separate subjects. It was most notable for students of different levels of prior attainment at intake, and for those of different ethnic backgrounds. Some evidence of differential effects was also found for socio-economic disadvantage and gender (for details see Thomas et al., 1997a).

Nonetheless, we found that, overall, *all* students in more effective schools and departments were likely to perform relatively well at GCSE, but some groups (e.g. those not socio-economically disadvantaged) performed especially well. In contrast, *all* students in ineffective schools and departments were likely to perform relatively poorly at GCSE, though the effect was less marked for some ethnic groups.

These results provide no evidence that more effective schools closed the gap in achievement between different student groups—they did not 'compensate' for society. Our conclusions are broadly in line with those of our earlier primary school study, which indicated that effective schools tend to 'jack up' the performance of all students (Mortimore et al., 1988a). However, they also show that, within schools, school and departmental effects (positive and negative) can be stronger for some groups.

- *If schools are differentially effective at the departmental level and/or for different groups of students, is the pattern of differences stable from year to year?*

We explored the stability of school and departmental effects across three years. All correlations between effects in different years were positive and significant but many were far from perfect (9 out of 21 being under 0.60, with a range from 0.38 to 0.92). Effects on total GCSE performance score were relatively stable from one year to another (correlations between 0.82 and 0.88), but effects on subject results were less stable, and French particularly unstable. As would be expected, correlations across three years (1990–1992) were lower than between pairs of consecutive years, pointing to the need to look at variations over longer time periods. Despite the large sample size of over 90 schools, the small numbers of students in particular groups in each year meant that it was not appropriate to examine stability in school/departmental effects for different student groups in detail.

Implications for judging school effectiveness

The results of Phase I demonstrate the need for studies of school effectiveness to use longitudinal data and multilevel techniques to identify the proportion of variance attributable to schools or departments, after making appropriate adjustment for the impact of relevant background factors (particularly prior attainment, but also other factors) at the student level. The benefits of investigating outcomes over several years is also apparent, so that changes over time can be modelled. Three-level models incorporating student (level 1), year (level 2) and school (level 3) enable the separation of school and year effects and provide better estimates of the relative progress made by students attending different schools (Gray et al., 1995).

Our results also demonstrate the value of using several measures, including total GCSE performance score (which exhibits greater stability in school effects over time) and separate subject scores, to provide a more comprehensive account of schools' academic effectiveness. The results also point to the complexity of making overall judgements about school effectiveness (see also Gray, 1990; Gray & Wilcox, 1995; Mortimore & Stone, 1991; Reynolds, 1995a; Reynolds et al., 1995; Silver, 1994, on the broader topics of making judgements about 'good' or 'bad' schools and evaluating performance). This project focused explicitly on *academic* effectiveness as measured by GCSE performance and the results indicate that a small number of schools were outliers (consistently academically more effective or ineffective over several years) but that, for most schools, the results were far less clear cut and some had mixed effects (effective and ineffective departments co-existing in the same school).

The results, in line with Goldstein and Thomas's (1996) conclusions, indicate that judgements about school performance and relative effectiveness need to be made with caution and there is little justification for 'league table' approaches to the presentation of performance data. Reference to the confidence limits attached to estimates of effectiveness is needed to establish the statistical significance of any apparent differences. It is thus possible to distinguish between schools with significantly better or worse than predicted results over a particular period, but inappropriate to rank results (Sammons et al., 1994c; Thomas & Mortimore, 1995).

In addition, the findings support and extend other secondary school analyses (Goldstein et al., 1993; Jesson & Gray, 1991; Nuttall et al., 1989) which point to the impact of differential effectiveness. We found evidence of significant internal variations in schools' academic effectiveness for different student groups. Findings concerning differential effectiveness have important implications for those concerned with equity issues in schooling. Differential effects were most notable for students with different levels of prior attainment and the results point to the importance of including finely differentiated measures of prior attainment in order to make adequate control for differences in intake (Jesson & Gray, 1991). Our findings on differential effectiveness point to the need to consider explicitly such internal variations in performance.

In our view, *effectiveness is best seen as a feature which is outcome and time specific*, because some schools are effective in promoting student performance in one subject matter domain but not in others, and some schools have significantly positive or negative effects in one year, but not others. In line with Gray et al.'s (1995) analyses, the results point to the importance of examining trends over time in order to identify outliers and those exhibiting improvement or relative decline.

In addition to adopting the criteria for adequate studies of schooling outlined by Scheerens (1992, 1995), we conclude that judgements about schools' effectiveness need to address three questions:

- Effective in promoting which outcomes?
- Effective over what time period?
- Effective for whom? (Sammons, 1995, p. 32).

Accounting for variations in effectiveness
The fifth question addressed was:

- *What factors to do with school status and processes relate to differences between secondary schools in effectiveness in promoting GCSE attainment? In particular, is there evidence that different factors and processes are important in promoting good results for different departments?*

The second and third phases of the research study focused on how to account for school and departmental differences in secondary schools' effects, both in terms of overall academic effectiveness and effectiveness in promoting performance in specific subjects using both qualitative and quantitative techniques.

In Phase II, detailed qualitative case studies of outlier schools and departments examined the characteristics and processes operating in more and less effective schools and departments (see Sammons et al., 1995a, 1995b, 1995e). The results indicated that both factors to do with school organization, management (including leadership) and culture, as well as departmental processes (particularly team work and the quality of teaching), were of importance in differentiating more and less effective institutions. There was no clear evidence, however, that different factors and processes were important in promoting good results for different departments. Moreover, factors such as choice of examination boards and grouping policies were not found to differentiate between more and less effective departments, although a general emphasis on examination entry and monitoring of performance was important. Conflict and personality clashes were a source of significant problems in less effective departments and—in the SMTs—of less effective schools. Shortages of qualified staff and difficulties in retaining staff were problems in some ineffective departments. In others, a core of long-serving, weak teaching staff were reported to be a source of difficulties. High levels of staff absence, low morale and low expectations were strong features of less effective schools and departments.

The analyses of interviews with HoDs, HTs and DHTs demonstrated the need to focus explicitly on the views and experiences of middle managers (a neglected group in school effectiveness research, as Brown & Rutherford [1995] note). The retrospective focus of the interviews proved illuminating in helping to identify factors related to change and improvement, as well as to effectiveness. Change in leadership (of HT or HoD) was found to be one factor of particular relevance. Schools from the 'mixed' group (in which both academically effective and ineffective departments co-exist in the same institution) were of particular interest, as case studies and provide rich subjects for those concerned with school improvement. They also indicate that in some schools one or two 'key' departments were perceived to be more effective and played a leading role for other departments (e.g. producing policy documents on matters such as marking or homework which were later adopted as school policy).

Aspects found to be of particular importance in the case studies were:

- The importance of school and departmental histories and the impact of change
- High expectations
- Academic emphasis—including examination entry policy and monitoring
- Shared vision/goals
- The HT's and HoDs' roles and leadership
- An effective SMT
- The quality of teaching
- Parental involvement and support

The Phase II results support Reynold's (1992) view on the value of using case study approaches in school effectiveness research. They are broadly in line with those reported by Harris et al. (1995) in their recent study of effective departments in six secondary schools in a West Country city. However, Harris et al. found that, although the schools in which the more effective departments were located were 'broadly supportive', this was not a major factor in their success. The results of our case studies draw more attention to the importance of the facilitating (or otherwise) nature of whole school context, the leadership of the HT and the role of the SMT. This may be a reflection of the selection of case studies (covering both more and less effective examples, rather than concentrating only on effective departments). Whilst the departmental level was undoubtedly very important, in some schools it was apparently 'easier' for all departments to function effectively, due to better leadership, a more supportive context, shared whole school emphasis on the importance of student learning and achievement, and the apparently mutually beneficial impact of successful departments supporting each others' efforts. Conversely, in other schools it was 'harder' for departments to be effective due to lack of overall leadership and shared goals and vision, poor expectations and inconsistent approaches. The results support Scheeren's (1992) view that higher level conditions (school and departmental) facilitate lower level conditions, particularly the quality of teaching, which impact directly on student outcomes.

The third phase was used to investigate, amongst a larger sample of schools and departments (n = 55), the applicability and generalizability of the results of the qualitative case studies. It involved a questionnaire survey of HTs and HoDs of English and mathematics (for details see Sammons et al., 1995a).

HTs' and HoDs' perceptions of factors which *ought* to be taken into account in judging school or departmental effectiveness, and their views of factors which influenced their school's and department's effectiveness, were analysed. Factors regarded as important for judging *school* effectiveness were: good progress for students of all ability levels; high quality teaching; high expectations of students; positive interpersonal relationships for staff and students; and the creation of a positive climate for learning.

Factors regarded as important in judging *departmental* effectiveness by HoDs were: quality of teaching; team work; commitment/enthusiasm of teaching staff; enjoyment/interest of students; and high expectations of students.

Views about what contributed to the effectiveness of their school and (for HoDs) their department and the barriers to greater effectiveness were also analysed. For HTs, a strong and cohesive SMT was cited most frequently. This was followed by staff and students' shared belief that the school is primarily a place for teaching and learning; the quality of the HTs' leadership; and high quality teaching. For HoDs the commitment and enthusiasm of teaching staff, good leadership by HoDs, students feeling valued as people, high quality teaching and staff stability in post were more important, although around half also drew attention to the positive impact of the HT and the SMT.

Our analyses revealed that a relatively limited set of process indicators accounted for most (and for some outcomes all) of the school level variation in GCSE results. There were also indications of greater similarity in findings concerning the relationships between school and departmental processes for English and total GCSE performance score than for mathematics (the Phase I results showed a stronger correlation between schools' effects on English and total GCSE score than between effects on mathematics and total GCSE score). This supports the view that English departments may have a particularly important impact on a school's overall academic effectiveness.

Overall, the findings from Phase III were broadly in line with those found from the qualitative case studies. However, Phase III drew more attention to the value of consistency and a student-centred approach. Nine interdependent aspects concerning mechanisms of school and departmental effectiveness were highlighted:

- High expectations
- Strong academic emphasis
- Shared vision/goals
- The HT's and HoDs' roles and leadership
- An effective SMT
- Consistency in approach
- Quality of teaching
- A student-centred approach
- Parental involvement and support

Whilst this project focused on academic effectiveness, it is relevant that HTs' and HoDs' evaluation of their school's performance in terms of non-academic outcomes (student behaviour, attendance and motivation) were significantly related to effectiveness at GCSE, especially total performance score. Behaviour, attendance and motivation are important outcomes in their own right and are likely to be influenced by, and themselves influence, academic performance.

Implications of the data

The findings point to the value of longitudinal data and multilevel techniques, the importance of making appropriate control for differences between schools in their student intakes (using adequate measures of prior attainment and relevant background factors, especially gender, socio-economic disadvantage and ethnicity), and the need to examine outcomes over several years. We found significant evidence of the importance of using both an overall measure of academic outcomes (such as total GCSE performance score) and performance in different subjects in order to obtain a comprehensive picture of academic effectiveness.

Growing concern has been expressed amongst politicians and the wider public about 'educational standards', particularly levels of literacy and numeracy over the last twenty years. Regular reports that school leavers lack the skills needed by employers still appear in the contemporary press. This concern is not unique to the UK system, although to practitioners it sometimes seems as though 'teacher bashing' is a peculiarly English phenomenon! (The term 'English' is used deliberately, for studies suggest that public satisfaction may be higher in Scotland). Visitors to countries such as the US, Canada, New Zealand or Australia, however, will also hear debates about 'failing schools' and falling educational standards that have a very familiar ring.

In fact, there is little hard evidence about whether educational standards have actually fallen—reliable information enabling comparisons over decades simply is not available. The tendency to look back to a mythical 'golden age' ignores the trend for many more young people to stay on at school and enter further and higher education, and there can be no doubt that access to educational qualifications has widened considerably, particularly for girls. The introduction of the GCSE, removing the two-tier GCE/CSE divide, is generally regarded as having had a beneficial impact, and a gently rising trend in GCSE performance has been evident over the last decade.

These improvements in educational opportunities should be welcomed and are a cause for celebration—but there is no room for complacency (see the Labour Literacy Taskforce, 1997, for example). Although we do not think there is convincing evidence that standards have fallen in the UK, international comparisons strongly suggest that our educational system is not working to maintain competitiveness with other nations as well as it should. Too few young people obtain vocationally relevant qualifications and, although substantially more enter higher education than previously, the proportion remains lower than in most post-industrial societies. It must, however, be recognized that international comparisons are fraught with difficulties (Goldstein, 1996). In areas such as mathematics, recent reviews suggest that our education system continues to serve more able students well, but that it has a much longer 'trailing edge' than is evident in many other countries, particularly the 'tiger' economies of the Pacific rim (Reynolds & Farrell, 1996). While the reasons which underlie these differences are likely to be complex and probably reflect cultural traditions and researching as much as variations in the processes of schooling, such international comparisons suggest that we should pay much more attention to ways of raising standards for average and below average students.

There is, therefore, a growing awareness that our current education system continues to serve the bottom 30 per cent of our young people relatively poorly. This has important equal opportunities as well as economic implications. Such students are over-represented in inner-city areas and there is considerable concern about the long-term social consequences of their educational under-achievement. Additionally, poor and ethnic minority students are geographically concentrated in such areas and thus are disproportionately affected. There are also growing gender differences in achievement at GCSE, which can be seen as the gateway or, for those failing to gain A–C grades, the stumbling block to continuing in education after age 16. Gender, ethnic and socio-economic factors do not operate in isolation, however, and in recent years the poor achievement of white working-class and Afro-Caribbean boys has attracted much media attention (Gillborn & Gipps, 1996; Sammons, 1995). Allied to problems of academic under-performance, there is growing concern about increasing behaviour and attendance problems in schools, both amongst the staff as well as the wider public (Barber & Dann, 1996). Tragedies such as the shooting of primary pupils at Dunblane and the murder of London head teacher Stephen Lawrence, and the well-publicized disruption at The Ridings School in Yorkshire, appear to have induced a sense of moral panic in the public at large. Moreover, there is growing evidence that the number of exclusions has risen from 1991 onwards (Gillborn & Gipps, 1996; *Times Educational Supplement*, 9 November 1996, p. 1).

There are, of course, strong links between students' academic achievement, motivation, behaviour, attendance and self-esteem. These links are often reciprocal, poor attainment increasing the risk of subsequent poor behaviour and attendance and vice versa (Mortimore et al., 1988a). As we have argued elsewhere, there are strong arguments for focusing on these links, since programmes which address only one aspect in isolation, be it academic achievement, attendance, behaviour or self-esteem, are liable to have less impact in the long term. A failure to address the needs of the 'trailing edge' has serious consequences for democracy and social cohesion, as is demonstrated by the rise of an increasingly alienated underclass of mainly male, young, unemployed people concentrated in decaying, inner-city environments with rising crime rates.

School effectiveness research has indicated that there are greater variations between schools in their effectiveness in the UK than in many other education systems where school differences are far smaller (Reynolds, 1995a). The results of our study of departmental differences in secondary school effectiveness are highly relevant to all those concerned with raising educational standards and school improvement. We have identified the existence of both statistically and—more importantly—educationally significant differences in academic effectiveness between schools. We have also highlighted the need to look at within-school differences in effectiveness, and our case studies showed links with behaviour and attendance patterns. Because of the nature of the student population we studied, our data are of particular relevance to those concerned with raising educational standards for average and below average groups, and to those committed to improving the quality of schooling in socio-economically disadvantaged and ethnically diverse urban areas.

School improvement has been defined as 'a strategy for educational change that enhances student outcomes as well as strengthening the school's capacity for managing change' (Hopkins, 1994a, p. 3). In this chapter, therefore, we will examine the implications of our research for the various partners involved in educational policy making and the delivery of education in schools, as well as for the consumers of the service—the students and their parents.

Implications for policy makers—government and LEAs

The last two decades have seen many important and controversial changes to the education system. For secondary schools the most significant have probably been those arising from the implementation of the Education Reform Act (1988) leading to greater autonomy and accountability, via the introduction of LMS and open enrolment, the national curriculum and associated national assessment (NC and NA) at KS3, and national publication of examination results from 1992—the so-called 'league table' policy. Changes in teacher pay and conditions (e.g. the introduction of directed time) and the creation of the Office for Standards in Education (OFSTED) and the development of a national frame-work for regular inspection on a four-year cycle have also been highly influen-tial, along with the identification of 'failing' schools and of those with serious weaknesses requiring 'special measures'.

Detailed discussion of these changes is beyond the scope of this chapter—see Barber, 1996a, 1996b, for recent analyses of these developments. In brief, how-ever, they have involved attempts to apply market forces to education as outlined in the White Paper, *Choice and Diversity* (Department for Education, 1992). It was claimed that the combination of open enrolment (with student numbers dri-ving funding formulae) and the publication of league tables of NA and public examination results would lead to the 'withering away' of 'poor' schools if they failed to improve, because parents would choose to send their children to schools with better results. Significantly, nothing was said about the impact of this poli-cy for the quality of education available to students attending these schools dur-ing this process of withering! In the early 1990s, government policy substantially reduced the powers of LEAs, including the abolition of the administrative body for the capital, the Inner London Education Authority in the capital (and the future and role of LEAs remained in some doubt). Government policy also reduced the LEA support available to schools, through both local management of schools (LMS) and the encouragement of schools to opt out of local control by becoming grant maintained (GM). The existence of greater diversity in schools (the previous Prime Minister's advocacy of a 'grammar' school in every town) was ostensibly designed to make schools more responsive to local needs and to allow greater consumer choice.

Although many of the changes outlined here were intended to make schools more autonomous and to encourage diversity, they also involved a great increase in the powers and responsibilities of the Secretary of State and greater central-ization and standardization (for example, of the curriculum, of funding arrange-ments, and a much higher profile for inspection). As a result, the trend towards greater autonomy of individual schools is in tension with the trend towards cen-tralization, standardization and control; likewise, the move towards increasing accountability at the individual school level and the reduction in powers of the LEA, which in turn erodes accountability to the local electorate. Furthermore, there is a tension between the policy of enhancing parental choice, and encour-aging diversity amongst schools in order to widen such choice, and the policy of promoting selection which inevitably enhances schools' abilities to choose students and, therefore, reduces options for the majority.

Our research contains a number of important messages for policy makers concerned with raising educational standards. These include implications for: the judgement of performance and mechanisms for ensuring accountability; the inspection process and teacher training; and the intake and researching of schools.

Judging school performance

It is evident from the findings of our secondary school research that schools do indeed differ in their effectiveness. Even within the relatively socio-economically disadvantaged and ethnically diverse context of inner London, some schools were much better than others at promoting their students' academic outcomes over several years. As the study illustrates, the differences for individual students in terms of GCSE results could be striking (at the most extreme, differences for the average student between six Grade Ds and six Grade Bs). Some students' future educational and employment prospects were significantly enhanced by their positive educational experiences, whilst others were much less fortunate. As in an earlier primary school study (Mortimore et al., 1988a), we can conclude that secondary schools also matter. Even in the face of very difficult circumstances, schools can have a beneficial impact on their students' lives. It is vitally important that schools receive feedback about their effectiveness, because such information can help them evaluate their performance, set targets, assist in school development planning and stimulate improvement initiatives.

League tables and value added

Our study also makes it quite clear that the current publication of raw 'league tables' of schools' public examination results is not justified as a mechanism for accountability. As we have shown, schools vary markedly in the nature of their student intakes and valid comparisons cannot be made without reference to this. There is a long tradition of sociological and educational research (for a review of this see Sammons et al., 1994c) which demonstrates the strength of relationships between students' background characteristics, particularly socio-economic factors such as parents' education, occupation and income, and their educational outcomes. It is unrealistic to expect schools to compensate for all the ills of society. Raw league tables make invalid comparisons because they are not conducted on a 'like with like' basis. Schools in affluent suburban areas are compared with those receiving students from very different backgrounds in inner-city areas. Such comparisons are likely to lead to complacency on the part of more advantaged schools and demoralization on the part of staff in schools serving disadvantaged areas which face very different challenges. We must stress that this is not to condone low expectations of students by staff in such schools. Rather, we argue that judgements about performance should take account of differences in intake so that comparisons are only made between schools receiving similar kinds of students.

One of the purposes of research was to explore how value-added approaches can be used to study school effectiveness. This technique focuses on student progress over time (for example, from secondary transfer at age 11 to the end of compulsory schooling) and seeks to separate a schools' contribution from that which relates to its intake, by controlling for prior attainment and other background factors. Such information shows whether students in a given school made more or less progress than similar students in other schools. We argue that such value-added information is much more useful to practitioners in schools than raw league tables, and also is more relevant to inspectors and those concerned with accountability and promoting school improvement. We believe strongly that the proper criteria for measuring school effectiveness is their impact on students' educational outcomes, and that measures of academic progress are an important indicator. Schools are thus held accountable for what they are designed to influence—students' progress—which can be seen as a fundamental purpose of education. Schools should not be held responsible for all the pre-existing inequalities in society (Mortimore et al., 1994c).

The Office for Standards in Education has shown some interest in the development of contextualized measures of secondary school performance (Sammons et al., 1994c) and, after some initial reluctance, the Department for Education (1995) and the School Curriculum and Assessment Authority (1995) have accepted the need for value-added measures. However, there has been considerable reluctance to take on board the message from school effectiveness research that, in addition to prior attainment, other factors to do with students' backgrounds (most notably socio-economic disadvantage as measured by eligibility for free school meals, but also gender) exert an influence. Our research shows that such factors continue to influence students' GCSE results. Ignoring such differences inevitably penalizes inner-city schools (Willms 1992; Sammons, 1994c) and does nothing to remove the link between socio-economic disadvantage and school achievement. In order to be accepted by practitioners, it is vital that school comparisons are seen to be fair.

Arguments against value-added approaches have stressed the need for 'simplicity' (although, complexity appears to be quite acceptable in other areas, such as economic modelling or police pay formulae!) There is, however, an important distinction between simplicity and the adoption of simplistic—but inappropriate—solutions. Value-added approaches have been used to give feedback about school performance for over a decade and, in our experience, both practitioners and parents accept the message that student progress is at the heart of an effective school. Examples of LEAs which have developed value-added indicators of performance include pioneering work by the former ILEA (later extended by the Association of Metropolitan Authorities), Lancashire, Shropshire, Suffolk, and Surrey. The Durham University system of examination analyses has also operated in many parts of the country and gives schools value-added feedback on A-level performance and, in some cases, GCSE. In our experience the development of such measures has been welcomed by schools, which are keen to obtain comparative feedback about their performance (FitzGibbon, 1991b, 1992; Thomas & Mortimore, 1996).

It is important to stress, however, that ranking schools on the basis of their value-added GCSE results (as is the practice in raw league tables) is not justified (Goldstein et al., 1993; Goldstein & Thomas, 1996; Sammons et al., 1993b). It is possible to identify schools in which students' GCSE results were significantly better or worse than predicted on the basis of intake. For many schools, however, GCSE results were in line with those predicted, and thus could not be differentiated. The fine distinctions implied by rank ordering are simply not statistically valid, as there may be no statistically significant differences between quite big clusters of schools.

In addition, our analyses of GCSE performance demonstrate that comparisons of schools based on only one measure (the percentage gaining five A–C GCSE grades) are inadequate. Even using value-added approaches, reliance on only one measure will obscure the existence of internal variations in effectiveness. As our results illustrate, there can be marked variations in effectiveness in different GCSE subjects, pointing to the importance of the departmental level of effectiveness. Although a few 'outliers' can be identified (broadly effective or broadly ineffective across a range of subjects), the situation is much more complex in most schools. Indeed, in some institutions we found highly effective and highly ineffective co-existing departments. The use of 'one overall measure' can obscure such internal variations. For most schools, simplistic distinctions such as 'good' or 'bad' are, therefore, inappropriate. We conclude that the concept of school effectiveness should generally be amended to that of school and departmental effectiveness.

Trends over time

Our research also highlights the need to look at school performance across several years, three years being the minimum required to identify trends and five providing a better picture (Gray et al., 1996). We argue that value-added information about trends is much more useful to practitioners as well as to parents (whose children usually spend five years in one secondary school before entering for GCSEs). It is also more relevant for inspectors concerned with judging the quality of education provided and with identifying areas for improvement.

The question of differential effectiveness is also relevant for those concerned with social justice and democracy. Is a school equally effective for different student groups or for boys or girls? How do those of different ethnic or socio-economic backgrounds and those who enter secondary schooling with below or above average prior attainment fare?

We recommend that either nationally or at LEA level, as is already done very successfully in some areas, appropriate value-added frameworks be developed which will provide schools with good quality comparative information about their performance on a year-by-year basis. Such information should use both an overall indicator (such as total GCSE performance score) and performance in core subjects (English, mathematics and science). In this context, we note the work of the SCAA value-added working group (SCAA, 1995). However, we believe that the attempt to use national assessment data for these purposes is problematic. Such measures were not designed with the requirements of establishing a value-added framework in mind and therefore may not provide sufficiently detailed information about student attainment on entry to secondary school. The use of standardized assessments in reading and mathematics, which are good predictors of later GCSE results, are infinitely preferable. IQ-type measures, particularly if not taken at entry, are also considered inappropriate, because they do not relate to the curriculum. Our study has demonstrated the continuing strength of socio-economic and other background influences. Value-added frameworks should be established which explicitly model such effects. Only in this way can we be confident that like is properly being compared with like.

Intake and researching of schools

School effectiveness research has revealed the importance of taking account of the differences between schools in their intakes. In our study we were able to demonstrate the existence of substantial differences between schools in the prior attainments of their students at age 11, as well as in measures of socio-economic and ethnic diversity. Although resources were not identified as a key factor influencing school effectiveness, some schools had experienced great difficulties in attracting and retaining experienced and qualified staff. This has obvious implications for the quality and consistency of students' learning experiences. Of course, such difficulties may be as much a symptom as a cause of ineffectiveness in some schools. Nonetheless, they remain powerful barriers to improvement. Sadly, in one of our studies drawn from the 'highly ineffective' group, finally having in-post the full complement of staff was cited as perhaps the major achievement of the new head's time in the school!

The challenges faced by schools in socio-economically disadvantaged areas require serious recognition. Ways of improving such schools' attractiveness to teachers need to be developed. Current policies—such as the publication of raw league tables—are likely to add to staff demoralization in such areas. This tends to discourage teachers from applying for jobs in these schools because of the risk of association with institutions which are more likely to be identified as 'failing' or requiring special measures. The rewards for head teachers in such schools also need to be improved, given the evidence reported in recent years of growing difficulties in attracting good candidates. Although resources are certainly not the answer to all educational problems, ways of ensuring that inner-city schools can attract and retain good staff at all levels need to be identified and given a high priority.

Experience of the educational priority policies of the 1970s suggests that it is important that additional resources do not reward schools with poor results (Sammons et al., 1983). Under LMS, however, there are restrictions which limit LEAs' abilities to direct additional resources to schools which serve students with additional educational needs. Some LEAs make no provision; many use crude measures of the percentage of students eligible for free school meals. The way such funding formulae are applied, however, means that students with the same characteristics in different areas will attract different resources to their schools (Sammons, 1993). An additional problem is that there is no mechanism for ensuring that any resources allocated to schools on the basis of their students' special needs are actually used to benefit those students—except in the case of statemented children. Given the strong links, illustrated by this study but also found in many others, between low levels of attainment at age 11 and students' GCSE results, and the impact of other factors such as low family income, we think there is a very strong case for the development of a national funding formula for schools. This should take into account the *risk* of low achievement and direct extra resources to schools which serve higher numbers of such students. This would remove the geographical 'lottery' which currently characterizes the operation of LMS. If such a formula were based on student intakes to school (e.g. at secondary transfer at 11, probably using low KS2 results as a basis), the danger of rewarding poor past performance would be eliminated. There would be an additional advantage to such a system, since it would help to counteract the 'market forces' pressure on schools to recruit high attaining, non-disadvantaged students who are likely to do well at GCSE and thus boost a school's raw league table position. To put it crudely, under the present system, schools which can recruit more than average numbers of middle-class girls will tend to shine; schools which have the most disadvantaged students cannot.

Of course, extra resources by themselves will be no guarantee of effectiveness (a point we discuss in more depth later). It is *vital* that such resources are specifically targeted at students in most need. This was a crucial weakness of earlier educational priority policies of the 1970s and 1980s (Sammons, 1993; Sammons et al., 1983), and remains a weakness in the way resources are allocated for special educational needs under LMS. Students falling below a certain level of performance could be identified as at risk of low attainment or viewed as entitled to extra provision (probably in literacy and numeracy), designed to bring low attaining first- and second-year students up to a specified level which would enable them to benefit more fully from the rest of the secondary curriculum. The design of special programmes for such groups, if used positively, could help to raise, rather than depress, teachers' expectations.

The ways in which resources could be so targeted have been clearly demonstrated by the success of the Reading Recovery programme with younger age groups (Sylva and Hurry, 1995). Given the strong link between poor attainment (especially in reading, and for boys) and low self-esteem, in addition to behaviour and attendance problems, intervention in the early years of secondary schooling and careful monitoring of student progress should have beneficial effects on a range of student outcomes, not only academic performance. The deliberate targeting of resources, on the basis of education need to benefit those students who are the 'trailing' edge in our system and who are at most risk of becoming the so-called 'disaffected (and disappeared)' (Barber, 1996a), would help to ensure that schools in the most difficult circumstances had better odds in the struggle to raise standards.

In this study we focus on the implications of our research for secondary schools in particular. Nonetheless, our other studies have pointed to the importance of primary education and the variations in effectiveness of such schools (Mortimore et al., 1988a). We have also drawn attention to the long-term impact of primary schools (Sammons et al., 1995c) on later GCSE results. Early identification of children with low levels of reading attainment in particular (for example, via

Reading Recovery schemes) will prove most cost-effective in the long term and enable students to progress into secondary schooling more readily (Sylva and Hurry, 1995). Again, the arguments we have made about the need to provide and target resources for secondary schools also apply to the primary sector.

Selection

Our research, as noted earlier, demonstrates the strong links between individual student intake characteristics and academic results. In addition, we found some indications of *contextual* effects related to the proportion of disadvantaged students (those eligible for free school meals) in a school, in spite of the fact that our sample came from an inner-city area well known for encouraging a balanced intake. The implication of our findings is that, in schools with a higher concentration of disadvantaged students, the performance of all students, regardless of their own background, tends to be depressed. This tendency was most evident for performance in English at GCSE, reflecting the stronger links between performance in this subject and background. We would argue that this tendency would be more pronounced in areas where there are greater variations between schools in their intakes, especially where there are selective schools.

The early *Fifteen Thousand Hours* study in inner London (Rutter et al., 1979a) and work in Scotland (Willms, 1986) has also drawn attention to the impact of socio-economic and academic balance in schools. Of course, schools' intakes vary greatly according to the socio-economic characteristics of their local catchment areas. But the influence of other factors, such as the availability of alternative schools, also has an important effect. Schools in middle-class suburbs usually have a more favourable academic balance. Even without selection, in some areas true 'comprehensives' may be hard to find. However, where selection operates, local comprehensives are creamed of the more able students. Current plans to increase schools' abilities to select their students (the most extreme being proposals for a grammar school in every town) inevitably will mean that the majority of other (non-selective) schools will have less balanced intakes.

As Mortimore (1995c) has argued, the beneficial influence of a balance of academically able students in a school 'gives a powerful boost to the ethos of the school and thus to its ability to be effective and promote progress'. Most teachers also value the opportunity for a genuine balance of teaching assignments (in this research we found that academic balance was an important issue for many respondents). Unfortunately, although research as well as practitioners' experience suggest that academic balance is desirable, the recent policy emphasis on diversity has promoted the opposite trend. Proposals to increase selection would, we believe, tend to increase the wide gap in performance (already wider in the UK than in many other countries) between the highest and lowest performing students rather than reduce it. This would exacerbate the problem of the 'trailing edge' of the bottom 30 per cent of students. Furthermore, as we have noted before, the variation between schools is also substantially larger in the UK than in many other systems. Increasing selection could thus also serve to widen the 'trailing edge' of schools as well as of students.

There is, unfortunately, no easy solution to this problem. How can the maximum academic balance of students be encouraged for the maximum number of schools, thus benefiting the academic achievement of the majority of students, whilst, at the same time, allowing the flexibility of parental choice? Can a balance between diversity and equity be encouraged which, as Barber (1996a) has suggested, will avoid the re-creation of a two-tier system of schools with the accompanying sense of failure for the majority of children at 11-plus, and the consequent reduction in their choice of schools which a fully selective system inevitably creates?

LEAs no longer have the power to intervene in admission arrangements in the way they once did. In these circumstances, how can a satisfactory overall pattern of schools be created? One possible solution may be to allow only partial selection of academically high attaining students (perhaps the maximum of 15 per cent currently allowed for GM schools), whilst at the same time allocating significant extra resources for those with additional educational needs. Targeting resources at the student level (as discussed above) would act as a powerful incentive to schools to maintain a wide balance in their intakes. It would also benefit students in schools serving areas in which there were, as a consequence of the social geography of the locality, higher numbers of disadvantaged and low attaining students.

Although it might not prove feasible to have a quota of low attaining students (as was tried with limited success in the former ILEA) by linking resources *directly* to the admission of low attaining students at secondary transfer, and ensuring they were specifically used to benefit those students the current powerful incentives to schools to recruit as many able students as possible would at least be reduced, if not eliminated. Moreover, the status of such students could be enhanced by specific recognition of their needs, if properly designed programmes were instituted. If the lowest scoring 20–25 per cent of students (in terms of national primary school KS2 assessments) were identified before secondary transfer, their choices of secondary schools might be enhanced. Clearly, in socio-economically disadvantaged areas, more students would be identified than would be the case in suburban areas. Yet this would help to recognize—and should help address—the additional challenges currently faced by such schools. If the results of primary school assessments were used, there would be little danger of rewarding low performing secondary schools, an important consideration if the aim is to raise national educational standards. Analysing the value-added scores for the low attaining group after a period of time in secondary school (from age 11 to KS3) would provide one method of evaluating whether the additional funds had helped improve performance for these students.

We reiterate—additional resources cannot by themselves raise standards. Our research was conducted amongst 94 inner London schools with broadly similar funding levels (a legacy of the former ILEA) and favourable resource levels in comparison with secondary schools elsewhere in the country. Researching levels were not found to differentiate the most and the least effective schools in our case studies, even though all respondents felt more resources would be beneficial. In terms of policy implications, we are not suggesting a dramatic increase in researching to finance the targeting of specific funds for the lowest attaining groups at secondary transfer. A modest increase in educational funding, however, would surely have a considerable psychological impact, especially if guaranteed to continue over several successive years. However, if (as we have proposed) a national pupil-based funding formula was developed, with an explicit and fairly substantial needs-based element, this would have a *redistributive* effect. We argue that it is this redistributive aspect which would create a tension between the current pressure on schools to maximize their numbers of high ability socio-economically advantaged students likely to perform well in league tables and pose fewer behaviour and attendance problems, and a direct financial incentive to recruit more low attaining, disadvantaged students. This tension, we think, would act as a powerful mechanism for encouraging schools to maintain a balanced intake which would, nationally, benefit the attainment of the majority of students.

The amount of the educational budget which should be allocated to enable such redistribution is a matter which would require consultation, but a figure of 15–20 per cent of the total allocated on the basis of pupil numbers might be sufficient.

Inspection

The creation of the Office for Standards in Education (Ofsted) in 1993 was a significant and ambitious policy initiative designed to serve two main functions—to promote accountability and to stimulate improvement. Matthews and Smith (1995) provide a clear account of the underlying rationale. Before Ofsted's inception, 'the inspection manual was a fairly closely guarded secret' (Wilcox & Gray, 1996, p. 139). Ofsted, to its credit, has sought to be open, via publication of its handbook and consultations prior to its revision in 1995. The Ofsted handbook can be seen to embody not only a model of inspection, but also an implicit model of the school (Wilcox & Gray, 1996).

The inspection system prior to 1993 could be criticized for its infrequency and, therefore, the remote possibility of identifying schools which were failing to provide a satisfactory education for their students. The opposite extreme has now been reached, with a four-year inspection cycle. Whether spending the large sums entailed is the best way to achieve school improvement remains to be proved (see Earley et al., 1996; Mortimore, 1996c). The current move to a six-year inspection cycle, with more frequent inspection of schools for which there is concern, is likely to prove more acceptable and manageable. Moreover, it should release additional resources which could be used to provide a higher level of support post-inspection than is currently the case. There are very good arguments for ensuring that inspections provide 'support as well as pressure' (Fullan, 1993; Stoll & Thomson, 1996). In our view, the separation of advisory and inspection functions is unfortunate and does not provide the best basis for post-inspection action planning.

Our study of secondary school effectiveness has, we think, important implications for the operation of the inspection process. The discussion of league
tables and accountability is clearly relevant to the judgement of educational
standards and quality of education in secondary schools. It is essential that
comparisons are made on a 'like with like' basis, given the consequences of
being categorized as a 'failing' school or one requiring special measures. The
inspection process should use information about student intakes (as provided
in the Pre-Inspection Context Indicators reports) to assist in the contextual-
ization of inspectors' judgements of performance (Sammons et al., 1994c).
Where available, value-added data or information about the attainments of
students at secondary transfer should be obtained to assist in this process and
schools should be encouraged to engage in internal monitoring of pupil
progress using such methods. Targeting and benchmarking, if contextualized,
may prove valuable stimuli for monitoring and focusing on improving educational standards.

The results of our analysis of the mechanisms underlying secondary and
departmental effectiveness support the emphasis given by Ofsted to the crucial
role of the management of schools. We identified the leadership of the head
teacher and senior management team as important factors which contribute to
the academic success of the school. Their influence operates through the
creation of a shared vision and goals, high expectations, and a climate which is
conducive to teaching and learning in the classroom. Concern with administrative and financial matters was not allowed to obscure the prime focus of the
school on students' outcomes. The development and consistent implementation
of whole school policies (marking, assessment, behaviour, homework) had a
high priority. Likewise, the establishment of effective mechanisms for the regular monitoring and review of student progress and outcomes was regarded as
important. The leadership sought to involve staff as well as to influence their
behaviour. Communication and consultation with staff was afforded a high priority and, as a result, in the more effective schools a sense of whole school
ownership of policies was engendered.

Our research also draws attention to the significant role of middle managers.
Heads of department played an important part in promoting GCSE subject
results. In some schools, both highly effective and highly ineffective departments
co-existed. The identification of lead departments may be one way to raise the
performance of others. Studies of school improvement suggest that it is important to build on and celebrate existing strengths whilst also targeting weaknesses. This can be a positive outcome of inspection and help to empower staff
managers and the governing body through recognition of the need to act to raise
standards in specific subjects.

The inspection process can be used to help clarify the role and responsibilities of heads of department and to identify training needs. Key features include
policy and consistent current examination entry, assessment and record keeping,
homework, marking and feedback to students, and the department's methods
for monitoring, reviewing and rewarding student progress. As with the school

as a whole, the individual department's history, especially of staff changes and shortages, will be highly relevant.

Getting the right balance of advice and inspection demands local knowledge at the level of the school and the LEA, as well as appropriate experience and skills. Good subject specialist advice will be particularly important for schools with difficulties in particular departments. The provision of post-inspection support by Ofsted is likely to make its commitment to promoting improvement more of a reality. It is also likely to improve schools' abilities to accept and act on the judgements made by inspectors.

The findings of our questionnaire survey indicated that the majority of those already inspected had found the process helpful rather than unhelpful. We suggest the process of significant self-evaluation and review, stimulated by the advance knowledge of when the school would be 'Ofsteded', is likely to have been at least as important as the inspection process itself. Ironically, in some schools, the prospect of inspection appeared to have engendered a sense of whole staff unity and encouraged a level of collaboration which was previously lacking. Whether this is sustained post-inspection may be another matter. For long lasting improvement, a change of culture from within the school is a necessary pre-condition (Stoll & Fink, 1996). Such a change in culture cannot be externally mandated, though appropriate advice and support may be highly beneficial.

The most workable and cost-effective system may prove to be a more flexible inspection system with specific criteria to trigger earlier inspection where deemed necessary (for example, in response to a declining trend in examination or NA results or in attendance, or an increase in indicators of behaviour problems, such as exclusions) but a longer inspection cycle for other schools and lighter reporting. For schools with severe difficulties, there may be a need for long-term—two to three years—external support to promote school improvement. Such support, however, should have a definite time scale and be evaluated carefully by means of clear targets and criteria. Although it is recognized that improvement may take several years for most schools, in extreme cases the power to close schools should be retained where problems continue unchecked for a specified period. Turning around 'failing' schools may prove too time-consuming or difficult in some instances and time is very costly to the students involved.

Ofsted has had a highly controversial first four years in operation. We consider it important that achievements in providing an external framework for evaluating schools should be built on. Whether the considerable resources involved are the best way to promote school improvement, however, remains open to question. A more flexible, somewhat less frequent, inspection cycle which combined support/advice as well as judgement would, we think, prove more efficacious. In our view, the highly political role adopted by its current chief inspector (in contrast to his predecessor) threatens to bring the system into disrepute and alienate teachers and senior managers. Without their support and good will, raising educational standards will be impossible. This controversial and adversarial approach is preventing the useful contribution which a more flexible inspection system could make to promoting good practice and improving opportunities for students.

Implications for practitioners in schools

Staff in schools are chiefly responsible for the quality of students' educational experiences. Our study shows that even in difficult circumstances they can and do make a difference. Where learning is valued and academic matters are seen to be relevant for all students, staff recognize that they can make an important contribution. School effectiveness research has consistently demonstrated that schools cannot lay all the blame for failure at the doors of parents and society, powerful though such influences can be (Mortimore, 1995a; Reynolds et al., 1994b).

Stoll and Fink (1996) have provided a definition of an effective school which links well with schools' interests in improvement. This covers four aspects:

- Promoting progress for *all* students beyond what would be expected, given consideration of initial attainment and background factors
- Ensuring that each pupil achieves the highest standards possible
- Enhancing all aspects of pupil achievement and development
- Continuing to improve from year to year (p. 28)

The senior management team

Unsurprisingly, our research drew attention to the importance of the senior management team (SMT) in promoting secondary schools' academic effectiveness. As Wallace and Hall (1994) have shown in their detailed study of different SMTs, it is essential that those in the SMT work together effectively as a team. They stated that lack of team work is the 'Achilles heel' of SMTs: 'together, team members make the team, individually they can break it. The culture of team work is no stronger than individuals' commitment . . . the onus is on every member to accept equal responsibility for making the SMT work' (p. 198). Our research supports this emphasis on the need for teamwork and on individual, as well as collective, responsibility for ensuring this.

In this section we highlight some of the most important practical messages for the SMT from our research.

Monitoring

There are a number of simple but informative ways in which individual schools can analyse their own data to enhance their monitoring capacity and this section provides some suggestions concerning this.

By linking information about students' prior attainment and later performance, we can investigate the value-added by the school. Where a school has access to information about its own results, set in the context of other schools and convening three or more years, changes in performance can be studied over time. In Figure 13.1 we show, for a sample of our schools, the trends in average prior attainment over three years (the mean LRT score) at secondary transfer. From such a plot, a school can see whether its intake is changing from year to year and also how it compares with other schools. In Figure 13.2 the trend in overall examination performance (i.e. the mean total GCSE score) is shown for the same three student cohorts at age 16. This illustrates an overall upward trend in GCSE results across most schools. Differences between schools in both prior attainment and GCSE outcomes are quite marked in both these plots. Only by looking at the relationship between the two can schools gain a better picture of their performance *relative to other schools with similar student intakes*.

The concept of value-added thus focuses on student progress, something which should be recognized as the heart of the educational process. Our study vividly illustrates the importance of monitoring pupil progress. Value-added results, taking into account students' prior attainment, can be used positively as part of the regular process of school self-evaluation and review. By concentrating on subject results as well as overall measures of performance, the SMT can identify areas of strength as well as weakness. They may also focus on identifying current levels of performance in key skills important for progress across the curriculum, such as reading and numeracy. Monitoring trends over time provides valuable information about school improvement as well as about student progress. Of course, information about performance cannot raise standards on its own. It is the *uses* to which such information is put that are vital. Value-added data can help the SMT to ask questions, to encourage reflection and to set realistic targets for improvement. These can be incorporated into the school's development plan. Analysing results for different pupil groups can help a school to establish whether it is equally effective for all its students and, if not, help to set priorities for the future. They can thus contribute to the school's equal opportunities policy.

Collecting detailed information about students' achievement at entry in key skills such as reading and numeracy is essential to help the school decide priorities for special needs provision. Early intervention to raise the performance of 'at risk' groups (for example, poor readers) will have long-term benefits for their academic outcomes and future life chances. Raising achievement levels in years 7 and 8 will also have positive effects on self-esteem and motivation, behaviour and attendance patterns, which, in turn, will influence later academic results. They will also convey messages about the school's commitment to raising standards and influence its culture, which, as we have argued, is a powerful influence on academic effectiveness.

Those working in schools should remember, however, that all performance data are retrospective and that it is quite possible that the results of future students may reveal a changing pattern. Crucially, this means that the widespread practice of predicting the GCSE grades of individual year 7 students on the basis of attainment at entry should be treated with some caution, as it is important that predictions do not depress teacher or student expectations.

Total GSCE scores over three years

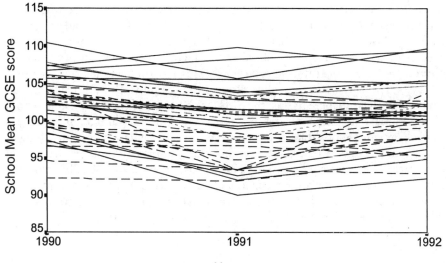

Figure 13.1. Differences between secondary schools in students' average total GCSE performance score for three GCSE cohorts (1990–92).

Prior achievement scores over three years

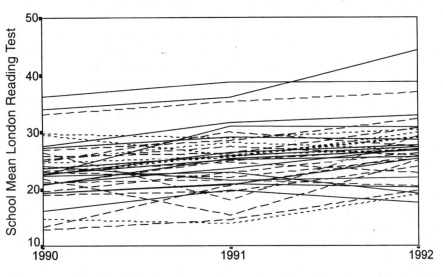

Figure 13.2. Differences between secondary schools in students' average prior attainment levels at secondary transfer for three GCSE cohorts (1990–92).

In addition to monitoring academic results, analysing information about behaviour/attendance and listening to the students' views (Ruddock et al., 1996) should be key activities for the SMT. In our view, there are three important aspects of school ethos and culture which are important for the academic effectiveness of secondary schools: order (behaviour policy and practice), task achievement (academic emphasis) and relationships (a student-focused approach). Ensuring a safe and orderly working environment in school is a necessary prerequisite for effective learning. Although all staff, both teaching and support, must contribute to this, the SMT are best placed to take a whole school view. Our case studies showed that improvement in 'interim outcomes', that is to say behaviour, motivation and attendance, may be evident before any changes in academic results occur. Collecting and using information about such social outcomes and about students' views also provides important feedback on the quality of students' educational experiences. Evidence of improvements in 'interim outcomes' can boost staff morale, raise expectations and help to maintain staff commitment to promoting academic outcomes in the long term.

Leadership

One clear message, from both our research and other school effectiveness studies, is the need for leadership. The HT has a particularly important role to play in exercising this. His/her leadership helps to establish a clear and consistent vision (agreed goals) for the school, which emphasizes the prime purposes of the school as teaching and learning and is highly visible to both staff and students; staff collaboration and involvement is emphasized; and the head teacher takes a keen interest in monitoring pupil progress and in the quality of teaching.

Although the head teacher is a key figure, our research also highlights the need for an effective SMT which promotes staff morale and exemplifies teamwork. The academically least effective schools in our case studies suffered from marked division between individuals and personality conflicts which prevented teamwork and cohesion of approach. The SMT should play an important part in promoting the shared vision and goals of the school, an academic emphasis and high expectations. The effective SMT recognizes the need for consistency in approach in terms of agreed policies and practice in the key areas of behaviour, rules and management, assessment and marking, homework, and parental involvement. It ensures high levels of staff consultation and involvement in the development of such policies. It is also deeply involved in the process of self-evaluation and review, monitoring the performance of different departments on a regular basis and encouraging them to give regular feedback to their students. The effective SMT thus seeks to promote a culture of continuous improvement in the school.

There is increasing recognition of the need for schools to become learning organizations in which all participants—SMT, HoDs and teachers, as well as students—are actively involved in learning. Southworth (1994) has drawn attention to some of the key features of a learning organization. He notes, 'what really holds members of staff together is a sense of shared values . . . the development of shared beliefs takes time and requires more than formal structures that invite staff to plan and evaluate together' (p. 71). Our research draws attention to the impact of school culture in creating academic effectiveness. Bush (1995) has noted the value of cultural models in his discussion of theories of educational management. He notes that cultural models provide a focus for organizational action and that there is a strong connection between the way we think and the way we act: 'Leaders may focus on influencing values so that they become closer to, if not identical with, their own beliefs. In this way they hope to achieve widespread support for, or 'ownership' of, new policies . . . An appreciation of the salience of values and beliefs, and the ritual that underpins them, is an important element in the management of schools and colleges' (p. 140).

Other authors have also highlighted the concept of culture. In their discussion of school development planning, Hargreaves and Hopkins (1993) argue that 'when research-based knowledge is put to the test of practice, the result will be more schools which educate *all* of their pupils' (p. 239). However, they also emphasize that a profound change in school culture is required for many schools to take on board the messages of school effectiveness research—that it is possible to raise the achievement of all children. Stoll and Fink (1996) likewise draw attention to the need to change school culture, although writing more recently in connection with schools in difficulty, they note that change takes time and there are 'no quick fixes'.

Inspection evidence has also drawn attention to the creation of a reflective, consultative, self-critical approach which has become 'enshrined in the school's culture'. Based on HMI visits to over 30 schools identified as good or improving and committed to quality management, Coleman and Matthews (1996) identified four common features: a marked capacity for self assessment; concern for the views of pupils and parents; effective strategies for improving teaching; and inspiring leadership and effective management.

Practical strategies for improvement
Discussion of the results of our study of secondary school and departmental effectiveness with practitioners suggests a number of practical strategies which the SMT can adopt to improve their school's effectiveness.

Explore staff views about the school's current goals and effectiveness
A number of questions can be used to initiate discussion and reflection amongst the SMT and staff as a whole. They can enable the SMT to examine the extent of shared vision/goals and to identify common perceptions of areas of strength and weakness. The questions we developed and piloted in our research may prove useful for the SMT in identifying important differences in focus between different groups (the SMT itself, HoDs, classroom teachers).

- What would you say are the principal educational goals that this school tries to achieve for its students? Have these changed over the last five years?

- Which factors do you think ought to be taken into account in judging the effectiveness of any secondary school?
- Which factors contribute most to the current effectiveness of this school?
- What (if anything) holds this school back from being more effective?

It is important to encourage all staff to focus on areas of success and achievement as well as on challenges or problems. Collecting and discussing staff views of major successes/achievements over a given time period (such as the last five years) and examining major problems/challenges which the school has faced can prove a useful exercise. Open discussion of the results of such a survey will help to identify areas of agreement as well as difference. Feeding the results into school development planning and identifying agreed specific foci for action (including staff involved, resources and time scale) are important components in an on-going process or cycle of self-evaluation/review—action—reflection—evaluation/review. Such a strategy can help to address feelings of powerlessness amongst staff and managers, which are often present in schools experiencing serious difficulties. Of course, very deep divisions may exist in some schools. Open discussion may appear to exacerbate some of these at first but some, perhaps unanticipated, areas of agreement may be found which can be built on and the deeper difficulties may be resolved as a result of the process of discussion.

Encourage the regular collection and use of information about students' educational outcomes
As well as the statistical analysis of results suggested earlier, regular reviews of samples of students' work can contribute to the monitoring of different departments and year groups. They can also help to establish whether assessment/marking and homework policies are being followed consistently and whether students get regular and constructive feedback on their performance and on how to improve their work.

Information about behaviour and attendance can be used to identify 'at risk' students who require greater particular pastoral care. Early intervention and ensuring that behaviour standards are agreed amongst staff and consistently applied is likely to be most effective where students themselves are involved in developing the school's code of conduct. A 'firm but fair' approach focusing on positive reinforcement strategies is most productive. No magic solutions are on offer but helpful approaches to attendance problems and behaviour difficulties have been described and applied (MacBeath, 1994; Watkins, 1995). Specific anti-bullying programmes may be appropriate for some schools.

Using questionnaire surveys of particular year groups is a strategy that is proving beneficial in an increasing number of schools. This strategy can help to identify whether significant numbers of students experience bullying and the context in which it occurs. Such surveys can also prove revealing in relation to students' views of academic matters such as homework, feedback on work, teacher–student relationships and teaching quality. As Ruddock et al. (1996) have argued, in many schools too little attention is given to listening to, and learning from, the students' voices. Seeking to find out about, and valuing, students' views can be an important first step in creating a sense of whole school identity and common purpose. An example of the way student attitudes can be measured by questionnaires and used as an important indicator of educational outcomes has been provided in an ongoing school improvement study in Scotland (Thomas et al., 1997).

Focusing attention on early identification of at risk students (in terms of behaviour and attendance), especially for those in years 7 and 8 before a pattern becomes firmly embedded, is also likely to be most fruitful and will have a beneficial impact on these students' later achievement. Given the known links between attendance and behaviour problems and poor academic achievement, efforts to identify and improve the basic skills of at risk students are likely to foster positive social outcomes, including self-esteem. This, in turn, will have a positive impact on learning.

Focus on staff morale
Poor staff morale is probably as much a symptom as a cause of ineffectiveness. There is no doubt from our research that this was an important issue for schools in our sample, and perhaps nationally, during the first half of the 1990s. Schools in the inner-city serve the most disadvantaged communities and, whilst not unique in this respect, serve above-average numbers of students with attendance, behaviour and learning difficulties. In raw league table terms these schools fare badly and annual press publication can prove demoralizing for teaching staff. Inner London schools, in particular, have experienced a range of major changes compressed into a relatively short period. In addition to all the major national educational changes related to the introduction of the national curriculum, national assessment, LMS, directed time and national Ofsted inspections, these schools simultaneously had to cope with the abolition of the ILEA. Not surprisingly, levels of stress related to the pace and pressure of external change were reported to be high and staff morale was felt to have been adversely affected.

Nonetheless, some schools coped with change far better than others and, in line with national trends, overall GCSE standards were rising. In particular, the number of students achieving no qualifications at all declined over time across the sample. Some schools also reported improving attendance, motivation and behaviour amongst their students. Linked with staff morale, poor staff attendance was also identified as a significant problem in a minority of schools. Unsurprisingly, high staff absence levels in the previous five years had a negative impact on students' progress, as measured by our value-added analyses.

Poor staff attendance was associated with low expectations and a tendency to blame external factors (especially students/parents/community) for the school's problems. Remedying unacceptably high levels of staff absence must be a high priority for the SMT, linked with the development of a shared vision and goals and with raising expectations. Encouraging departments to cover for absent colleagues wherever possible and ensuring that classwork and homework are set and marked can help to maintain some continuity for students. Poor attendance may not only be evident amongst classroom teachers, of course. Where HoDs or members of the SMT itself have a poor attendance record over an extended period, action by the head teacher and other SMT members, perhaps involving the governing body, will be needed. High levels of staff, as well as of student, absence have a powerful impact on the culture of any secondary school and demonstrate that teaching and learning are not regarded as the highest priority of the school. As well as conveying an adverse message to students about the value of education, high staff absence rates directly affect the quality and continuity of students' educational experiences.

Working with middle managers
One method of enhancing academic success at GCSE was evident from our case studies. It concerned a strong SMT commitment to working closely with HoDs, particularly new ones and those whose departments were not considered to be achieving as well as others in the school. Learning from the good practice developed in other particularly effective departments was another strategy (for example, adopting a particularly effective department's marking or homework policy for the whole school). It is notable that, in interviews, HoDs stressed the benefits of clear *whole-school policies* on behaviour, assessment and marking and homework which were followed in *all* departments.

In the sample of schools as a whole we found that many HoDs wanted a clearer definition of their role and greater involvement with the SMT in decision making. Regular department reviews (one per term) may prove to be a useful mechanism for encouraging such involvement and for providing HoDs with both recognition for current achievements, pressure for improvement where necessary and support. Pairing departments may also prove beneficial if conducted sensitively.

In connection with the need for a clearer definition of their role, the Teacher Training Agency's (TTAs') work on the development of a National Professional Qualification for Subject Leaders (NPQSL) is highly relevant. The qualification is intended to provide a framework for the training, development, assessment and accreditation of such post holders. The stated objectives of the qualification is to help to identify and describe national standards. One of the key principles outlined in the TTA consultation document was that it should be rooted in school improvement and should build on current best practice in effective schools and outside education. We return to this topic in more detail in the next section, when we focus on implications of our research for HoDs. For school management and leadership we suggest that the SMT may find that the development of national standards and a national professional qualification will help to provide the greater clarity about roles and responsibilities needed by HoDs, as well as improving their status. It may prove to be a valuable mechanism for encouraging HoDs to focus on establishing and ensuring high standards of teaching and learning in their subject, for contributing to policy development in the school and evaluating its impact.

We welcome the fact that the proposed NPQSL lays great stress on monitoring and promoting standards of student achievement. We believe this should help to foster the academic emphasis and high expectations which our research shows are essential components of the institutional culture of academically effective schools.

Heads of department

Our study explicitly sought to investigate the nature and extent of internal variations in school effectiveness. Its findings demonstrate that, although a small number of schools were found to be consistent outliers (either academically very effective or ineffective), for *most* schools the picture was far more complicated, with significant differences at the subject level over three consecutive years. We analysed information about performance in terms of the three core areas of the national curriculum—English and English literature, mathematics, and science (highest grade in any science subject). We also obtained details for French and history, because these subjects were taken by larger numbers of students in our sample than any others. In some schools results were highly mixed, with ineffective and effective departments co-existing in the same institution. This clearly demonstrates the importance of the subject department in any discussion of secondary school academic effectiveness. Going beyond earlier work (Luyten, 1995; Smith & Tomlinson, 1989; Witziers, 1994), we related information about school and departmental processes to students' GCSE results.

Our case studies of six schools and 30 different subject departments provide rich qualitative insights into what enabled some departments to be more effective in promoting their students' achievement than others. By studying both consistently more effective and less effective departments, and by focusing on change over a five-year period, we achieved a better understanding of factors which contribute to, or are barriers to a greater effectiveness. We also obtained important insights into the processes and factors which influence change and foster improvement. Our questionnaire survey of HoDs enabled us to test out the qualitative findings using a larger sample.

HoD leadership

The leadership role of the HoD was found to be important but all too often ill-defined. HoDs have the primary responsibility to monitor pupil progress and raise achievement levels for all students of their subject. To achieve this it is important that they create or maintain a shared vision of their subject and foster amongst their department's teachers high expectations for *all* students.

Good record-keeping and a clear assessment and marking policy, which facilitates the monitoring of individual students' progress and those of different student groups both within and across years, is a characteristic of more effective departments. As well as oral comments, marking, tests and records of achievement all provide opportunities to give students constructive feedback on their performance and, more importantly, on how to improve the quality of their work. HoDs who monitored the setting and marking of homework and quality of classwork—by looking at lesson plans and via observation—were better able to ensure consistency in the implementation of departmental and school policy.

Regularly examining samples of students' workbooks and GCSE coursework and having discussions with students provide valuable sources of information for HoDs to help evaluate the performance of their department.

Monitoring pupil progress over several years helps HoDs to identify areas of success or of under-achievement. Investigating trends over time is essential to establish evidence of improvement. Obtaining information about student attainment at entry gives a baseline for plotting later results (annually or at KS3) as well as linking to final GCSE performance. It is important that such information is recorded at the level of the individual student. In addition to examining their own school's data, it is valuable for HoDs to compare the department's performance with that of other departments elsewhere using value-added measures (these may be available at the LEA or via consultancy projects such as the NFER).

If value-added data are not available, it may prove possible to compare the department's results with those of other schools known to serve a similar catchment area (for example, predominantly ethnically diverse inner city with a high proportion of students who do not speak English as a first language or mainly middle-class suburban with few students eligible for free school meals). This can help to give HoDs an indication of relative performance on a contextualized or 'like with like' basis. Such comparisons can enable challenging but realistic targets to be set for improvement based on past performance and performance of similar schools. The Department for Education and Employment, Ofsted and SCAA are currently showing much interest in the way benchmarking and target-setting can be used to help schools identify realistic goals for their improvement. In particular, SCAA is exploring ways of providing schools with information about the performance of schools from similar groups (i.e. according to their profile in terms of specific social indicators). In the absence of value-added measures, this may well prove helpful for more rigorous school self-evaluation and more accurate target-setting.

The HoDs of more effective departments attached considerable importance both to team building and to actual teamwork in their departments. In contrast, the absence of teamwork was frequently cited as a source of difficulty in the less effective departments. Low morale and high staff absence, as might be expected, were more common in departments which lacked a clear direction and a team spirit. Analysing performance data, however, is only one important activity for HoDs.

In our study, we found that effective HoDs often sought to lead by example in a variety of ways, including teaching and expressing high expectations of both staff and students. They also sought to ensure that departmental policies were developed through a process of discussion, which helped promote a sense of common ownership. Regular departmental meetings to discuss policies and practice and to evaluate student progress were seen to be important in fostering teamwork, identifying areas for improvement and setting targets, as well as for discussing departmental policies. The ability to listen to staff and to maintain constructive relationships was seen by many HoDs to be an essential part of their work. Personality conflicts and 'dead wood' (uncommitted members of staff who were not felt to pull their weight) were a feature of the less effective case studies. Shortages of staff and high levels of absence were also seen as major barriers to greater effectiveness by this group.

Quality of teaching

There was strong evidence, as would be expected, that the quality of teaching is a crucial component of departmental effectiveness. Important factors which our research suggests can form a helpful basis for departmental reviews include the following:

- Work focus of lessons (are most students on-task most of the time?)
- Strong academic emphasis
- Clarity of goals for student learning
- Student responsibility (independent learning is encouraged)
- Lessons generally challenge students of *all* ability levels
- Teacher enthusiasm
- Effective classroom control
- High teacher expectations for student performance and behaviour
- Promptness in starting and finishing lessons
- Regular monitoring of student progress
- Consistently applied marking policy
- Homework given a high priority and homework policy consistently applied by all teachers
- Teachers' knowledge of the content of the subject and of the GCSE syllabus

These are all aspects of teaching which might form a useful basis for the observation of lessons both by the HoD and by other subject teachers. Conducted with sensitivity and honesty, observations could provide a valuable opportunity to discuss teaching approaches, to identify training needs and to give constructive feedback for all subject teachers, including the HoD. Further consideration of teaching approaches is given in the section on implications for classroom practitioners.

Questions which may prove helpful in stimulating discussion at the departmental level include the following:

- Which factors do you think ought to be taken into account in judging the effectiveness of any department?
- Which factors contribute most to the current effectiveness of this department?
- What, if anything, holds the department back from being more effective?

Examining boards

Our research provided little support for the view that the particular examining board chosen was a significant factor in determining departmental effectiveness. Indeed, amongst our case studies, examples of the most and least effective departments used the same boards and syllabus. Factors which were more important related to covering the syllabus, ensuring students had completed the required coursework, entering students for examinations whenever possible (as well as, of course, the quality of teaching and staff expectations).

Ability grouping

Likewise, the use of ability grouping did *not* emerge as a key feature in relation to academic effectiveness. None of our sample of schools used rigid streaming, preferring instead the more flexible approach of setting for specific subjects and specific year groups. Most schools set students into ability groups for years 10 and 11 (the GCSE period). We found that some of the less effective case studies, which had used mixed-ability approaches, planned to introduce more setting in the hope of raising standards. In other schools, good value-added results had been achieved in a mixed ability context—although some of their staff thought the use of setting from year 9 onwards might lead to further improvements. From the questionnaire survey, we found setting from a younger age (years 7 or 8) for all subjects was associated with greater effectiveness in overall GCSE results, but this was not identified as a key factor in the multilevel analysis. Moreover, in mathematics—the subject in which setting by ability was most common—a greater use of setting from a younger age was weakly negatively associated with effectiveness.

We can conclude, therefore, that the search for prescriptive and, we suggest, simplistic organizational solutions concerning the merits of streaming or ability grouping versus mixed ability approaches are unlikely to be the key to raising performance. The quality of teaching, high expectations, an academic emphasis and good student–teacher relationships and classroom control are much more important. Whatever approach to student grouping is adopted, it is important that departmental staff are involved in the decision-making process, that they share common goals, and that a department's policies are agreed and consistently applied by all its teaching staff.

Classroom teachers

As we have noted elsewhere, our research has a vitally important and positive message for classroom practitioners. It demonstrates clearly that individual schools and departments can and do make a difference to secondary students' progress between the ages of 11 and 16 years. Even in some of the most disadvantaged LEAs in the country, individual schools and departments were much more effective than others. Although students' background characteristics exert a powerful influence, which needs to be recognized, the quality of teaching and educational experiences at secondary school can significantly raise achievement levels and affect the subsequent life chances of students. Teachers do make a difference.

Due to the retrospective nature of our research, we did not observe teaching in individual classes in any of our sample of schools. We cannot, therefore, evaluate or make detailed comments about specific teaching practices. Nonetheless, the evidence from both the case studies and questionnaire surveys confirms the importance of high-quality teaching as a vital determinant of academic effectiveness to both SMTs and HoDs.

Purposeful teaching, creating a learning environment and high expectations are seen as indicators of high-quality teaching. It is, of course, vital to recognize that teachers do not operate in isolation. Other aspects we have already referred to concerning the SMT and middle managers facilitate (in effective schools) the teaching and learning process in individual classrooms. The combination of leadership and management, organization and policy, goals and expectations influences the school's and individual departments' cultures. We can conclude that a more supportive environment for classroom practitioners and for teaching and learning is provided by:

- Effective leadership
- Shared vision/goals (fostering consistency of practice, and collegiality)
- A clear focus on monitoring student progress, and departmental reviews
- A student-focused approach (with positive staff–student relationships and emphasis on students' rights and responsibilities

Teaching styles
In the light of the recent resurrection of the teaching styles debate, following the publication of international reviews which highlighted the UK's poor performance in mathematics (in particular, Reynolds & Farrell, 1996), it is important to note that, on the basis of available evidence, no one 'style' can be seen to be more effective than others. Indeed, our experience in the field indicates that teachers' practice is far more complex than simplistic notions of teaching style, such as formal versus informal, allow (Mortimore, 1993b; Sammons, 1995d). Elsewhere, on the basis of an extensive review of school and teacher effectiveness literature, we observed 'in our view debates about the virtues of one particular style over another are too simplistic and have become sterile. Efficient organization, fitness for purpose, flexibility of approach and intellectual challenge are of greater relevance' (Sammons et al., 1995e, p. 25).

Factors which the present research indicates are relevant for effective classroom practice point to the importance of teachers' knowledge of the curriculum and of pedagogical, school and classroom processes, as well as their skills in organization, analysis, synthesis, presentation management, assessment and evaluation. There are no easy recipes or blueprints for 'good teaching'. Teachers need to blend together skills and knowledge for particular purposes, taking into account the context of the age, prior attainments and interests of a particular class of students. Imagination, creativity and sensitivity are also needed to communicate with, and to inspire, students (Mortimore, 1993b).

While there is no prescription for good teaching, the benefits of a fairly structured approach, of teacher enthusiasm, positive student–teacher relationships, clear planning and good order and control in the classroom for promoting students' academic achievement were evident from comments by head teachers, deputies and HoDs in our research, and are in accord with the results of reviews of the school and teacher effectiveness literature (Sammons et al., 1995e). From our case studies, it was apparent that five years previously in many departments there had been concern about variability of teaching quality between individual teachers. In the less effective departments, in particular, concerns about lack of interest and relevance to students, over-reliance on a passive role for students in lessons, and too much emphasis on students working individually in isolation were perhaps best characterized by comments like 'death by a thousand work-sheets'. Lack of preparation, little academic emphasis, low expectations and unclear goals were also criticized and, in some instances, poor behaviour man-agement by teachers was a serious handicap.

Reflecting on personal practice
Particular features which were found to be associated with academic effective-ness were noted earlier under implications for middle managers. These were sug-gested as a helpful basis for departmental reviews. They can also, we think, provide useful pointers for teacher reflection on their own practice, and for observations and constructive critique of colleagues in terms of three activities: planning, management and feedback.

Planning
- Teachers' knowledge of the content of the subject
- Teachers' knowledge of the content of the GCSE syllabus in use
- Clarity of learning goals
- Homework policy consistently applied
- Strong academic emphasis
- Lessons which challenge students of *all* ability levels

Management
- Work focus of lessons (most students on-task most of the time)
- High teacher expectations for student performance and behaviour
- Student responsibility (independent learning is encouraged)
- Effective classroom control
- Promptness starting and finishing lessons
- Teacher enthusiasm (for subject and teaching)
- Quality of teacher–student relationships

Feedback
- Assessment information used for regular monitoring of student progress
- Emphasis given to providing students with constructive feedback (verbal and written)
- Consistently applied marking policy

Implications for students and parents

A concern for equity, promoting the educational achievements of *all* students regardless of their gender, ethnic or socio-economic status, has been—and continues to be—a driving force in school effectiveness research. As Reynolds (1995a) has argued, the impact on students is the 'touchstone' for school effectiveness research. In earlier chapters, we have highlighted the ways in which some schools and individual departments were able to promote students' progress during their time at secondary school.

Our research has focused on secondary schools' academic effectiveness at GCSE, although we have also noted the important interdependencies between attainment, behaviour, attendance, motivation and self-esteem. We have not attempted to address the concept of a 'good' school (interesting discussions of this have been made by writers such as Silver [1994], and Gray & Wilcox [1995]). We doubt whether agreement on what constitutes a 'good' school could be achieved or would be desirable. Parents and students, quite rightly, will have their own views on this, reflecting their particular interests and values. However, whilst we would acknowledge that a good school will be much more than an academically effective one, we remain convinced that academic effectiveness is a *necessary*, if not sufficient, condition (Sammons & Reynolds, 1997).

The prime purpose of schooling, we argue, is the promotion of pupil progress. The concept of value added—the school's particular contribution to the progress a student makes while attending his or her secondary school—is thus essential to allow informed judgements about a school's performance to be made. In our experience, parents are keenly aware of the importance of measuring progress and are anxious to receive regular and comprehensible information about this from their child's school. Parents recognize the significance of the 'high stakes' assessment by public examination at GCSE and the implications of success or failure for their children's later education and employment prospects. Many realize that current raw league tables may not provide a good guide to school effectiveness, but the absence of other comparative published material means that such tables are still consumed avidly. Given this, we believe our study of departmental differences in secondary school effectiveness has important implications and messages for both parents and students which we will attempt to summarize here.

Choosing schools

Our research has examined internal variations in secondary schools' performance over three years. When we focus on the value added by schools (taking into account differences between schools in their intakes of students at 11 years), it is quite clear that crude distinctions, such as a 'good' or 'bad' school, are inappropriate for the vast majority. Over three years, only a very small number of schools were found to be highly effective across the board and very few to be consistently ineffective. In some schools, 'average' overall GCSE results may mask the existence of significant subject variations. Highly effective and ineffective departments can co-exist in the same institution.

Raw league tables, which only show the percentage of the 15-plus age cohort attaining five A–C grades, cannot tell parents and prospective students how a school performs, nor about particular subjects; for example, those in which a child has shown an aptitude or interest at primary school. Nor are raw league tables able to demonstrate whether a school is differentially effective for some student groups, such as boys or girls or different ethnic groups. Yet this sort of detailed information is of interest to prospective parents and students.

Our research shows that, in the real world, judgements about school performance are complex (Sammons, 1996). We believe that steps to provide non-statistical information about the value added by schools to students' progress would be more useful than crude league tables. Developments in school effectiveness research will provide more accurate information about school effectiveness. Parents would not need great statistical expertise to interpret value-added results presented as a profile of measures. Using such a form of presentation would avoid all the misleading properties of raw ranked league tables which appear to show differences between individual schools but which are statistically invalid. By presenting results for key core subjects (such as English and mathematics) and by including total GCSE performance score as an overall indicator, a broader picture of schools' academic effectiveness could be given. In addition, we suggest that results be presented for at least two—but preferably three—consecutive years, so that trends can be seen.

Of course, it must be stressed that schools are subject to change and over time a school may improve its performance or, alternatively, decline. When students and parents choose a secondary school, even the best value-added indicators of examination results can only give a *retrospective* indication of performance. There is no guarantee that the school which is performing above expectation now will still be in this position in six years' time when prospective students take their GCSE results. In our view, value-added information is probably most useful for schools to encourage rigorous self-evaluation and review, to guide target-setting and to help evaluate the success of improvement initiatives. Nonetheless, in an open and democratic society it is only right that value-added information is made available in addition to raw results (Tomlinson et al., 1988).

In addition to information about examination results, we believe, as do many parents that discussion with the parents of students already at schools which their child might attend should be encouraged. Details about attendance and behaviour will be relevant, as well as visits to the school, informal observations in and around the school and talking to current students. Published inspection reports can also be a useful source of information.

Parents with children in primary school will need to consider the benefits of proximity, maintaining primary school friendships and the pupils' views about secondary schools. However, we believe that the factors which our research highlights as important for promoting academic effectiveness (described in earlier chapters) also provide an excellent basis for parents in evaluating what they see in their school visits, and provide pointers which may be helpful (for example, on homework policy and practice, subject setting, assessment and the code of practice on student behaviour.)

It must be remembered that, in many ways, the concept of parental choice can be rather misleading. Parents have a right to express a preference for a particular school but cannot be guaranteed a place if the school is popular. Where a school is over-subscribed, schools will make choices according to specific criteria. For some schools (e.g. church schools or grant-maintained schools) criteria can differ. It should also be remembered that, in many areas of the country, there may in practice be very little choice because of the practicalities of transport to and from the school. Where selection exists, choice will be restricted, with schools selecting students rather than parents choosing schools. Parents with a better knowledge of the education system and with access to a car will usually be able to exercise greater choice than others.

In addition, whilst parents have some (usually restricted) choice, it is important to remember that parents have no say about individual teachers. In a typical secondary school career a student may be taught by perhaps 30 or more different teachers. Inevitably, some students will respond better when taught by particular teachers. From our research, the school's culture or ethos is perhaps the key factor parents and students should attempt to judge when visiting potential schools. The features of school culture which we found were important in determining academic effectiveness were:

- Academic emphasis
- Behaviour of students
- Quality of the relationships between students and teachers

Parental involvement

Much research has pointed to the value of parental involvement in their children's education, both at home (especially in the early years) and at school. However, such research has tended to focus on pre-school and primary school children. Our study demonstrates that parental involvement is also important at the secondary level. Some schools in our research were better able to involve parents and had a more positive attitude towards their potential contribution. Parents have an important role in encouraging and supporting their children's efforts right through secondary school. Many, however, would welcome clear advice from, and encouragement by, the school concerning practical strategies for helping their children. The more effective schools in our case studies tended to harness parents' commitment by, for example, encouraging them to monitor students' homework (such as by signing a diary regularly), sending home newsletters, and providing systematic feedback about students' progress and achievements. These schools were also likely to be proactive about enlisting at an early date parental support concerning behaviour or attendance problems. Celebrating student achievements (by letter or certificate) is just as important as involving parents when things go wrong. More effective schools, as MacBeath (1994) has argued, tend to be better at making demands on parents as well as at providing them with opportunities for involvement and ensuring a welcoming atmosphere in the school.

Parental contracts have received considerable publicity in the UK in the wake of the Labour Party's commitment to them. We doubt whether such contracts are legally enforceable but, in principle, we feel that stressing both the rights and responsibilities of parents as well as students may be one way in which schools could help to maximize parental support and involvement to the benefit of young people's secondary education.

Postscript

The key message from our research concerns the positive impact secondary schools can have, even in disadvantaged areas, on students' academic performance. What schools and teachers do really can make a difference. We believe that our findings are relevant to all those interested in school improvement and hope they will stimulate reflection by both policy makers and practitioners. It is important to recognize that there are no solutions or magic recipes for school effectiveness. It is also clear, however, that our research does not support the 'back to the 1950s' lobby which argues that traditional approaches (streaming, selection, whole-class teaching, caning, uniforms) are the solution to all our educational ills. Although it is important to recognize that schools are in many ways non-rational organizations that are resistant to external pressure for change, we believe that—by focusing on the different components of the school's culture and by monitoring student progress, and departmental and whole-school performance—educational standards can be raised. Involving students and parents, seeking their views and addressing their concerns, is also vitally important. This chapter suggests that—where expectations are high, where all participants share the view that their school is primarily a place for teaching and learning, where student progress is not only encouraged and celebrated but seen as the 'touchstone' for evaluating school, departmental and teaching practices—improvement will follow.

14

Current Impact and Future Potential of Effective Schools

Introduction

I gave my inaugural lecture as director of the Institute of Education in February 1995. I had taken up my post as the ninth director on the 1 August 1994 and I wanted to present this lecture during my first year in office. I wished to restart the tradition of inaugural lectures and I was aware of the importance of modelling. I realized that my senior colleagues would be more willing to deliver inaugural or professorial lectures if I had already established the pattern. I used the opportunity to survey the field in which I had researched for so long and to reflect on both its achievements and its limitations. The original lecture included two extra sections: one on the history of the Institute and one on inaugural lectures in the field of education.

My title has been chosen as a device to draw together my research work and that of my many associates in this university and elsewhere and the mission of this institute in the context of contemporary educational policy making. The entire scope of the mission cannot be included: its range extends from education in the early years of childhood through to further, higher and continuing education and training. It also encompasses our substantial involvement in international education, whilst my research has been mainly concerned with primary and secondary schools in this country. Nor, of course, can I hope to do justice to the mass of contemporary policies that govern our educational system.

I shall structure the lecture and thereby limit its scope by posing five questions:

- What do we mean by effective schools?
- What has been the impact of school effectiveness work?
- What is the future potential of work on school effectiveness and school improvement?
- Does the education system help or hinder effectiveness?
- What should be the role of a university?

What do we mean by effective schools?

Schools, and the philosophers and providers of schooling, according to Professor Harold Silver, have always been concerned with outcomes. Silver has traced the history of what is sometimes called the school effectiveness movement from Plato—with his concern that the 'overseers of the state (be) prepared by right education'—and has noted the various schools created for bureaucrats, religious leaders, choristers, lawyers and craftsmen through the ages right up to modern times (Silver, 1994, p. 11). Like my colleague Dr Andy Green (Green, 1990), Silver notes the late arrival of an English national system of schooling. He also recounts some of the pioneering attempts at quality assurance instituted by Her Majesty's Inspectors (first appointed in 1839), including, in response to the question 'in which country do we live?', the answer from a child considerably ahead of his or her time: 'Europe'.

Silver also comments on the four-point scale ('excellent', 'good', 'fair' and 'bad') drawn up by the Newcastle Commission as part of the payment by results code. Not surprisingly, perhaps, the evidence to the Commission confirmed the variability of standards in schools (cited in Silver, 1994, p. 32). Much later, evidence about school differences came from the 'emergence to prominence of the sociology of education in the late 1950s in Britain and the discovery of poverty in the United States in the early 1960s' (Silver, 1994, p. 76).

Studies investigating the efficacy of initiatives to combat poverty, increase opportunity and pursue equality were commissioned in both countries. Culminating in the work of Coleman et al. (1966) and Jencks et al. (1972), the conclusion of the research endeavour was the view that schooling could play only a minor role in countering the influence of social class and family background.

The difficulty those in the education world had with this conclusion led to the promotion of research studies which sought to disentangle the effects of what the school tried to do from the influence of what the student brought into the classroom. This quest—strongly motivated by a moral concern for disadvantaged children and the seemingly limited opportunities available to them—led to the creation of the school effectiveness movement inspired in the United States by the late Dr Ron Edmonds's catch phrase 'all children can learn'

(Edmonds, 1979) and, in the United Kingdom, by the pioneering work of Professor (now Sir) Michael Rutter.

School effectiveness researchers, recognizing that schools do not receive uniform intakes of students but that some take those who come with high levels of prior achievement and are equipped with many advantages, whilst others predominantly receive those who lack these benefits, have sought to distinguish the impact of the school from the dowry brought by the student. We have had to find a way to describe an *effective* school. Accordingly, my definition is: 'a school in which students progress further than might be expected from a consideration of its intake' (Mortimore, 1991a, p. 9).

The term *effectiveness*, defined in this way, rather than by the simpler adjectives *good* or *successful*, does not imply that all students from disadvantaged backgrounds are likely to do badly in examinations. Some disadvantaged students will, of course, perform well in spite of—or even because of—their disadvantage for, as we know from many individual cases, adversity can promote motivation. What the definition indicates, however, is that, all other things being equal, disadvantaged students, as a group, are less likely to do well than are their more advantaged peers in any kind of assessment which is highly competitive. It is surely not surprising that in an examination such as the GCSE, with only 50 per cent or so gaining the higher grades, those who have had material advantages since birth—better housing, health care and diet, stimulating toys, access to books, parental expertise and encouragement and, if necessary, extra coaching—will be more likely to do better than those who have not.

Of course, advantages and disadvantages do not always cluster quite so readily and high expectations, talent and motivation are not evenly distributed. The overall patterns, however, are clear, as can be seen from so many studies in this country and elsewhere. Factors to do with disadvantage are likely to explain, for example, much of the difference between inner urban and suburban school results. Urban students are not less intelligent, nor are urban teachers less able than their suburban counterparts, but the examination results reported in the most recent league tables illustrate a considerable gulf between schools in these different contexts. Disentangling the effects of the students, the schools and the social context is difficult, as Smith and Tomlinson (1989), Teddlie (1994) and many of my colleagues here at the institute can vouchsafe.

Studies of effective schools

Studies of variation between individual schools can be simple or complex, cross-sectional or longitudinal, national or international. The simpler, short-term studies take little or no account of the differences in the characteristics of students at entry to the school. The more complex designs endeavour to do so and to use this information to compensate—as far as possible—for these differences. From a researcher's point of view, the ideal investigation into the specific effects of a school would entail an experimental design in which representative groups of students were randomly assigned to different schools. However, at a time when parental choice is seen not merely as desirable but almost as a right, such a design is usually considered impossible and statistical adjustment has been used to compensate for any systematic differences in the student intake of schools.

The extension of multiple regression into multilevel modelling (Paterson & Goldstein, 1991) has solved many of the technical problems associated with the measurement of progress. Regrettably, there appears to be a strong view held by some influential educationalists, parts of the press and some of the public that educational measurement—unlike, for instance, economic measurement—must always be simple and, all too often, this appropriate technique, able to provide a reasonable estimate of the *value added* by the school, is rejected in favour of less suitable methods, as the recent debate over league tables has demonstrated (SCAA, 1994). Nevertheless, in a number of different countries serious attempts continue to be made by researchers to judge the *effectiveness* of schools.

It is the quest to identify the characteristics of more effective schools that has driven researchers to undertake complex studies, often over many years. My own involvement in this field began in 1975, when I was recruited by Professor Michael Rutter into a team of four researchers (two of whom now work at this institute) to investigate the effects of 12 inner-city secondary schools (Rutter et al., 1979a). After nearly three years of highly stimulating intensive work, carried out in collaboration with the staff of the schools, we satisfied ourselves and a great number of practitioners, even if not all the research community (the first *Bedford Way Paper* of this institute was dedicated to a critique of the study's findings, Tizard, 1980), that there were systematic differences between schools' outcomes, not only in terms of students' examination success but also in attendance rates, behaviour ratings and delinquency records. We also sought to correlate our sampling of the various approaches to organization, learning and welfare—what we termed the school's processes—to the outcome measures.

In undertaking this latter task, we were looking for a theory to explain why some of these schools, rather than others, were effective. The theory that emerged was that the most effective schools tended to have a more positive ethos, that is to say they were more positive about students and about learning than were the other schools. Of course there were other factors which helped. One of these was having a balanced intake.

> The implication is that the outcomes are likely to be most favourable when there is a reasonable balance of academically successful children who are liable to be rewarded by their good attainments at school and, therefore, who perhaps are more prone to identify with the school goals and aims. When the proportion of less able children becomes too high, this will mean that a preponderance of the students will fail to achieve examination success and hence may see themselves as not achieving anything useful at school. (Rutter et al., 1979a, pp. 159–60)

I was fortunate in being in a position to play a role in the adaptation and extension of this research design with a sample of primary schools whilst working as Director of Research and Statistics for the Inner London Education Authority from 1978–1985. Our research team (which included two other current members of the institute's staff) replicated the central finding that schools had different levels of effectiveness and that inner-city schools receiving disadvantaged students could still be effective in promoting progress.

Because we had started with a truly random sample, used a longitudinal design, collected a wide range of data and employed the emerging multilevel modelling statistical techniques being developed by my colleague, Professor Harvey Goldstein, we were reasonably confident of the validity of the differences that we found between schools. Our faith has been justified by the subsequent re-analysis of the data which replicated the original findings (Sammons et al., 1993b). We were also able to extend the theoretical explanation of the differences in outcomes of the schools. We suggested that both *given* variables—such as the size of the school and the ratio of students to teachers—and the *policy* variables, reflecting the decisions of those within the school, could make a difference.

We identified a number of what we termed key factors concerned with both whole-school and classroom processes. These factors have been much debated since the publication of our findings in 1986 (and in book form in 1988). They and those of other prior and subsequent studies have recently been collected by a team working at this institute.

These factors should not be seen as a blueprint for effectiveness. They have not been conclusively proved to be essential but, given the consistency of their identification by researchers working in different countries and employing different methods, the probability of their importance is clear. The way they are enacted, of course, will vary between schools. The number of studies that have been reviewed to create the list of factors is large (approximately 160). Those wishing to find more exhaustive reviews should consult Reynolds et al. (1994b) or Northwest Regional Educational Laboratory (1990).

What has been the impact of school effectiveness work?

Having recently returned from the seventh International Congress of School Effectiveness and Improvement in the Netherlands, it would be easy to overclaim in answer to this question. Researchers, policy makers and practitioners from 50 or so countries meeting to exchange ideas and good practice and engaging in practical and theoretical discussions makes for a stimulating environment. Endeavouring, however, to put aside any halo effects of this experience, I would wish to make seven comments on the usefulness of this field of study. In my judgement school effectiveness research has:

- Moderated over-deterministic sociological theories about home background

- Qualified an over-reliance on psychological individualistic theories about learning
- Focused attention on the potential of institutional influences
- Provided—as a result—a more optimistic view of teaching and renewed attention on learning concerns and on school management
- Advanced the methodology of the study of complex social effects
- Stimulated many experiments in school improvement
- Contributed to theories of how students learn in particular school settings

Social background theories
The works of Coleman et al. (1966) and Jencks et al. (1972), as noted earlier, have frequently been used to demonstrate that school influences are small in comparison to those concerned with socio-economic status. Whilst this is undoubtedly true in relation to student *attainment* (and could hardly be otherwise in view of the enormous range of life conditions experienced by young people), it is not completely true in relation to student *progress*. Thus, in our junior school study we were able to explain (in a statistical sense) approximately 25 per cent of the variance between students in progress in comparison to only 5 or so per cent which we were able to trace to home background (Mortimore et al., 1988a).

Individual psychological theories of learning
Elsewhere I have addressed issues that link theories of learning and of teaching with school effectiveness (Mortimore, 1993a). I believe that an approach which focuses predominantly on the individual learner is of limited value. The recognition by school effectiveness scholars that individuals develop in a complex context of family, peer and school influences—with phases of development being differently affected by some factors rather than by others—not only accords with other theories but is crucially important in its own right and has many implications for practice.

Institutional effects
The late Jack Tizard, an eminent professor at this institute (and one of my doctoral supervisors), was one of a small group of researchers who early on recognized the scope of institutional effects (Tizard et al., 1975). Focusing on hospitals, childrens' homes, nurseries and approved schools, he and his colleagues formulated a methodology (later developed by Professor Michael Rutter) by which, having selected a range of appropriate outcomes and using a process known to researchers as backward mapping, they sought to tease out the characteristics of the institution which were associated with positive or negative effects. Although the application of the technique has mostly been used by school effectiveness researchers, it has considerable scope for research into special school provision, further education and, indeed, universities (Mortimore, 1991b).

Teaching as an optimistic activity

The research evidence provides support for the positive role of head teachers and teachers and for school and classroom influences. Of course, those who work in schools in the most disadvantaged areas have a difficult task. As I have already noted, it would be curious if the enhanced life experiences of some young people did not predispose them to doing better than their less advantaged peers in any competitive performance. But part of the impact of school effectiveness research and its associated school improvement activities has been to provide hope—and fairer ways of judging the results of their efforts—to head teachers, teachers and their colleagues in urban areas (see, for instance, House of Commons, 1994).

The methodology of studying complex social effects

The status of school effectiveness investigations has been well documented in recent years (Reynolds et al., 1994b; Scheerens, 1993). As with any developing field, there have been demands for clearer conceptualization, the use of more sophisticated statistical techniques, better sampling methods, more appropriate outcomes and better ways of linking outcomes to processes. Considerable progress on these fronts has been made and a methodology of *value added* has been developed. This term refers to the 'relative boost a school gives to a student's previous level of attainment' (Sammons et al., 1995d). It enables the identification of those schools which, despite receiving disadvantaged intakes of students, are able to promote outstanding progress. Similarly, this technique permits the head teachers of schools which receive favourable intakes, but which fail to promote progress commensurate with similar schools, to review their success (Thomas & Mortimore, 1994) and, perhaps of even greater significance, enables departmental differences within schools to be studied (Sammons et al., 1995d).

Experiments in school improvement

At an international conference at this institute in 1992, much of the territory of school improvement was laid out. The conference papers, published in *Managing Schools Today*, included reports on Canadian (Stoll and Fink, 1993), American (FitzHarris, 1993) and British experiences (Taggart, 1993). The first of a series of *Bulletins* from our recently founded International School Effectiveness and Improvement Centre (ISEIC) describes the features of improvement programmes and lists what have been termed the doors to improvement: *collegiality* between staff; awareness of *research* into effective schools; knowledge of *site-specific* data on the school; *curriculum initiatives*; and developments in *pedagogy* (Joyce, 1991).

In drawing up a programme for the work of the ISEIC, we have sought to take forward two related strands of work. First, we have endeavoured to extend the corpus of knowledge about the implications for school improvement of school effectiveness work. We have done this through projects such as the Lancashire examination analysis (Thomas & Mortimore, 1994) and the study commissioned by the Office for Standards in Education on how best to make sense of examination results using surrogate background variables (Sammons et al., 1994c). We have also undertaken studies funded by the Economic and Social Research Council on secondary school and subject department differences, primary school development planning, and the innovative use of staff in city technology colleges. The centre has also benefited from the contribution of Professor Harvey Goldstein and his constantly developing work on multilevel modelling.

Our second strand of work focuses on methods of supporting schools working on improvement programmes. A group of associates, drawn from the senior ranks of the education service, work with us on a variety of programmes in collaboration with individual schools and local education authorities. Currently, we are involved in 20 projects with many scores of schools and LEAs. In addition, we co-ordinate a network of 250 or so individual and corporate members.

We recognize that the use of the term 'improvement' could imply that only failing schools need to work with us. We reject this view and use the term as a shorthand for an international body of research and associated developments concerned with raising the quality of education. For us, the crucial characteristic of the work is that the initiative stems not from government diktat nor from any academic or inspectorial orthodoxy but 'rather from a commitment to view the staff of schools themselves as the agents for change' (Hillman & Stoll, 1994).

In a recent survey commissioned by the Office for Standards in Education, Professor Michael Barber of Keele University identified 60 urban school improvement projects currently taking place within the United Kingdom. These projects vary from one concerned with A-level achievement in Dagenham to youth work for young people at risk in Cambridge (Barber, 1994). Themes from these projects include raising achievement, assessment processes, improving the behaviour of students, the mentoring of teachers, measures to reduce bullying, maximizing the value of homework and many others. In all, over 80 per cent of the projects are focused on raising achievement levels and over two-thirds employ some kind of indicators to examine effectiveness.

At the Netherlands conference, Dr David Hopkins (of the Cambridge Institute of Education) welcomed the coming together of teachers from different countries, involved in improvement programmes, in order to analyse what they had been doing, compare progress and obtain feedback from an experienced evaluator. (Two of the teams reporting on their work are collaborating with colleagues from our centre.) Dr Hopkins has proposed a number of *desiderata* for future school improvement work in order to maximize its opportunity to help teachers (Hopkins, 1995). It remains to be seen whether people will follow Hopkins's suggestions and whether the suggestions will lead to the desired effects.

Theoretical basis
Although school effectiveness and school improvement work have been led, in general, by empirical investigations, there has been an increasing preoccupation with the need for the development of an underpinning theory. This lack of a

sufficiently specific theory has been compensated for, in part, by the use of a range of other theories culled from psychology (in particular, child development), management science, sociology and, more recently, the literature on institutional change. The need for an integrated theory, however, remains. One of the first models is that produced by a school effectiveness researcher from the Netherlands, Professor Jaap Scheerens (1990). In his model, Scheerens endeavours to link *inputs* to the school and *outputs* from it with *processes* drawn from both classroom and school levels within a specified *context*.

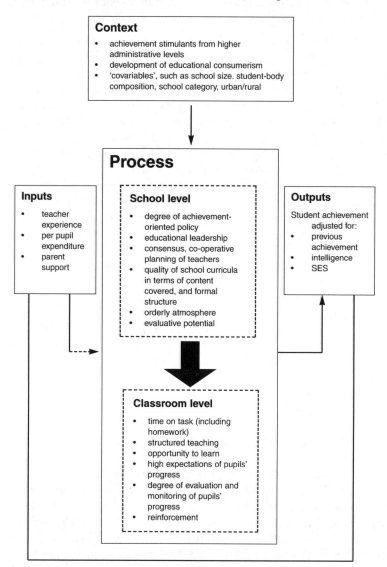

Figure 14.1.   A theoretical model.

Drawing on the latest thinking of Scheerens (1995), it may be helpful to consider our interest in theory under six separate headings:

- Conceptual clarification (i.e. what do we mean by terms such as 'effectiveness')
- Explanations and predictions of positive student outcomes
- Mechanisms of improvement
- Delineation of models
- Contingency effects and unintended consequences of different models
- Relationships with established social scientific and educational theories

Considerable progress has been made on the first and second components. On the whole, researchers in this field talk the same language and, as I have indicated, are in a position to explain a number of positive outcomes. With regard to the third component, after a period in which the differences between effectiveness research and improvement projects failed to be recognized (Clark et al., 1984), researchers are now studying how these mechanisms might operate (Hopkins, 1995; Stoll, 1992). We are also endeavouring to describe more accurately the various models of both effectiveness and improvement.

It is, perhaps, in relation to the fifth and sixth components that least progress has been made. Identifying contingency effects and predicting the probability of unintended consequences of particular initiatives are difficult tasks. Not only do researchers make wrong predictions but, at times, governments have created policies which have led to the opposite of what was intended or which have produced unwelcome side effects.

Work which relates school effectiveness to other theories also needs to be carried out. Scheerens has begun this to do this with a detailed account of the relevance of public choice theory to school improvement (Scheerens, 1992). Others who have sought to contribute to the formulation of theories in this field of study include: Coleman and Collinge (1991), Slater and Teddlie (1992), and Hopkins (1994b). A recently completed institute study which reports the empirical testing of six postulates to do with how best to help schools in their improvement strategies will, we hope, also make a contribution to this area (MacGilchrist et al., 1995).

What is the potential of school effectiveness and improvement?

As I have tried to illustrate, we need to learn more about how improvement takes place. We are not seeking to create a recipe book—schools are far too complex for such an approach—but rather to tease out the underlying processes of change. Scholars such as Fullan (1992a), Huberman (1993) and Louis and Miles (1991) have identified a number of facilitating or inhibiting factors, but there are insufficient British studies of equivalent status. The follow-up study to *Fifteen Thousand Hours* (Maughan et al., 1990; Ouston et al., 1991) provides us with some ideas, but we need more case studies of the genesis of effective schools. It is encouraging, therefore, that the final project of the National Commission on Education is devoted to uncovering how some schools have succeeded against the odds. Twelve teams (each consisting of an educational researcher and representatives from the business world and the community) are engaged in fieldwork trying to identify the reasons why chosen schools are successful in the face of disadvantage. Howard Davies of the Confederation of British Industry and Sarah Portway of IBM are currently part of this project and are engaged with me in drawing up a case study of a school in South London.

We also need to resolve a number of technical research issues which impinge upon both effectiveness and improvement studies. In the paper presented by my colleagues and I at the Desmond Nuttall Memorial Conference last year (Mortimore et al., 1994c), for instance, we drew attention to three such issues: the (lack of) stability of results over time; the possibility of differential effects within the same school; and the effects of context on school performance. Since then we have carried out further work on these issues. We have taken forward our thinking, particularly with regard to the first issue. Working with the same sample of schools, we have looked at trends in examination value-added scores over three years (Thomas et al., 1995a) and have found that the overall results of schools are indeed relatively stable, but that this overall stability conceals a considerable amount of change within various subjects: what we have termed the 'swings and roundabouts effect'. This operates through results in some subjects improving and thus compensating overall for the deterioration, from one year to another, in other subjects. We also found interesting overall patterns with, for instance, history showing the greatest stability from one year to another, and French the least. We now need to establish why these patterns occur and to try to ascertain whether it is something intrinsic to the subjects, the way they are examined or the manner in which they are taught which is most likely to account for the differences between them.

In terms of increasing our knowledge of how best to help and support schools to improve, we now need research on the efficacy of:

- Different models of intervention (ranging from the sympathetic outsider seeking to increase insights, through the provision of feedback, to the Education Association which—as a last resort—will assume the statutory powers of the governing body and head teacher)
- Different strategies of action (focusing immediately on the classroom learning and teaching or approaching this, indirectly, through the governing body and the management arrangements)
- Different ways to ensure the optimum match of the intervention strategy to the circumstances and context of the school. My colleague, Dr Louise Stoll, has recently been considering how best to link the 11 factors for effective schools (noted earlier) with school improvement routes which include specific actions for heads and teachers to carry out (Stoll & Mortimore, 1995). We now need to test these actions in carefully evaluated projects.

Of course, we need to remain conscious that what suits the schools of today might not suit those of tomorrow. Technological developments are certain to make a difference (Wood, 1993). The ability to connect with other learners any-where in the world, to use virtual reality to explore geographical and historical phenomena and the opportunity to experience personal coaching through inter-actional multi-media packages must enhance the opportunity for better learn-ing. I remain sceptical, however, as to whether such developments will, in fact, make schools, as we know them, completely redundant (Mortimore, 1994c).

School effectiveness and school improvement still need further research and development in order to clarify some conceptual issues and to improve some technical mechanisms. In general, though, this field of scholarship, in which the institute has been so heavily involved, has been productive in academic terms in this country and abroad. It has also been successful in eliciting the interest of some policy makers and a number of practitioners. It remains to be seen, of course, how much this work will actually change the way teachers and students behave in schools, but it has already taken us some way towards developing a methodology of improvement.

We need also to draw out the lessons for school improvement from the recently completed study on school development planning carried out by my colleagues Dr Barbara MacGilchrist, Jane Savage and Dr Charles Beresford and myself. Our data show that, although development planning is being undertak-en and is absorbing a great deal of time and energy, only in a minority of cases is the plan *corporate*. By this term we mean that it involves the full staff, is co-ordinated with all the other planning issues in the school and that it impacts upon the opportunities for learning in the classroom. We have characterized the development plan in other schools as *rhetorical* (mainly fine words), as *singular* (where it appears to be the property of the head teacher) and as *co-operative* (where it has some of the properties of the corporate plan but has not yet reached the classroom) (MacGilchrist et al., 1994).

The emphasis on improving the learning opportunities for students is a char-acteristic of the best school improvement projects currently being undertaken in both primary and secondary schools. Yet I believe that it is in the primary sec-tor that schools can make the most difference. A recent follow-up of the *School Matters* cohort has shown that the primary school effect had not been washed out by five years in secondary schools (Sammons, 1995). The ongoing study by my colleagues confirms the presence of a 'strong persisting influence on sixteen-year-olds' achievement' (Goldstein & Sammons, 1994).

Primary schools, however, have often been regarded as the Cinderella of the education system. Certainly their levels of funding and average size of class are far less generous than their secondary counterparts. Paradoxically, a recent review of class size suggests that it may be with the youngest primary students that the best return from an investment in smaller classes can be obtained (Blatchford & Mortimore, 1994).

In terms of achievement levels of primary schools, our research—carried out during the 1980s—found considerable variation between what teachers saw as acceptable, and identified secondary teachers as being nonplussed at how to cope with such differing levels of achievement in their intakes. Many primary schools, of course, were extremely ambitious for, and had high expectations of, their students, but others did not. We found that intellectual challenge was a characteristic only of the most effective schools.

Now that we have a national curriculum with an entitlement for students, this variation ought to be less of a problem, but it will undoubtedly take time for new levels of achievement to be seen as appropriate and—in some cases—to be considered possible. We should not waste a moment. Professor Maurice Galton of Leicester University argues that primary schools will not be improved 'by reducing the demands of a national curriculum and providing a moratorium for teachers to master the various programmes of study and the revised assessment procedures' (Galton, 1995, p. 52). Instead, he proposes that teachers need to build up their own understandings of the nature of the knowledge they are endeavouring to teach and their knowledge about 'how children think and learn'.

Certainly there is scope for raising standards—as publication of the national curriculum tests indicate. My view is that we need to attend much more to the key skills of reading and mathematics, though it is important to stress that this should not be to the major detriment of other curriculum subjects. Professor Robin Alexander of Leeds University has recently stressed the need for schools to follow a wide-ranging curriculum which will give them 'the broader skills which will enable them to cope with the complexities and tensions of life in a pluralist and divided society' (Alexander, 1994).

Professor Bob Slavin of Johns Hopkins University, the author of a leading-edge intervention programme in the United States, is also concerned that schools should make the most of the opportunities of early learning. He has argued that, unless children master the basic skills of reading and mathematics, they will be unable to develop whatever talents they might have (Slavin et al., 1989; 1994). Slavin uses an approach which draws on the Reading Recovery work of Dame Professor Marie Clay. Clay was a visiting professor here for two years and established a Department for Education/Institute of Education collaborative programme for a national programme of Reading Recovery.

This highly structured, individualized programme seeks to enable children experiencing reading problems at the age of six to catch up with their peers through a brief, but intensive, period of individual help (Hobsbaum & Hillman, 1994). Our work with this programme is being evaluated through a grant from the School Curriculum and Assessment Authority. Initial findings are positive.

Unless reading is put right at an early stage, the problem becomes increasingly difficult to solve. The Secondary Transfer Study, in which a number of my colleagues and I were involved during the 1980s, showed clearly that the biggest handicap to students' subsequent progression was their reading difficulties: 'their educational outcomes and . . . their future employment prospects, clearly underline the importance of identifying those with reading difficulties at an early stage and responding appropriately to their needs' (Alston & Sammons, 1986).

I also wish to argue for a new focus on the teaching of primary mathematics. Our recent research evidence shows that the years of junior schooling are important for the whole school career of the student. Yet we know that, in many primary schools, the subject is being taught by teachers who not only lack formal qualifications in mathematics but who are, in certain cases, insecure in their grasp of its essential principles. The Ofsted evidence on primary mathematics is uneven. The annual report for 1992/93 draws attention to 'weaknesses in using and applying mathematics generally' (pp. 10–11) but is more critical of teachers' lack of knowledge and understanding of science, and the report on the fourth year of the monitoring programme of the national curriculum found that 'in three-quarters of the lessons standards of achievement were satisfactory or better' (p. 4). A new annual report is about to be published.

A current debate between academics over whether the mathematical competences and understandings of undergraduates have declined, however, has caused my colleague from King's College, Professor Margaret Brown, to argue that, whilst the curriculum, in her view, is now generally suitable, 'it is the way it is taught that causes the problem' (Brown, 1993). Brown believes a shortage of trained mathematics teachers means that students are being taught by some teachers who do not have a confident grasp of the subject. Given the moratorium on curriculum change that has been agreed, following the acceptance of Sir Ron Dearing's review, this is an opportune moment for head teachers and governing bodies to consider their approach to these vital subjects—though they may need some support at national level if work on reading and mathematics realistically is to be put on a new footing.

Does the education system help or hinder effectiveness?

The next question is whether the national educational system helps or hinders schools in their search for improvement. I am conscious that to leave the world of the school and to comment on 'the system' is to leave the scientific security of academia with its known confidence intervals and take to shark-infested waters! I have no wish to involve myself in political comment for its own sake, and have sought to distance the institute from party political bias, but it is impossible to discuss the system of schooling in the abstract. It is also foolish to imagine that schools can do it all alone: as our Emeritus Professor Basil Bernstein (1970) famously commented, 'education cannot compensate for society'. Of course, I recognize that politicians have a legitimate interest in education: the system consumes over 30 billion pounds of our national budget, it represents the largest state intervention into the lives of citizens, and it is the main vehicle for the transmission of values and of our national culture.

Furthermore, the system has changed greatly over the last seven or eight years. The Education Reform Act of 1988, for instance, re-wrote the relationship between central and local government educational policies, introduced a national curriculum and created a system of local management for schools. It also introduced the concept of the social market to schools and colleges and, with subsequent legislation, introduced a new system of school inspections.

A great deal has been written by academics about the impact of this legislation, much of it critical, as the recent edited collection by my colleague, Professor Sally Tomlinson of Goldsmith's College, illustrates (Tomlinson, 1994). My personal view is that an overall evaluation is unhelpful: many changes were sorely needed; others were introduced on ideological rather than educational grounds and, as often happens, have created further problems. It is, of course, always difficult to introduce change. As Professor Michael Fullan of Toronto University observes, 'one must always fight against over-control on the one hand and chaos on the other' (Fullan, 1993). In our case, it must also be recognized that the costs, both in terms of wasted revenue and the well-being of many practitioners, have been considerable.

The system of today is very different to that of ten years ago. In some ways it ought to be more supportive of school improvement: local management has enhanced the power of head teachers and governing bodies to control their own destinies; new-style inspections will be more regular and will provide more accurate feedback; there is a new energy and dynamism among some school staff.

On the other hand, the new system has also created some serious problems which, rather than supporting school improvement, can sabotage it. I will focus on just one example concerning the promotion of diversity. The British school system has always been diverse, with a small but powerful group of independent schools and the co-existence of denominational and county, single-sex and mixed schools. Moreover, recent legislation has sought to increase its diversity by creating grant-maintained schools, technology schools and city technology colleges and by enabling existing comprehensive schools to opt for the power to select at least some of their student intake.

The 1992 White Paper expressed the view that 'more diversity allows schools to respond more effectively to the needs of the local and national community' (Department for Education, 1992). Diversity, a popular concept much lauded in political speeches, obviously has advantages in terms of its potential sensitivity to popular pressures and through its propensity to encourage innovations and experiments. It also has a down side in that it disturbs the equilibrium of systems. Quite simply, a single governing body choosing—and being permitted—to change its school's character, in effect, can alter the perceived character and status of all other schools in the neighbourhood through a domino effect.

Does this matter? It matters if you believe that the equilibrium is worth preserving. If, however, you believe that the whole system needs to be reformed, then diversity is irresistible: introduce it, encourage those with imagination to take advantage of it and see what has been achieved when the dust has settled! But of course life is not this simple. There are likely to be casualties amongst students and teachers. The extent of these casualties will depend on whether the introduction of a new school—or type of school—funded in a different way or according to different standards, poses a threat to more traditionally established schools and to the professionalism of their teachers (Hargreaves, 1994).

Is a negative reaction simply a question of envy or resentment at not being where the action is? In my judgement, there can be legitimate grounds for governors, head teachers and teachers feeling aggrieved. For example, if a new or restructured school takes away resources from the existing schools in the area, eclipses them with its enhanced building (or resourcing levels) and thereby reduces their community esteem. For those who for years have dedicated their efforts to serving students in particular schools, especially if these are in inner-city disadvantaged neighbourhoods, the introduction of diversity and a market economy brings few rewards. Seeing newly established rival institutions being better funded and certainly better housed must be a sore test of their commitment to the state education system.

Yet I am also sympathetic to the views put forward by head teachers and teachers from those city technology colleges and grant-maintained schools with whom I work. They have shown me that innovation is stimulating, that being sponsored brings energy and commitment as well as resources. For the first time in a long while, they feel excited by the potential of schooling and by their own ability to improve their school.

The challenge for the system of how to maintain these positive attitudes and this achievement, without too high a price being paid by all those students and teachers who are likely to remain in less innovative settings and on whom the quality of the major part of the system depends, is daunting. A fine balance has to be struck. This tension may be eased with the introduction of a common funding formula which ensures a level playing field approach to resources.

Otherwise there is a danger that, with the British sensitivity to status differences, the result of a policy of diversity may simply be an even more refined pecking order of schools which, in effect, may make school improvement more difficult for most head teachers and governors.

What should be the role of the university?

This Institute, and many other university departments of education, have played an important role in carrying out relevant research, synthesizing and interpreting findings from a range of studies of school effectiveness and working collaboratively with practitioners on school improvement programmes. (See, for example, the new School Improvement Centre at the University of Bath and the ongoing Improving the Quality of Education for All project run by the Cambridge Institute of Education.) Is this enough or are there other tasks they should be performing? Before answering this question, it may be helpful to comment on the role of the university in general.

One of the roles of a university is to create 'a knowledge of first principles and relations rather than of mere facts', as John Henry Newman wrote in 1852. Central to the role of this institute is 'the promotion of new ideas in policy and professional practice grounded in its research and teaching expertise'. Over the last hundred or so years, this university has amply fulfilled its role, as the number of Nobel and other prize winners illustrates. This institute, too, has played its part in generating ideas for educational change and a number of my predecessors, and many of our professors, have been in the forefront of educational thinking.

In recent times, however, much of the thinking role has been taken over by governments and their agencies. Of course, I am not arguing against governments acting intelligently but simply pointing out that there has been a growing tendency in our field for university thinking to be ignored or accorded a lower status. Academics have sometimes reacted by focusing exclusively on criticizing governments and this has led to them being seen as either totally negative or in thrall to the opposition parties.

I do not believe this development has been good for the policy makers. Governments have created special policy units and have supported independent groups outside of academia, but in some (but not all) cases this has created a tendency to propagate ideas based more on ideology than on research evidence (Brown, 1993). It has also led governments into policy developments based on insufficiently tested ideas. In the field of education this precipitation has exacted a heavy price from our national budget (over half a billion pounds in the case of the national curriculum and its associated assessment programme).

If this analysis of the sidelining of universities by policy makers is correct, one has to ask how such a situation came about? The historians of tomorrow will no doubt provide fuller answers, but my interpretation of developments in education over the last twenty or so years is that both governments and universities must share the blame. Governments have been impatient, they have become over-ideological, they have fallen into the trap of thinking that they must know best, and they have focused on the short term.

Governments have become impatient

The 1987 consultation document was followed far too promptly, in my judgement, by the 1988 Education Reform Act. Comment and information received from thousands of academics and practitioners could not be assimilated in time and had to be ignored. We know, thanks to the painstaking research of Haviland (1988), that, had some of this advice been followed, a more cost-effective process could have been adopted. Similarly, as a member of the steering group of the first KS1 (key stage 1) assessment project, I know that the deadlines inflicted on the development teams were impossible. The teams did their best, but the work would have benefited from less pressure. Such haste made no sense, was a poor use of resources and stored up trouble for the future (Black, 1994). As it happened, it did not matter, because the government changed its policy on the testing model.

Governments have become over-ideological

This is not the place for a full discussion of ideology or of the current reliance on the notion of education as a social market and there are others far better qualified than me to comment on these topics (Bridges & McLaughlin, 1994; Chubb & Moe, 1990; Le Grand & Bartlett, 1993; and my colleague Dr Geoff

Whitty, 1992). I simply want to make the point that such a dependence on one idea makes any government vulnerable. A less ideological approach, which accepted that some aspects of the education system were suited to a market approach—and that such an approach was probably long overdue—would probably have better served those wanting change. Such an approach, however, would have to accept that other aspects would not benefit from the introduction of market principles but needed planning on an area, even a national, basis.

Thinking that one always knows best

This is a very natural state both for individuals and for governments. It is also dangerous. We have seen how the political imperative to create a particular type of assessment could not be delivered; it was just not technically possible to do so. Similarly, politicians in a number of different countries have discovered that, despite their considerable powers, their wishes can be frustrated if the people on whom they depend are not convinced of the reasonableness of the policy. It is possible to abolish organizations and it is certainly possible to create new bodies and give them wide powers. But it is not possible to legislate for excellence or to guarantee that all teachers will approach the national curriculum with enthusiasm and energy.

Governments have focused on the short term

The education of an individual takes a long time: at least 11 years of statutory schooling, together with pre-schooling and post-school training at work, often over an extended period. It is unrealistic, therefore, to expect changes in the education system to take place very rapidly. Of course this is frustrating and can be an excuse for procrastination. But governments avoid facing up to this reality at their peril. Fullan (1993) and many others have warned of the dangers of rash reforms. Similarly, some developments take time to 'bed down' before their impact is felt. An example is the Reading Recovery Programme, where the preliminary results, in this country, are extremely encouraging. The government has invested directly, and through the local education authorities, in the programme's success. It hardly seems sensible on any grounds, therefore, to withdraw support now that the scheme is working well and the early investment is beginning to pay off. It is not just like any other initiative: it is one of the most promising means of raising national standards. It is expensive, as is any individual coaching. But if a child can be cured of reading problems, for the equivalent of the costs of administering a statement of special educational needs, that must represent good value for money.

It would be wrong to blame the government exclusively for the situation I have described; universities too must accept some responsibility. I repeat—the historians will write their accounts in due course. I suspect, however, that some of the factors which have led policy makers to see the work of university departments of education as generally irrelevant have been the inability of academics to work to time-scales which correspond more closely with policy needs, their failure to engage sufficiently with the real-life problems of schooling, and the tendency to engage in what seem, to the outside world, to be rather esoteric debates.

The inability of university academics to work to time-scales which fit with policy needs

Different kinds of institutions have different rhythms of working and, in previous times, it seemed that the rhythm of the university could not be adjusted to fit with that of the school. Certainly, when I was the Director of Research and Statistics for the Inner London Education Authority during the 1980s, working in a climate where research was taken very seriously, I soon learned the lesson that policy makers need to have research evidence at the time of their debates and that a delay in the production of a report—however excellent—would render it of little value if it missed the crucial debate. I also learned how difficult it must have been for universities to fit in with such a timetable for, despite the many offers of help from academics or graduate students, we were able to collaborate on only a limited number of occasions.

The failure of university academics to engage in the real-life problems of schooling

This is an easy criticism to make and one which might be seen as unfair, since large-scale projects need funding and this is generally outside academic control. Nevertheless, in my experience, there is a tendency for academics to focus on peripheral issues and ignore the main questions. There is, for instance, a lack of high-quality research on both learning in the classroom and on effective teaching, yet there have been numerous studies on issues of less relevance. This may be because educational researchers have been afraid to tackle the big issues without first developing their skills on smaller projects. In a profession with so poor a career structure, researchers may well have moved into teaching or other jobs before they felt equipped to deal with the major studies that need to be done. There is, after all, a dearth of full-time posts for professionally qualified researchers. But the problem of peripheral research has certainly been exacerbated by poor judgement and a lack of a sufficiently detailed knowledge of schools and schooling.

The tendency of university academics to engage in esoteric debates

Reynolds (1995a) has described how, in his judgement, the sociology of education was weakened considerably by academics engaging in fundamental debates before their collective knowledge base was sufficiently robust to bear the pressure; a process which did not take place to such an extent in the United States or in mainland Europe. In the field of educational research there is a tendency to do the same: to focus on such issues as whether, for instance, studies of school effectiveness and studies of school improvement work in the same or in different paradigms. Valid and important though such a distinction is, there is the danger that this issue becomes the major focus and distracts from studies to improve the quality of learning.

Theoretical and methodological matters are essential subjects for researchers to debate but, if this is seen by practitioners to be the major focus of educational research, it is likely to be deemed irrelevant to most schooling issues. Practitioners will communicate this negative view to policy makers and, as a result, academics will fall out of favour with both groups. This is likely to be more of a problem in the field of education than in other areas, because the common experience of schooling gives non-researchers considerable knowledge of the field. There is an assumption, therefore, that all problems can be solved with common sense: a comforting, but not necessarily true, sentiment.

A related problem is the lack of a tradition within the teaching profession of keeping up with the field—whether in a specialist subject area or in pedagogy itself. I hope this attitude is changing and would encourage researchers to write in professional, as well as in academic, journals and in our excellent trade press. I would also encourage practitioners to include such reading as part of their professional development.

The way forward

With a new Secretary of State for Education, this is surely the time for a new relationship to be formed between academics and policy makers. We have seen the alternative and it does not work. Of course, lessons have been learned by both parties and practice has changed. In the light of such changes, we should be able to create a more effective system which better serves our society's needs and which is likely to help more schools to improve.

This means academics in universities playing a fuller part in the promotion of new ideas; formulating policies and calculating their respective advantages and disadvantages; testing out ideas for unintended consequences; and sharing in the evaluation of initiatives based on such policy changes. It means governments listening to academics; dispensing with what my colleague from King's College, Professor Stephen Ball, has termed the 'discourse of derision' (Ball, 1990). It might also be helpful for everyone if a forum in which academics, civil servants and practitioners could discuss important educational issues (like the former Central Advisory Councils) were to be established.

Academics, in turn, must be prepared to engage more in the world of schools. This will involve addressing important policy issues (including those dilemmas in which hard decisions have to be made) and working to timetables which, wherever possible, fit with policy makers' needs.

This country faces an uncertain future. At a time of increasingly global trade it will have to compete with other nations in which the cost of labour is relatively low. The advance of technology makes it likely that industry will only need small numbers of highly skilled workers rather than its traditional large-scale work force. We face a climate in which, according to Charles Handy, 'Britain will never be "Great" again, in the sense that she could be a world power or economic force . . .' (Handy, 1994).

Yet, as in other developed nations, it still seems prudent to educate as many of each generation as we can, to as high a level as possible, both in anticipation of new, as yet unthought of, employment opportunities and in order to ensure the continuation of our democratic culture. For those who are not likely to have the opportunity for a full-time career, the need to develop their self-efficacy may be even more powerful than for their working peers. Yet, in those areas of the country where there has been chronic unemployment, we have failed so far to find an alternative means of motivating young people and of inculcating self-respect. In such circumstances, the need for school improvement and for energy and commitment from all who work in, or with, them is crystal clear.

Let us, therefore, continue to support schools with our work on effectiveness and improvement and through our involvement in policy formulation and analysis. As we move towards the millennium—and the centenary of this institute—I hope that the comments of Ernest Barker, a former principal of King's College, may still be echoed by future generations of school students:

> 'My school . . . taught me to work, to read, and to think. It gave me great friendships. It filled me entirely and utterly for nearly the space of seven years. Outside the cottage, I had nothing but my school; but having my school I had everything'. (Barker, 1953)

Postscript

This chapter addresses issues beyond the scope of school effectiveness research. Such issues go right to the heart of schooling, involving, as they do, the governance of education and the tensions between policy makers, practitioners and academics. The comments which I made about the lack of trust between politicians and universities are as relevant in the United Kingdom under a Labour government as they were under a Conservative administration in 1995. These matters must be resolved if our national system is to improve. The evidence produced by the school effectiveness studies demonstrates the importance of a school climate which is positive and in which rewards are more common than punishments. Similar characteristics should govern the education system as a whole.

15

The Relationship Between School Effectiveness and School Improvement[1]

Introduction

One of the 'roads' that I signposted in chapter ten was that of school improvement, which I described as a productive offshoot of the research on school effectiveness. By the mid 1990s it was clear that school improvement had developed its own distinct paradigm. In the publication on which this chapter is based, Louise Stoll and I tried to spell out the common and the differing characteristics of the two fields. Louise Stoll had been a field officer on the School Matters project. As a direct result of this experience, she had been seconded to a school district in Ontario which was about to begin a major programme of school improvement. The secondment was so successful that she worked for five years in Canada and was involved in a series of school improvement ventures before returning to England and to an academic post at the Institute of Education. The tutorials for her doctoral thesis—which I supervised and which was based on the work she had undertaken in London and in Canada—were frequently held in airports and at international conferences as our paths crossed. Because of her work experience, Louise Stoll was able to provide a unique link between the school effectiveness tradition of London and the school improvement and educational change studies that Michael Fullan, Andy Hargreaves and others were developing in Toronto.

---

1 The first author of the original publication upon which this is based is Louise Stoll.

Background

The last decade has seen a burgeoning of interest in the twin fields of school effectiveness and school improvement by politicians, policy makers and practitioners. For some, the drive has been to raise standards and increase accountability through inspection and assessment measures, believing that the incentive of accountability and market competition will lead to improvement. Alternatively, reform and restructuring have led many people in schools to create their own agenda and to ask, 'How do we know that what we are doing makes a positive difference to our pupils?' and 'What can we do to provide pupils with the best possible education?'

This paper explores the paradigms that underpin notions of school effectiveness and school improvement. We start with their definitions and aims. Key factors of effectiveness and improvement are examined and fundamental issues discussed. We conclude with a description of attempts to link the two areas of work.

School effectiveness—definition and aims

A definition of 'effectiveness' is 'the production of a desired result or outcome' (Levine & Lezotte, 1990). School effectiveness researchers aim to ascertain whether differential resources, processes and organizational arrangements affect student outcomes and, if so, how. Ultimately, school effectiveness research searches for appropriate and reliable ways to measure school quality. The concept of 'effectiveness' forces choices to be made among competing values. While some people choose a narrow approach, with an emphasis on basic skills, others perceive schools' aims to be more diverse. There is a difference between those who believe that the chief focus of effectiveness should be equity, in particular raising standards for students 'at risk', and those who are committed to increasing standards for all students. Both approaches are important and can, to a certain extent, be combined. In this paper we define an effective school as one in which students progress further than might be expected from consideration of its intake.

Research on school effectiveness

School effectiveness studies largely came about in reaction to the view that home background had a far greater influence on a child's development than did the school. The studies sought to distinguish the impact of family background from that of the school, to ascertain whether some schools were more effective than others and, if so, to identify which factors contributed to the positive effects. Earlier studies, criticized for lack of generalizability and for methodological inadequacies, gave way to more sophisticated designs. Currently, school effectiveness researchers devote considerable attention to issues of measurement of student outcomes, stability and continuity of school effects, differential effectiveness and context specificity.

Value-added analyses
'Value added' is a technique designed to make fair comparisons between schools. It yields estimates of average progress for each institution. To assess the 'value' added by the school, it is essential to adjust for various background factors and for prior attainment by the individual student. To assess effectiveness of different schools without taking such information into account is like comparing apples with oranges. Unless schools are compared on a 'like with like' basis, judgements are neither fair nor valid. In Britain, to an increasing extent, schools, local education authorities, the media and, recently, the government have been looking at how to establish measures to be used in the analysis of educational outcomes (Department for Education, 1995). These measures range from simple disaggregation of academic results and attendance information (presented, for example, by gender, year and ethnic background) to the use of sophisticated multilevel modelling techniques.

The increasing consensus from political parties on the need for account to be taken of context in the analysis of schools' performance is welcome. While this is a step in the right direction, unresolved issues remain around the use of the concept of value added. Three will suffice here.

First, there is little agreement as to what academic measures are suitable for baseline assessment of pupils at the start of infant and junior school. Moreover, many tests are inappropriate for young children.

Secondly, current league tables and many of the available value-added analyses focus on examination and test results and on attendance. Whilst pupil attitudes increasingly are seen as an important aspect of a school's performance, less work has been undertaken by researchers on the corresponding value-added analysis. Furthermore, the world beyond school increasingly seeks young people who can display a wide range of skills and aptitudes, including the ability to solve problems and to be flexible, creative and co-operative. These attributes have received scant attention in terms of the measures generally used in schools.

Even when value-added analyses are used to produce 'adjusted' league tables, results need to be interpreted cautiously, because confidence intervals for school 'effects' are wide. This means that many schools cannot be separated reliably and that only schools or departments at the extreme ends of the spectrum can be identified as performing much better or worse than predicted (Goldstein & Thomas, 1995).

Stability and continuity in schools' effectiveness
Despite variations in estimates of the stability of school effects over time, there is general agreement that, when judging a school's effectiveness, it is important to take account of students' performance over a period of years.

The evidence also suggests the lingering effect of primary school throughout a students' career in secondary school. This highlights the importance of 'getting it right' at primary school. Much attention has been paid to secondary schools, the first port of call for Ofsted inspectors and the first target for league tables. The research evidence, however, implies that it is too late to leave effectiveness until secondary school. The academic building blocks must be in place during the primary years.

Schools' effectiveness for different pupils and those taking different subjects

In certain schools some students of different ethnic or social-class backgrounds or prior attainment levels tend to do better than others. Some departments are also more effective than others in promoting better results. This suggests that the overall concept of effective versus ineffective schools may be too simplistic to describe the dimensionality of schools' effects and has led to more detailed study of departmental effectiveness in secondary schools (Sammons et al., 1994b).

It has become increasingly clear, from studies of schools serving students from different social-class backgrounds and in international attempts to replicate one country's findings elsewhere or to examine the same factors in a different country, that 'what works' in one context may lack relevance in others. This has implications for the generalizability of research findings.

School improvement—definition and aims

The goals of school improvement have begun to move closer to those of school effectiveness, as the importance of student outcomes is increasingly acknowledged. The most frequently quoted definition of school improvement emanates from the International School Improvement Project (ISIP):

> 'a systematic sustained effort aimed at change in learning conditions and other related internal conditions in one or more schools, with the ultimate aim of accomplishing educational goals more effectively' (van Velzen et al., 1985).

This definition stresses the importance of careful planning, management and continuity, even in the face of difficulties. It also emphasizes a focus on teaching and learning, as well as the need to support organizational conditions. Additionally, the intricate relationship between school improvement and change is highlighted. Indeed, all school improvement involves change, although it cannot be assumed that all change leads to improvement. A more recent definition of improvement views it as 'a distinct approach to educational change that enhances student outcomes as well as strengthening the school's capacity for managing change' (Hopkins et al., 1994).

Research on school improvement

In the 1960s, 'school improvement' innovations from outside were frequently introduced to schools in a top-down manner. The original targets were organization and curriculum, with student-oriented outcomes as the goal. Lack of teacher commitment to this approach, however, led to a new improvement paradigm in the 1980s. This celebrated a 'bottom-up' approach, using practitioner, rather than external, knowledge. The focus shifted from the school to the teacher, although the improvement attempt was 'whole-school' oriented. Thus, school self-evaluation and school-based reviews were emphasized, as the process of change became the focus of studies. This process-oriented 'journey', however, did not always lead to actual improvement in students' achievement. Accordingly, the late 1980s saw a renewed emphasis on the evaluation of both processes *and* outcomes.

The 1990s have seen a further movement in this direction, exemplified in the approach of the Improving the Quality of Education for All (IQEA) project at the University of Cambridge Institute of Education (Hopkins et al., 1994). The project involves measurement of student outcomes but is chiefly concerned with the classroom-level and school-level processes that lead to such outcomes. The improvement strategies also blend the research and practitioner knowledge that has come to be associated with the school improvement movement, but with a greater emphasis on working *with*, rather than *on*, schools.

The process and outcomes of improvement

School improvement involves change. Most researchers have described three broad phases of the change process. The first, *initiation*, incorporates the process that leads up to the decision to change. The second, *implementation*, consists of early experiences of putting innovations into practice. The third, *institutionalization*, describes whether or not innovations are embedded into ongoing practice. Fullan (1991) adds a fourth state, *outcome*, which refers to a variety of results, including the impact on students, teachers, the organization and school-community relations. Generally the outcomes represent the extent of improvement measured according to specified criteria.

The actual process of improvement has been described as the determining, by the school, of priorities which are then formulated into a coherent strategy. Once the strategy is underway, problems tend to arise that lead to resistance or 'internal turbulence'. This causes a slowing down of progress and to frustration, often leading to abandonment of the original priority in favour of a new one. Change is notoriously 'messy' and time-consuming. When faced with problems, however, people in 'moving' schools respond by adapting their teaching, learning and organizational conditions. This, in turn, changes the school's culture and enables them to surmount the difficulties.

Characteristics of the innovation, individuals and organization

Superficial solutions, or 'bandwagons', have been demonstrated not to work or to lead to unnecessary overload. Successful innovations meet a defined need, are clear, frequently complex and of high quality. Essentially, change has to be worth the effort. Change also rarely involves single innovations. Rather, several ideas and activities are involved simultaneously. The skill lies in the ability to weave the various activities into a coherent whole (Stoll & Fink, 1996).

Various individual and organizational factors have also been demonstrated to be influential, and to indicate the school's readiness for change. Individual factors include teachers' concerns, interests, needs and skills, as well as their psychological states. Organizational factors include the innovation's compatibility with the school's culture, increasingly recognized as a fundamental influence on school improvement.

Routes to improvement
There has been a reluctance to offer 'hard-and-fast' rules for school improvement, because of schools' individual contexts and cultures. Joyce (1991) described five different 'doors' suggested by proponents of school improvement. We have updated this metaphor to look at current improvement doors being opened in Britain. Some of these doors are being opened from the inside:

- *Collegiality*—the development of cohesive and professional relations within and beyond schools and efforts to improve the culture of the schools
- *Research*—the use of research findings on school and classroom effectiveness and school improvement
- *Self-evaluation*—the collection and analysis of school and student data, action research in classrooms and staff appraisal
- *Curriculum*—the introduction of self-chosen curricular or cross-curricular changes or projects
- *Teaching and learning*—the study, discussion and development of teaching skills and strategies (such as flexible learning and co-operative group work)
- *Partnerships*—activities and projects that involve parents, community representatives and agencies, LEAs, business and industry, higher education, TECs and educational consultants
- *School development planning* (see below)

Other doors are opened by those outside the school:

- *Inspection*—after a visit by an inspection team, the generation of action plans to address those areas highlighted for improvement
- *Provision of 'value-added' data* (linked with league tables)—LEA staff and/or higher education partners/consultants can adjust assessment information to take account of prior attainment and background factors. This enables schools to see to what extent they have boosted students' progress
- *External projects*—similar to partnerships, except the impetus for change comes from outside, for example an LEA-led project or HE-led research project
- *Quality approaches*—emanating from business and industry, they include Total Quality Management (TQM) and Investors in People (IIP)
- *National curriculum* (and associated assessments)—the assumption is that the need to master subjects promotes curriculum development and the practical experience of administering assessments creates understanding of, and new ideas for, assessment

Joyce argues that adherence to just one approach is inadequate and that major school improvement efforts need to open all internal doors. The reality of the 1990s suggests that many external doors are also opened. Opening any of these doors, however, without attention to the culture (or cultures) and organizational conditions of the school, is unlikely to lead to real improvement.

A report commissioned by Ofsted found 60 urban school improvement projects around England (Barber et al., 1995). These projects vary in their approach and can be seen to open different doors. Some have a specific curriculum focus; for example, 'Impact Mathematics' in Haringey LEA or the City Reading Project in Oxford LEA. Others have their origins in LEA data collection and analysis; for example, in Nottinghamshire, Shropshire and Suffolk. Examples of improvement through partnership include Business Compacts in Cleveland, Enfield and Barnet, the Middlesborough Community Education project and Parental Involvement in the Core Curriculum in Tower Hamlets.

One approach that offers the opportunity to simultaneously open all doors is the school-based development process. There are many varieties of approach. In Britain its origins lie in school self-review and the approach is now exemplified in the school development planning model. An early prototype was the Guidelines for Review and Internal Development in Schools (GRIDS) (McMahon et al., 1984). This was a voluntary process which schools were encouraged to adapt. Its focus was on internal review (rather than external accountability), leading to development for improvement. The process was directed at the whole school rather than individual teachers or small groups. Throughout the world, subsequent models have followed a broadly similar format, although some have now become mandatory and accountability-linked. Unlike many of the other doors, the process provides an improvement strategy that includes an audit of needs, the setting of priorities, the means for implementation and evaluation.

Factors identified by school effectiveness and school improvement

Whilst it is acknowledged that no simple combination of factors produces an effective school, several reviewers have identified certain common processes and characteristics of more effective schools and those seen to have improved. In a recent review, British and North American research literature has been summarized and a list provided of key factors or correlates of effectiveness (Sammons et al., 1995e). These factors are neither exhaustive, nor necessarily independent of each other. They offer, however, a useful summary of the most common factors found to be associated with effective schools. Such factors provide a picture of what an effective school looks like. What they cannot explain, however, is how the school became effective. This is the domain of school improvement. Despite the differences in approach and orientation of the two fields of endeavour, their findings are, for the most part, complementary. We have adapted Sammons's factors to incorporate the factors that have been identified as leading to school improvement (see below). Whilst the school effectiveness factors represent a snapshot of what one would see in an effective school, the school improvement factors (or conditions) are the focus of an overall change strategy.

Resources

Much school effectiveness and school improvement literature ignores the issue of resources. This is because, in a number of studies, the schools in the sample have similar levels of funding and—as a result—there is too little variability to distinguish between them on the financial dimension. This should not be taken as evidence that resource levels are not important—an argument robustly presented by at least one American educational economist (Hanushek, 1986). The common view amongst British researchers is that resources help but do not guarantee effectiveness. There is little support for the view that reducing levels of funding will improve the performance of students, teachers or schools. One area in which resource levels have been widely debated is class size.

Current research and development activities

Given the complementarity of the factors identified by school effectiveness and school improvement, it is perhaps surprising that until recently in Britain there has been an 'intellectually and practically unhealthy' reluctance on the part of the two communities to join forces (Reynolds et al., 1993). In contrast, in North America practitioners and policy makers have worked with researchers to draw on studies from both traditions and to link the two areas through improvement efforts. In 1988 schools in almost half of the United States' school districts (approximately 6,500) were engaged in such projects. The last few years, however, have seen a change in Britain, with a range of research and development activities deliberately established to bridge the divide. These encompass action research projects, networks, courses, indicator development and analysis, support materials, and dedicated centres.

Action research projects
Many of the LEA-sponsored urban improvement projects outlined by Barber et al. (1995) attempt to evaluate outcomes as well as processes. Three such examples are the Raising Achievement and Participation project (Sheffield), the Schools Make a Difference (SMAD) project (Hammersmith and Fulham) (Myers, 1995) and the Lewisham School Improvement project, a partnership between Lewisham schools, the LEA and the Institute of Education at London University (Stoll & Thomson, 1996). Somewhat different is the Improving School Effectiveness project, funded by the Scottish Office Education Department (MacBeath & Mortimore, 1994). A team of researchers from Strathclyde University and the Institute of Education are working with 80 primary and secondary schools to ascertain the value added by schools to a range

of student outcomes. At the same time, 24 of these schools are supported in improvement efforts in three areas: school development planning; teaching and learning; and the development of a 'moving school' ethos. These processes will be monitored in more depth in a sample of schools.

Networks
A variety of national and local networks have been started around the UK. The School Improvement Network at the Institute of Education has been created to enable educators throughout Britain to share experiences and ideas, discuss common difficulties, reflect on fundamental issues related to school improvement, and access important research findings which can be translated into practice. Members receive newsletters, research summaries and a contact list and attend meetings. Other school improvement networks are operated by Dorset LEA and Bretton Hall in Wakefield. A network for school effectiveness and improvement researchers, funded by the Economic and Social Research Council, meets twice a year.

Courses
The Institutes of Education of both London and Cambridge Universities and the Universities of Birmingham and Bath offer accreditation for practitioners involved in school effectiveness and improvement initiatives. Specifically-designed higher degree courses, for what has become an increasingly popular field of study, are also available in some universities.

Indicator development and analysis
Value-added analyses services are provided by several universities (particularly the Institute of Education and the Universities of Newcastle and Sheffield) and by LEAs to help schools examine in context their academic results and, in some cases, students' attitudes. Attitude surveys have also been developed by the University of Keele, the National Foundation for Educational Research and the Scottish Office Education Department to help schools collect baseline information from students and parents.

Information packs
Several guidelines, videos and resource packs have been produced on various aspects of school improvement.

Dedicated centres
The International School Effectiveness and Improvement Centre (ISEIC) at the Institute of Education aims to draw on, extend and link the school effectiveness and improvement knowledge by engaging in: developmental work and action research with schools engaged in effectiveness and improvement projects; and research, in collaboration with a variety of partners (including other higher education institutions, LEAs, education consultants and government agencies). A Centre for School Improvement has been established at Bath University.

Activities include seminars, school-specific improvement audits, development consultancy and summer workshops.

Future needs
Despite these positive ventures, many challenges still face those involved in school effectiveness and school improvement. It is well known that successful change is not a speedy process: realism about what schools may be able to achieve in one year is necessary. Students, however, only have one period of their life in statutory schooling. It is of the utmost importance, therefore, to determine ways in which the pace of improvement can be accelerated and some results be seen in months rather than years. While hardly any studies have demonstrated improvements over such a short time-scale, some programmes have shown remarkable success. At primary level, for example, considerable gains in reading have been demonstrated over a one-year period, using the Reading Recovery programme (Hobsbaum & Hillman, 1994). At secondary level, GCSE results in science and mathematics have increased considerably as a result of Cognitive Acceleration Through Science (Adey & Shayer, 1994). In the United States, the 'Success for All' programme has led to significant improvements, including lasting effects in reading achievement and fewer pupils being 'kept down' for another year or referred for special education support (Slavin et al., 1994). These are only three of several methods that appear to have a powerful impact on achievement in a short time. Further work is needed urgently to identify strategies which can speed up the improvement process.

Although some school effectiveness studies have focused on the classroom, until recently the orientation was directed more towards school level factors associated with effectiveness. Similarly, since the 1970s, school improvement has tended to pay greater attention to school-level processes. Recent school effectiveness studies, however, argue that most of the variation among students is due to classroom variation. It is clear, therefore, that school and classroom development need to be linked. One key implication is that teachers need to take a 'classroom exceeding perspective' while at the same time the head teacher needs a 'classroom perceiving perspective' (MacGilchrist et al., 1995). Another implication is the need to examine how classroom and whole-school strategies are linked.

Analyses of school effectiveness and improvement projects internationally demonstrate the increasing agreement on the processes necessary for successful school improvement. A fundamental idea is that improvement should come from within, even if outside change agents are involved in supporting change. This requires people within the school to take charge of the change process. It has become apparent, from improvement efforts over the last few years, that this approach works well for the 'moving' schools—or even for those average schools that display readiness for change. It is less successful, however, with struggling schools or, particularly, with schools in crisis. For such schools, more direct intervention may be necessary. Further research and case studies are needed to determine the steps which may help a struggling school to improve.

The theoretical basis which underpins our knowledge of what makes schools effective and how they improve remains inadequate. In particular, the interconnection between school and classroom improvement is not well described, and a better understanding of the impact of the school's context and its readiness for change is needed.

In Britain, the word 'schooling' is usually used to denote education for those between the ages of 5 and 16 years. For effectiveness and improvement, such cut-off points are unhelpful. It is important to stress that these concepts relate to all academic institutions, including nurseries, post-16 colleges, universities and, indeed, institutions catering for adult continuing learners.

All the issues we have raised point to the need for further case studies and large-scale intervention studies of effectiveness and improvement. We think it is particularly important to attempt improvement in struggling schools, with a focus on classroom strategies and how these are related to schools' organization and management. Case studies need to be carried out in all phases, in a variety of contexts, and to incorporate measurement of a range of outcomes.

Postscript

Since this paper was first published, school improvement efforts have flourished. In the UK, the idea that schools could improve their effectiveness in promoting student progress was adopted by both government and opposition parties in the run-up to the 1997 general election. In many ways, that was what those of us working in the field had sought. After so many years of attempting to get across our message to a largely uninterested government, we now saw the principles of our work being embraced across the political divide. Delight at this situation was tempered, however, by a concern that policy makers might go too far and see school improvement as the only factor which could be manipulated. The converse of school improvement is school deterioration, and there was a tendency for policy makers inappropriately to blame teachers working in schools which did not appear to be improving, even though their good sense should have told them that in the bounded world of public examinations, one school's progress is likely to be accompanied by another school's regression. As noted in chapter thirteen, the temptation to blame proved irresistible. In chapter eighteen I will discuss these issues in greater detail.

16

The Burntwood School Case Study[1]

Introduction

In 1991, the then president of the British Association for the Advancement of Science—Sir Claus Moser—proposed at the annual meeting of the Association the establishment of a Royal Commission to review the state of education and training and to create a vision for its medium and long-term future. The idea of a Royal Commission was rejected by the government of the day, but there was sufficient support from the learned societies for the proposal to be taken forward. The result was the formation of the 'National Commission', funded by the Paul Hamlyn Foundation. I was asked to join the Commission's Research Committee and—together with a number of eminent researchers—served for the two years of its existence. The Commission's report—Learning to Succeed—provides, in my judgement, one of the clearest analyses of the British education system ever written. Unlike so many official reports, it includes many references to published UK and international research. One of the projects associated with the commission was a study of schools which 'succeeded against the odds'. I helped develop the idea of this project and I undertook, with two members of the business community—the Director General of the Confederation of British industry and the then Head of Corporate Affairs at IBM—the case study which makes up this chapter.

---

1 Original paper written by Peter Mortimore, Howard Davies and Sarah Portway.

Background

Burntwood School was formed in 1986 by the amalgamation of two neighbouring girls' schools. In 1992 it became grant maintained, for a reason markedly dissimilar from that of most schools that made application for that status:
Burntwood wanted to continue to offer a broad and balanced curriculum, contrary to the LEA policy of developing specialist or magnet secondary schools.
The success of this multi-ethnic school can be judged not only from the fact that
it is heavily over-subscribed but also from its excellent academic record.

Introduction and our approach

We began our task by formulating a strategy. We wished to meet representatives
of all the key players: the principal and the senior management team; the governing body; the staff; and the students. From these representatives we wished
to hear whether they considered the school to be successful and, if they did,
what particular factors contributed to this success. In order to deploy our limited resources to the best effect, we agreed to specialize: Howard Davies would
focus on management and organizational issues; Sarah Portway would focus on
the way the school responded to parents and the community; and Peter
Mortimore would focus on the academic life of the school.

We wanted the opportunity—no matter how limited—to see the school at
work, in order to sense its ethos and, if possible, to observe the learning and
teaching taking place. We also wanted to find a way to tap into the views of
ordinary Burntwood students in order to supplement our interviews and observations.

What information was collected?

During the course of our investigations we visited the school on seven separate
occasions and met with approximately 130 individuals. We had discussions with
governors, the principal and her senior management team, staff and students
from three year groups (9, 10 and 11) and the sixth form. Observations were
made of teaching in classes in years 7, 9 and 10 and on one of the two days in
the year in which the students were given specific academic counselling on their
reports.

We called upon the National Foundation for Educational Research (NFER)
to help us capture the views of students. In 1993, on behalf of the National
Commission on Education, the NFER had drawn up a questionnaire to elicit
attitudes to schooling from a representative national sample of just under 1,000
year 9 students. We commissioned the NFER to use this questionnaire to collect information from the whole of the year 9 group in Burntwood. This information would give us an idea of what Burntwood students thought about

schooling and it would also enable us to make comparisons with the national sample.

In addition, we analysed much of the paperwork associated with the school, including the prospectus, annual report, various brochures, policy documents, discussion papers and minutes of meetings.

The nature of our evidence

We were conscious that our task of uncovering the ways in which this school achieved its success necessitate dealing predominantly with the perceptions of its students, teachers and governors. We needed, therefore, to take all appropriate steps to ensure the validity and reliability of these perceptions.

With regard to information given to us by the students, we think the overwhelming agreement between the opinions expressed by the relatively small groups which we met and the NFER survey of year 9 provides sufficient confirmatory evidence to assure us of its validity.

With the groups of governors and staff we had no way of testing how fairly we could generalize from their views and had to rely on the technique—common in the social sciences—of triangulation, whereby we compared the views of different groups on the same issues. If the governors, the principal and the senior management team were all to indicate the same interpretation of school policy, there could be little doubt of its reality for the school. Similarly, if students and staff both drew attention to a particular aspect of the school organization which they saw as positive, it seemed sensible for us to pay attention to it. Of course, in some areas of our enquiry we would expect there to be genuine differences between the experiences and views of staff and students—for example, over the policy on uniform, which staff thought was reasonable but students thought was excessive.

In general, we consider that the objective evidence about outcomes and the more subjective views we gathered about the school fitted well together and gave us a broadly realistic picture of Burntwood School as it is today.

Background and history of the school

Burntwood was founded as a new school in 1986 following the amalgamation on the site of two neighbouring girls' schools. The building occupies a site of 13 acres of attractive grounds and was awarded an architectural prize in the 1950s. It consists of campus-style buildings. Two blocks house teaching rooms. There are dining rooms, science and technology areas, a library, a physical education block containing three gymnasia and a swimming pool, and a separate sixth-form suite.

The two schools that were amalgamated to create Burntwood had been very different. One was committed to mixed ability teaching, the other used a banding system; one had uniform, the other did not; one was run along democratic, the other on more authoritarian, lines. Yet despite these obvious differences, the amalgamation and formation of the new school is generally acknowledged to have been highly successful.

Two factors are thought to have helped what, in other circumstances, has often proved to be a very difficult task. Paradoxically, one factor was a delay in the appointment of a new principal. For one term the new staff, assisted by a talented and experienced advisory head teacher, had the unusual opportunity to plan the school. This involvement and collegial planning seems to have left its mark and is still apparent in the staff's willingness today to take on planning issues. The other factor was that the chosen principal had no previous connections with either school. She did not bring with her old loyalties, and genuinely could seek to create a new institution which would draw on the best aspects of both of the former schools.

The school became grant maintained in January 1992 following a rejection by the governors of the LEA's plans for specialist secondary schools. The governing body wished to preserve the ability of the school to offer a broad and balanced curriculum. The vote to opt out of the control of the local authority was supported by 80 per cent of the parents and 60 per cent of the staff. Two grants, of £500,000 and £800,000 for capital developments, have enabled the facilities for technology and for science to be brought up to modern standards. The enhanced technology resources include a state-of-the-art languages suite in which the latest developments are available to students and teachers.

Catchment and the community

The immediate neighbourhood of the school consists mainly of Victorian residential property. There is a large hospital adjacent to the site. Although most of the school's students live within the borough of Wandsworth, the shape of the borough means that many have an awkward journey to and from the school. The route is not well served by buses and, unusually for inner London, there is no underground station within the vicinity of the school. There is a bus specially scheduled for before and after school, but the lack of good, normal transport links has a negative effect on after-school activities and on parents' attendance at meetings.

Admissions policy

The school admits 283 new students each year. Until 1995, all students were admitted without reference to their ability. Because the school receives about 70 per cent more applications than it can take, it offers places according to three criteria, based on having a sibling already at the school, special medical or social grounds and proximity to home.

Parents are invited to visit the school and meet the staff and students. For those who are unable to visit the school during the day, sessions are arranged during an evening and on a Saturday. All students who are offered a place at the school are invited to attend special interviews and are given an induction day and evening in the July prior to their starting at the school. Some students enter the sixth form directly.

From 1995 onwards, the school has been permitted to admit up to 90 places on the basis of ability. Girls whose parents wish to enter them for this competition are required to take quantitative, non-verbal and verbal reasoning tests.

The students

There are currently 1,500 students aged 11 to 18 at the school. Two hundred are in the sixth form. They come from 60 or so different primary schools. Eighty per cent of them live in the local borough. About 70 per cent have family backgrounds from minority ethnic groups.

The staff

There are currently ninety-five members of the teaching staff, although they are not all full-time. The principal, 3 deputy principals and 4 senior teachers make up the senior management team. Fifteen of the teachers are men. A third of the teachers were members of the staff of one of the two amalgamating schools. There are also 28 support staff.

The governing body

There are 21 governors, including the principal; 5 are parent governors and 2 are teacher governors. The remaining 14 governors represent the business community, the local community, journalism and education. Only one governor remains from either of the two amalgamated schools.

The principal

The current principal has been in post since the creation of the new school in 1986. Prior to this, she was the deputy head teacher of a high-profile comprehensive school in west London and, for 12 years before that, had worked in secondary schools in Haringey, Oxfordshire and inner London. The principal is a fellow of the Royal Society of Arts, a fellow of the Management Centre at the Roehampton Institute of Higher Education, a member of the BBC Council for Educational Broadcasting and a non-executive director of Wandsworth Community Health Trust.

The school's publications

The prospectus gave details of the history of the school, its facilities, its curriculum, organization of time, the extra-curricular opportunities and administration and included a section for parents. The text was clear and there were excellent photographs of life in the school. The prospectus also contained a supplement which listed the names and qualifications of staff, and provided a detailed breakdown of courses and the information required for the Parents' Charter, including a full analysis of examination results.

The official annual report from governors to parents was similarly well produced. It provided a description of life during the last school year. Dealing in particular with sensitive topics such as religious education, sex education and (anti-) bullying measures, the school strove to explain its policies clearly and succinctly. The attendance figures were reported. The document also provided a considerable amount of information on the work of the governing body and its sub-committees and included a full income and expenditure account for the school. The development plan priorities for the next year were listed and included the key policy of striving to raise achievement.

Details were given of outings to the theatre, exhibitions, museums and other special events of the school's sporting activities, musical achievements (including two choirs and an orchestra) and of additional clubs in mathematics, science, computing, languages and technology. Finally, school journeys and field trips in England as well as to Venice, Paris and Madrid were listed.

The school today

The school budget for 1994 to 1995 is £3.8 million. The average class size is 24. The students follow the national curriculum and a special extended curriculum for students of marked aptitude. There is setting by ability in most subjects. Special support is provided for those whose first language is not English and for those with special learning needs. Music, drama, dance and art activities are encouraged. There is a student council. The latest attendance figures for the school show that only 7.7 per cent of the total available schooling was missed because of authorized absence and a mere 0.2 per cent through non-authorized absence.

Student intake

According to the report on the school inspection carried out by Her Majesty's Inspectors in 1990 (the year of entry of the current year-11 students), 'the school takes about one half of its students from economically disadvantaged areas, and the remainder from areas described as neither prosperous nor economically disadvantaged'. One third of the students are entitled to free school meals. Although no data are available, anecdotal evidence suggests that a much smaller proportion of parents own or have access to a car than is normal in this part of London. Forty per cent of the current student body speak a language other than English at home.

In terms of the educational performance of the student intake, the school regularly commissions an analysis by the Research and Evaluation Unit of the local borough. This shows that reading scores have fluctuated around the national average but in recent years have been significantly below the average for girls. Mathematics scores have been below, or just at, the borough average. Scores in abstract reasoning have also been around the borough average but the proportion of girls in the most able group has declined. Interestingly, the educational performance of those students coming from outside the borough has, in recent years, been considerably worse than that of local students.

The characteristics of the intake of the school, therefore, whilst not approaching the levels of disadvantage of some inner-city schools, are below average in national terms.

Student outcomes

The 1994 examination results show that almost 50 per cent of students obtained five or more of the higher (A–C grades) in the General Certificate of Secondary Education (GCSE); this is also the national average for girls. Ninety-two per cent of all students obtained one or more of the higher grades and almost 89 per cent obtained five or more of the A–G grades in the GCSE examinations. Given the somewhat disadvantaged nature of its intake, the school appears to be academically successful and to be providing a substantial value-added component to the achievement of its students.

In comparison to the success achieved by the school in the GCSE results, the 'A' level results seem disappointing. The average 'A' level points score achieved by each student was 8.6 (the equivalent of one grade D and two grade E passes or a combination of A/S levels). One factor influencing this result is the struggle the school has had, up until now, to retain its most able students in the face of competition from two successful tertiary colleges in neighbouring boroughs. In addition, 41 students gained good qualifications in vocational examinations.

The indicators of success are, therefore:

- An oversubscribed entry
- Very low average absence rates
- GCSE results above the national average
- Higher than average participation in further education (though not necessarily in the school)

Students' attitudes

As noted earlier, we invited the NFER to repeat the National Commission's survey of the attitudes of year 9 students. The full findings from the national survey are reported by Keys and Fernandes (1993). The findings from the national survey enable a reasonable comparison to be made of the attitudes of the Burntwood students and those of female students in general.

The main topics covered in the NFER questionnaire were:

- Background variables, including: gender; surrogate measures intended to provide an approximate indication of the cultural level of the home; perceived ability and behaviour in school; post-16 educational intentions; and attitudes towards school and learning (including views about the value of school and school work, liking for school, interest and boredom with school work, and opinions on the purposes of schooling)
- Perceptions of teachers and lessons, including: liking for teachers; teachers' support of students' learning; teachers' maintenance of discipline; individual discussions with teachers about school work; and liking for different types of lessons
- Students' self-reported behaviour in and out of school, including: behaviour in school; punishments; truancy; participation in lunch-hour or after-school activities; reading for pleasure; length of time spent doing homework, and watching television or videos
- Perceptions of parental interest and home support, including: parents' opinions about the value of education; parental interest in students'/their children's progress at school

The NFER report made the following points. Compared with the national sample of girls:

- The Burntwood girls were more likely to believe in the value of school and education and to believe that their school should teach them what would be useful for their future careers. They were also more likely to agree that school work was worth doing and that homework was important in helping them to do well and more likely to say they intended to continue their education after year 11. However, they were slightly less likely to express positive attitudes towards their school and less likely to intend to stay on in the sixth form of their own school.
- The Burntwood girls were more likely to say that their teachers praised them when they produced good work. They were more likely to say that they talked to their teachers about their work, but less likely to say that they talked to their teachers about their future careers. The Burntwood girls were less likely to say that they liked all or most of their teachers.
- The Burntwood girls were more likely to say that they behaved well in school, but also more likely to say that they had received punishments (such as lines, detentions or being kept in). The Burntwood girls were more likely to say that discipline in their school was too strict and that there were too many rules. Their greatest objections were to rules concerned with school uniform.
- The Burntwood girls were less likely to say that they had played truant this year and slightly less likely to say they had been bullied.
- The Burntwood girls were more likely to say that they worked hard at school but had slightly lower perceptions of their own ability and of their teachers' perceptions of their ability.

- The Burntwood girls spent more time each day on homework and slightly less time reading for pleasure; they also spent more time watching TV and videos (but this could have been because the Burntwood survey took place in the winter, whereas the national survey took place in the summer).
- The Burntwood parents were seen by the daughters as slightly more supportive of the school, but there were no differences in the perceptions of the two samples in terms of parental interest in their future.

These results provided us with some fascinating information about the school. They illustrate the positive way in which learning, good behaviour and academic achievement are viewed by the parents, students and teachers. They also show us that the strictness associated with the teachers (and probably needed in order to achieve these good outcomes) is not always appreciated by the students.

Similarly, the finding of a commitment to further education and a willingness to transfer to a college at 16 also illustrates the difficulties of retaining students in a single-sex school situated within relatively each reach of large co-educational colleges with good reputations.

The National Commission's factors related to success

The school rated highly in relation to the ten features of success described in *Learning to Succeed* (NCE, 1993).[2] There was manifestly strong positive leadership exerted by the principal and senior staff. We were also impressed with the good atmosphere that we experienced in the school. The physical environment had been enhanced and the grounds of the school were well kept (interestingly the students were critical of the appearance of the buildings and they felt the grounds could be tidier). From our discussions with the teaching staff, we identified a clear and consistent focus on learning. High expectations were held on behalf of students who were, themselves, expected to take responsibility for their learning and to participate fully in the life of the school.

It was difficult at the early stages of our inquiry to know whether there were well-developed procedures for assessing the progress of students, whether there were rewards and incentives to encourage success, and whether parents were encouraged to involve themselves in their daughters' education. It was clear, however, that the staff provided several extra-curricular activities to suit students' interests and to expand their opportunities.

---

2   The Commission adapted the factors from Mortimore (1993a) and added 'Extra curricular activities which broaden pupils' interests and experiences, expand their opportunities to succeed, and help to build good relationships within the school'.

The search for an explanation of effectiveness?

The preceding sections provide the background with which we began our series of visits (apart from the NFER pupil attitude survey, which reported later on in our programme). We accepted that Burntwood was an effective school in that it was achieving reasonably good academic results with an intake of students that was somewhat disadvantaged. Our job, therefore, was to collect as much information as we could in order to tease out the reasons for its success against the odds.

We have chosen to group the reasons that we identified mainly under the headings of 'values' and 'mechanisms'. We do so because we wish to draw attention to the way the school staff endeavour to link the school mission with very practical ways of achieving that mission. We are conscious that other, equally satisfactory, ways of organizing the material could have been found.

Values

Clarity of aims and ethos of the school

We think the clarity of the aims of the school (built around the mission statement of the school: 'the best education today for the women of tomorrow') is crucial to the success of the school. We have been struck by the commitment of staff, students and governors to the principles and values embodied by the school community. The use of the school name as an adjective (and, at times, as an abstract noun) is a good example of the way this commitment reveals itself ('. . . a Burntwood identity' and '. . . that is not very Burntwood').

The way students appear to accept and identify with the school's aims and values seems to us likely to encourage their acceptance of responsibility and to create general goodwill. Compared to students elsewhere, they are more likely to see the value of education in general, even though they complain about the strictness of the school.

We have also considered the particular ethos of the school. In our view, the Burntwood ethos is now a self-reinforcing system in which high expectations and enthusiasm generally lead to positive and constructive attitudes to learning and to better-than-average behaviour. These positive attitudes appear, to us, to be exhibited by both staff and most of the students (not all students are positive, as the survey demonstrated) and to result in generally constructive and warm relationships. These are recognized and valued by the governors.

Focus on learning and achievement

The focus on learning throughout all aspects of the life of the school appears to be fundamental. It is apparent in the literature about the school. It was apparent in the sample of lessons observed. It was stressed in discussions with all our respondents. It appears to have been the dominant driving force of the school since its creation.

As evidence of the commitment to learning of the school governors and staff and of a lack of complacency, we noted that two of the three major priorities listed in the current school development plan are focused on the curriculum and on the organization of learning.

We considered it significant that the pastoral support system is nested in an academic structure. We also found that the parental involvement in the school is primarily focused on the educational development of their children.

We think these factors help to translate the rhetoric about learning into reality. The fact that teachers and managers demonstrate their shared understanding of the priority of learning over all other activities powerfully influences the ethos of the school. In comparison with other institutions which we know, there appears to be remarkably little evidence of territorial battles being waged between different segments of the school community.

The time and attention given to the reporting on progress also impressed us. The systems appear well thought out and effectively executed. The students obviously value the feedback they receive.

It became clear to us that not only is learning valued but also that the ethos of the school celebrates achievement. Governors, teachers and students all stressed the positive attitude to achievement that has been established and which is constantly reinforced. Learning is valued for its own sake but is also seen as the key to achievement. Students want to succeed in public examinations and thus equip themselves to do well in a career. The large amount of homework undertaken—with over 20 per cent of year 9 students reporting over three hours each night, in comparison with a national figure of less than 2 per cent—illustrates the point.

High expectations

Expectations affect everyone involved with the school and are reflexive in their nature: they work in both directions. The governing body, for example, has expectations of the principal, but she, in turn, has expectations of it. The governors have taken their role in the school very seriously. Led by their chair, they have participated in both collective and individual training programmes which have given them the opportunity to develop their contribution to Burntwood.

Similarly, both staff and students have expectations about the way the other party will behave towards them. The Burntwood Agreement, signed by each new student, parent and the principal of the school, lays out the rights and responsibilities of each party and is, in effect, a formal expression of these expectations.

We have been struck forcibly by how frequently we heard high expectations being expressed of other people in the school. An extension of the policy on expectations has just been formulated—on the principle that successful education requires students to co-manage the process. (We were surprised, therefore, that the NFER survey showed, on average, that Burntwood students had lower perceptions of their ability—and of their teachers' perceptions of this—than was the case nationally.)

We were impressed that both students and staff have had the opportunity to make explicit their expectations about the other party. We have come across schools where the teachers had produced expectations about their students but not where the process was reciprocal. We learned that, initially, some members of staff felt uneasy about the wisdom of providing an opportunity for students to comment on staff behaviour. We understand this uncertainty and commend the staff for taking the risk. The highly positive reactions to the exercise that we elicited from students augurs well for future interactions between staff and students. The involvement of students in the formulation of the policy on expectations is an indication of the strength of the school's collective confidence.

We have also been struck by how 'hard-nosed' the expectations policy is. It even provides guidance on what happens if either students or staff fail to meet their expectations. It seems to us that exercises of this sort provide an excellent basis for the creation and maintenance of a positive ethos. We are conscious, however, that it takes time and energy to carry it through and that, to a certain extent, the ethos will have to be re-created from time to time as new students and new teachers join the school.

Focus on quality

We observed only a minute proportion of the school's teaching and discussed the matter with only a fraction of those involved, but the impression that we have gained, and which was supported by the views of students, is that the general quality of teaching in the school is high. We see the quality of teaching as being a supremely important aspect of the life of the school. Because it is high, the students feel confident in the ability of the staff to support their learning. In turn, because the students expect good teaching, the staff are more likely to continue to deliver it and, therefore, to gain more satisfaction in their daily work. The system thus becomes self-reinforcing.

We also detected a sense of healthy competition between members of departments and among 'clusters' (a group of departments) over the promotion of good teaching. This acts as an incentive to individual teachers who do not want to let down the side—or their students.

Striving for quality does not stop with teaching. The school takes obvious pride in the way it presents itself and the quality of its collective behaviour. The carefully maintained grounds and the politeness and efficiency of the student receptionists illustrate a sense of professionalism and a quiet confidence in the way the school conducts its activities. Again, we were struck that the students—in comparison to their peers in other schools—did not judge the building to be particularly clean and tidy. This may, of course, reflect a more critical stance or higher expectations than found elsewhere.

Collegiality

We were impressed by the existence of a particular form of collegiality amongst the staff. This collegiality appears to operate at both the department and cluster level as well as across the school as a whole. Given the dispersed nature of the buildings, and the tendency of staff to take breaks in their cluster room, the collective, whole-school feeling is perhaps surprising and even paradoxical. Our impression is that the basis of this form of collegiality is a strong commitment to the underpinning values of the school.

We are conscious that some staff feel the pressure to be task-centred is so great that it does not allow time for social activity. This can be counter-productive in that problems that might be sorted out informally in staffroom conversation have to be resolved through the use of memos or formal meetings. At the same time, we know there is a view that one of the benefits of life at Burntwood is the absence of a strong staff-room culture with its attendant rivalries and cliques.

It seems to us that the single-sex composition of the school and the predominance of women in senior positions on the staff provides a strongly unifying focus (encapsulated in its mission statement) for this girls' school. Given the mood in society generally, that women need to assert their entitlement to an equal opportunity for achievement, this focus appears to generate considerable energy which the school is able to channel towards achievement.

Comradeship is also discernible amongst the students. Tolerance, patience, the valuing of diversity and a pride in the corporate success of the school were obvious amongst the representatives of the student body that we met. We are conscious that we have had the opportunity to discuss these issues with only a very small number of students. Without exception, those students were positive and articulate; we recognize that others may be different. The survey of the whole of year 9, however, made clear that, whilst there is a range of opinion on most issues, the views of those we talked to generally reflected the views of the majority of students.

Mechanisms

Leadership

It seems clear that the stable and secure leadership exhibited by the principal is a key factor in the success of the school—the absolutely key factor, according to some respondents. The determination of a respected leader to push the achievements of the school to the maximum appears to us also to be a major factor in the success of the institution. We have not had the opportunity to study in detail the style of leadership adopted, but we have heard from our respondents that commitment, attention to detail and high expectations are three of the characteristics much in evidence. We believe that the ability to judge the quality of job applicants is also important, and there is evidence that the principal possesses this skill to a high degree and uses it most effectively. A vital characteristic of leadership, in our judgement, is the way the principal is able to delegate to, and support, the various post-holders with leadership roles within the school. We think this has led to a willingness to take ownership of developing school policies and is clear evidence of staff appreciation of this support.

Deciding who does what, in terms of the leadership of a large organization, is obviously crucial. We think the skill of knowing when the decision needs to be taken by the whole staff, the middle managers, the senior management team or by the principal herself is extremely valuable. The evidence given to us suggests that, on the whole, decisions have been taken correctly. There is also evidence that the principal's habit of thanking and congratulating staff for particular achievements is highly reinforcing. We were interested that this began as a joke (with the principal using stationery with the picture of a tiger), but that it has become part of the school tradition. Now tiger-sticker head teacher awards are highly sought after.

Management

The school is clearly managed very efficiently. A senior manager with a financial background was recruited at deputy principal level and has invested his time and energy in creating good systems and sound financial policies. The organization appears well structured and professional: communications are generally clear; responsibilities are well defined; and services are managed competently. There is a strong corporate identity that appears to have been reinforced, if not created, by a number of related elements, including the logo, the uniform and the newsletter. The general view seems to be that this strong corporate identity helps the school on what are sometimes called short-term reinforcers of appropriate behaviour and also promotes successful functioning. A considerable amount of corporate effort appears to be invested in rewarding students and staff for outstanding achievement or particular efforts. We think this is a sensible strategy and consider that the benefits for the school repay considerably the efforts of the principal and senior staff.

We were also interested that the school appears—collectively—to be able to cope well with change. The transition to grant-maintained status appears to have been smooth. The recent change of entry policy to include a selected group of pupils might have caused considerable turbulence but appears not to have done so. Similarly, we have been struck by the way administrative systems are regularly changed and improved.

Communications

In many institutions, one of the most common complaints is about the lack of good communication. This has not been the case at Burntwood. Communications appear to be good, and it is obvious that considerable time and energy have been invested in creating and developing appropriate channels. Examples of such channels are the cluster meetings and the feeding of views up to the senior management team and, reciprocally, from the senior staff down to the clusters. Special consultation exercises, such as the diagnostic windows sheets (surveys which the principal uses to take a 'rain check' on staff views of different aspects of the school), are also used fairly frequently.

Monitoring

We are only too conscious that the systems we have seen require careful monitoring in order to retain their effectiveness. Whether it is the amount and quality of homework being undertaken by the students, the level of GCSE results or the quality of the individual feedback given in the biennial reporting sessions, there appears to be evidence of good monitoring systems at work. The frequency of monitoring does not appear to be resented; it seems that both staff and students see its value and appreciate its purpose within the overall goals of the school.

Participatory decision-making

As we have noted earlier, we were impressed by the amount of participatory decision-making that takes place. The advantages of this can readily be seen in the high proportion of the staff accepting ownership for policy decisions. Because the debates surrounding those decisions have been well conducted and there have been opportunities for exploring the advantages and disadvantages of particular courses of action, the decisions appear to have been made on rational grounds even in areas of policy which, in other schools, have been seen as highly emotional. The involvement of students in decision-making (where appropriate) also appears eminently sensible, as do the attempt to seek, and listen to, the views of parents.

Parental and community involvement

The relationship of the school with parents is deemed important and is still being developed. The strategy to engage parents in year groups and in the educational processes of the school is clearly sensible. We suspect that, if the achievement of all, or a substantial majority, of the student body is to be raised significantly, current strategies for parent involvement will have to be enhanced.

The relationship with the community, however, appears still to be at a relatively *ad hoc* level. There are examples of links with local businesses (for example, through the British Telecom scheme and GNVQ programmes), but these do not yet seem to be part of a fully planned outreach programme.

In our judgement, the school has pursued an intelligent policy in seeking to establish its emphasis on learning as its major priority. It may be that it is now at a stage to develop its outreach potential in a rather more co-ordinated way.

Other contributory factors

Grant-maintained status

The circumstances in which the school became grant maintained are unusual. A Wandsworth Borough strategy for the creation of specialist schools, modelled on North American magnet schools, was rejected by the governing body (and, incidentally, by all other governing bodies of secondary schools), the parents' consultative committee and the principal.

The governors of Burntwood then acted in order to protect the autonomy of a girls' school to offer a broad and balanced curriculum. The result was that a school which—had it been located in another part of the country—might well have rejected grant-maintained status, embraced it in order to protect its character. This history, together with the extra funds made available because of the change of status, has proved uniquely favourable to the development of the school. Significant changes in the philosophy of the school have occurred without a great deal of disruption or ideological tensions. The school has remained in harmony with itself.

The first year of the new status is said to have been an exhilarating one. The services of the LEA were not missed greatly. Only educational psychologists, welfare personnel and one adviser (who is carrying out an evaluation of the appraisal system) have been carried over from the old to the new system. Under grant-maintained status, small but significant changes have been introduced at a speed previously deemed to be impossible. There is a feeling that the school is now free to develop, unhampered by political agendas.

The decision to apply to the Secretary of State for permission to accept 30 per cent of the entry on the basis of academic selection was taken on pragmatic grounds by the governing body as the only way to protect the balanced intake of the school.

Buildings and site

The advantages of a relatively large site with its extensive landscaping and its campus-style environment are considerable. Games facilities on-site also increase the attractiveness of the school. The buildings, which in the 1950s were considered outstanding, are considerably better than those of many other urban schools. Recent capital grants to improve and extend the facilities have enhanced the opportunities open to students of the school.

Where next?

Maintenance and enhancement of current standards

As we have made clear, we believe that this school is successful and that it has succeeded against the odds in an exceptional way. We have sought to explain our understanding of why the school is in this position. Given the investment we have made in seeking to understand the institution, it would seem foolish not to go one step further and identify three further challenges.

In our view, the first challenge will be the maintenance and enhancement of current standards. Given the pressures on urban schools with disadvantaged intakes, sustained effort is required even to stand still. The work of an effective school succeeding against the odds is never over, as, each year, new students and new staff will join and will have to be convinced that success is within their grasp. These newcomers will not share ownership of the way the school functions, even though they may well have been attracted by it. They will need to be socialized into the norms of Burntwood. The way we have described the school's ethos as a self-reinforcing system illustrates the importance of continuity. Continual efforts and further innovations involving new staff and students are essential.

The sixth form
The current size of the sixth form of about 200 students has enabled it to function. In our judgement, it is not really large enough to flourish. In order for the school to offer a sufficiently broad choice of 'A' levels, GNVQs and other vocational qualifications, a larger sixth form base would be beneficial.

We have been impressed by the way in which the school has changed its strategy on the sixth form. Whereas at one time the policy was to isolate sixth formers and imitate the ethos of a self-standing mini sixth form college, the current view of staff is that this was counter-productive. Such a sixth form could not compete with other, much larger colleges in neighbouring boroughs and able students constantly drifted away.

The new policy seeks to strengthen—rather than to diminish—the links between the sixth form and the rest of the school. Rather than focusing on the separateness of the sixth form, the school now seeks to integrate it with the rest of the school and to provide opportunities for leadership for older students. It aims to impose prefectorial duties and to associate these sixth formers with a class of younger girls.

Families from minority faith groups find these arrangements attractive and safe for their daughters. Where there is a strong preference for an all-girls' education, the arrangement is also likely to be attractive to other families. We think, therefore, that with this strategy the school may well be able to expand its sixth form and to provide a firmer academic setting for the study of both 'A' levels and GNVQs.

For this strategy to succeed, however, it will be necessary to raise the current levels of achievement. More top A and B grades will be needed if the school is to establish itself as a serious rival to the local colleges and to independent schools. Currently, as we have noted, the achievement at 18 is not as impressive as at 16, and this is clearly a weakness. In our view, the senior management team would be wise to review 'A'-level teaching techniques and ensure that appropriate staff are recruited in order to bring about an improvement.

Outreach
We learned of a number of interesting activities involving local business companies but were struck by the lack of an overall policy for outreach work. We recognize that the first priority for a school must be its focus on learning and achievement within the curriculum. Since (with the caveats noted earlier) this appears reasonably secure—at least up to the age of 16—we think now could be the time to improve and consolidate relationships. Links with local companies could be enhanced and pupils' work experience integrated into this arrangement. Staff work experience in different fields might also be included, if this was deemed appropriate.

Parents

It might also be the time to rethink the school's policy towards parents. It will obviously be necessary to reconsider any new policy in the knowledge of the difficulties that many families have in getting to school functions because of work or family commitments and poor evening public transport. Innovative approaches may need to be undertaken. It might, for instance, be worth making a series of Burntwood videos to accompany options choices or applications to the sixth form. The promising results of year-group, as opposed to whole-school, parents' meetings will need to be evaluated and, if appropriate, further developed.

Conclusions

Like almost every other school in the country, Burntwood is not perfect, and we have set out three areas in which we think improvements are both necessary and possible. Nevertheless, we wish to reiterate that, in our judgement, success has been achieved. One of the key ingredients of success has been the ability of the leadership of the school to motivate the staff to plan for further improvements. It is this continual seeking for improvement that we see as the main source of energy in the school.

In carrying out an investigation of this sort, and in writing a positive report on the school, we are aware that we may be encouraging complacency. We trust that the staff will resist this temptation and—with the knowledge that we have been impressed—continue to strive for excellence and to refuse to accept that anything less is good enough for their students. Urban schools are demanding places in which to work. Successful ones demand more of both staff and students than is sometimes thought reasonable. For the students, however, such schools can have a very powerful positive influence on their life chances. At a time of such radical changes in patterns of work and in society in general, the benefits of attending an effective school are likely to be of even greater value for urban pupils coming from disadvantaged backgrounds. This is why schools which succeed against the odds are important and why governing bodies, head teachers and their staff deserve to be congratulated on their success.

Postscript

The experience of carrying out this study was both interesting and valuable. Reviewing the effectiveness of a school and, even more so, endeavouring to analyse and explain the reasons for its effectiveness in the company of two people not used to the world of schools, was extremely challenging. Striking, however, was the level of agreement in our judgements. We did find Burntwood effective. As noted in this chapter, we traced its success to a mixture of factors which included its leadership and efficient administrative sys-

tems. Perhaps most remarkable was the level of trust exhibited in the school community. The principal showed that she trusted her colleagues and, collectively, they all trusted the students—even to the point of allowing them to specify the behaviours they expected of teachers. Seeing this reinforced my own conviction of the importance of trust in all aspects of education. I believe it underpins high expectations of achievement as well as of behaviour.

17

The Drive Primary School Case Study[1]

Introduction

The publication on which this chapter is based developed from a Department for Education and Employment (DfEE) commission. The International School Effectiveness and Improvement Centre at the Institute of Education was asked to undertake a series of case studies of schools which, having failed their inspection, managed to turn themselves around. Our task was to uncover how they had done so. Alma Harris and I immersed ourselves in the records of the history of the inspection and its aftermath and then interviewed staff, students, parents and the chair of governors. We went to the school with some trepidation—unsure as to how keen the staff who had undergone such a traumatic experience would be on the investigation. We need not have worried.

The school

The Drive County Primary School is located in the Felling district of Gateshead. Unemployment in the neighbourhood is above the national average and 56 per cent of the pupils are eligible for free school meals. There are no students from ethnic minority backgrounds in the school. Predominantly, the students (from 3

---

1 My co-author in the original publication on which this is based is Alma Harris.

Table 17.1. Results of the Drive's 1986 National Curriculum Assessment Tasks.

| Key Stage 1 | Teacher assessment | | Test results | |
% Level 2	The Drive	National	The Drive	National
Reading	53	79	54	78
Writing	46	77	46	80
Speaking	54	85	–	–
Mathematics	77	79	77	78
Science	69	84	–	–

| Key Stage 2 | Teacher assessment | | Test results | |
% Level 4	The Drive	National	The Drive	National
English	38	56	50	48
Mathematics	56	54	56	44
Science	56	64	63	70

to 11 years) live in local-authority housing in the surrounding area. Most will have attended the school's nursery unit. The time allocated to teaching each week is 20 hours for the nursery, 21 hours for reception and Key Stage 1 (KS1) and 23 hours for Key Stage 2 (KS2). Levels of attendance at the school are fairly high (92.3%) and no students have been permanently excluded in the past year. The results in the National Curriculum Assessment Tasks taken in 1996 (when compared with national data for 1995) show that students at key stage 1 at the Drive are likely to be achieving well below the national average, except for mathematics where (despite the majority performing below average on non-verbal reasoning tests) they achieve at the national average level.

The results for KS2 present a rather different picture. They suggest that the Drive students are performing better than average in English and mathematics tests and in the teachers' assessment of mathematics.

The school's motto, introduced since the Ofsted inspection, is 'Learn and Grow'. This symbolizes the school's newly-found emphasis on high-quality teaching and effective learning for all students. The head teacher and staff work in an active partnership with governors and the LEA. Both parents and students express enthusiasm for the learning opportunities for pupils and optimism about the future of the school. The hard work of the head teacher, the staff and the governors has clearly changed the reputation of the school in the community. The Drive is now a 'moving' school. It is a happy place, where the achievement of students is celebrated and where the head is seen as the leading professional. Staff morale is high and parents are involved and supportive. The governing body works effectively and efficiently. The buildings and the external environment are safe places for children. Overall, we found the school to be a thriving, positive and innovative place in which to learn.

The Ofsted report

The school was identified as failing when it was inspected in January 1994. The inspectors found that standards in the nursery were satisfactory and, in some respects, good, but that standards were in line with national expectations *only* in science and art at KS1 and were below average in *all* subjects at KS2.

The inspection report also stated that:

- The leadership and management of the school were weak, with poor and inconsistent planning
- The budget, though adequate, was poorly managed and failed to meet the school's priorities
- Curriculum policies were poor and staff responsibilities unclear, with the result that the requirements of the national curriculum were not being met
- The quality of teaching was generally unsatisfactory (in some cases poor) and there was a lack of monitoring and evaluative procedures
- teaching time was badly used and assessment information was not used to plan further tasks
- Too little emphasis was given to the spiritual and cultural development of the students

On the positive side, the inspectors found that the social and moral development of students was promoted adequately, teachers cared about their charges' welfare and standards of behaviour were generally satisfactory.

A number of key issues for action by the school community were identified by the inspection team. These included five major challenges:

- Imposing effective leadership
- Ensuring adequate coverage of the national curriculum
- Implementing detailed schemes of work for all subjects
- Establishing a series of management systems
- Dealing urgently with all matters of health and safety

Reactions to the Ofsted report

News of the inspectors' criticisms of the school were reported in the local newspaper. Parents were surprised but did not manifest any obvious signs of panic or of discontent. The staff were shocked and—initially—considered the decision to be unfair. The head teacher agreed to take early retirement at the end of the academic year and was on sick leave from April to August.

The LEA moved rapidly to appoint a new head teacher and an advertisement appeared in late February 1994. Interviews were held in April and the new head teacher began work on 3 May. As the deputy head was also on sick leave from soon after the inspection until she, too, took early retirement in January 1995, the LEA seconded two successive acting deputies for this period. (Both went on to obtain senior appointments in other schools.)

Prior to the inspection, the governors had played little part in the running and development of the school. They had not been encouraged to be proactive, as all decisions had been dominated by the head teacher. They were initially surprised by the decision to fail the school but accepted the judgement and set about working with the deputy director of the Local Education Authority to draw up an action plan. The plan was sent to the Department for Education and Employment in April, shortly after the new head had been appointed but before she started work at the school. It included the endorsement of a new mission statement for the school, as well as a statement that '. . . the school could, once again, become a school of quality and high standards. . .'

The format of the plan was clear and simple:

- Each action statement relates to one of the key five actions identified by the inspectors
- Each action has a named 'person responsible' in addition to proposed starting and completion dates
- The resources necessary for each action are itemized
- Success criteria are indicated
- The responsibility for monitoring the progress of each action is allotted

A shortened version of the action plan in pamphlet form was sent to all parents.

The school remained in the *Special Measures* category for 29 months. It was 'released' following a *sixth* re-inspection during June 1996.

The process of improvement

Improvement had been achieved by a process of systematic change and development based on the principal goals of improving the effectiveness of teaching and thus (by inference) the quality of learning in the school.

The key to the school's success appears to reside in a multi-layered approach to school improvement. A shared belief among teachers, governors, parents and the LEA that it was possible to turn the school around clearly assisted the process of recovery. The core components of this process of recovery and improvement appear to us to be:

- Involvement of the governing body
- Early support from the LEA
- Effective leadership and management by the head teacher
- Developing and monitoring the quality of teaching and learning
- Staff development and training
- The establishment of a positive learning culture and school environment

Involvement of the governors and the LEA
The absence, or virtual withdrawal, of senior management not only meant that LEA officers frequently took on the leadership of the school but that the drawing

up of the action plan was left to the governing body (tutored by the LEA). In the process of formulating and refining the action plan and in co-opting new members (including an international authority on school effectiveness from Newcastle University), the governing body re-established its own function within the school. The action plan which it produced was of high quality and undoubtedly the willingness of governors to accept responsibility for it helped in the process of recovery. The governing body, for the first time, was able to offer firm strategic direction to the staff. With a less secure head teacher, this active role could have led to difficulties. As it was, the new head and the governing body formed a strong partnership and were able to provide accountability and leadership. This partnership was welcomed by staff and parents.

The need to appoint a new deputy provided the opportunity for the head and the governors to work together in a rigorous selection process. This helped to ensure a high calibre appointment of someone able actively to support the improvement process within the school. Interestingly, the appointee was an existing member of staff who had joined the school just after the inspection which had led to the introduction of special measures.

The LEA was highly supportive throughout the period of change, despite the fact that its initial nominations for new governors for the school were not deemed to be acceptable to the Secretary of State. In addition to playing a major part in the formulation of the action plan, the LEA dealt extremely rapidly with the appointment of a new head teacher. On the subsequent advice of this new head teacher, the LEA abandoned a series of inspections, parallel to those mounted by OFSTED, in favour of less formal feedback and encouragement.

Effective leadership and management
Prior to the initial inspection, it had been widely acknowledged by staff, governors and parents that the leadership in the school was weak. The subsequent inspection report endorsed this view and highlighted this factor as a major problem for the school. The report also revealed that there were severe inadequacies in the various mechanisms of management. The appointment of a new head teacher provided an opportunity to overhaul the entire organization of the school.

The new head made an immediate impact upon the school in several ways. A senior management team (SMT) was created. This gave a visible message that, henceforth, leadership was to be shared and that a new approach to management had been adopted. The SMT comprised the head, the acting deputy head and a curriculum co-ordinator (who subsequently became the new deputy). Each member had specific roles and responsibilities within the team (for example, policy development, staff development and assessment).

The head also interviewed every member of staff in order to gain an insight into their perspectives and understanding and anxieties surrounding the inspection findings. These interviews made staff feel that the head had listened to them and that they were valued. They also enabled the head to judge the potential capacity for change within the staff.

The head sought to implement the action plan by giving responsibility to working parties, composed of staff and governors, for specific areas of development and change. These working parties reinforced the sense of shared responsibility for change and gave teachers, who had previously felt powerless, a sense of direction, purpose and—most importantly—ownership in the development and progress of the school.

Some staff were encouraged to assume different responsibilities in order to experience new teaching challenges. The head personally provided support to such colleagues by teaching alongside them. Her frequent monitoring and observation of class teaching made staff more aware of the variable quality of their own teaching. Where staff were not performing adequately, the head's response was to turn to professional development and training rather than simply to blame or criticize individuals. Her style of leadership was firm but encouraging and her own skill as a teacher meant that she was respected and emulated.

We consider that the head teacher's positive attitudes and well-developed skills were key factors in transforming the school. Staff were inspired and motivated by her approach and example. The teachers felt that the firm and purposeful leadership exhibited by the SMT had made the school 'a different place' and that its members had 'turned the school around by enthusiasm and example'.

Developing and monitoring high quality teaching and learning

Teachers, in the past, had worked in isolation with little idea of how their teaching contributed to the overall quality of teaching and learning in the school. The majority of changes and new initiatives introduced in the school focused directly upon improving the quality of teaching and learning. From the whole-school development plan, through the schemes of work, to actual lesson plans, the central aim was to improve pupils' learning and to raise levels of achievement. An important initial step in this endeavour was encouraging teachers to work together.

The absence of any whole-school ethos and common standards of acceptability before the inspection meant that students' work had been highly variable in both quantity and quality. Initial staff discussion of standards, therefore, focused upon staff expectations of students in the context of assessment in the core subjects and the use of standardized verbal and non-verbal reasoning tests. Teachers worked in groups to compile the school assessment portfolio and, whilst doing so, shared views about what was an acceptable standard of performance at different ages and abilities. This collaboration helped create a set of shared norms and values for the staff.

Working groups were also set up to plan different areas of the curriculum. These groups devised plans and schemes of work to ensure curriculum coverage. In addition, specialist subject co-ordinators were appointed by the head to ensure continuity, progression and coherence across the different year groups and curriculum areas. A considerable amount of the head's time and energy was devoted to training and working alongside the co-ordinators.

Whilst, at times, all these changes proved difficult for teachers to accept, the enthusiastic support of the head meant that curriculum planning and co-ordination mechanisms were successfully implemented. These mechanisms have been translated into two-week schedules used by each teacher. This detailed level of planning is accompanied by a rigorous system of self-assessment. The plans act as a catalyst for change but have also proved to be a means of self-review and evaluation.

Other mechanisms for systematic school-wide monitoring and evaluation of teaching and learning have also been put in place. Regular review has become a feature of school life. Evidence is collected from a wide variety of sources to inform the head, governors, teachers and parents about the progress of individual students. The school monitors both outcomes—such as test scores—and processes—such as the work of the teacher in the classroom. The openness within the school created by the head ensures that such review is not seen as threatening but rather as a necessary part of *sustaining* improvement. A new system of appraisal focuses on providing teachers with feedback and assisting their professional development.

A whole-school assessment policy was devised by the teachers to ensure the flow of consistent information between year groups and different subject areas. This assessment policy has been translated into regular classroom procedures and practice. The new assessment system incorporates a *Record of Achievement* which is used as a means of sharing criteria for judging students' work. It has been used by the school to focus target-setting and review.

Staff development and training

The inspection report highlighted weaknesses in teaching across the school. In response to this criticism, the head gave priority to staff development and training. This focused primarily upon improving teaching practices and extending teaching repertoires.

A number of strategies were put in place. First, staff were encouraged to attend INSET sessions which focused on subject teaching in particular. It was evident from the report that the teaching in core subjects in some classes needed serious attention. Second, staff were encouraged by the head to visit other schools and observe teachers in different contexts. This strategy worked well and was appreciated by teachers, who considered it broadened their view of teaching. Third, the head taught some classes and modelled different teaching methods and approaches. Staff were encouraged to observe these sessions and to discuss different teaching strategies and approaches with her. Lastly, teachers were encouraged to team-teach and to observe each other's lessons. This *partnership* approach was an effective form of professional development, leading to greater confidence and competence in teaching.

The investment in staff development proved to be a most valuable resource in achieving and sustaining school improvement. The staff development strategies instigated by the head encouraged teachers to talk about teaching and to share different methods and strategies with each other. Structured INSET was another important contributor to improvements in teaching, as it resulted in experimentation and the refinement of different teaching approaches. Most importantly, the head teacher *believed* that staff could improve and she demonstrated high levels of trust in the staff at all times.

Producing a positive school environment and learning culture

A number of important factors contributed to a change in the school culture. The change was described by teachers and parents in terms of a more positive environment and 'a place where learning happens'. The external environment of the school was substantially improved through the removal of a dangerous earth slope, the redesign of the play area and by the provision of outdoor seating. The involvement of students in the design of the play area was an important indicator that they too could influence change.

The LEA provided extra funds towards the redecoration and some refurbishment of the buildings which were further enhanced by the teachers mounting imaginative and colourful displays of students' work. The teachers also strove to make their classrooms stimulating and interesting places in which pupils could learn. There was widespread evidence of students' high quality work.

Changes to the external and internal physical environment were complemented by changes in relationships between students and staff. The introduction of a stated behaviour policy meant that teacher–student relationships were less fraught, because discipline procedures were clear to all. A *merit scheme* was introduced in order to develop praise as the method for student control and the means to good behaviour. Parental involvement in the school increased quite dramatically and a number of community projects were developed.

Changes in the external and internal conditions of the school resulted in a change of culture. At the external level, support from the LEA, governors and parents proved instrumental in the maintenance and development of the school. At the internal level, improvements in student behaviour and in their attitudes to learning, teaching quality and staff development all contributed to raising the standards of teaching and learning. The school moved from a position of failure—where staff relationships were poor, leadership was weak and morale was low—to a position where confidence, trust and high standards contribute to improved teaching and learning.

Key themes

- The need for early intervention
- The need for leadership for improvement
- Expectations and trust as engines of change
- An inspection model which fosters challenge rather than dependency

The need for early intervention

This case study demonstrates the need to intervene in the management of schools with serious weaknesses. It is clear (albeit with the benefit of hindsight) that, when earlier visits by HMI and an LEA inspection team had rung warning bells, insufficient efforts were made to support the school. At that time, however, there was no generally accepted policy for dealing with a 'failing' school and certainly few precedents of schools in such circumstances being threatened with closure. Today, in a different climate where there is more public discussion of inspection reports and a much 'harder-nosed' interpretation of accountability, the LEA would be likely to intervene at the first sign of serious difficulties. Furthermore, today's governing body would have a different conception of its role (and of the workload that such a role involves) and would be more likely to demand that the LEA do something about the management of a school in difficulties. That such attitudes and actions were not evident in 1994 is regrettable but hardly surprising, given the assumptions and views about the management of schools which prevailed at that time.

Need for leadership for improvement
The key to the improvement strategy of this school was the appointment of a new head teacher. The school was lucky to attract an application from a very experienced candidate who had the necessary personal and professional skills to do the job. As is obvious from the account we have given, however, the new head realized that there was a need both for leadership to be distributed throughout the staff and for the governing body to have a role in the management of the school. That said, it is abundantly clear that the head has been at the heart of the change and improvement in the school.

Expectations and trust as 'engines' of change
Although there have been changes in the school staff, it is highly significant that the majority of teachers remained in post at the school. They have changed their practice and have thus demonstrated that they had the capacity to develop skills in the new climate of learning that the head created. This has a positive lesson for school improvement: change is possible.

Inspection—the challenge or the dependency model
This case study cannot, by itself, justify the DfEE's policy on failing schools but it lends considerable credence to it. Without the routine inspection, the Drive School might have been permitted to continue on its path of failure for some considerable time. Under the government's special measures, all those involved with the school were brought up short and made to face the reality of the situation. They did so and, as a direct result, the school has improved beyond all recognition. The policy has worked and those responsible should take pleasure in its success.

The policy of special measures, however, also has an associated danger: schools' staffs can be made dependent upon external judges. Staff who have been found to be failing—especially when this judgement comes as a surprise— lose confidence and become deskilled. They learn to rely overmuch on the feedback of the returning inspectors. Yet, in examining follow-up reports on the progress of this school over the 29 months of its duration on special measures, it is difficult not to question the consistency of judgements. It is hard for the staff or governors to challenge this (lack of) consistency, for the inspectors have absolute power over the future of the school. Arguing with the judgements may lead only to an extension of the time on special measures. In this case, the appointment by the governing body of such an experienced head teacher—with no previous connections with the failing school—meant that she was strong enough to avoid the dependency trap, but the lesson needs to be learned.

Conclusions

The results of the students in the national curriculum Key Stage tests are reasonable and will, hopefully, improve. Both the attitude towards learning and the behaviour of students are positive. Staff have had to come to terms with a hard lesson but have done so with remarkably good grace and now demonstrate many of the skills of accomplished teachers. The head teacher is a gifted and highly experienced professional. The governing body has found a role and works well with the LEA. Students and their parents are positive about the changes and believe in the ability of the school to nurture talent and inculcate sound values. We believe that the Drive Primary School can now look forward with confidence to a successful future.

Postscript

I enjoyed our visit to the Drive school. The head teacher was clearly a talented educator. She was also a natural social psychologist. She was recruited after the school had been judged to have failed, but she did not reject the staff she inherited. Instead, the head teacher built up their strengths and gave them new skills. Through her sensitive approach the school was turned round. This is a very different strategy to 'blaming and shaming'. It rests on high expectations, trust and patience. What applies to the staff of this school surely applies to staff and students in schools everywhere. Again, observing the developments in this school reinforced my belief in the importance of psychologically sound approaches to changing behaviour; the literature shows that praise is a much more effective engine of change than punishment.

18

Can School Improvement Overcome the Effects of Disadvantage?[1]

Introduction

Those of us who have worked in the field of school effectiveness and school improvement over the last twenty or so years have seen a sea change in central governments' attitudes. Initially, there was mild interest but a refusal to see any implications for the way central government worked. (It is only fair to note that some local government authorities had grasped the significance of the findings and had drawn on these whilst working with schools in their jurisdiction. Their attempts to use this information, however, were often stymied by the relentless pressure of central government for reforms and, during the last ten years, the forcible introduction of a 'market' into the educational system). During the last couple of years of the previous Conservative administration and the first months of the new Labour government, however, attitudes have changed. Policy makers have seized upon the notion of school improvement and it is now being promulgated as the major means of lifting educational standards. For us researchers this long-awaited recognition is pleasing, but it has its dangers. Like all new converts, there is an element of zealotry in the government's attitudes and expectations. Schools do make a difference—as I have been arguing for nearly twenty years—but they are not alone in the impact they have on children's lives. Family backgrounds, the views and attitudes of peers

---

1 My co-author in the original publication on which this is based is Geoff Whitty.

and the social and economic contexts in which schools have to operate also have an effect. It is certainly true that schooling should be easier to influence than family, peer or broader social and economic trends, but this does not invalidate their influence. In particular, the effects of poverty and other forms of disadvantage cannot easily be dismissed as irrelevant just because some schools in disadvantaged areas are able to promote exceptional progress. This 'occasional paper' was co-written with another colleague—Geoff Whitty—in order to present such views. The immediate stimulus was a comment in a lecture expressing regret that those working at the Institute on School Effectiveness did not collaborate with their institute colleagues in the Sociology of Education. This paper is the result.

Despite the previous government's refusal to acknowledge the importance of the relationship between social disadvantage and educational achievement, stark differences in the lives of pupils with different family backgrounds have not gone away, nor has the problem of knowing how best to deal with them. According to some commentators, this topic has been 'almost a taboo subject in public policy debate in recent years' (Smith & Noble, 1995, p. 133). Teachers who have dared to mention the subject have been branded defeatist or patronizing for even considering that social background can make a difference. With the election of a new government, it is surely time to re-open this important public policy debate.

In schools—especially in those with high proportions of disadvantaged pupils—the issue is of crucial importance, although many of us, including teachers and governors, are unclear about the best approach to adopt. If the problem in the past has been low expectations, should we now ignore disadvantage in the hope that students themselves will find the necessary strengths to overcome their problems? Should we rely on adopting, and trying to instil, high expectations for students' achievement or are such 'hands off' approaches doomed to failure, no matter how genuinely they are intended to help disadvantaged students?

The lessons of history are not hopeful. While some outstanding individuals have achieved the highest levels despite (or, in some cases, motivated by) their inauspicious home backgrounds, most formal education systems have failed students whose families are disadvantaged (Davie et al., 1972; Douglas, 1964; Essen & Wedge, 1982; Gorman & Fernandes, 1992; Mortimore & Mortimore, 1986; Osborne & Milbank, 1987; OECD, 1995). Paradoxically, those who have had most to gain from education have often been the least able to do so.

In recent years the problem has been exacerbated by the introduction of a requirement to publish examination and test results which have been turned, by the press, into crude league tables. Parents are being encouraged to use these results to judge the quality of schools, despite the absence of any relevant information about the background or prior achievement of students as they enter the schools. It is thus in schools' interests to avoid admitting disadvantaged students who—in the absence of extra resources—would be likely to perform poorly and thus worsen the position of the school in the league tables. Such 'hard to teach' students are often only welcome in schools which are undersubscribed and which are desperate for extra students in order to increase their financial viability. Unfortunately, many such schools are already coping with problems to do with the low morale of staff and students and are not—except in exceptional cases—in a strong position to 'lift' the achievement of disadvantaged students.

Meanwhile, our society appears to be deeply confused about the relationship of disadvantage to patterns of achievement. In particular, there is confusion over how much underachievement is due to the actions of individuals and how much to the influence of the school or the attitudes of the wider society. In this paper, we will try to clarify some of the issues by exploring what we do know about disadvantage and the impact it can have on the life of school students. We will also evaluate some of the remedies that have been adopted in attempts to try to change patterns of disadvantage. Finally we will outline other approaches that appear *prima facie* to offer hope for this group of students and discuss both their advantages and their limitations.

Social disadvantage

Fifteen years ago Mortimore and Blackstone commented that 'The concept of social disadvantage is not easy to define partly because it is a relative concept, tied to the social context of time and place' (1982, p. 3). Townsend (1996) sees poverty in the same relative way, as '. . . the absence or inadequacy of those diets, amenities, standards, services and activities which are common or customary in society'. In an attempt to provide objective measures, studies carried out by the National Children's Bureau on the effects of disadvantage adopted three 'hard' criteria: membership of a large or a single-parent family; being in receipt of a low family income; and living in poor-quality housing (Essen & Wedge, 1982). The Organization for Economic Co-operation and Development draws attention not only to the multiplicative effects of such factors (with one form of disadvantage often leading to the experience of other forms) but also to the fact that much of the impact is felt disproportionately by women (OECD, 1995).

A graphic account of what being poor is actually like has been reported by Oppenheim (1993):

> Poverty means going short materially, socially and emotionally. It means spending less on food, on heating and on clothing . . . Poverty means staying at home, often being bored, not seeing friends . . . not being able to take the children out for a treat or a holiday. . . (p. 4)

Despite the general improvement over recent years in most people's living standards, conditions have worsened for a significant minority. According to Walker and Walker (1997), the number of people living in poverty (50 per cent of average national earnings or less) has shown a three-fold increase since 1979 and now stands at one quarter of the population. Our country has been exceptional in that the difference between the 'haves' and the 'have nots' seems to have resulted from official policies designed to lift the constraints affecting the rich. These policies have also sought to penalize the poor in the interests of freeing them from a so-called 'dependency culture'. 'Britain stands out internationally in having experienced the largest percentage increase in income inequality between 1967 and 1992' (Dennehy et al., 1997, p. 280).

The proportion of children living in poor households is now 32 per cent, compared to the European Union average of 20 per cent (Eurostat, 1997). Researchers from the Thomas Coram Research Unit estimate that about one third of children now live in households with no full-time earner (Brannen et al., 1997). For many such children, life is grim:

> Children from poor homes have lower life expectancy and are more likely to die in infancy or childhood; they have a greater likelihood of poor health . . . a greater risk of unemployment, a higher probability of involvement in crime and enduring homelessness. (Holtermann, 1997, p. 26)

What impact does social disadvantage have on children's educational opportunities?

Almost by definition, children from disadvantaged backgrounds are more likely than other children to live in a worse environment. Of course, disadvantage exists in rural areas, as it does in estates on the fringes of many of our cities, but it is often in the inner city that the worst problems are found in this country. High density living is not, in itself, a bad thing—many people choose to live in this way—but it tends to mean living in greater proximity to crime and drugs and it frequently means living in poor-quality housing. As noted by Holtermann (1997), social disadvantage is also frequently associated with poorer health. Children tend to be physically weaker and have less energy for learning than their peers. They are also more likely to be emotionally upset by the tensions in their lives. Finally, they are less likely to have the opportunity for study and for educational help at home. These are just the conditions in which children will be vulnerable to low levels of self-efficacy: 'an inability to exert influence over things that adversely affect one's life, which breeds apprehension, apathy, or despair' (Bandura, 1995a, p. 1). They, in turn, will work against children's development as effective school learners and, ultimately, according to Wilkinson (1997), their chance of a long healthy life.

Whether the impact of disadvantage on a particular child's education is lasting or not will depend on their own resilience as well as on how much their parents are able to shield them from the effects of disadvantaging circumstances. We know from studies of educational priority programmes that the effects of disadvantage are cumulative. Each new factor adds to the problem. This became starkly evident in a recent study of the educational consequences of homelessness with which one of us was involved (Power et al., 1995).

Remedies already tried

There have been a number of distinct approaches to the amelioration of the effects of poverty on educational opportunities. We will focus, for the time being, on education-centred measures, although we shall point later to the limitations of these. One approach rests on the concept of *meritocracy*. First taken seriously with the introduction of public examinations for officials in the mid-nineteenth century, the concept has subsequently underpinned the widely-held assumption that those with talents would rise to the top through public competition. It was used to justify the scholarship ladder introduced at the turn of the century, formed the basis of the 11-plus selection procedure and, most recently, the assisted places scheme. It has also informed the thinking behind public examinations generally. The evidence from studies of social mobility shows that such a meritocratic approach does help overcome the effects of disadvantage by promoting some individuals with outstanding talents. What such studies also show, however, is that, although this works for some, it fails to do so for many more (Brown et al., 1997). The philosophy of 'plucking embers from the ashes' of inner-city deprivation (cited in Edwards et al., 1989) does nothing to improve the standard of education for those left behind. The sorts of choice and competition strategies introduced by the Conservative government with the avowed aim of equalizing opportunities for all families, regardless of where they lived, seem only to have polarized provision even further (Whitty, 1997a).

The second approach has been characterized by the use of *compensatory mechanisms*. These include individual benefits, such as free school meals, uniform grants and other special measures for low-income families. The problem with individual benefits is that the levels of funding have always been relatively modest and have thus been unable to compensate for the major differences in the conditions of children's lives (Smith & Noble, 1995). Compensatory mechanisms have also included the allocation of additional resources to schools, such as in the Educational Priority Area (EPA) programmes of the 1960s and 1970s, when extra payments were made to schools with high proportions of disadvantaged students (Halsey, 1972; Smith, 1987). One drawback of school-wide schemes is that targeting is necessarily inefficient: some advantaged students will gain access to extra resources within the chosen schools, whilst many disadvantaged students, in other schools, will fail to do so (Acland, 1973; Plewis, 1997). However, there may still be cost-effective benefits, as work concerned with the development of 'at risk' registers of birth disorders, carried out over twenty years ago, shows (Alberman & Goldstein, 1970). Later versions of the EPA idea, adopted by the (former) Inner London Education Authority, provided extra resources on a sliding scale rather than on an all-or-nothing basis (Sammons et al., 1983). The local management formulae approved over the last few years, however, allow little scope for radical positive discrimination.

The third approach to combating disadvantage involves the creation of *intervention projects,* potentially open to all students, but which have mainly been used with the disadvantaged with a view to accelerating their educational development. Such projects include: in the United States, the High Scope programme, which promoted active child learning (Weikart, 1972); the Comer Approach, which addresses children's health and social, as well as their educational, needs (Comer, 1980); and Success for All (Slavin et al., 1993), seen as one of the most promising approaches to overcoming the educational effects of disadvantage (Herman & Stringfield, 1995). In New Zealand, Clay has developed the Reading Recovery Programme, a structured approach to overcoming early reading failure which has been shown to be effective for disadvantaged students (Clay, 1982; Rowe, 1995). In Latin America, there have been a number of initiatives based on the work of the late Paulo Freire. There has also been an interest in capitalizing on research which demonstrates that intellectual tasks can be found in the everyday activities of disadvantaged children (see, for instance, Nunes et al., 1993). In the United Kingdom, the Early Years nursery study, which focused on ways of increasing children's capacity to learn (Athey, 1990) has also claimed some success; a series of British parent involvement schemes designed to encourage children and parents to read together (see, for example, Tizard et al., 1982) has been shown to have positive effects; and a Scottish project on the use of homework has demonstrated gains in disadvantaged areas (MacBeath & Turner, 1990).

Despite the enthusiastic support of teachers and local authorities in the UK for each of these projects, official support and hence widespread implementation has been strictly limited. The Reading Recovery Programme, for instance, was trialed in an English LEA and introduced more widely in a highly systematic way. It had £14 million spent on it through government grants and obtained positive evaluations from a carefully controlled experiment (Hobsbaum, 1995; Sylva & Hurry, 1995). Nevertheless, it was dropped from government priorities after three years, just as its impact was beginning to be felt. Furthermore, the Early Years study by Athey has never been promoted widely, despite some evidence that its application might even lessen the gap between disadvantaged and other pupils. These interventions have the ability to change student outcomes, but their potential benefits have not been exploited nor have the limits to their efficacy been properly investigated. In particular, we need to know whether these approaches are especially advantageous with disadvantaged students to the extent that they would help close the achievement gap even if used with *all* students.

Although these approaches clearly can combat the individual consequences of disadvantage to some degree, they have so far failed significantly to alter the established differential patterns of achievement in this country. There remains a strong negative correlation between most measures of *social disadvantage* and *school achievement,* as even a cursory glance at the league tables of school-by-school results demonstrates (Smith & Noble, 1995). Why is this so? First, there is the obvious fact that what has been done in compensatory and supplementary activity remains slight in comparison with the impact of the cumulative advantages of growing up in an advantaged home. It would be odd if having warmer, more spacious accommodation, more nutritious food, better health, greater access to books, educational toys and stimulating experiences, and more informed knowledge about how the system works did not confer considerable advantage in any tests or examinations.

Second, it should not be forgotten that measures of educational achievement are determined by competition within the tradition of a meritocracy. Thus, even though there has been a rise in achievement, as recorded by the General Certificate of Secondary Education results (from 22 per cent in 1980 to 44.5 per cent in 1996 gaining the five high grades usually deemed the mark of success), more than half the age group still does not succeed at this level (DfEE, 1996). Given this reality and the factors noted earlier, it would surely be surprising if those with disadvantaged backgrounds succeeded in equal proportions to their more advantaged peers.

Examination success is not, of course, rationed, and the official examination boards would be quick to refute any suggestion that they worked within strict norms, but it would be naïve to think that expectations established over many years could be set aside other than by a slow incremental progression. The annual chorus of 'more must mean worse' ensures that the scope for disadvantaged candidates to join the successful group is likely to remain strictly limited, whatever improvements are made to their absolute levels of achievement.

The report *Learning Works: Widening Participation in Further Education* (Kennedy, 1997a) has drawn attention to the evidence that it is those who are already well qualified who go on to earn more and to demand and get more learning.

So there remains a need to do a great deal more if an often-declared goal of our education system—to help every child, regardless of family background, achieve up to the limits of his or her potential—is to be realized.

What else can be done?

Two possible avenues forward are often seen as mutually exclusive alternatives. One builds on the work in school improvement that has been pioneered as a result of research into school effectiveness. The other is more fundamental and demands change not only to the nature of educational practice but also to the broader social and cultural contexts within which education takes place. We believe that an effective strategy for tackling disadvantage requires movement on both fronts.

Change through school improvement

The roots of school improvement lie in twenty years of research into school effectiveness carried out mainly in England, the Netherlands and the United States (Hopkins et al., 1994). The central tenet of school improvement is that the responsibility for change must lie in the hands of the school itself (Stoll & Fink, 1996). In contrast to centrally driven projects, those working in school improvement believe that the head teacher, staff and school governing body— having listened to the views and advice of school inspectors, consultants or researchers—are well placed to decide how best to improve their own institutions (Mortimore, 1996a).

Evaluations of established improvement projects show that they tend to have a common pattern (Stoll & Fink, 1996). Initially, the school improvement team carry out an audit of the current state of the school: the students' outcomes (including behaviour as well as attainment), the curriculum, the pedagogy, the management of learning, behaviour and resources, and the state of the premises. In the light of such investigations, the team draws up an action plan to enhance the good and repair the bad. Although problems are sometimes obvious, it is often difficult precisely to diagnose their cause. The team has to make a series of hypotheses about what has probably caused which outcome, and what might—if changed—produce a different result. This is far from being an exact science and in the third stage—the evaluation—the team may discover that many outcomes are the result of a complex web of influences and, furthermore, that some changes have produced unintended negative results.

School improvers know they cannot create a recipe book—schools are far too complex for such an approach (Stoll & Myers, 1997). They have sought, rather, to identify and make use of the underlying processes of change. Writers such as Louis and Miles (1990), Fullan (1991) and Huberman (1992) have identified a number of facilitating or inhibiting factors which affect the process. Fullan, for instance, lists a number of warnings about change which he urges head teachers to heed: that change is not easy, that conflict and disagreement will be inevitable and that not all colleagues will embrace it. Fullan stresses that heads should expect these outcomes and not be caught unawares if they occur in reaction to change efforts.

Two questions arise from this brief review of improvement strategies: can school improvement help schools which have high proportions of disadvantaged students and can it help individual disadvantaged students?

Can improvement projects help schools with high proportions of disadvantaged students?

The National Commission on Education (NCE, 1996) undertook a project designed to uncover how some schools with disadvantaged students had improved and succeeded against the odds. Eleven teams (each consisting of an educational researcher and two representatives from the business world or the community) carried out fieldwork to identify why particular schools were successful in the face of disadvantage. In the school case study carried out by one team (Mortimore et al., 1996), we were particularly impressed with the quality of the leadership team and the way it had trusted the majority of the staff to create a set of school aims around the idea of achievement. Students were committed to learning and staff held high expectations about examination performance and social behaviour. The confidence of the teachers in the good sense of the students—even to the radical point of encouraging them to draw up a code of what they expected of the staff—was impressive.

Maden and Hillman's (1996) discussion of the findings from all the case studies in the project emphasizes the importance of: a leadership stance which builds on and develops a team approach; a vision of success which includes a view of how the school can improve; the careful use of targets; the improvement of the physical environment; common expectations about students' behaviour and success; and an investment in good relations with parents and the community. Maden and Hillman note how a crisis in the life of the school can become a catalyst for successful change.

What the project demonstrates is that committed and talented head teachers and teachers can improve schools, even if such schools contain a proportion of disadvantaged students. In order to achieve improvement, however, such schools had to exceed what could be termed 'normal' efforts. Members of staff have to be *more committed* and *work harder* than their peers elsewhere. What is more, they have to maintain the effort so as to sustain the improvement. There can be no switching on the 'automatic pilot' if schools are aiming to buck the trend. We must, however, be aware of the dangers of basing a national strategy for change on the efforts of outstanding individuals working in exceptional circumstances.

Further evidence about the ability of schools with disadvantaged students to improve comes from the first tranche of case studies published by the Department for Education and Employment (DfEE, 1997b). These studies describe some of the ways in which improvement was brought about in schools which had failed their Ofsted inspections. In contrast to much of the rhetoric about resources not mattering, what stands out is the impact of the extra resources invested by the LEAs in their efforts to turn the schools round.

Can school improvement projects help individual disadvantaged students?

Evidence from a recent study of the value-added results from one local authority shows that some schools are able—once all background factors have been taken into account—to 'lift' the GCSE results by the equivalent of a change from seven grade Ds to seven grade Bs (Thomas & Mortimore, 1996). MacGilchrist (1997) also argues forcefully that some of the special interventions (noted earlier) which have been mounted to support the learning of students with special difficulties—and, in many cases, disadvantaged backgrounds—demonstrate that more schools, given adequate support, could help such students. She notes, however, that these opportunities have not been sufficiently exploited.

In theory, researchers should be able to estimate fairly precisely how many individual students have been helped by their schools to overcome the effects of personal disadvantage. By addressing the GCSE results of secondary schools and noting their intake information from five years before (for example, what was student attainment at the end of primary schooling and how many students were eligible for free school meals), it should be possible to estimate some value-added scores for their schools in relation to other institutions. Those which had raised the achievement of their 'disadvantaged students' significantly beyond what had been achieved by similar students in other schools could be assumed to have helped, especially, this group of students. The results could then be aggregated to provide an estimate of the likely total number of disadvantaged students that have been helped by the efforts of school improvement. Retrospective investigations could then attempt to explore how the schools had helped these students and, in particular, whether improvement had been the result of a planned programme or whether it had occurred seemingly spontaneously. Other information, such as whether the 'disadvantaged' group had been a particularly high or low proportion of the total, could also be collected, so as to inform us about the importance of the educational context in which a student learns.

Unfortunately, such an investigation remains a theoretical possibility because not only would it be difficult to ensure that one really was 'comparing like with like' but also because there is not a suitable national database which brings together accurate intake and examination outcome data. It is worth noting, anyway, that attributing causal effects to particular initiatives in complex organizations such as schools is always likely to be difficult. Analysis of American statistical evidence suggests that achievement gains are often too readily attributed to a particular initiative when there may well be entirely different explanations, such as a change of intake (Henig, 1994). Without appropriate data and suitably robust analytical techniques, therefore, the evidence for the ability of schools to help individual disadvantaged students has to rest on theory and on the historical evidence of those institutions which, in the absence of alternative explanations, do appear to have bucked the trend.

Cultural and structural change

Sociologists of education have frequently been critical of work on school effectiveness and school improvement. For example, Angus criticizes it for failing 'to explore the relationship of specific practices to wider social and cultural constructions and political and economic interests' (1993, p. 335). He argues that it 'shifts attention away from the nature of knowledge, the culture of schooling and, most importantly, the question of for whom and in whose interests schools are to be effective' (p. 342). Hatcher (1996) sees school improvement as downplaying the significance of social class, with similar consequences. In this context, even the very term 'disadvantage' can serve to hide the structured inequalities of class and race and actually contribute to the 'colour-blindness' of recent education policy (Gillborn, 1997).

Can changes in curriculum and assessment help?
Angus's questions suggest that the curriculum itself may be implicated in perpetuating disadvantage by marginalizing the culture of the least powerful groups in society. There is certainly a case for broadening the scope of what counts as legitimate knowledge in schools (Comer, 1980; Whitty, 1985). Some of the national curriculum orders have been criticized for adopting an unduly narrow view of worthwhile knowledge and ignoring the pluralism and multiculturalism of late twentieth-century Britain (Ball, 1993).

Although some of these issues will need to be addressed by the new government, individual schools can also play some part in the way they choose to interpret the national curriculum and they need to be mindful of this opportunity to help the disadvantaged. Trying to counter the cultural bias of current curricular arrangements and making schools more 'inclusive' of diverse communities is sometimes seen as a watering down of standards. Yet, schools that are successful with students from a variety of backgrounds recognize that high standards can be achieved in a number of ways. While some learning goals need to be tackled by all students in the same way, others can be achieved through a variety of routes that take account of different backgrounds. This is not the same as adjusting standards to the lowest common denominator. It is an unacceptable option, especially in the light of the increasing globalization of labour and the need to ensure that young people from the United Kingdom can compete with their peers from elsewhere in the world.

Nevertheless, such considerations also demand that we find ways to ensure that a greater proportion of our young people can succeed. This may require a restructuring of the assessment system. Can we design a progression system so that a much higher proportion of candidates reaches the currently accepted level of success? The experience of assessing the progress of students through the national curriculum is not very promising and efforts to combine a student's need for diagnostic assessment with a system need for certification and monitoring have generally proved unsatisfactory for each of these needs. There are a number of ways in which our national approach to assessment could be improved: the standards set for performance could be better defined; feedback could be more positive; a range of performance tasks and modes could be provided (Gipps, 1994). It has to be borne in mind, however, that such improvements would be more likely to lift 'overall' standards than specifically help the disadvantaged. This would be helpful to our national standards of achievement and is to be greatly encouraged, but clearly does not address the particular problem of the disadvantaged.

It is sometimes suggested that the print-based culture of schools is in itself an obstacle for disadvantaged students and that this might be overcome by the new information technologies. It is too early to know whether these will provide dramatic new opportunities. So far, few schools have had the resources to invest in adequate equipment and too few teachers have been fully trained in its use. Experiments in particular schools in the United States and in Australia need to be evaluated before we would know whether the technology will provide radically more powerful ways of learning. But while it is possible that IT may help, in particular, students from disadvantaged backgrounds, we have to remember that IT is shaped by the same social forces as other more obviously social phenomena. For example, any potential benefits for disadvantaged students may be offset by the fact that those from advantaged families are more likely to have access to IT equipment in the home and thus to develop the relevant 'know-how' sooner. Furthermore, the internet, often proclaimed as a democratic medium which eradicates social distinctions, is actually used mainly by white middle-class males and this has consequences for the material available on it (Kenway, 1996).

Addressing the impact of the wider society

Whatever changes occur in the curriculum and means of assessment, it seems inevitable that schools will be affected by their role within a wider society which still maintains social divisions and a powerful sense of hierarchy. A particular criticism of school improvement work is that it has tended to exaggerate the extent to which individual schools can challenge such structural inequalities. Whilst some schools can succeed against the odds, the possibility of them all doing so, year in and year out, still appears remote, given that the long-term patterning of educational inequality has been strikingly consistent throughout the history of public education in most countries.

Doubts have recently even been cast on whether Sweden, usually seen as a shining exception, has actually succeeded in bucking this particular trend in recent years (Erikson & Jonsson, 1996). Although there are different theories about how the social and cultural patterning of educational outcomes occurs (Goldthorpe, 1996), these patterns reflect quite closely the relative chances of different groups entering different segments of the labour market. Accordingly, whilst it might be possible, for example, for the ethos of a particular school to help transform the aspirations of a particular group of students within it, it seems highly unlikely that all schools could do this in the absence of more substantial social changes.

As noted earlier, one of the depressing findings is that the *relative* performance of the disadvantaged has remained similar even when the absolute performance of such groups has improved. Just as poverty is a relative concept, we are faced with a situation in which educational success also appears to be partly relative. A large-scale longitudinal study of primary schools carried out by one team (Mortimore et al., 1988b) found that no school *reversed* the usual 'within-school' pattern of advantaged students performing better than the disadvantaged. However, some of the disadvantaged students in the most effective schools made more progress than their advantaged peers in the least effective schools and even did better in absolute terms. Yet, encouraging as this is, it would appear that, if all primary schools were to improve so that they performed at the level of the most effective, the difference between the overall achievement of the most advantaged social groups and that of the disadvantaged might actually increase.

At secondary level, schools only rarely overcome the relative differences between the performance of different social groups, as the latest evidence on differential school effects demonstrates (Thomas et al., 1997). Moreover, despite the optimism of some school improvement literature, it is still difficult to counter the conclusion to be drawn from a reading of the pioneering *Fifteen Thousand Hours* research (Rutter et al., 1979a) that, if all schools performed as well as the best schools, the stratification of achievement by social class would be even more stark than it is now. This would happen because socially 'advantaged' children in highly effective schools would achieve even more than they might do in a less conducive environment and the gap between them and their less advantaged peers would increase.

The recent report of the Literacy Task Force (Literacy Task Force, 1997) seemed to recognize the existence of such problems but perhaps underestimated the resource implications of overcoming them. The problems and dilemmas facing schools with large numbers of disadvantaged students, compared with those with advantaged intakes, are much greater than current policies recognize (Proudford and Baker, 1995; Thrupp, 1995, 1997b). This suggests a continuing need for positive discrimination and the effective targeting of human and material resources. Smith et al. (1997) recommend three sets of actions to support schools in disadvantaged areas. They argue that, because of the competitive market that has been created, education in poor areas must not be considered in isolation. Given the existence of this competitive market between schools, they recommend a stronger interventionist role for the LEA. They suggest that 'choice' is too blunt an instrument for improvement and recommend the targeting of resources to schools in disadvantaged areas and possibly a transfer of resources from inspection to school improvement.

Robinson claims that educational measures are unlikely to alleviate the impact of disadvantage. He rightly sees the tackling of social and economic disadvantage as more likely to succeed, arguing that 'a serious programme to alleviate child poverty might do far more for boosting attainment AMD literacy than any modest interventions in schooling' (Robinson, 1997, p. 17). Unlike Robinson, however, we believe more up-to-date evidence shows that schools *can* make some difference. Schools with disadvantaged students can lift achievement levels, provided those who work in them invest the energy and the dedication to maintain momentum even whilst working against the grain. Within any school, however, the powerful factors associated with a more advantaged home background appear, in general, to be paramount and evident when we look across the education system as a whole. It is, therefore, important for government, LEAs and school governors to set challenging goals, but it is also important to be clear about the limits of school-based actions. Setting unrealistic goals and adopting a strategy of 'shame and blame' will lead only to cynicism and a lowering of morale amongst those teachers at the heart of the struggle to raise the achievement of disadvantaged pupils.

Tackling disadvantage beyond the school

Grace has argued that too many urban education reformers have been guilty of 'producing naïve school-centred solutions with no sense of the structural, the political and the historical as constraints' (Grace, 1984, p. xii). If schools alone are unable to close the gap between the disadvantaged and their peers, are there other institutions or agencies that can do so? Clearly, if disadvantage has multiple causes, tackling it requires strategies that bring together multiple agencies that more usually work in isolation. There have, of course, been a number of initiatives that have sought to do this in targeted areas (see Wilmott &

Hutchinson, 1992), but the recent 'marketization' of housing, health and education appears to have provided disadvantaged families with less rather than more co-ordination of services (Power et al., 1995). A major priority for the new government must surely be to provide incentives for effective multi-agency work to counter disadvantage.

This is not just a matter of ensuring greater efficiency in the delivery of public services, important as that is. Considerable concern has been expressed recently about a decline in 'social capital' in modern societies, with an alleged breakdown in relationships of trust and supportive social networks. Furthermore, there is growing evidence of the damaging effects of vast differences in social capital between different communities (Wilkinson, 1996). Arguably, this has been made worse by recent policies which treat education as a consumer right rather than a citizen right and thereby undermine the notion that education is a public good and the responsibility of the whole community (Whitty, 1997b). Yet Coleman's analysis (1988) suggests that the social capital of a community, as well as that of families and schools, can have an important bearing on the educational achievement of its children. Policies that may appear to have little to do with education, such as community development or the building of 'healthy alliances', might therefore actually contribute to the raising of achievement in schools. Thus, statutory agencies could usefully assist voluntary associations in developing networks within the wider community that support the work of schools, at the same time as bringing other benefits to the community. Current initiatives around the concept of 'healthier schools' are one example of this and it will be important to evaluate their impact on school effectiveness in disadvantaged areas (Toft et al., 1995).

The enhancement of social and cultural capital in disadvantaged areas also requires that more be done to provide opportunities for learning beyond the years of compulsory schooling. Traditionally, this has been one of the tasks of further education colleges and adult institutes committed to continuing life-long learning, but these institutions and their clientele have too often been marginalized within the system as a whole.

Lifetime Learning (DfEE, 1996b) tries to focus public debate on the importance of lifelong education and training, but there are other ways in which, in our view, the government could help disadvantaged people extend their education. These include: a radical revision of its approach to studying whilst unemployed; an extension of tax exemptions for all in post-compulsory training; an equalization of treatment of part-time and full-time students; support for a national credit-based education and training framework; and the provision of increased child care to support learning opportunities for part-time and temporary workers.

Kennedy (1997a) lists a number of detailed recommendations for government, the Training and Enterprise councils and individual further education colleges. These include: the launching of a lottery-funded government campaign for the creation of a learning nation; the redistribution of public resources towards those with less success in earlier learning; the encouragement of company funded learning centres for adult workers; and the creation of a unitized system for recognizing achievement (the Pathways to Learning project).

Kennedy also argues (Kennedy, 1997b, p. 3) that drawing more people into the community of learning is not only central to economic prosperity but also 'one of the most effective ways of tackling social exclusion'. She claims that 'we have been seeing the most terrible separation between rich and poor over the past decades and education has a vital role in redressing the consequences of that division'. This requires 'a redistribution of public resources towards those with less success in earlier learning'.

Changes such as those proposed above would ease the financial costs for those who needed to make up in their own time for an unsatisfactory experience of schooling. Such opportunities are necessary if more people are to continue their education and, in particular, if the disadvantaged are to play any part in the formation of a learning society. They are only likely to succeed, however, in the context of a culture—as well as a structure—of inclusiveness. Yet much of our previous history of education has been built on a culture of exclusiveness. It is how to change this culture that probably represents the new government's greatest challenge.

One of the ways to alter this culture is to invent new approaches which bring together partners from across society rather than seeing problems as being solely in the realm of the education service. The government, in its first White Paper, has proposed a pilot programme of up to 25 Education Action Zones in areas with a mix of under performing schools and the highest levels of disadvantage (DfEE, 1997b). Such action zones will have at their centre a forum of local parents and representatives from local business and community interests in which an action plan and targets will be formulated, implemented and monitored. It remains to be seen how these develop and whether their existence does indeed channel more help and energy into the target areas whilst avoiding the pitfalls of the old 'educational priority' areas. Nevertheless, the idea seems worth pursuing, provided each zone's forum includes all relevant constituencies and provided there is a significant redistribution of resources into these areas.

Conclusions

In this paper we have spelled out our interpretation of the educational problem faced by students from disadvantaged families in our society. We have found— with some notable exceptions—that school students with such backgrounds do less well than their peers, hardly a surprising finding in a competitive system. We have also shown that previous governments have failed to exploit what knowledge there is about how to combat the problem. In particular, we have described how a number of the co-ordinating initiatives and intervention strategies that appear to have had some success in other countries have been ignored. Furthermore, some of those that have been adopted and shown to have benefits have inexplicably been allowed to wither. Meanwhile, the advantaged have sometimes gained even more than the disadvantaged from those initiatives that have been pursued. The effect of this is that the advantaged become more so and the disadvantaged—without the help and support of focused extra help—slip further behind. Thus the conventional pattern of outcomes is maintained—with the advantaged at the top and the disadvantaged (with some exceptions) at the bottom. So can there be a solution to this set of problems?

The re-engineering of the educational system, so that disadvantaged groups can succeed, will not be easy. As Bernstein (1970) noted nearly thirty years ago, 'education cannot compensate for society'. Nor is education's role in helping to change society well understood. Probably the single most significant factor that currently distinguishes the most academically successful schools (even if not the most 'effective' ones in value-added terms) is that only a small proportion of their students come from disadvantaged homes. To that extent, policies which tackle poverty and related aspects of disadvantage at their roots are likely to be more successful than purely educational interventions in influencing overall patterns of educational inequality. Yet, if dynamic school improvement strategies can be developed as one aspect of a broader social policy, then they will have an important role to play on behalf of individual schools and their pupils.

What we have been concerned to stress in this paper is that society needs to be clearer about what schools can and cannot be expected to do. As we have tried to demonstrate, the relationship between individuals, institutions and society is complex and blaming schools for the problems of society is unfair and unproductive. Nevertheless, demonstrating that opportunities for some disadvantaged students can be changed in particularly effective schools—even if the disadvantaged as a group still remain behind their peers—can itself help to transform a culture of inertia or despair. It is this transformation that those who work in the field of school improvement are seeking. Schools with high proportions of disadvantaged students need extra support. Teachers who choose to work in these schools—because they want to help the disadvantaged—need their commitment recognized and supported rather than being 'blamed', as has happened so shamefully in the past.

In short, we do not consider that there is any single factor which could reverse long-standing patterns of disadvantage but neither do we regard such patterns as an unchangeable fact of life. We believe that our society must—through government actions as well as grass-roots initiatives—begin to adjust the balance between individuals' opportunities and their social responsibilities so as to develop a more equal society. Society should not have to cope with what Wilkinson terms the 'corrosive effects of inequality' (Wilkinson, 1996).

With such a perspective, we consider four clusters of immediate action to be vital:

- Better coordination of the work of the support agencies by the government and by local authorities
- Early interventions which provide additional educational opportunities for the disadvantaged, funded from an increased education budget

- Reconsideration of the approaches to learning and teaching used with disadvantaged students
- Extra support for students with disadvantaged backgrounds in school improvement programmes

Even with these actions, we accept that there is unlikely to be a sudden reversal of long-established patterns of disadvantage or any significant long-term change in the absence of concurrent strategies to tackle poverty and disadvantage at their roots. We do consider, however, that the current waste of human resources caused by the educational failure of those with disadvantaged backgrounds is unacceptable in a modern society. We urge the new government to make a fresh start. We believe that, if it could focus its energy on this problem and set a new tone by working with local authorities, the teaching and other caring professions, it would have a better chance of achieving change than previous governments. Future generations of school students from disadvantaged families would stand to benefit, but the real gain would be the creation of a better educated society more likely to surmount the challenges of the twenty-first century.

Postscript

In this paper we sought to strike a balance between lauding the positive effects of schooling and warning of the negative effects of disadvantage. We recognized from the numerous studies we reviewed that, for many school students, both influences were important. The fortunate students would experience a positive 'pull' from their schools and an equally positive 'push' from their families' social and economic background. The unfortunate, however, may suffer from a double negative influence. In some cases, the push/pull influences can be in opposite directions, thus placing individual students in extraordinarily difficult situations with some pulled towards academic success by the school whilst being pushed back by other influences and others being pushed forward by their family in the face of the negative pulling back by the school.

The implications of this chapter for the way we judge effectiveness are important. Schools must not use disadvantage as an excuse for their failure to promote achievement wherever this is possible. But neither must policy makers allow the existence of 'particularly effective schools' to cover up their own inability to improve the social and economic conditions of many families. Finally, 'blame' needs to be treated with extreme caution. In my judgement it will seldom be appropriate as a tool of social policy. It is particularly inappropriate when it is used to compare the results of those working with the 'hardest to teach' students and the fewest resources to those of schools which are able to select talented and motivated students.

19

Criticisms of School Effectiveness[1]

Introduction

This chapter is based on a riposte to a series of critical articles included in a book published this year by the Institute. Some might see it as counterproductive for the Institute, which has been responsible for much of the most important work in this field, to promote a collection of critical articles. This would—in my view—be a misjudgement. Social science needs to criticize itself. Its concepts, methodologies and theories (whether explicit or implicit) must remain open to scrutiny if progress is to be made. That said, if criticisms appear unfair or misguided, they need to be countered or rejected.

Research in the social sciences is frequently difficult to undertake. Parents and children tend not to live in towns nor to attend schools in patterns that fit easily with research designs. The reality of uneven, overlapping, mixed contexts and subjects provide researchers with considerable methodological challenges and—for those working with quantitative methodologies—the need for statistical techniques that can cope with such complexity.

Because social and educational research is difficult there is a tendency to see criticism as unfair or inappropriate. This is wrong. Of course some critics will be fired by ideological fervour and some will be ignorant of the work that they

---

1 The original work on which this chapter is based was co-authored with Pam Sammons.

seek to criticize, but others will be motivated by a healthy desire to challenge accepted findings. We believe that research in education and the other social sciences develops and improves through critical review and through the challenge and refutation of both findings and theories. That said, we—and surely researchers in general—expect criticism of our work to be undertaken seriously, reported even-handedly and presented in a way which avoids personal attacks. It is surely only fair that those who seek to criticize should first have studied the major works in the field in detail. It is not good enough to cite secondary sources nor is it good scholarship simply to make serious allegations without presenting supporting evidence.

At the institute we have sought to develop a reasoned approach to a critique which focuses on the methodology of the research in question and, whilst it may challenge its conclusions, endeavours to avoid personal attacks on the author. This is the approach which some of us at the institute tried to adopt when we published a critique of some recent Ofsted research (Mortimore & Goldstein, 1996). This approach, however, did not save us from an emotional and vituperative riposte by a journalist in a national newspaper (Phillips, 1996).

School effectiveness provokes criticism from all quarters: our research peers; politicians of all parties; and, most recently, from the head of Ofsted (Woodhead, 1997). We are grateful to the editor for the opportunity to reply to those critics who have contributed to these papers, but we obviously cannot answer on behalf of the many researchers, in this country and elsewhere, who have written about this field of inquiry. We will respond, therefore, drawing—where this seems appropriate—on our own research studies carried out over the last twenty or so years. We are pleased to note, however, that school effectiveness research has also been welcomed by both practitioners and academics.

We will not attempt to respond to every critical comment that has been made in any of the papers. We have discussed many of the general issues over the years (Mortimore, 1991b, 1995a; Mortimore et al., 1988a, 1988b, 1988c; Sammons et al., 1993b) and some similar points have already been answered in the autumn edition of *Forum* (Sammons et al., 1996b) and in the *Cambridge Journal of Education* (Sammons & Reynolds, 1997).

Furthermore, we will not address a number of technical points which have been addressed in detail in Goldstein's publication on the limitations of league tables (Goldstein & Speigelhalter, 1996). Instead we have selected the key generalizable issues and will endeavour to deal with these. We are sure that this will not resolve all the concerns that have been raised and we welcome continued dialogue on what we deem to be an important area of research.

Definitions of effectiveness

A number of critics challenge the basic concept of 'effectiveness'. Our view, which we have consistently applied to our research over the years, is that some operational definition of effectiveness is necessary for empirical research.

Accordingly, we have tried to set the achievement of students within the context of the capacity of the school to promote progress. This is because we recognize that schools do not receive uniform intakes of students. Some schools take those who come with high levels of prior achievement or with considerable social advantage, whilst others predominantly receive students who lack these benefits. We have sought to find ways to distinguish the impact of the school from the 'dowry' brought by the student. One definition we have used is that an effective school is: 'a school in which students progress further than might be expected from a consideration of its intake' (Mortimore, 1991a).

This definition is built on the premise that an *expectation* for any particular school intake group can be calculated on the basis of the average levels of achievement recorded by students with different background characteristics in a population or a large sample of schools. More effective schools are those which exceed this expectation. Less effective schools are those where students do less well than expected on the basis of their given characteristics. Scott, in his criticism of the definition, slips from our focus on *the school* to *teaching* and claims that we argue 'pupils are only being effectively taught if their achievements go beyond what would normally be expected of them'. This is a subtle change but an important one which distorts our argument.

Two assumptions lie at the heart of the definition given above: that any student's outcome in a given performance test will be related to both his or her individual characteristics and background *and* to the quality of their total school experience, including the teaching that they have received; and that those schools in which students systematically perform markedly better than the average for the whole population of the schools—once the individual characteristics and background differences have been taken into account—are *prima facie* likely to be better than the others. We term such schools effective. They may receive students who are exceptionally talented or very ordinary. The students may have done well or badly in previous educational settings. Nevertheless, these differences should not by themselves affect the effectiveness or otherwise of the school.

The definition we have quoted is still used quite widely, although it has been elaborated in a number of cases (see, for instance, Stoll & Fink, 1996). Stringfield and Reynolds have adopted a commercial concept and used the phrase 'high reliability organizations' to illustrate their view of effective schools (Reynolds, 1995b).

A different type of definition which we have sometimes used attempts to deal more explicitly with the impact of family background:

> An effective school regularly promotes the highest academic and other achievement for the maximum number of its students, regardless of the socio-economic backgrounds of their families. (Mortimore, 1996a)

These definitions share similarities. They focus on the *capability* of the school to make a difference. They can also cope with the reality that the playing field for students' performance is seldom level and that progress for some students—and for some schools—will be harder than for others.

The concept of effectiveness is not simple but it provides a way of describing schools which is not dependent on either their intake or their outcomes alone—but on the relationship between them both.

Methodology of effectiveness

The concept of effectiveness depends on the ability of researchers to integrate data on the intake characteristics of students and data on their outcomes. Both are important and any choice of variables is bound to be open to debate. We have tended to use prior achievement at the end of a previous phase of schooling as our favoured intake variable and have fine-tuned its effects with information on students' background characteristics and—if appropriate—with the contextual effects made up of the aggregated impact of individual characteristics (Goldstein et al., 1993; Gray et al., 1990; Mortimore et al., 1988a, 1988b; Sammons et al., 1993a, 1994c; Thomas & Mortimore, 1996).

Twenty years ago, our earlier studies had to make use of rudimentary standardization procedures but, in recent times, the development of multilevel modelling (MLM), able to take account of the nested nature of educational data has made the process much more reliable when large samples are available (Paterson & Goldstein, 1991). MLM represents a way in which valid and reliable judgements can be made about particular sets of results. In particular—and in marked contrast to the use of crude league tables—it demonstrates that a relatively small number of schools can be distinguished with *significantly* better or worse results than others at any particular time or, if results are available, over a period of years.

White, from a philosophical viewpoint, argues that the effectiveness of a school will be self-evident (White, 1997). On the basis of the analysis of hundreds of schools over a number of years (for example, see Thomas & Mortimore, 1996) we disagree. We are convinced that only empirical research is capable of teasing out—in a reliable way—the relationship between the intake and outcomes. Our recent study of secondary school departments has indeed shown quite different levels of effectiveness for different subjects. We found evidence, for example, that in some institutions highly effective and ineffective departments co-existed (Sammons et al., 1996c). As a result of this and other research, we have drawn attention to the need to consider complexities in the judgement of school performance and have highlighted the need to ask three key questions:

- Effectiveness for which outcomes?
- Effectiveness over which period of time?
- Effectiveness for whom?

We have thus sought to extend the concept of effectiveness to include the dimensions of consistency, stability and differential effects (Sammons, 1996).

The choice of outcomes

A number of critics raise the point that school effectiveness researchers have focused exclusively on a limited range of academic outcomes. Scott goes further and raises the distinction, drawn from studies of language, between competence and performance (Scott, 1997). We accept that we have not attempted in any of our work to diagnose the underlying competence of students. How could anyone have done so? On the other hand, we have collected and used a much broader range of outcomes than most critics acknowledge and we intend to use more. We have used, in addition to reading and mathematics tests, practical mathematics tasks, speaking assessments and writing assignments, as well as measures of self-concept, attitude to school, attendance and behaviour (Mortimore et al., 1988a, 1988b) and are currently engaged in a large-scale study in Scotland with the University of Strathclyde, in which we are collecting a number of potential attitudinal outcomes (Robertson et al., 1996).

Of course, the outcomes which we have adopted cannot encompass the whole of a child's development. It is true that, as Winch notes, we have largely ignored the individual aims of schools. This is because we found, in *Fifteen Thousand Hours* (Rutter et al., 1979a) and *School Matters* (Mortimore et al., 1988a) that the amount of variation between the aims that schools articulated was, in fact, relatively small.

We reject the criticism that the academic outcomes we have used are not those desired by parents. Of course, parents want schools to give their children other training and experiences in addition to good examination results. Moreover, there are class differences in the way parents choose schools (Gerwitz et al., 1995). We have as yet to meet—in any of our extensive studies of parental attitudes and behaviours—many who would sacrifice good examination results for the other benefits. For example, a survey conducted for ILEA found that 78 per cent of parents thought it was 'very important' that schools should provide their child with qualifications and only 2 per cent thought that the school was not important for future job prospects and further or higher education opportunities (ILEA, 1984).

We also take issue with the criticism that the differences between schools' academic outcomes (although statistically significant) may be so slight that they do not warrant much attention. We have identified differences which are both statistically and, more importantly, educationally significant in a number of our studies. For example, in our recent analysis of secondary school academic effectiveness, the difference between the most and least effective schools (after controlling for intake) reached 12 GCSE points—equivalent to the difference between six grade Bs and six grade Ds for an individual student with an average level of prior attainment at age 11. Such differences have important implications for further and higher education, as well as for employment prospects.

> Although the differences in scholastic attainment likely to be achieved
> by the same student in contrasting schools is unlikely to be great, in

> many instances, it represents the difference between success and fail-
> ure and operates as a facilitating or inhibiting factor in higher educa-
> tion. When coupled with the promotion of other prosocial attitudes
> and behaviours and the inculcation of a positive self-image, the poten-
> tial to improve the life chances of students is considerable.
> (Mortimore, 1995b, p. 357)

The neglect of process

Some critics accuse us of ignoring the observable *processes* of schooling. Elliot
(1996), in particular, appears to believe that if the processes are 'good' then the
outcomes will look after themselves (p. 206). We dispute this on the grounds
that educationalists still know relatively little about the relationship between
teaching and learning for any individual student. Clearly, the two are related
but the relationship is neither simple nor direct (Mortimore, 1993a). Not all
learning occurs in schools. Moreover, as Winch (1997) has argued, schools cannot be held accountable for that which they cannot influence (p. 3). By focusing
only on observable processes, researchers could radically misinterpret what students had learned. For this reason the 'touchstone' for school effectiveness studies remains the impact on students' educational outcomes (Reynolds, 1995). We
think it is difficult, without reference to this touchstone, to evaluate different
approaches to classroom organization and teaching. Without it, decisions about
what constitutes 'good' practice would be made on the basis of personal taste
or would depend on the whim of an 'expert'. Even the latest *Framework for
Inspection* adopted by Ofsted has student outcomes as one of its main criteria.

Our recent review of *Key Characteristics of Effective Schools* illustrates the
existence of a growing body of research (we included over 160 studies in our
review) which has investigated processes and identified a common core of findings (Sammons et al., 1995e). For those who have not studied the methodological details of *School Matters*, can we also point out that the majority of the
project's time was spent observing classroom and school processes rather than
collecting outcomes (Mortimore et al., 1988a). Nonetheless, having stated our
commitment to the use of outcomes, we accept the criticism that—in comparison with the number of studies focusing only on outcomes—some school effectiveness research could profitably devote more time and attention to process
factors.

The linkage between outcomes and processes

White (1997) and Scott (1997) both raise the point that many of the factors
associated with effectiveness are self-evident and that logical deduction rather
than empirical research could have identified them. We believe this view is quite
wrong. The correlates identified through multilevel modelling as associated with

effectiveness—at the school or department level—are far from self-evident. Fielding (1997, p. 2) quotes the phrase: 'empirical illustrations of tautological truths', but he too is wide of the mark. Like both the head of Ofsted and Davies, he may *believe* it can all be explained by 'common sense' but he offers no evidence for this claim. There can be many different versions of common sense, as Winch (1997, p. 15), citing Gramsci, explains. How can anyone decide, other than by careful empirical research, which is the version most likely to be true? The danger with the counter view (that it is all common sense) is that this provides abundant opportunities for prejudices and particular hobby horses to be exercised. In the *Fifteen Thousand Hours* study (Rutter et al., 1979a), we listed a number of common sense items that were *not* supported by the evidence!

A lack of concern with equity

A number of critics (notably Davies, 1997; Elliott, 1996 and Fielding, 1997) accuse us of ignoring questions of equity. We reject this criticism which—as far as we can ascertain—has been made without any accompanying evidence. Those who have read such classic studies as the article by Edmonds (1979) will know that the very foundation of school effectiveness is a concern for equity. In terms of our own work, a major section of *School Matters* dealt with the lack of equity in outcomes (Mortimore et al., 1988a). A follow-up study explored, over a nine-year period, the changes occurring within gender, socio-economic and ethnic groups (Sammons, 1995).

The negative impact of social and economic disadvantage on students' educational opportunities is a constant theme in our work (Mortimore, 1995c, 1995d, 1996b; Mortimore & Goldstein, 1996; Sammons et al., 1994c). Our research and that of colleagues has paid increasing attention in recent years to the concept of differential effectiveness (Goldstein 1993; Nuttall et al., 1989; Sammons et al., 1993c, 1996d; Thomas et al., 1995).

If, by their criticism, Davies and the others are suggesting that, by controlling for such factors as race, class and gender, we have removed the possibility of examining for bias, they are also wrong—as we intend to illustrate in the concluding section of this paper chapter.

White (1997, p. 9) argues for the adoption of such school goals as 'becoming self-directing citizens of a liberal, democratic society'. We believe that there are good arguments for emphasizing literacy, numeracy and examination achievement, since much research (for example, by the Basic Skills Unit) demonstrates that functional illiteracy and lack of numeracy prevent substantial numbers of adults from engaging in everyday activities (reading bus or train timetables, newspapers, understanding official documents), as well their obtaining employment. These barriers effectively prevent—or at best impede—participation in the democratic processes. We argue, therefore, that academic effectiveness is a necessary, though not, in itself, a sufficient condition for—using any acceptable definition—a good school. (See also discussions by Gray &

Wilcox, 1995.) We are happy to continue our search for further factors which we can use in our school improvement work, but we reject the accusation that we have ignored the dimension of equity.

Ideological commitments

Fielding (1997) echoes the accusations made by both Hamilton (1996) and by Elliot (1996) that school effectiveness researchers are supportive of most aspects of government policy and that we are uncritical of the educational reforms of recent years. Fielding castigates us for: 'The occupation of a political site which is by turns naïve or opportunistic, and at worst complicit in a divisive model of schooling' (Fielding, 1997, p. 2).

We are surprised at this view. We trust that those who have read our corpus of work or heard our various presentations will accept that such a view is manifestly untrue. From the discussion in the chapter of *School Matters* (Mortimore et al., 1988a), through the Director's Inaugural Lecture (Mortimore, 1995a), to the most recent conference presentation (Sammons et al., 1997), our stance has been *evaluative*: critical where our accumulated data or analyses suggest that the policy or practice is wrong and supportive where they suggest it is right. Nor have we been afraid to present our views in the public domain. Our criticisms and those of our colleagues about league tables, for instance, have been on record for a number of years (Goldstein, 1993; Mortimore et al., 1994c; Sammons et al., 1993c). Indeed, it is notable that our work for Ofsted on contextualizing school performance by taking note of the important impact of socio-economic disadvantage (Sammons et al., 1994c), although initially welcomed, was later rejected by the head of Ofsted (*Times Educational Supplement*, 1996, p. 1).

More seriously, Fielding quotes Elliott's accusation that research studies into school effectiveness are the: 'products of an ideological commitment, rather than research, which merely provides a legitimating gloss to mask this fact' (Elliott quoted in Fielding, 1997, p. 2). How can anyone who understands research methodology—and who has taken the trouble to study our publications and the way we work—make such an unfair accusation? As we have noted, we have not been afraid to speak out whenever our accumulated findings have provided reliable evidence. The descriptions of the methodology that we have used and the caveats that we have employed can be found in our various publications. We reject—utterly and completely—this accusation and challenge its makers to provide evidence for the statement or to withdraw it.

Conclusions

We believe that a number of conclusions can be drawn from theoretical papers about school effectiveness and school improvement. First, the field needs further development. More complex models are needed to reflect the complexity of the educational processes and the difficulties of studying it (Sammons, 1996). Whilst we can appreciate the value of simplicity, we feel that an oversimplistic approach is likely to mislead both practitioners and policy makers.

Second, the crude anti-quantitative attitudes which appear amongst some of the articles need to be reconsidered. Davies's comment, for example, that 'effectiveness studies often dehumanize students by reducing them to intake variables' is extreme and illustrates a gulf of understanding between her and researchers like ourselves. In our view, the use of multilevel modelling has enabled us to tease out the impact of a school on pupils with quite different educational backgrounds and to make the case on their behalf. We do not accept that the use of our data could *dehumanize* pupils more than any description or measurement does. We maintain that the availability of sophisticated data is actually more likely to *help* rather than harm those people from whom it is collected, hence the arguments in favour of ethnic or gender monitoring in relation to both educational and employment statistics. In general, we seek to use a range of quantitative and qualitative methods in our work, depending on the nature of the problem and the theoretical approach being employed. We believe that a combination of approaches can often be more fruitful than reliance on either in isolation.

Third, we have been surprised at the use of phrases such as Fielding's 'hegemony of school effectiveness' (Fielding, 1997, p. 2). Although the number of academics and practitioners interested in school improvement has increased remarkably over the last few years, the number of British researchers working in the field of school effectiveness remains remarkably small. Of those that do so, only a very few have undertaken any large-scale empirical work. To talk of a hegemony, therefore, appears exaggerated and partisan. Indeed, we think it highly regrettable that the country has experienced so much ideologically-driven change with so few opportunities for objective evaluation. The creation of different kinds of schools, open enrolment and the encouragement of selection cry out for investigation *within a school effectiveness framework*. Only in such a way can the claim that changes in the type of schools will lead to higher standards be properly evaluated.

We also regard it as essential that practitioners are fully involved in efforts to improve the quality of education given to young people. As we have observed in relation to recent legislative changes:

> Excellence cannot be mandated by politicians or bureaucrats. Government, central or local, would do well to realize this and ensure that any legislative framework that is created is likely to stimulate and elicit from those most involved ownership, commitment and dedication rather than learned helplessness and resentment. (Mortimore, 1995b, p. 357)

Finally, we wish to continue the debates with policy makers, with practitioners and with our fellow researchers. An area as important to the lives of people as education must be *contestable* and this includes the methods we employ to study its quality and impact (Mortimore & Stone, 1991). We believe fervently (ironically, in view of some of the criticisms reported earlier) that academics should be able to challenge the views of their peers and of the government and its officials. We do not advocate a negative, responsibility-free, critical approach. Our preferred mode of operation is through constructive criticism within a context of a commitment to improvement. Ultimately, however, we must be prepared to draw on the principle of academic freedom to stand up for what our evidence tells us is true.

This does not give us or any other academics *carte blanche* to make political judgements on the government's or the opposition's policies. We recognize that we have no greater standing than any other citizen. In a democracy all can comment on such matters and it is only when we speak as scholars—basing our remarks on the accumulated findings of our field of study over many years or on our special training in the evaluation of evidence (Goldstein, 1997)—that we can make any claim to special authority. On such occasions, however, we have a duty to speak out. The 'truth versus power' debates (as a recent article in an American journal so eloquently put it) may not be particularly comfortable for the dissenting academic, but must prove worthwhile in the end.

Postscript

Since this chapter was written, other criticisms have been raised by Lauder et al. (1998). They criticize what they term a 'received model' of school effectiveness work for:

- *underestimating the limits of schooling to achieve success without resources*

This is a point dealt with in the previous chapter. It might be fair to aim the criticism at policy makers but few researchers subscribe to the view that resources are unimportant and, in my own work, I have always stressed that, whilst an increase in resources does not guarantee effectiveness, its impact on the lives of students and teachers is usually to the good.

- *overestimating the ability of school to affect life chances*

I recognize that there will be limits to what schools can do. As Lauder et al. claim, 'working-class students may start from a lower level of prior achievement and achieve more relative to their middle-class counterparts and still not compete on equal terms'. This is undoubtedly true but the existence of well established 'achievement markers' (such as five A*–C grades in the GCSE examination) in the English system means that the 'working-class' students who clear this hurdle will improve their chances of doing well even if they never catch up with their middle-class peers.

- *being dominated by the political agenda*

This is a similar criticism to that made by Hamilton and Elliott in the chapter. It is easily countered by the early chapters of this book, which were written prior to the positions assumed by the recent administrations. As I have argued, it took many years for the policy makers to catch up with the message of the researchers. Having finally done so, they now seek to overclaim the research results.

- *lacking theory*

The lack of adequate theory has been one of the consistent themes of the writing in this book. Chapters eight, nine, ten and fourteen specifically addressed the issue. Of course it is fair to ask why—if I thought theory was so important—I had not, over the years, devoted more time to it. The honest answer is that I probably should have done so. Of course the theory of why some schools are more effective than others has been addressed. The various processes described in the early chapters, the specific mechanisms and the characteristics which have been listed throughout this book are all theoretical constructs of effectiveness and have been incorporated into work by, for instance, Scheerens (1995) or Scheerens and Bosker (1997). The theory of school improvement has—up to now—been neglected rather more. Theories of educational change such as those proposed by Gross et al. (1971) and by Fullan (1991) cover the ground to some extent, but they need to be amended in the light of the recent experience of school failure and 'turnaround' in England.

- *assuming staff and students will respond to the rational use of rewards and sanctions and thus to re-engineering possibilities*

Lauder et al. accuse school effectiveness researchers of ignoring the argument made twenty years ago by Willis (1977) that 'working-class' students have often made a rational decision to reject 'compliance' for 'credentials'. This point is fair: most school effectiveness studies do start with the assumption that students want to succeed. If, for any reason, this is not the case, then many of the strategies of school improvement are likely to fail. The key point is the one raised in the last chapter, by Geoff Whitty and myself, that the system needs to permit as many as possible to succeed—albeit at different speeds with different amounts of support and to different levels.

Criticism is essential to the growth of any field of research. I hope this chapter has illustrated that it has to be taken seriously, but that if it is inaccurate or unjust it can be answered authoritatively. Critics must, if they are to have an effect, actually study the works they seek to condemn. Academic writing, through its use of detailed references, reveals whether or not this has happened and exposes critics who have failed to do their necessary homework. The criticism which must be taken seriously is that which is knowledgable, able to point to a defect in method, analysis or interpretation and—ideally—suggest ways of improvement. Many of the criticisms of Fifteen Thousand Hours were of this kind and led to improvements in subsequent studies. Like theatre critics occasionally challenged to direct plays, critics of educational research should, from time to time, get their hands dirty with empirical research. Despite the massive interest in the field of school effectiveness, the number of actual studies involving the collection of data from students and teachers in schools remains remarkably small.

20

The End of the Story: Policy, Practice and New Directions

The previous chapters have been based on articles and papers written over the last twenty years about my research into school effectiveness. They encompass work undertaken, with colleagues, mostly when I was working in two colleges of the University of London—the Institute of Psychiatry and the Institute of Education—and during the time I worked for the Inner London Education Authority. The purpose of this final chapter is to:

- Comment on the progress made in this field of research in school effectiveness and school improvement over the last twenty years
- Assess the implications of the field for both policy and practice
- Sketch out an agenda for further work which can draw together the strands of academic progress, policy formulation and improvements in practice

Progress since 1977

Over the last twenty years, the field of school effectiveness has developed dramatically. It has grown from a pioneering methodology used by a couple of far-sighted researchers unknown to each other—in the United Kingdom and in the United States—to an international network of researchers, policy makers and practitioners. Re-reading the research reported in the early chapters makes clear just how perspicacious were Michael Rutter and Ron Edmonds.

It has taken successive British governments twenty years to absorb the lessons which emanated from the conclusions of *Fifteen Thousand Hours* and ten years to begin to absorb those of *School Matters*. If the governments of the day had acted upon those lessons, many of the 'tough' actions thought necessary today might have been avoided. Had previous governments heeded what researchers were telling them about, for example, the negative effects of unbalanced intakes to schools, the difficulties of measuring progress precisely, the benefits of school self-evaluation, whole-school policies and parental involvement, they might by now have accomplished many of the outcomes currently being rather desperately sought. Moreover, the justification for change would have stemmed from evidence arising out of independent research, carried out with the active support of teachers, rather than from 'top-down' political agendas. We will never know for certain how much could have been achieved and how much has been lost, but I suspect that the recent clamour for early retirements and the current low levels of professional morale and of recruitment could have been avoided.

The research has contributed a number of new understandings about the way schools work. Many of these are now generally accepted—as the foregoing chapters of this book have indicated. Six of the most significant, in my judgement, are:

- Recognition that schools can make a difference (for better or for worse) to the life chances of students
- The need, when judging a school, to take account of its intake
- Disadvantage and its relationship to school improvement
- The importance of achieving an academic balance in the intake of students
- Recognition of the importance of leadership in schools
- The creation of 'outcome-based' school improvement strategies

Schools can make a difference

As the chapters dealing with findings from *Fifteen Thousand Hours*, *School Matters* and *Forging Links* have demonstrated, and as the literature review of chapter eight has endorsed, schools can make a measurable difference to the life chances of students. This is not to claim that schools *determine* outcomes—students have varying degrees of talent, motivation and commitment—but simply to illustrate that schools which 'promote' effective learning are likely to supplement the attainments that would have been achieved by their students. On average—as reported here—the school improvement is small but highly significant: the difference between 7 Grade Ds and 7 Grade Bs in the English system (Mortimore, 1997). This improvement does not, of course, downplay the insidious influence of disadvantage—and chapter eighteen spelled out the counterbalancing forces of a disadvantaged home and an effective school. It does, however, contradict the doom-laden claims that schools are impotent and that students' life chances are unaffected by the years spent in education. Were such claims true, the justification for a high-quality—or indeed any kind of—publicly funded education system would be seriously dented. In contrast, the research evidence justifies the creation of a high-quality service. This should be good news for all students. It will make the most difference to the disadvantaged even though—as a group—they achieve the least. This is just one of the many paradoxes which research in the field of school effectiveness has revealed.

The need to take account of intake

As was made abundantly clear in chapters four and five, schools differ enormously in the nature of their student intakes. Some recruit those who have much higher than average prior performance levels whilst others admit all who apply, even if this means taking in high proportions of those who are the hardest to teach. The theories of school effectiveness and of school improvement are still being formulated, as I have noted in earlier chapters. It is already clear, however, that schools differ in effectiveness because of what their head teachers and staff do *and* because of their intakes and other 'givens', related to their resources, structure and position in the local pecking order.

What has emerged from the studies is that exceptional schools can be effective, whatever circumstances they face. Some schools which serve disadvantaged areas have shown (as in chapter sixteen) that they can succeed, whatever the odds against them. The research could only reveal this, however, because it was able to disaggregate the effects of the school from the effects of its intake. Without such information, 'good' schools would simply be those which received 'good' students. One of the fundamental claims of those working in the area of effective schools research is that an effective school (or an effective department) is one which succeeds with its intake—whatever it is like.

Disadvantage and school improvement

Chapter eighteen laid out the arguments on this crucial topic. Disadvantage does impact upon students' life chances but many students can overcome it if sufficient help is provided. Whether, in the current economic climate, many societies will be prepared to invest the resources in this cause remains to be seen. Such a mission involves the advantaged groups giving up some of their privileges. Democratic governments that pursue such a course of action are vulnerable to sudden loss of support. What chapter eighteen argues, however, is that, without such actions, the disadvantaged groups will stay locked behind their peers and their children will be unlikely to break the pattern. This is not only unacceptable for individuals but economically unwise in modern societies which need a general raising of learning capabilities across their populations.

Whilst exceptional schools in areas of disadvantage can succeed against the most unequal odds, many others need some extra component if they are to flourish with the most 'difficult to teach' students. This component can take the form of additional resources; supplementary professional help such as a school social worker or extra classroom assistants (Mortimore et al., 1994a); the most gifted teachers; or simply extra time for students (such as an additional year of secondary schooling). In one or another of these ways, such schools need to find a method of nurturing their students and bringing them up to the same starting line from which more advantaged students begin their schooling.

The idea of measuring schools on the basis of the progress—rather than just on the end attainment—of their students may not sound very radical, but it underpins many of the recommendations stemming from the work reported in this book. Indeed, the idea of receiving a commendation for progress when one's actual achievement is modest could be construed as insulting and as implying a lack of ability—as some parents have discovered. Whilst it is entirely appropriate to judge students on their achievements rather than on their progress, such a strategy does not work if one is judging a school. The fair judgement of schools requires something more—a measure of the progress a school makes with a particular group of students. It is this measure which is the most likely to reveal something about the school's effectiveness.

The research also shows that it is more difficult to turn around a school which has a student body made up predominantly of the disadvantaged. It is not impossible—and there are some striking examples of this achievement in the English system—but it is foolish to pretend that the social background of students makes no difference. We know—from UNESCO and OECD studies as well as from British work—that middle-class families are able to extract more out of any educational situation. The benefits of economic and social advantage, as well as the 'cultural capital' of knowing how the system works, mean that their children have a head start in any competitive educational system. Ways of helping the children of the disadvantaged so that the gap between them and their more affluent peers is reduced are always likely to be difficult to identify. The case of parental involvement is illustrative of this. Introduced with a central, if not prime, aim of helping disadvantaged children, it was taken up with great enthusiasm by the middle classes with the result that the gap—far from reducing—actually grew. As chapter eighteen argues—new ways operating along the twin tracks of school improvement and better social conditions for the poor and disadvantaged need to be developed if this situation is ever to be altered.

Achieving an academic balance of students

The research shows clearly that schools which have a reasonable academic balance of ability in their intakes have great advantages over those which do not. Replication in New Zealand of this important finding has recently been reported by Thrupp (1997a). Having a balance of ability in a school's intake does not guarantee that schools always succeed. Some with advantaged students still fail to challenge their learners and, as a result, underachieve. Yet, because their students can fairly easily achieve what appear to be reasonable results, they are seldom seen as failing and, as a consequence, many remain complacent. In contrast, other schools—provided they receive a minimum of students for whom successful schooling is possible—will exceed all normal expectations. It is having a balance which is important and yet, at a time when parents expect to be able to choose a school, this is hard to achieve. For 'advantaged' English parents, choosing schools has become one of the ways in which they can perpetuate their own privileged status for their children. Of course, it has always been the case that those with sufficient resources could ensure an exclusive set of peers for their children—either by moving house to an appropriate school's catchment area or by paying for private schooling. This is one of the options in a country where private schools co-exist alongside the state system. By instituting parental choice for state schools, policy makers no doubt hoped to capture the motivation of ambitious parents. This they did—but they also created the opportunity for the advantaged to consolidate their position without paying fees.

In making these points, I am not condemning parents for doing the most natural thing—trying to improve the life chances of their children. I am simply pointing out that in choosing a school a parent is also choosing his or her children's companions and that, if some schools attract more than their share of advantaged—and generally easier to teach—students, then other schools will suffer the loss of such students. In the early days of comprehensive schools, a proportion of relatively 'advantaged' parents, committed to the comprehensive ideal, voluntarily renounced the opportunity to have their children educated exclusively with children from similar backgrounds and opted for all-ability schools in order to improve the system as a whole. These parents accepted that their own children's subsequent attainments may be slightly lower than they would have been in a more select or selective environment but they doubtless hoped that their children's experience of growing up with a cross-section of the population would bring its own benefits and that their participation would improve the system overall.

The actions of these parents—working against the natural benefits of their class for the general good—was derided in the heyday of Thatcherism. The majority of the press joined in an anti-comprehensive campaign which has proved near-fatal. So-called comprehensive schools (without any balance in their intake) have been compared on strictly academic grounds to selective schools—or to genuine comprehensives—and have been found wanting. Parents have been encouraged to think exclusively of what is best for their children and school communities have been encouraged to press for every advantage, regardless of the consequences for other schools. The result has been a rising tide of dissatisfaction and a lengthening list of those appealing about their failure to obtain the school of their choice.

The research findings on school differences must bear some responsibility for increasing the desire of parents to choose schools. We researchers did, after all, tell parents that the school could make a significant difference to a child's academic results. The research also suggested a solution to the problem—creating schools with balanced intakes. Sadly, only half the message of the research seems to have been absorbed—perhaps to the cost of the English nation as a whole. A situation in which increasing numbers of parents demand—and expect to gain—access to the first school of their choice is bound to cause disappointments. Taking their information from ranked league tables inexorably leads to more and more parents desiring fewer and fewer schools and results in an increasingly unsatisfactory situation. Unlike material goods, the production of places in favoured schools cannot be increased *ad infinitum* (the most prestigious independent schools have not expanded greatly nor sought to produce duplicate institutions). A better solution surely is to try to raise the standard of as many schools as possible, so that 'choice' becomes less of an imperative and balance is easier to achieve.

The recognition of the importance of leadership in schools

Schools differ in effectiveness, in no small measure, because of the actions of their head teachers. The leadership skills required to create a school which actively promotes learning through effective teaching and has a climate which is positive and which encourages efficacy amongst its students are considerable. The various lists of the characteristics of effectiveness that have emerged over the last two decades point to such institutions being led by head teachers with vision, creativity, educational knowledge and social and management skills.

The UK policy of 'local management' has built on earlier ideas of whole-school policies. This policy has necessitated head teachers taking on many functions previously undertaken by the local authority. The change has generally been popular with head teachers and is seen as good for schools. As the research reported in this book has shown, the *contextual* influence of a particular school on a student's achievement—and on his or her self-esteem—can be powerful. Young people appear to take significant account of the school's regard for them, independently of the status of the institution. This is why in the 1970s, when selection was the norm, educational researchers found evidence that those in the lowest streams of high-status schools still felt themselves to be failures, despite their objective knowledge that, in comparison with their peers in other schools, they were probably high achieving. Why this was so is not clear, though work on 'efficacy' by the American psychologist—Bandura—provides some clues: 'Perceived self-efficacy refers to beliefs in one's capabilities to organize and execute the courses of action required to manage prospective situations . . . Successes build a robust belief in one's personal efficacy. Failures undermine it, especially if failures occur before a sense of efficacy is firmly established' (Bandura, 1995b, pp. 2–3).

A number of the other characteristics which have been identified as being associated with effectiveness are concerned with classroom practice and with the processes of learning and teaching within the school. High expectations, the use of structured sessions in which the available time is used to the maximum, teaching which is intellectually stimulating and which challenges students, communicating with the whole class rather than with individuals, good record keeping and parental involvement have all been found to contribute to the creation of a positive climate in which learning is valued and achievement is seen as the norm. These characteristics represent a considerable challenge for head teachers.

The creation of 'outcome-based' school improvement

Until the school effectiveness research, school improvement projects had generally focused on altering the processes without paying attention to the effects of

these changes on the outcomes of the students. The advent of the major studies
of effectiveness in the United States and the United Kingdom changed all this.
The studies spawned a new field of development, outcome-based school
improvement, which has seized the imagination of many practitioners and
policy makers as well as researchers. At a time when so many nations are grasp-
ing the crucial importance of education for their development in the third mil-
lenium, school improvement is seen as an appropriate vehicle for change. This
does not mean it is an easy field—far from it. School improvement is extremely
demanding—as the analysis in chapter fifteen and the two case studies have illustrated.

School improvement is emerging as one of the most dynamic areas in social
policy. Whilst official bodies such as Ofsted, the local education authorities and
consultants from universities all have their parts to play, the main thrust has to
come from the school community. There is a growing body of knowledge about
the ways in which schools can turn themselves around. The detail given in chapter seventeen illustrates the need for effective leadership and management,
improved teaching skills and enhanced self-confidence in the establishment of a
positive learning culture. Many of these components are the same as those which
distinguished the school which succeeded 'against the odds' described in chapter sixteen. This school provided an excellent model of trust by allowing students, for example, to set out their expectations of staff.

Head teachers of improving schools face particular challenges as they prepare for the future. They will need to:

- Sustain the dedication of colleagues at a time when there is widespread
  general criticism of schools
- Develop new ways of teaching which will tap into new ways of learning
- Exploit as fully as possible the opportunities of new information and com-
  munications technology
- Find new ways of supporting the disadvantaged

As the foregoing chapters have revealed, there are no 'quick-fix solutions' to
these challenges. In my judgement, the school effectiveness research has provided the best analysis to date of what school leadership actually means. It is now
up to bodies such as the Leadership Centre at the Institute of Education to experiment with training programmes, expert systems and networking techniques in
order to support head teachers and other school leaders in coping with them.

The implications of school effectiveness for educational policies

The last twenty years illustrate both the sense and the nonsense of educational
reforms. In England, numerous legislative changes have succeeded in unsettling
the world of education. As a result, there has been a radical change of attitudes
amongst some teachers. There is a greater emphasis on achievement and many
schools are now imbued with a positive spirit. Local management has brought

a new sense of ownership over resources, property and school planning in general. Many of the schools which were already advantaged when the reforms were introduced have made great strides. Some have received considerable extra funding and some have increased their capacity to select incoming students. These schools and their teachers have benefited considerably from the changes.

For the system as a whole, however, the picture is very different. Hours of precious time have been wasted dealing with bureaucratic demands which have added little to the central activities of learning and teaching. A national curriculum and its allied assessment system have been created and frequently revised—at considerable public expense. The former system of school inspections has been replaced. Morale in much of the profession has fallen and many experienced and talented teachers and head teachers have chosen to leave teaching as a direct result of these changes. Many aspects of schooling have been made subject to market pressures and a clear pecking order of schools has been established. For those schools at the bottom of the pecking order, life has become much harder as the proportion of 'hard-to-teach' students has increased.

As was argued at the start of this chapter, many of the negative outcomes of educational reform could have been avoided had successive government administrations listened to the findings of research more closely. That they have not done so is probably due to the need, in a predominantly two-party democracy, to dominate public debate with new policies. Listening to educational researchers is not as macho an activity as taking a legislative bill through the political machinery. That said, one of the purposes of this book is to identify the role of research into school effectiveness rather than to complain about missed opportunities.

In my opinion, in order to capitalize on the positive—and to limit or abolish the negative—consequences of change, policy makers should

- Sustain their emphasis on school improvement
- Stop blaming schools which have disadvantaged students for not achieving
- Listen to what research has to say about positive reinforcement
- Create a less harsh inspection system, based on self-evaluation
- Provide—wherever possible—extra resources for schools, including new technology

Sustain the emphasis on school improvement

School improvement is now accepted as a viable framework underpinning a range of school-specific strategies. It should be further supported. As these chapters have made clear, school improvement works best when head teachers and their staff take full responsibility for it: when they are in the driving seat—with policy makers, administrators, inspectors and researchers providing support. It is crucial, however, that policy makers desist from claiming that school improvement—by itself and in the absence of extra resources—can solve all problems. Whilst this might be true in 'advantaged' schools which receive highly gifted students, it is certainly not true in disadvantaged situations. The case studies of schools which have been turned around—and the reports by those involved in the process—illustrate that the operation of rapid improvement needs considerable resources. Detailed figures are not available because it has not been in the interest of either central or local government to reveal how much the process of 'turnaround' actually costs. In my judgement, however, it is likely to be a sum equivalent to approximately a third of the annual budget for the school and is likely to be more if the cost of paying off former head teachers or other staff is taken into account. Nor is this the only extra expenditure that is needed. It needs to be recognized that schools which have failed—however partially—because of the intrinsic difficulties of the area or the nature of their intake, will cost more to run. The additional time, the social work back-up and the smaller groups which I have argued for carry extra costs. This must surely be a sound investment if the school could be improved and 'failure' and its effects on students, staff and the community be avoided.

Stop blaming the schools with disadvantaged students

As all the empirical evidence reported in this book has made clear, it is unfair to blame those who work with the most disadvantaged students—who can be amongst the hardest to teach. For these students to reach the national average, (an average made up predominantly of those who are not disadvantaged) represents a remarkable achievement. Given that any average represents a central point in a wide spectrum of attainment, disadvantaged students achieving this level will have had to leapfrog over many of their more advantaged peers. Whilst this is possible and is achieved by a minority of extremely highly motivated individuals, supported by the sometimes superhuman efforts of their dedicated teachers, it is a pious hope to assume that it can be achieved by the majority of the disadvantaged.

This is not to be patronizing about the disadvantaged but simply to recognize that such students have to compete with their peers in what amounts to a schooling race in which they begin from way behind the starting line. Of course, outstanding children from disadvantaged homes can occasionally win: individuals manage to overcome all hurdles. The overwhelming majority, however, need extra help or longer time if they are to complete the course successfully. In a competitive situation, the accumulated advantages of better diet, health care, housing and many other material benefits, to say nothing of the competitive edge and 'know-how' that is given to the children of families that are already educationally successful and who possess the social capital and efficacy to make the system work for them, are of enormous benefit.

Teachers who choose to work with those who lack the natural and material resources of the advantaged need support, not blame. Otherwise they will take the easy way out and forsake the needs of the disadvantaged and seek to attract 'easier-to-teach students' to their schools. I have come across a number of schools which have successfully done so. Their outcomes improve but this is not the result of changes in their teaching or in the management of the school. It is simply the effect of a changed—and less advantaged—intake. As Gewirtz (1997) argues: 'Within the current educational regime governed by the discourses and technologies of the market and performativity, 'good management' is in large part defined as the ability to transform the socio-economic and linguistic make up of a school . . . what it is effectively doing is producing a redistribution of students amongst schools. It cannot address the root causes of educational underachievement.'

If the blaming policies are continued, it is likely that:

* The gap between successful (and perhaps effective) schools serving advantaged communities and those schools perceived to be unsuccessful (even though some may be effective in relative terms) will increase
* Astute head teachers will seek to improve simply by attracting 'easier-to-teach' students through careful marketing and publicity
* The already perceptible problem of declining teacher recruitment will reach crisis proportions

Listen to what research has to say about positive reinforcement

The idea of using 'blame' to motivate people is currently popular in a number of countries and is used by police and justice systems in the United States and the United Kingdom. I have come across little evidence of its success. The psychological literature, instead, points towards the use of praise and reward as drivers of change. Teachers and students both need and respond well to them. Policy makers would do well to heed this lesson—promulgated by some leading business gurus and already evident in the management techniques of many successful companies. Although populist actions such as taking a 'tough line' on teachers may win voters in the short term, any policy based on poor theory is likely to fail in the long run. The theory that 'blaming' works best rests on an assumption that humans will be shamed into more productive or harder work. It depends on those culpable being able to find better ways of working. In contrast, current work on brain scanners, whilst still in its early stages, suggests that when people are put under such pressure they respond defensively and their brain reduces its activity, in effect 'shutting down'. Far from becoming more productive, people are likely to lose confidence and to become increasingly deskilled. In contrast, praise and rewards appear to enhance the human brain—to enable it to be creative. Furthermore, those teachers who are already working extremely hard but are overwhelmed by the nature of the challenge facing them feel extremely resentful when they are wrongly blamed for the poor results of their students. Rather than achieving more, they are likely to succeed less. Blaming policies based on bad theory should be dropped. If they are maintained, but still fail to achieve the desired results, they will surely be applied by a disappointed electorate to the policy makers who have used them so freely.

Create a less harsh inspection system around the idea of self-evaluation

Inspection arrangements in English schools need to be amended. Apart from being seen by many teachers as punitive—and too ready to blame schools which receive the 'hardest-to-teach' students in the most disadvantaged areas of the country—inspection teams are too distant from the day-to-day, week-by-week realities of the school. As indicated by the research findings, a more productive form of inspection would involve self-review by a team from the school, supplemented by experienced and knowledgable 'outsiders'. Provided that emergency arrangements could trigger an instant inspection by an external agency, the normal procedure should start with a self-review. This could give the staff the opportunity to monitor and evaluate the strengths and the weaknesses of their own performance. This 'formative' inspection would benefit from what appears to be a natural phenomenon of the social sciences: that those closest to the collection of data learn most from its subsequent analysis and are thus in the best position to implement change.

Provide extra resources including new technology for schools
These chapters have illustrated that resources do not—by themselves—guarantee effectiveness. There is, however, no evidence that I know of which shows that a reduction of resources leads to more effective schooling. Even Hanushek—the most forthright critic of studies arguing for extra resources—argues that there is little correlation between spending on education and its outcomes. Hanushek maintains that, whilst 'teachers and schools differ dramatically in their effectiveness' (1986, p. 1159), the results indicate that 'there is no strong or systematic relationship between school expenditures and student performance' (p. 47). In particular he has claimed that there is no strong evidence that '(low) student–teacher ratios, (good) teacher education, or teacher experience have the expected positive effects on student achievement' (1989, p. 47). Hanushek's conclusions have been attacked by Hedges et al. (1994) on the grounds of inadequate data, inappropriate methodology and, most seriously, biased reporting of results. Until we have more routine cost-benefit analyses of schooling—able to take sensitive account of educational factors—we will not have a clear view of the precise importance of resources. It seems to me, however, that both those who argue that since there is as yet no proven link to quality there is no need for extra investment and those who argue that no improvement is possible without extra resources are wrong. Extra resources generally help most endeavours and a nation that is seeking improvements will do well to provide them. It is encouraging that, in the United Kingdom, the government has identified extra money and is seeking to find other sources of funding for schools.

In terms of new technology, it is also encouraging that the government is intending to broaden schools' use of new technology. As noted in chapter eleven, the potential opportunities for better learning are extremely exciting. Some schools have already discovered the motivational effects of access to expert systems, communications with other learners and everlastingly patient electronic skill trainers. Few have yet explored the opportunities of virtual reality for learning about, for example, science or geography, but they will, in time.

What is now needed is the opportunity for experiments in pedagogy which will deal with information and communications technology as a natural learning tool rather than an exotic extra. The Future Learning Centre at the Institute has been designed to carry out just such a programme of work.

The implications for practitioners of school effectiveness research

The chapters in this book have identified a number of lessons for practitioners. Many—for instance to do with school management and the behaviour of head teachers—have already been elaborated. In terms of guiding principles, the following three underpin many of the behaviours of those responsible for schools:

- Learning must lie at the heart of the school
- The school must function as a collective unit
- School culture must be positive

Learning must lie at the heart of the school

This may appear a trite phrase—surely learning has always been at the heart of schooling? Curiously, however, my experience of twenty years of research into the effects of schooling demonstrates that this is not necessarily the case. Schools certainly focus on teaching—people worry about how to introduce information, how to present the curriculum and how to assess students' outcomes. But the other side of the coin—learning—is seldom considered in as thorough a fashion. Partly, this is because of the absence of adequate learning theories. The most developed of these are often perceived as too behaviourist, saying more about laboratory trained rats than about young people. The gap between neurological theories—what happens in connection with the chemical and electrical changes in the brain when new information is absorbed—and psychological theories, dealing with, for instance, attitudes towards particular kinds of knowledge or the social context of learning—remains wide. Furthermore, there is a marked contrast between the ease with which young people master 'real-life learning'—to do with sport, pop music, driving a car or social interactions—and 'school learning'. It is this contrast which presents one of the most challenging opportunities for educationists today. Were we to find a way of tapping into the learning mode that young people use in ordinary life, we could powerfully improve the efficiency of school learning.

There are signs to indicate whether learning (as opposed to teaching) actually does lie at the heart of a school. These signs include whether learners:

- Have high expectations about their teachers
- Are given detailed guidance on the objectives of courses
- Have access to information which is independent of teachers
- Can attend classes other than those offered in the national curriculum
- Are encouraged to offer advice to teachers

Other signs include whether teachers:

- Hold high (in relation to intake) expectations for learners

- Regularly discuss ways in which students can improve their learning
- Observe each other's classes in order to judge how helpful the teaching is for learning
- Give students detailed feedback and advice on learning strategies
- Listen to student feedback

The school must function as a collective unit
The research evidence shows schools can make life much easier for students if they function as collective units. From the findings provided in chapter two about institutions other than schools through to that about secondary school departments given in chapter thirteen, the message is abundantly clear: a single clear mission helps both the inmates and the staff. Consistency of approach also makes life more manageable for both parties. In terms of schooling, the laying down of clear expectations and norms of behaviour as school-wide policies and practices provides helpful limits which can be internalized by both teachers and students.

School culture must be positive
Culture is difficult to define and many commentators on this subject offer different emphases. Schein, for instance, argues that many of the different interpretations lack any basic assumptions and beliefs which define 'in a basic "taken for granted" fashion an organization's view of itself and its environment' (1985, p. 6). Handy defines culture as 'the feeling of a pervasive way of life, or a set of norms' and argues that 'in organizations there are deep-set beliefs about the way work should be organized, the way authority should be exercised, people rewarded . . . dress, and personal eccentricities' (1993, p. 181).

An oft-quoted definition by Deal and Kennedy—'the way we do things round here' (1993, p. 14) was considered too superficial by Lawton, who wrote that, 'for the term school culture to be used in a meaningful way, it must refer to the beliefs, values and behaviour of the teachers, including the head teacher' (1997, p. 40). In a study of associate (non-teaching) staff in English city technology colleges, the following definition was used to draw attention to the importance of such staff in colleges: 'School culture consists of the beliefs, values and behaviour of the head, the teachers and the associate staff of the institution' (J. Mortimore, 1997).

The findings from the studies of school effectiveness suggest that students also need to be added to the list. It is the beliefs, values and behaviours of *all* involved with the school which will determine whether the culture is predominantly positive or not. This will be the case if:

- Learning for its own sake is valued and achievement is expected and rewarded
- Individuals are accorded dignity and people are trusted

Learning for its own sake is valued and achievement is expected and rewarded
In an age dominated by the ready provision of information—on the internet, in newspapers and magazines and on radio and television—the ability to learn efficiently is paramount. No one can be an expert for very long. All of us are having constantly to learn new skills and update our personal knowledge bases. The days in which we learned mainly whilst we were at school and then lived out our working lives on the basis of this early learning are over. Hence the need to discover new methods of learning which are more efficient than traditional approaches.

The learning of new languages provides a neat illustration of this need. Until fairly recently, adult learners who wished to acquire a new language would join a class and operate in a similar way to the manner in which he or she had struggled to master languages whilst at school. More recently, language schools have experimented with new approaches involving intensive one-to-one conversation classes, the use of audio-visual material and submersion into native language groups. We now have three models of language learning: a natural acquisition process used by very young children growing up in linguistic communities; school language teaching; and more radical approaches designed mainly for business and diplomatic purposes. Whilst these will share some common features, they also differ in significant ways.

Young children learn very easily but tend to show resistance to formal learning as they progress through school. We need to overcome this resistance. Somehow we have to find ways of evoking in school students the same enthusiasm and learning capability that very young children and—at times—highly motivated adults display.

We also need to ensure that schools both expect and reward achievement. The criticisms sometimes put forward by right-wing thinkers that egalitarian approaches eschew the celebration of achievement that cannot be open to all are based on crude stereotypes. On the other hand, some schools that I have visited appear to downplay achievement unnecessarily. As with most educational strategies, there is a balance to be struck.

Individuals are respected and accorded dignity and people are trusted
The research indicates that the social context of where learning takes place is important. For reasons we do not yet fully comprehend, we seem to learn better in some contexts than in others. The optimum condition appears to be when we are motivated, at ease and rested. Learning when we are bored, anxious or fatigued appears more difficult. Hence the need for students to feel secure whilst at school. School bullying has its own literature which lies outside the remit of this book. It does have lessons, however, for school effectiveness. If either children or adults are oppressed or persecuted they are not going to be in the mood for effective learning. Furthermore, the modelling for other learners within an institution which tolerates such behaviour will be powerful and negative.

Trust between colleagues and between teachers and students is important. Again, as with the earlier point about learning, we do not completely understand the neurological and psychological processes involved, but when people trust others they are expressing high expectations and this itself is motivating. We know that being trusted appears to free up energy. It allows us to risk failing and therefore to take greater risks which, in turn, may allow more adventurous thinking and liberate us from particular mind-sets.

One possible clue lies in the work undertaken at the University of Chicago by Csikszentmihalyi (1975; Csikszentmihalyi & Csikszentmihalyi, 1988). Csikszentmihalyi (1975) describes the phenomenon of 'flow', whereby an individual becomes utterly absorbed in his or her task, even to the point where they lose all consciousness of time. According to the author the experience involves 'intense involvement, deep concentration, clarity of goals and feedback, loss of a sense of time, lack of self-consciousness and transcendence of a sense of self . . . recognized in more or less the same form by people the world over' (p. 365). Numerous studies have been undertaken by Csikszentmihalyi and his collaborators recording the experience of flow in a variety of experiences. Learning appears to be one of the activities best able to stimulate flow.

Thus, a school culture in which individuals trust and respect each other, which has high expectations about the ability of students (and teachers) to learn easily and which operates efficiently, represents an ideal model for school effectiveness.

An agenda for further work

After twenty years work in the area of school effectiveness, readers might well ask what else needs to be done? Both primary and secondary schools have been thoroughly investigated and the findings carefully integrated with comparable work from around the world. Our latest study on secondary school departments and on differential effectiveness has broadened the methodology to include a number of qualitative techniques and has cast light on many of the variabilities of school functioning. The work on school improvement and, in particular, the case studies of schools working against the odds or recovering from failure have shown how academic research can inspire practice-based projects. I have recently been—or am currently—involved with several studies outside the scope of this book: in school development planning (with Barbara MacGilchrist, Jane Savage and Charles Beresford), in the use of associate staff (with Jo Mortimore and Hywel Thomas) and with grouping practices in secondary schools (with Judy Ireson, Sue Hallam and Sarah Hack).

I am also involved with a large-scale study of school effectiveness in Scottish primary and secondary schools, which is being undertaken by a team from Strathclyde University led by John MacBeath in collaboration with colleagues from the Institute of Education. In an unusual methodology, 'critical friends' from the research team, over a two-year period, have worked closely with a subsample of schools on improvement tasks. As a result, this study has the potential to reveal some of the ways that schools can become more effective (MacBeath & Mortimore, 1997).

Despite this activity, there is still much to be done. In particular, we need to discover more about how learning actually takes place and to uncover the optimal conditions for its growth. We need to identify what triggers motivation and we need to unearth how the state of flow described earlier can be evoked in busy—and sometimes noisy—schools. We also need to experiment with how computers can be used to support learners.

Unlike some academics, I do not believe the death of the school is imminent. Even though it will be possible for well-off families to have far superior equipment in their homes to that available in schools, I do not think more than a minority will wish to keep children out of school. The majority, I believe, will want their children to experience collective school life and to learn the rules of social order in a civilized setting serviced by trained professionals, rather than to remain at home with them—particularly if they are part of the new breed of 'home-workers'. Some parents will opt out of schools and researchers will have an interesting task studying the intellectual and the social accomplishments of home-educated, in comparison to school-educated, students.

Conclusion

Compiling this book has been a pleasure—although at times a daunting one. Linking the chapters and commenting on their relevance involves both looking back and looking forwards—a privilege not often afforded to researchers. Reading articles written nearly a quarter of a century earlier is always risky— ideas change and language evolves. Examining which ideas have developed and which have been ignored has been fascinating; hindsight provides the opportunity to pass a verdict on the quality of the work. On the whole, I have been struck by how the empirical research has stood up. It has passed the acid tests of applicability and replication. I am delighted, too, that the academic thrust of research into effectiveness has shifted towards practitioners' leadership of improvement work.

I wish to take this opportunity to thank the various funding bodies which have contributed to the costs of the research reported in this book. I hope you feel you have achieved good value for money and that you will continue to fund studies in this important field of research.

My final words must be of appreciation. To my early research mentors, my first co-researchers—who inducted me into the world of research—my various collaborators over the years in so many projects and to the head teachers, staff and students in all the schools which have been involved in the many different studies, I offer my sincere thanks for time, support and ideas. I have learned much from all of you. In our search for school effectiveness we have worked well together and shown that partnerships between colleagues and between academics and practitioners can work well.

This twenty-year story shows how researchers and practitioners have changed the way people think about schools and schooling. All that is needed is for policy makers to listen to the whole message and to have the courage to heed it. The *Road to Improvement* will never be easy but, when all the partners work well together—and do not become distracted by blaming or criticizing each other—the ensuing powerful synergy can improve schools. Even the most effective schools cannot compensate for all the other inequalities of peoples' lives, but they offer the best chance we have of enabling more and more of our population to achieve their potential and thus to create a nation at peace with itself.

References

Acland, H. (1973) 'Social determinants of educational achievement: An evaluation and criticism of research', Ph.D. thesis, University of Oxford.

Acton, T. (1980) 'Educational criteria of success: Some problems in the work of Rutter, Maughan, Mortimore and Ouston', *Educational Research* 22 (3): 163–9.

Adey, P. & Shayer, M. (1990) 'Accelerating the development of formal thinking in middle and high school students', *Journal of Research in Science Teaching* 27: 267–85.

Adey, P. & Shayer, M. (1994) *Really Raising Standards: Cognitive Intervention and Academic Achievement*. London: Routledge.

Ainley, J. & Sheret, M. (1992) 'Effectiveness of high schools in Australia: Holding power and achievement', paper presented to the International Congress for School Effectiveness and Improvement, Victoria, British Columbia.

Ainscow, M. & Hopkins, D. (1992) 'Aboard the moving school', *Educational Leadership* 50 (3): 79–81.

Aitken, M., Anderson, D. & Hinde, J. (1981) 'Statistical modelling of data on teaching styles', *Journal of the Royal Statistical Society* 144 (4): 419–61.

Aitken, M. & Bennett, T.N. (1980) *A Theoretical and Practical Investigation into the Analysis of Change in Classroom Based Research*. Final report to the SSRC, HR5710.

Aitken, M. & Longford, N. (1986) 'Statistical modelling issues in school effectiveness studies', *Journal of the Royal Statistical Society* (Series A) 149 (1): 1–43.

Alberman, E.D. & Goldstein H. (1970) 'The "at risk" register: A statistical evaluation', *British Journal of Preventative Medicine* 24 (3): 129–35.

Alexander, R. (1994) 'Innocence and experience: Reconstructing primary education', *ASPE Papers No. 5*. Nottingham: Trentham Books.

Alexander, R., Rose, J. & Woodhead, C. (1992) *Curriculum Organisation and Classroom Practice in Primary Schools: A Discussion Paper*. London: Department of Education and Science.

Alston, C. (1988) 'Improving secondary transfer', *Secondary Transfer Project Bulletin 17*, RS 1200/88. London: Research and Statistics Branch, Inner London Education Authority.

Alston, C. & Sammons, P. (1986) 'Reading attainment and progress', *Secondary Transfer Project Bulletin 14*, RS 1071/86. London: Research and Statistics Branch, Inner London Education Authority.

Angus, L. (1993) 'The sociology of school effectiveness', *British Journal of Sociology of Education* 14 (3): 333–45.

Archer, E. & Montesano, P. (1990) 'High school academies: Engaging students in school and work', *Equity and Choice* (Special Report), Winter, 16–17.

Armento, B.J. (1980) 'Review of '*Fifteen Thousand Hours*', *Educational Researcher* 9 (8): 27–8.

Athey, C. (1990) *Extending Thought in Young Children*. London: Paul Chapman Publishing.

Atkinson. J. (1957) 'Motivational determinants of risk-taking behaviour', *Psychological Review* 64: 359–72.

Averch, H., Carroll, S., Donaldson, T., Kiesling, H. & Pincus, J. (1972) *How Effective Is Schooling? A Critical Review and Synthesis of Research Findings*. Santa Monica, CA: Rand Corporation.

Badger, B. (1992) 'Changing a destructive school', in D. Reynolds & P. Cuttance (eds.) *School Effectiveness: Research, Policy and Practice,* pp. 134–53. London: Cassell.

Bailey, R. (1979) 'Education myths are exploded', *Nottingham Evening Post,* 22 March.

Baldwin, J. (1972) 'Delinquent schools in Tower Hamlets: I. A critique', *British Journal of Criminology* 12: 399–401.

Ball, S.J. (1990) *Politics and Policy Making in Education.* London: Routledge.

Ball, S.J. (1993) 'Education, Majorism and "the curriculum of the dead"', *Curriculum Studies* 1 (2): 195–214.

Bandura, A. (1974) 'Behaviour theory and the models of man', *American Psychologist* 29: 859–69.

Bandura, A. (1992) 'Perceived self-efficacy in cognitive development and functioning', paper presented to the American Educational Research Association, San Francisco.

Bandura, A. (1995a) 'Exercise of personal and collective efficacy in changing societies', in A. Bandura (ed.) *Self Efficacy in Changing Societies.* Cambridge: Cambridge University Press.

Bandura, A. (1995b) *Self Efficacy in Changing Societies.* Cambridge: Cambridge University Press.

Bandura, A., Ross, D. & Ross, S. (1961) 'Transmission of aggression through imitation of aggressive models', *Journal of Abnormal Social Psychology* 63 (3): 575–82.

Barber, M. (1988) 'What makes a good school?', *Teacher* 23 May: 8.

Barber, M. (1994) *Urban Education Initiative: The National Pattern* (Report for the Office of Standards in Education). Keele: University of Keele.

Barber, M. (1996a) *The Learning Game: Arguments for an Education Revolution.* London: Victor Gollancz.

Barber, M. (1996b) *The Curricula, the Minister, His Boss and Her Hairdresser.* London: Curriculum Association.

Barber, M. & Dann, R. (eds.) (1996) *Raising Educational Standards in the Inner City: Practical Initiatives in Action.* London: Cassell.

Barber, M., Denning, T., Gough, G. & Johnson, M. (1995) 'Urban education initiatives: The national pattern', paper presented to the Ofsted Conference on 'Access and Achievement in Urban Education: Nature of Improvement'. Bromsgrove, London: HMSO.

Barber, M. et al.?? (1997), *A Reading Revolution: How We Can Teach Every Child to Read Well.* London: Literacy Task Force.

Barker, E. (1953) *Father of the Man.* London: Oxford University Press.

Bashi, J. & Sass, Z. (1992) *School Effectiveness and School Improvement: Proceedings of the Third International Congress on School Effectiveness and School Improvement.* Jerusalem: Magnes Press.

Bashi, J., Sass, Z., Katzir, R. & Margolin, I. (1990) *Effective Schools—From Theory to Practice: An Implementation Model and Its Outcomes.* Jerusalem: Van Leer Institute.

Bates, S. (1988) 'Right wingers set out to teach Baker a lesson', *Daily Mail,* 21 March.

Bayliss, S. (1988) 'Vital research threatened by plan to abolish ILEA', *Times Educational Supplement,* 25 March.

Bennett, S.N. (1976) *Teaching Styles and Pupil Progress.* London: Open Books.

Bennett, S.N. (1987) 'Changing perspectives on teaching–learning processes', *Oxford Review of Education* 13: 67–79.

Bennett, S.N. (1988a) 'The effective primary school teacher: The search for a theory of pedagogy', *Teaching and Teacher Education* 4 (1): 19–30.

Bennett, S.N. (1988b) 'What about the teaching?', *Times Educational Supplement*, 25 February.

Beresford, C., Mortimore, P., MacGilchrist, B. & Savage, J. (1992) 'School development planning matters in the UK', *Unicorn* 18 (2): 12–16.

Berger, M. (1972) 'Modifying behaviour at school', *Special Education* 61 (June): 18–21.

Berger, M., Yule, W. & Rutter, M. (1975) 'Attainment and adjustment in two geographical areas: II. The prevalence of specific reading retardation', *British Journal of Psychiatry* 126: 510–19.

Bernstein, B. (1970) 'Education cannot compensate for society', *New Society* 387: 344–7.

Black, P. (1994) 'Alternative education policies: Assessment and testing', in S. Tomlinson (ed.) *Educational Reform and its Consequences*, pp. 129–36. London: IPPR/Rivers Oram Press.

Blakey, L. & Heath, A. (1992) 'Differences between comprehensive schools: Some preliminary findings', in D. Reynolds & P. Cuttance (eds.) *School Effectiveness: Research, Policy and Practice*, pp. 121–33. London: Cassell.

Blatchford, P. & Mortimore, P. (1994) 'The issue of class size for young children in schools: What can we learn from research?', *Oxford Review of Education* 20 (4): 411–28.

Bliss, J., Firestone, W. & Richards, C. (1991) *Rethinking Effective Schools*. New Jersey: Prentice Hall.

Bloom, A. (1987) *The Closing of the American Mind*. New York: Simon & Schuster.

Bloom, B. (1976) *Human Characteristics and School Learning*. New York: McGraw Hill.

Blum, R. (1984) *Onward to Excellence: Making Schools More Effective*. Portland, OR: Northwest Regional Educational Laboratory.

Bollen, R. & Hopkins, D. (1987) *School Based Research: Towards a Praxis*. Leuven, Belgium: Academic Publishing Company (ACCO).

Bondi, L. (1991) 'Attainment in primary schools', *British Educational Research Journal* 17 (3): 203–17.

Boseley, S. (1986) 'Traditional teaching values vindicated by ILEA study into pupils' achievement', *Guardian,* 15 April.

Bosker, R. & Scheerens, J. (1989) 'Issues and interpretations of the results of school effectiveness research', *International Journal of Educational Research* 13 (7): 41–52.

Boydell, D. (1988) 'Review of *School Matters: The Junior Years*', *Educational Research* 30 (3): 235–6.

Boyson, R. (1979) 'Secret shame of Britain's schools', *News of the World*, 18 March.

Brandsma, H.P. & Knuver, J.W. (1989) ' Effects of shool and classroom characteristics on pupil progress in language and arithmetic', *International Journal of Educational Research* (Special Issue, *Developments in School Effectiveness Research*) 13 (7): 777–88.

Brannen, J., Moss, P., Owen, C. & Wale, C. (1997) *Mothers, Fathers and Employment: Parents and the Labour Market in Britain, 1984–1994*. London: DfEE, Institute of Education.

Bridges, D. & McLaughlin, M. (1994) *Education and the Market Place*. London: Falmer Press.

Brimer, A., Madaus, C., Chapman, B., Kellaghan, T. & Wood, D. (1978) *Sources of Difference in School Achievement*. Slough, Buckinghamshire: National Foundation for Educational Research.

Brookover, W. & Lezotte, L. (1977) *Changes in School Characteristics Co-incident with Changes in Student Achievement*. Michigan: East Lansing Institute for Research on Teaching, Michigan State University.

Brophy, J. & Good, T. (1974) *Teacher/Student Relationships: Causes and Consequences*. New York: Holt, Rinehart & Winston.

Brown, C. & Wing, J. (1962) 'A comparative clinical and social survey of three mental hospitals', *Sociological Review Monograph* 5: 145–71.

Brown, M. (1993) *Clashing Epistemologies: The Battle for Control of the National Curriculum and its Assessment*. London: King's College.

Brown, M. & Rutherford, D. (1995) *Successful Leadership for School Improvement in Areas of Urban Deprivation: A Framework for Development and Research*. Birmingham: Universities of Birmingham and Manchester.

Brown, P., Halsey, A.H., Lauder, H. & Wells, A. (1997) 'The transformation of Education and Society: An introduction', in A.H. Halsey, H. Lauder, P. Brown & A. Wells (eds.) *Education, Culture, Economy and Society*. Oxford: Oxford University Press.

Bruner, J. (1966) *Towards a Theory of Instruction*. New York: W.W. Norton.

Bush, T. (1995) *Theories of Educational Management* (2nd edition). London: Paul Chapman Publishing.

Caldwell, B. & Spinks, J. (1988) *The Self Managing School*. Lewes: Falmer Press.

Cannan, C. (1970) 'Schools for delinquency', *New Society* 427: 1004.

Carr, W. (1986) 'Theories of theory and practice', *Journal of Philosophy of Education* 20 (2): 177–86.

Carroll, J.B. (1963) 'A model of school learning', *Teachers College Record* 64: 723–33.

Central Advisory Council for Education (1967) *Children and their Primary Schools* (Plowden Report). London: HMSO.

Chapman, J. & Stevens, S. (1989) 'Australia', in D. Reynolds, B. Creemers & T. Peters (eds.) *School Effectiveness and Improvement: Proceedings of the First International Congress, London 1988*, pp. 47–61. Groningen: RION Institute for Educational Research / Cardiff: School of Education, University of Wales.

Chrispeels, J. (1990) 'Allies in educational reform: Review of J. Rosow', *School Effectiveness and School Improvement* 1 (1): 229–31.

Chrispeels, J. (1992) *Purposeful Restructuring*. London: Falmer Press.

Chrispeels, J. & Pollack, S. (1989) 'Equity schools and equity districts', in B.Creemers, T. Peters & D. Reynolds (eds.) *School Effectiveness and School Improvement: Proceedings of the Second International Congress, Rotterdam*, pp. 295–307. Lisse, The Netherlands: Swets & Zeitlinger.

Chubb, J. & Moe, T. (1990) *Politics, Markets and America's Schools*. Washington DC: Brookings Institute.

Clare, J. (1986) 'Schools of scandal', *Listener*, 31 July.

Clark, B.R. (1985) *The School and the University*. Berkeley, CA: University of California Press.

Clark, D., Lotto, L. & Astuto, T. (1984) 'Effective schools and school improvement: A comparative analysis of two lines of enquiry', *Educational Administration Quarterly* 20 (3): 41–68.

Clark, T. & McCarthy, D. (1983) 'School improvement in New York: The evolution of a project', *Educational Researcher* 12 (4): 17–24.

Clarke, K. (1992) '*Reform of initial teacher training*', North of England Conference address, 4 January. London: Department of Education and Science.

Clarke, R.V. & Cornish, D.B. (1972) 'The controlled trial in institutional research', *Home Office Research Studies No. 15*. London: HMSO.

Clarke, R.V. & Cornish, D.B. (1977) 'The effectiveness of residential treatment for delinquents', in L. Hersov, M. Berger & D. Shaffer (eds.) 'Aggression and anti-social behaviour in childhood and adolescence', *Journal of Child Psychology and Psychiatry, Monograph Series*, No. 1. Oxford: Pergamon.

Clarke, R.V. & Martin, D.N. (1971) *Absconding from Approved Schools*. London: HMSO.

Clay, M.M. (1982) *Observing Young Readers*. New Hampshire: Heinemann.

Clay, M. (1985) *The Early Detection of Reading Difficulties*. London: Heinemann.

Clegg, A. & Megson, B. (1968) *Children in Distress*. Harmondsworth: Penguin.

Coleman, J. (1966) *Harvard Educational Review, Special Issue* 38 (1): 7–22.

Coleman, J. (1988) 'Social capital in the creation of human capital', *American Journal of Sociology* 94 (Supplement): 95–120.

Coleman, J., Campbell, E., Hobson, C., McPartland, J., Mood, A., Weinfeld, F. & York, R. (1966) *Equality of Educational Opportunity*. Washington, DC: National Center for Educational Statistics/US Government Printing Office.

Coleman, J., Hoffer, T. & Kilgore, S. (1982) *High School Achievement*. New York: Basic Books.

Coleman, M. & Matthews, P. (1996) 'Initiative or strategy: The chicken and the egg of school improvement', paper presented at the British Educational Research Association Conference, University of Lancaster.

Coleman, P. & Collinge, J. (1991) 'In the web: Internal and external influences affecting school improvement', *School Effectiveness and School Improvement* 2 (4): 262–85.

Comer, J.P. (1980) *School Power: Implication of an Intervention Project*. New York: Free Press.

Comer, J.P. (1991) 'The Comer school development program', *Urban Education* 26 (1): 56–82.

Contenta, S. (1988) 'Putting schools to the test: A simple 12-question quiz', *Toronto Star*, 16 April.

Cornish, D.B. & Clarke, R.V. (1975) 'Residential treatment and its effects on delinquency', *Home Office Research Studies, No. 32*. London: HMSO.

Cox, C.B. & Dyson, R.E. (eds.) (1969a) *Black Paper I: Fight for Education*. London: The Critical Quarterly Society.

Cox, C.B. & Dyson, R.E (eds.) (1969b) *Black Paper II: The Crisis in Education*. London: The Critical Quarterly Society.

Cox, C.B. & Dyson, R.E. (eds.) (1970) *Black Paper III: Goodbye Mr Short*. London: The Critical Quarterly Society.

Cox, C.B. & Dyson, R.E. (eds.) (1975) *Black Paper 1975: The Fight for Education*. London: Dent.

Creemers, B. & Lugthart, E. (1989) 'School effectiveness and improvement in the Netherlands', in D. Reynolds, B. Creemers & T. Peters (eds.) *School Effectiveness and Improvement: Proceedings of the First International Congress, London 1988*, pp. 89–103. Groningen: RION Institute for Educational Research / Cardiff: School of Education, University of Wales.

Creemers, B., Peters, T. & Reynolds. D. (1989) *School Effectiveness and School Improvement: Proceedings of the Second International Congress, Rotterdam*. Lisse, The Netherlands: Swets & Zeitlinger.

Creemers, B., Reezigt, G. & Van der Werf, M. Proposal for a research programme on 'school-effectiveness', personal communication.

Creemers, B. & Scheerens, J. (eds.) (1989) 'Developments in school-effectiveness research', *International Journal of Educational Research* 13: 689–825.

Crone, L., Lang, M. & Franklin, B. (1994) 'Achievement measures of school effectiveness: Comparison of consistency across years', paper presented at the annual meeting of the American Educational Research Association, New Orleans.

Cross, C.T. (1990) 'National goals: Priorities for educational researchers', *Educational Researcher* 19 (8): 21–4.

Csikszentmihalyi, M. (1975) *Beyond Boredom and Anxiety*. San Francisco: Jossey-Bass.

Csikszentmihalyi, M. & Csikszentmihalyi, I. (1988) *Optimal Experience: Psychological Studies of Flow in Consciousness*. New York: Cambridge University Press.

Cuttance, P. (1985) 'Methodological issues in the statistical analysis of data on the effectiveness of schooling', *British Educational Review Journal* 11 (2): 163–79.

Dalin, P. (1989) 'Reconceptualising the school improvement process: Charting a paradigm shift', in D. Reynolds, B. Creemers & T. Peters (eds.) *School Effectiveness and Improvement, Proceedings of the First International Congress, London 1988,* pp. 30–45. Groningen: RION Institute for Educational Research / Cardiff: School of Education, University of Wales.

Daly, J. (1990) 'Time to stop the nonsense', *Times Educational Supplement,* 14 February.

Daly, P. (1991) *How Large Are Secondary School Effects in Northern Ireland?* Belfast: School of Education, Queen's University.

Dancy, J. (1979) *Fifteen Thousand Hours: A discussion, Perspectives* 1. Exeter: Exeter University.

Danziger, K. (1971) *Socialisation*. Harmondsworth: Penguin.

Davie, R., Butler, N. & Goldstein, H. (1972), *From Birth to Seven*. Harlow: Longman.

Davies, J. (1988) 'Review of *School Matters: The Junior Years*', *British Educational Research Journal* 15 (1): 95–6.

Davies, L. (1997) 'The rise of the school effectiveness movement', in J.White and M. Barber (eds.) *Perspectives on School Effectiveness and School Improvement,* pp. 25–40. *London:* Institute of Education.

Deal, T. & Kennedy, A. (1993) 'Culture and school performance', *Educational Leadership* 40 (5): 14–15.

Delamont, S. (1976) *Interaction in the Classroom*. London: Methuen.

Dennehy, A., Smith, L. & Harker, P. (1997) 'Not to be ignored: Young people, poverty and health', in A. Walker & C. Walker (eds.) *Britain Divided: The Growth of Social Exclusion in the 1980s and 1990s*. London: CPAG.

Department for Education (1992) *Choice and Diversity: A New Framework for Schools*. London: HMSO.

Department for Education (1995) *Value Added in Education: A Briefing Paper*. London: DfE.

Department for Education and Employment (1996) *Education Statistics*. London: HMSO.

Department for Education and Employment (1996). *Lifetime Learning: A Policy Framework*. London: DfEE.

Department for Education and Employment (1997a) *Excellence in Schools*, Cm 3681. London: HMSO.

Department for Education and Employment (1997b) *The Road to Success*. London: Institute of Education/DfEE.

Department for Education and Employment (1997c) *Statistical News*, 386/97. London: DfEE.

Department of Education and Science (1983) *Statistical Bulletin*, 16/83. London: DES.

Department of Education and Science (1991) *Development Planning: A Practical Guide, School Development Plans Project 2*. London: DES.

Dixon, C.W. (1986) *History of the University of London Institute of Education, 1932/1972*. London: Institute of Education.

Doe, B. (1980) 'Second thoughts on the Rutter ethos', *Times Educational Supplement*, 13 June.

Domanico, R. & Cenn, C. (1992) 'Creating the context for improvement in New York City's public schools', paper presented to the Quality of Life in London/New York Conference, London.

Doran, A. (1979) 'Do as I do—not as I say', *Evening News*, 22 March.

Dorr-Bremme, D. (1990). 'Culture, practice and change: School effectiveness reconsidered', in D. Levine & L. Lezotte (eds.) *Unusually Effective Schools: A Review of Research and Practice*. Madison, WI: National Center for Effective Schools Research and Development.

Douglas, J.W.B. (1964) *The Home and School*. London: MacGibbon & Kee.

Dunkin. M. & Biddle, B. (1974) *The Study of Teaching*. New York: Holt Rinehart & Winston.

Dweck, C. & Repucci N. (1973) 'Learned helplessness and reinforcement responsibility in children', *Journal of Personality and Social Psychology* 25 (1):109–16.

Earley, P., Fidler, B. & Ouston, J. (1996) *Improvement Through Inspection: Complementary Approaches to School Development*. London: David Fulton.

Ecob, R. (1985) *Multilevel Mixed Linear Models and Their Application to Hierarchically Nested Data*. London: Research and Statistics, Inner London Education Authority.

Ecob, R., Sammons, P. & Mortimore, P. (1986) 'Methods of analyses used in the ILEA Junior School Project', in *Junior School Project Technical Appendices, Appendix 3: 1*. London: Research and Statistics, Inner London Education Authority.

Economist (1979) 'Schools count', 31 March.

Edmonds, R. (1979) 'Effective schools for the urban poor', *Educational Leadership* 37 (1): 15–27.

Edmonds, R. (1982) Personal communication.

Edmonds, R. & Frederiksen, J. (1979) *'Search for Effective Schools: The Identification and Analysis of City Schools that are Instructionally Effective for Poor Children'*, ERIC Document Reproduction Service No. ED 170 396. Cambridge, MA: Harvard Graduate School of Education, Center for Urban Studies.

Education (1986) 'ILEA primary progress', Document of the Week, 18 April.

Education (1988) 'What a good school can do', Document of the Week, 25 March.

Edwards, T., Fitz, J. & Whitty, G. (1989) *The State and Private Education: An Evaluation of the Assisted Places Scheme*. Lewes: Falmer Press.

Eggleston, J. (1977) *The Ecology of the School*. London: Methuen.

Einsiedler, W. (1992) 'The effects of teaching methods, class methods and patterns of cognitive teacher pupil interactions in an experimental study in primary school classes', paper presented to the International Congress for School Effectiveness and School Improvement, Victoria, British Columbia.

Eiser, J. & Van der Pligt, J. (1988) *Attitudes and Decisions*. London: Routledge.

Elliott, J. (1996) 'School effectiveness research and its critics: Alternative visions of schooling', *Cambridge Journal of Education* 26 (2): 199–223.

Ellis, W. (1986) 'Importance of primary education underlined', *Financial Times*, 15 April.

Elvin, L. (1987) *Encounters with Education*. London: Institute of Education.

Erikson, R. & Jonsson, J.O. (eds.) (1996) *Can Education Be Equalized? The Swedish Case in Comparative Perspective*. Boulder, CO: Westview Press.

Essen, J. & Wedge, P. (1982) *Continuities in Childhood Disadvantage*. London: Heinemann.

Eurostat (1997) Reported in the *Guardian*, 28 April.

Evening Standard (1988) 'Social class', *Evening Standard*, 21 March.

Fielding, M. (1997) 'Beyond school effectiveness and school improvement: Lighting the slow fuse of possibility', in J.White and M. Barber (eds.), *Perspectives on School Effectiveness and School Improvement*, pp 137–160. London: Institute of Education.

Finlayson, D. & Loughran, J. (1976) 'Pupils' perceptions in high and low delinquency schools', *Educational Research* 18 (2): 138–45.

FitzGibbon, C. (1991a) 'A-levels: Corrective comparisons', *Managing Schools Today* 1 (2): 44–5.

FitzGibbon, C. (1991b) 'Multilevel modelling in an indicator system', in S.W. Raudenbush & J.D. Willms (eds.) *Schools, Classrooms and Pupils: International Studies of Schooling from a Multilevel Perspective*. San Diego, CA: Academic Press.

FitzGibbon, C. (1992) 'School effects at A-level: Genesis of an information system', in D. Reynolds & P. Cuttance (eds.) *School Effectiveness Research: Policy and Practice*. London: Cassell.

FitzHarris, B. (1993) 'School improvement: The American way', *Managing Schools Today* 2 (7):24–8.

Fogelman, K. (1984) 'Problems in comparing examination attainment in selective and comprehensive secondary schools', *Oxford Review of Education* 10 (1): 33–43.

Fogelman, K., Goldstein, H. & Ghodsian, M. (1978) 'Patterns of attainment', *Educational Studies* 4 (2): 121–30.

Fraser, B. (1989) 'Research synthesis on school and instructional effectiveness', *International Journal of Educational Research* 13 (7): 707–20.

Fullan, M. (1982) *The Meaning of Educational Change*. New York: Teachers' College Press.

Fullan, M. (1991) *The New Meaning of Educational Change*. London: Cassell.

Fullan, M. (1992a) 'The evolution of change and the new work of the educational leader', paper presented at the Regional Conference of the Commonwealth Council for Educational Administration, Hong Kong.

Fullan, M. (1992b) *Successful School Improvement*. Toronto: OISE Press.

Fullan, M. (1993) *Change Forces: Probing the Depths of Educational Reform*. London: Falmer Press.

Fullan, M., Bennett, B. & Rolheiser-Bennett, C. (1990) 'Linking classroom and school improvement', *Educational Leadership* 47 (8): 13–19.

Gage, M.L. (1978) *The Scientific Basis of the Art of Teaching*. New York: Teachers' College Press.

Galloway, D. (1976) *Case Studies in Classroom Management*. London: Longman.

Galloway, D., Martin, R. & Willcox, B. (1985) 'Persistent absence from school and exclusions from school', *British Educational Research Journal* 11 (2): 51–61.

Galton, M. (1988) 'Writing effectively about school effectiveness', *Oxford Review of Education* 14 (3): 377–9.

Galton, M. (1995) *Crisis in the Primary Classroom*. London: David Fulton.

Galton, M. & Simon, B. (1980) *Progress and Performance in the Primary Classroom.* London: Routledge & Kegan Paul.

General Accounting Office of the United States (GAO) (1989) *Effective School Programs: Their Extent and Characteristics.* Washington, DC: GAO.

Gewirtz, S. (1997) 'Can all schools be successful? An exploration of the determinants of school "success"', paper presented at the British Educational Research Association Annual Conference, York.

Gewirtz, S., Ball, S. & Bowe, R. (1995) *Markets, Choice and Equality in Education.* Buckingham: Open University Press.

Gideanse H. (1981) Letter to the Editor, *Educational Researcher* 10 (1):28.

Giles, A. (1975) 'School organisation and its relationship to discipline', unpublished paper.

Gillborn, D. (1997), 'Young, black and failed by school: The market, education reform and black students', *Journal of Inclusive Education* 1 (1): 65–87.

Gillborn, D. & Gipps, C.V. (1996) 'Recent research on the achievements of ethnic minority pupils', in *Ofsted Reviews of Research.* London: Office for Standards in Education.

Gipps, C.V. (1992) *What We Know about Effective Primary Teaching.* London: Tufnell Press.

Gipps, C.V. (1994) *Beyond Testing: Towards a Theory of Educational Assessment.* London:Falmer Press.

Glaser, R. (1976) 'Components of a psychological theory of instruction: Towards a science of design', *Review of Educational Research* 46 (1): 1–24.

Glass, G. (1977) 'Integrating findings: The meta-analysis of research', *Review of Research in Education* 5: 351–79.

Glyn, T., Crooks, T., Bethune, N., Ballard, K. & Smith, J. (1989) *Reading Recovery in Context.* Wellington, New Zealand: Department of Education.

Goddard, D. & Leask, M. (1992) *The Search for Quality.* London: Paul Chapman Publishing.

Goffman, E. (1961) *Asylums: Essays on the Social Situation of Mental Patients and Other Inmates.* New York: Doubleday.

Goldstein, H. (1980) '*Fifteen Thousand Hours*: A review of the statistical procedures', *Journal of Child Psychology and Psychiatry* 21 (4): 364–6.

Goldstein, H. (1984) 'The methodology of school comparisons', *Oxford Review of Education* 10 (1): 69–74.

Goldstein, H. (1986) 'Multilevel mixed linear model analysis using interactive generalised least squares', *Biometrika* 73: 43–56.

Goldstein, H. (1987) *Multilevel Models in Educational and Social Research.* London: Charles Griffin.

Goldstein, H (1993) 'Assessing group differences', *Oxford Review of Education* 19 (2): 141–50.

Goldstein, H. (1996) 'Relegate the leagues', in *New Economy.* London: Dryden Press.

Goldstein, H (1997) 'A response to Hargreaves on "evidence based educational research"', *Research Intelligence* February (59): 18–20.

Goldstein, H., Rasbash, J., Yang, M., Woodhouse, G., Pan, H., Nuttall, D. & Thomas, S. (1993) 'A multilevel analysis of school examination results', *Oxford Review of Education* 19 (4): 425–33.

Goldstein, H. & Sammons, P. (1994) *The Influence of Secondary and Junior Schools on 16–Year Examination Performance: A Cross-classified Multi-level Analysis*. London: Institute of Education.

Goldstein, H & Spiegelhalter, D (1996) 'League tables and their limitations: Statistical issues in comparisons of institutional performance', *Journal of the Royal Statistical Society, A* 159 (3): 385–443.

Goldstein, H. & Thomas, S. (1995) 'School effectiveness and "value added" analysis', *Forum* 37 (2): 36–8.

Goldstein, H. & Thomas, S. (1996) 'Using examination results as indicators of school and college performance', *Journal of the Royal Statistical Society, A* 159 (1): 149–63.

Goldthorpe, J.H. (1996), 'Class analysis and the reorientation of class theory: The case of persisting differentials in educational attainment', *British Journal of Sociology* 47 (3): 482–505.

Good, J. & Brophy, J. (1986) 'Social and institutional context of teaching: School effects', in *Third Handbook of Research on Teaching*. New York: Macmillan.

Gordon, P. (1980) *The Study of Education Inaugural Lectures, 1*. London: Woburn Press.

Gorman, M. & Hargreaves, M. (1985) *Talking Together: NFER/ILEA Oracy Survey*. Slough: NFER.

Gorman, T. & Fernandes, C. (1992) *Reading in Recession*. Slough: NFER.

Gow, D. (1988) 'ILEA survey downgrades social factors in pupil attainment', *Guardian*, 23 February.

Grace, G. (1984) *Education in the City*. London: Routledge & Kegan Paul.

Gray, J. (1981) 'A competitive edge: Examination results and the probable limits of secondary school effectiveness', *Educational Review* 33 (1): 25–35.

Gray, J. (1983) 'Questions of background', *Times Educational Supplement*, 8 July.

Gray, J. (1989) 'Multilevel models: Issues and problems emerging from their recent application in British studies of school effectiveness', in R. Bock (ed.) *Multilevel Analysis of Educational Data*. New York: Academic Press.

Gray, J. (1990) 'The quality of schooling: Frameworks for judgement', *British Journal of Educational Studies* 38 (3): 204–23.

Gray, J. (1995) 'The quality of schooling: Frameworks for judgement', in J. Gray & B. Wilcox (eds.) *Good School, Bad School*, pp. 11–30. Buckingham: Open University Press.

Gray, J., Goldstein, H. & Jesson, D. (1996) 'Changes and improvements in schools' effectiveness: Trends over five years', *Research Papers in Education* 11 (1): 35–51.

Gray, J. & Hannon, V. (1985) *HMI's Interpretation of School Examination Results*. Sheffield: Division of Education, University of Sheffield.

Gray, J., Jesson, D., Goldstein, H., Hedger, K. & Rasbash, J. (1995) 'A multilevel analysis of school improvement: Changes in schools' performance over time', *School Effectiveness and School Improvement* 6 (2): 97–114.

Gray, J., Jesson, D. & Jones, B. (1984) 'Predicting differences in examination results between local education authorities: Does school organisation matter?', *Oxford Review of Education* 10 (1): 45–68.

Gray, J., Jesson, D. & Sime, N. (1990) 'Estimating differences in the examination performance of secondary schools in six LEAs: A multilevel approach to school effectiveness', *Oxford Review of Education* 16 (2): 137–58.

Gray, J. & Jones, B. (1983) 'Disappearing data', *Times Educational Supplement*, 15 July.

Gray, J. & Jones, B. (1985) 'Combining quantitative and qualitative approaches to studies of school and teacher effectiveness', in D. Reynolds (ed.) *Studying School Effectivenes*, pp. 103–15. Basingstoke: Falmer Press.

Gray, J., McPherson, A., & Raffe, D. (1983) *Reconstructions of Secondary Education: Theory, Myth and Practice Since the War*. London: Routledge & Kegan Paul.

Gray, J. & Wilcox, B. (eds.) (1995) *Good School, Bad School: Evaluating Performance and Encouraging Improvement*. Buckingham: Open University Press.

Green, A. (1990) *Education and State Formation*, New York: St Martin's Press.

Gregory, K. & Mueller, S. (1980) 'Leif Ericson Elementary School, Chicago', in W. Duckett (ed.) *Why Do Some Urban Schools Succeed?*, pp. 60–74. Bloomington, IN: Phi Delta Kappa.

Gross, N., Giacquinta, J.E. & Bernstein, M. (1971) *Implementing Organizational Innovations*. New York: Basic Books.

Grygier, T. (1975) 'Measurement of treatment potential: Its rationale, method and some results in Canada', in J. Tizard, I. Sinclair & R.V.G. Clarke (eds.) *Varieties of Residential Experience*, pp. 141–70. London: Routledge & Kegan Paul.

Guy, C. (1988) 'Best school formula is a tough equation', *New Zealand Herald*, 29 November.

Hagedorn, J. (1988) 'Great expectations', *Times Educational Supplement*, 25 March.

Hallinger, P. & Murphy, J. (1985) 'Instructional leadership and school socio-economic status: A preliminary investigation', *Administrator's Notebook* 31 (5): 1–4.

Hallinger, P. & Murphy, J. (1986) 'The social context of effective schools', *American Journal of Education* 94 (3): 328–54.

Hallinger, P. & Murphy, J. (1987) 'Instructional leadership in the school context', in W. Greenfield (ed.) *Instructional Leadership*, pp. 179–202. Boston, MA: Allyn & Bacon.

Halsey, A.H. (ed.) (1972) 'Educational priority', in *EPA Problems and Policies, 1*. London: HMSO.

Hamilton, D. (1996) 'Peddling feel-good fictions: Reflections on key characteristics of effective schools', *Forum* 38 (2): 54–6.

Handy, C. (1993) *Understanding Organisations* (fourth edition). London: Penguin Books.

Handy, C. (1994) *The Empty Raincoat: Making Sense of the Future*. London: Hutchinson.

Hannon, P., Weinberger, J. & Nutbrown, C. (1991) 'A study of work with parents to promote early literacy development', *Research Papers in Education* 6 (2): 77–98.

Hanushek, E. (1986) 'The economics of schooling: Production and efficiency in public schools', *Journal of Economic Literature* 24: 1141–77.

Hanushek, E. (1989) 'The impact of differential expenditure on school performance', *Educational Researcher* 18 (4): 45–65.

Hargreaves, A. (1994) *Changing Teachers: Changing Times*. London: Cassell.

Hargreaves, D. (1967) *Social Relations in a Secondary School*. London: Routledge & Kegan Paul.

Hargreaves, D. (1995a) 'School effectiveness, school change and school improvement: The relevance of the concept of culture', *School Effectiveness and School Improvement* 6 (1): 23–46.

Hargreaves, D. (1995b) 'Inspection and school improvement', *Cambridge Journal of Education* 25 (1): 117–25.

Hargreaves, D. & Hopkins, D. (1989) *School Development Plans Project: 1. Planning for School Development*. London: Department for Education and Science.

Hargreaves, D. & Hopkins, D. (1991) *The Empowered School*. London: Cassell.

Hargreaves, D. & Hopkins, D. (1993) 'School effectiveness, school improvement and development planning', in M. Preedy (ed.) *Managing the Effective School*, pp. 229–40. London: Oxford University Press/Paul Chapman Publishing.

Harris, A., Jamieson, I. & Russ, J. (1995) 'A study of "effective" departments in secondary schools', *School Organisation* 15 (3): 283–99.

Hartnett, A. & Naish, M. (eds.) (1986) *Education and Society Today*. Lewes: Falmer Press.

Hatcher, R. (1996) 'The limitations of the new social democratic agenda', in R. Hatcher & K. Jones (eds.) *Education after the Conservatives*. Stoke-on-Trent: Trentham Books.

Haviland, J. (1988) *Take Care Mr. Baker*. London: Fourth Estate.

Heal, K. (1978) 'Misbehaviour among school children', *Policy and Politics* 6: 321–32.

Heath, A. & Clifford, P. (1980) 'The seventy thousand hours that Rutter left out', *Oxford Review of Education* 6 (1): 3–19.

Heath, A. & Clifford, P. (1981) 'The measurement and explanation of school differences', *Oxford Review of Education* 7 (1): 33–40.

Hedges, L., Laine, R. & Greenwald, R. (1994) 'Does money matter? A meta-analysis of studies of the effects of differential school inputs on student outcomes: An exchange, Part 1', *Educational Researcher* 23 (3): 5–14.

Henig, J.R. (1994) *Rethinking School Choice: Limits of the Market Metaphor*. Princeton: Princeton University Press.

Her Majesty's Inspectorate (HMI) (1982) *The New Teacher in School: Matters for Discussion, 15*. London: HMSO.

Her Majesty's Inspectorate (HMI) (1988) *The New Teacher in School*. London: HMSO.

Her Majesty's Stationery Office (HMSO) (1988) *Education Reform Bill*. London: HMSO.

Herman, R. & Stringfield, S. (1995) *Ten Promising Programmes for Educating Disadvantaged Students*. Baltimore: John Hopkins University.

Hess, J. (1992) *School Restructuring, Chicago Style: A Midway Report*. Chicago, IL: The Chicago Panel on Public School Policy and Finance.

Hillman, J. & Stoll, L. (1994) 'Understanding school improvement', in *School Research Matters, School Improvement Network's Bulletin 1*. London: Institute of Education.

Hobsbaum, A. (1995) 'Reading recovery in England', *Literacy, Teaching and Learning* 1 (2): 21–39.

Hobsbaum, A. & Hillman, J. (1994) *Reading Recovery in England*. London: The Reading Recovery National Network, Institute of Education.

Holtermann, S. (1997) 'All our futures: The impact of public expenditure and fiscal policies on children and young people', in A. Walker & C. Walker (eds.) *Britain Divided: The Growth of Social Exclusion in the 1980s and 1990s*. London: CPAG.

Hopkins, D. (1987) *Improving the Quality of Schooling*. Lewes: Falmer Press.

Hopkins, D. (1994a) 'School improvement in an era of change', in P. Ribbins & E. Burridge (eds.) *Improving Education: Promoting Quality in Schools*, pp. 74–91. London: Cassell.

Hopkins, D. (1995) 'Towards effective school improvement', keynote address at the International Congress for School Effectiveness and School Improvement, Leeuwarden, The Netherlands.

Hopkins, D. (1994b) *Towards a Theory for School Improvement*, ESRC Seminar, Sheffield.

Hopkins, D., Ainscow, M. & West, M. (1994) *School Improvement in an Era of Change*. London: Cassell.

Hough, J.R. (1991) 'Input–output analysis in education in the UK: Review essay', *Economics of Education Review* 10 (1): 73–81.

House of Commons (1986) *Achievement in Primary Schools: Third report from the Education, Science and Arts Committee*. London: HMSO.

House of Commons (1994) *Performance in City Schools*, Minutes of Evidence, 22 June. London: HMSO.

House of Representatives (1986) *Proceedings and Debates of the 99th Congress*, second Session. Washington, DC: Congressional Record.

Huberman, M. (1992), 'Critical introduction', in M. Fullan *Successful School Improvement*. Buckingham: Open University Press.

Huberman, M. (1993) 'Linking the practitioner and researcher community for school improvement', *School Effectiveness and School Improvement* 4 (1): 1–17.

Huberman, M.A. & Miles, M.B. (1984) *Innovation up Close: How School Improvement Works*. New York: Plenum Press.

Hull, C.L. (1952) *A Behaviour System*. New Haven, CT: Yale University Press.

Husen, T., Tuijnman, A., & Halls, W. (1992) *Schooling in Modern European Society*. Oxford: Pergamon.

Ichheiser, G. (1943) 'Misinterpretations of personality in everyday life and the psychologist's frame of reference', *Character and Personality*, 12, pp. 145–60, cited in R. Farr & S. Moscovici 'On the nature and role of representations in self's understanding of others and of self', in M. Cook (ed.) (1984) *Issues in Person Perception*, pp. 1–27. London: Methuen.

Inner London Education Authority (1983) *Race, Sex and Class*, Festival Hall Seminar, 1981. London: ILEA.

Inner London Education Authority (1984) *Improving Secondary Schools* (The Hargreaves Report). London: ILEA.

Inner London Education Authority (1985) *Improving Primary Schools* (The Thomas Report). London: ILEA.

Inner London Education Authority (1987) *Informing Education: Report of the Committee of Inquiry into Freedom of Information appointed by the ILEA* (The Tomlinson Report). London: ILEA.

Ishewood, J. (1988) 'Viewpoint', *Sunday Times*, 10 April.

Izbicki, J. (1986) 'Best schools give priority to 3Rs', *Daily Telegraph*, 15 April.

Jagger, T. (1979) 'The school factor', *Education*, 25 May.

Jencks, C., Smith, M., Ackland, H., Bane, M., Cohen, D., Gintis, H., Heyns, B. & Micholson, S. (1972) *Inequality: A Reassessment of the Effect of Family and Schooling in America*. New York: Basic Books.

Jesson, D. & Gray, J. (1991) 'Slants on slopes: Using multilevel models to investigate differential school effectiveness and its impact on pupils' examination results', *School Effectiveness and School Improvement* 2 (3): 230–47.

Johnson, B. & McAthlone, B. (eds.) (1970) *Verdict on the Facts*. Cambridge: Advisory Centre for Education.

Jones, A. (1976) 'Coping in the school situation', in C. Jones-Davies & R.G. Cave (eds.) *The Disruptive Pupil in the Secondary School*, pp. 56–86. London: Ward Lock.

Jowett, S. & Baginsky, M., with MacDonald. M. (1991) *Building Bridges: Parental Involvement in Schools*. Windsor: NFER/Nelson.

Joyce, B. (1986) *Improving America's Schools*. New York: Longman.

Joyce, B. (1991) 'The doors to school improvement', *Educational Leadership* 48 (8): 59–62.

Junior Education (1986) 'Effective schools', 10 (7), July.

Kemble, B. (1979) 'Your good school guide', *Daily Express*, 22 March.

Kemble, B. (1988) 'The school matters—official', *Evening Standard*, 14 March.

Kennedy, H. (1997a) *Learning Works: Widening Participation in Further Education*. London: FEFC.

Kennedy, H. (1997b) 'The report', *Guardian Education*, p. 2–3, July 1.

Kenway, J. (1996) 'The information superhighway and post-modernity: The social promise and the social price', *Comparative Education* 32 (2): 217–31.

Keys, W. & Fernandes, C. (1993) 'What *do* students think about school?' A Report for the National Commission on Education. Slough: National Foundation for Educational Research.

King, R., Raynes, N. & Tizard, J. (1971) *Patterns of Residential Care: Sociological Studies in Institutions for Handicapped Children*. London: Routledge & Kegan Paul.

Kysel, F., Varlaam, A., Stoll, L. & Sammons, P. (1983) *The Child at School: A New Behaviour Schedule*. London: Research and Statistics, Inner London Education Authority.

Lacey, C. (1970) *Hightown Grammar: The School as a Social System*. Manchester: Manchester University Press.

Lacey, C. (1974) 'Destreaming in a "pressurised" academic environment', in J. Eggleston (ed.) *Contemporary Research in the Sociology of Education*, pp. 148–66. London: Methuen.

Lauder, H., Jamieson, I. & Wikeley, F. (1998) 'Models of Effectiveness: Limits and capacities', in R. Slee, G. Weiner & S. Tomlinson (eds.) *School Effectiveness for Whom? Challenges to the School Effectiveness and School Improvement Movement*, pp. 51–69. London: Falmer.

Lawton, D. (1997) *Promoting Improved Teaching and Learning: Policy Lessons*, Background Paper for OECD Secretariat, Paris: OECD.

Lazar, I. & Darlington, R. (1982) 'Lasting effects of early education: A report from the consortium for longitudinal studies', *Monographs of the Society for Research in Child Development* 195: 47.

Le Grand, J. & Bartlett, W. (1993) *Quasi-markets and Social Policy*. Basingstoke: Macmillan.

Levine, D. & Lezotte, L. (1990) *Unusually Effective Schools: A Review and Analysis of Research and Practice*. Madison, WI: National Center for Effective Schools Research and Development.

Lezotte, L. (1989) 'School improvement based on the effective schools research', *International Journal of Educational Research* 13: 815–25.

Light, P. & Butterworth. G. (eds.) (1992) *Context and Cognition: Ways of Learning and Knowing*. London: Harvester Press.

Light, R. & Smith, P.V. (1971) 'Accumulating evidence: Procedures for resolving contradictions among different studies', *Harvard Educational Review* 41 (4): 429–71.

Literacy Taskforce (1997) *A Reading Revolution: Preliminary Report of the Literacy Taskforce*. London: Institute of Education.

Little, A. & Mabey, C. (1972) 'An index for designation of educational priority areas', in A. Shonfield & S. Shaw (eds.) *Social Indicators and Social Policy*, pp. 67–93. London: Heinemann.

Little, A. & Mabey, C. (1973) 'Reading attainment and social and ethnic mix of London primary schools', in D. Donnison & D. Eversley (eds.) *London: Urban Patterns, Problems and Policies.* London: Heinemann.

Louis, K.S. & Miles, M. (1990) *Improving the Urban High School.* New York: Teachers' College Press.

Luyten, H. (1994a) 'Stability of school effects in secondary education: The impact of variance across subjects and years', paper presented at the annual meeting of the American Educational Research Association, New Orleans.

Luyten, H. (1994b) 'School size effects on achievement in secondary education: Evidence from the Netherlands, Sweden and the USA', *School Effectiveness and School Improvement* 5 (1): 75–99.

Lutyen, H. (1995) 'Teacher change and instability across grades', *School Effectiveness and School Improvement* 1 (1): 67–89.

MacBeath, J. (1994) 'A role for parents, students and teachers in school self-evaluation and development planning', in K.A. Riley & D.L. Nuttall (eds.) *Measuring Quality: Education Indicators—United Kingdom and International Perspectives*, pp. 100–21. London: Falmer Press.

MacBeath, J. & Mortimore, P. (1994) 'Improving school effectiveness: A Scottish approach', paper presented at the annual conference of the British Educational Research Association, Oxford.

MacBeath, J. & Mortimore, P. (1997) 'School effectiveness: Is it improving?', paper presented at the Tenth Annual Congress of School Effectiveness and School Improvement, Memphis.

MacBeath, J. & Turner, M. (1990) *Learning out of School: Homework, Policy and Practice*, a research study commissioned by the Scottish Education Department. Glasgow: Jordanhill College.

McCormack-Larkin, M. & Kritek, W. (1982) 'Milwaukee's project RISE', *Educational Leadership* 40 (3): 16–21.

McGaw, B., Banks, D. & Piper, K. (1991) *Effective Schools: Schools that Make a Difference.* Hawthorn, Victoria: Australian Council for Educational Research.

MacGilchrist, B. (1997) 'Reading and achievement', *Research Papers in Education* 12 (2): 157–76.

MacGilchrist, B., Mortimore, P., Savage, J. & Beresford, C. (1995) *School Development Planning Matters.* London: Paul Chapman Publishing.

MacGilchrist, B., Myers, K. & Reed, J. (1997) *The Intelligent School.* London: Paul Chapman Publishing.

MacGilchrist, B., Savage, J., Mortimore, P. & Beresford, C. (1994) 'Making a difference', *Managing Schools Today* 3 (9): 7–8.

McMahon, A., Bolam, R., Abbott, R. & Holly, P. (1984) *Guidelines for Review and Internal Development in Schools (Primary and Secondary School Handbooks).* York: Longman/Schools Council.

McNamara, D. (1988) 'Do the grounds for claiming that school matters, matter?', *British Journal of Educational Psychology* 58 (3): 356–60.

MacPherson, A. & Willms, D. (1987) 'Equalisation and improvement: Some effects of comprehensive reorganisation in Scotland', paper presented at the annual meeting of the American Educational Research Association.

Madden, J. (1976) cited in R. Edmonds, 'Effective schools for the urban poor', *Educational Leadership* 37 (1): 15–27.

Maden, M. & Hillman, J. (1996) 'Lessons in success', in National Commission on Education, *Success Against the Odds*, pp. 312–363. London: Routledge.

Mandeville, G. (1987) 'The stability of school effectiveness indices across years', NCME paper. Washington, DC: NCME.

Marjoribanks, K. (1979) *Families and their Learning Environments: An Empirical Analysis*. London: Routledge & Kegan Paul.

Marks, J. (1986) 'I explore the alibi of our failing schools', *Daily Mail*, 22 April.

Marks, J., Cox, C. & Pomian-Srzednicki, M. (1983) *Standards in English Schools*. London: National Council for Educational Standards.

Matthews, P. & Smith, G. (1995) 'Ofsted: Inspecting schools and improvement through inspection', *Cambridge Journal of Education* 25 (1): 23–34.

Maughan, B., Mortimore, P., Ouston, J. & Rutter, M. (1980) *'Fifteen Thousand Hours*: A reply to Health and Clifford', *Oxford Review of Education* 6 (3): 289–303.

Maughan, B., Pickles, A., Rutter, M. & Ouston, J. (1990) 'Can schools change: I. Outcomes at six London secondary schools', *School Effectiveness and School Improvement* 1 (3): 188–210.

Merton, R. (1968) 'The self-fulfilling prophecy', in R. Merton (ed.) *Social Theory and Social Structure* (revised edition), pp. 475–90. London: Collier MacMillan.

Miles, M.B. & Ekholm, M. (1985) 'School improvement at the school level', in W. Van Velzen, M.B. Miles, M. Ekholm et al. (eds.) *Making School Improvement Work*, pp. 123–80. Leuven: ACCO.

Miles, M., Saxl, E. & Lieberman, A. (1988) 'What skills do educational "change agents" need? An empirical view', *Curriculum Inquiry* 18 (2): 157–93.

Millham, S., Bullock, R. & Cherrett, P. (1975) *After Grace, Teeth*. London: Human Context Books.

Monks, T.G. (1968) *Comprehensive Education in England and Wales*. Slough: NFER.

Mortimore, J. (1997) 'Innovatory staffing practices in city technology colleges', unpublished PhD thesis, London University.

Mortimore, J. & Blackstone, T. (1982a) *Disadvantage and Education*. London: Heinemann.

Mortimore, J. & Blackstone, T. (1982b) *Education and Disadvantage*. London: Heinemann.

Mortimore, J. & Mortimore, P. (1984) 'Parents and schools', *Education* 164, Special Report 5 October.

Mortimore, J., Mortimore, P. & Chitty, C. (1986) 'Secondary school examinations: The helpful servants, not the dominating master', in *Bedford Way Papers, 18*. London: Institute of Education.

Mortimore, P. (1977) 'Schools as institutions', *Educational Research* 20 (1): 61–8.

Mortimore, P. (1978) 'The study of institutions', *Human Relations* 31 (11): 985–99.

Mortimore, P. (1979) 'The study of secondary schools: A researcher's reply', in *Perspectives 1*. Exeter: Exeter University.

Mortimore, P. (1982) 'Underachievement: A framework for debate', *Secondary Education* 1 (2): 3–6.

Mortimore, P. (1989) 'ILEA Research', *Primary Teaching Studies* 5 (2): 98–107.

Mortimore, P. (1990) 'The front page or yesterday's news: The reception of educational research', in G. Walford (ed.) *Doing Educational Research*, pp. 210–33. London: Routledge.

Mortimore, P. (1991a) 'The nature and findings of research on school effectiveness in the primary sector', in S. Riddell & S. Brown (eds.) *School Effectiveness Research: Its Messages for School Improvement*, pp. 9–19. Edinburgh: HMSO.

Mortimore, P. (1991b) 'School effectiveness research: Which way at the crossroads?', *School Effectiveness and School Improvement* 2 (3): 213–29.

Mortimore, P. (1991c) 'Effective schools from a British perspective: Research and practice', in J. Bliss, W. Firestone & C. Richards (eds.) *Rethinking Effective Schools*, pp. 76–90. New Jersey: Prentice Hall.

Mortimore, P. (1992) 'To teach the teachers: Teacher training for effective schools', in J. Bashi & Z. Sazz (eds.) *School Effectiveness and Improvement: Proceedings of the Third International Congress for School Effectiveness*, pp. 160–73. Jerusalem: Magnes Press.

Mortimore, P. (1993a) 'School effectiveness and the management of effective learning and teaching', *School Effectiveness and School Improvement*, 4, 4, 290–310.

Mortimore, P. (1993b) 'Managing teaching and learning: The search for a match', in M. Smith & M. Busher (eds.) *Managing Educational Institutions: Sheffield Papers in Educational Management*, pp. 59–79. Sheffield: University of Sheffield.

Mortimore, P. (1994) 'A glimpse of tomorrow', *Managing Schools Today* 3 (9): 11–13.

Mortimore, P. (1995a) *Effective Schools: Current Impact and Future Possibilities*, Director's Inaugural Lecture, 7 February 1995. London: Institute of Education.

Mortimore, P. (1995b) 'The positive effects of schooling', in M. Rutter (ed.) *Psycho-Social Disturbances in Young People: Challenges for Prevention*, pp. 333–63. Cambridge: Cambridge University Press.

Mortimore, P. (1995c) 'The balancing act', *Education Guardian*, 28 February.

Mortimore, P (1995d) 'Better than excuses', *TES*, July.

Mortimore, P. (1996a) 'Partnership and co-operation in school improvement', paper presented at the Association for Teacher Education in Europe Conference, Glasgow, Scotland.

Mortimore, P (1996b) 'Redressing disadvantage', Lewisham Head Teachers' Conference, Hythe.

Mortimore, P. (1996c) 'We should inspect our obsession with failure', *Independent*, 25 July.

Mortimore, P. (1997) 'Can effective schools compensate for society?', in A.H. Halsey, H. Lauder, P. Brown & A.S. Wells (eds.) *Education: Culture, Economy, Society*, pp. 476–87. New York: Oxford University Press.

Mortimore, P. & Blatchford, P. (1993) *The Issue of Class Size*, NCE Briefing 12. London: National Commission on Education.

Mortimore, P., Davies, H. & Portway, S. (1996d) *Burntwood School: A Case Study*. London: National Commission on Education/Routledge.

Mortimore, P., Davies, J., Varlaam, A. & West, A. (1983) *Behaviour Problems in Schools: An Evaluation of Support Centres*. London: Croom Helm.

Mortimore, P. & Goldstein, H. (1996) *The Teaching of Reading in 45 Inner London Secondary Schools: A Critical Examination of OFSTED Research*. London: Institute of Education.

Mortimore, P., MacGilchrist, B., Savage, J. & Beresford.C. (1994a) 'School development planning in primary schools: 'Does it make a difference?', in D. Hargreaves & D. Hopkins (eds.) *Development Planning for School Improvement*, pp. 162–72. London: Cassell.

Mortimore, P. & Mortimore, J. (1986) 'Education and social class', in R. Rogers (ed.) *Education and Social Class*. Lewes: Falmer Press.

Mortimore, P., Mortimore J. & Thomas, H. (1994b) *Managing Associate Staff*. London: Paul Chapman Publishing.

Mortimore, P., Mortimore, J., Thomas, H., Cairns, R. & Taggart, B. (1992) *The Innovative Uses of Non-Teaching Staff in Primary and Secondary Schools Project*. London: Institute of Education/Department for Education.

Mortimore, P. & Sammons, P. (1987) 'New evidence on effective elementary schools', *Educational Leadership* 45 (1): 4–8.

Mortimore, P. & Sammons, P. (1988) 'Snapshots of a pupil's path to progress', *Guardian*, 24 February.

Mortimore, P., Sammons, P. & Ecob, R. (1988c) 'Expressing the magnitude of school effects: A reply to Peter Preece', *Research Papers in Education* 3 (2): 99–101.

Mortimore, P., Sammons, P., Ecob, R., Hill, A., Hind, M., Hunt, M., Stoll, L., Clark, J. & Lewis, D. (1985) 'The ILEA junior school study: An introduction', in D. Reynolds (ed.) *Studying School Effectiveness*, pp. 117–35. Lewes: Falmer Press.

Mortimore, P., Sammons, P., Stoll, L., Lewis, D. & Ecob, R. (1986a) *The ILEA Junior School Project: Summary Report*. London: Research and Statistics, Inner London Education Authority.

Mortimore, P., Sammons, P., Stoll, L., Lewis, D. & Ecob, R. (1986b) *The ILEA Junior School Project: Main Report Parts A, B, C and Technical Appendices*. London: Research and Statistics, Inner London Education Authority.

Mortimore, P., Sammons, P., Stoll, L., Lewis, D. & Ecob, R. (1987a) 'The ILEA junior school project: A study of school effectiveness, I', *Forum* 29 (2): 47–9.

Mortimore, P., Sammons, P., Stoll, L., Lewis, D. & Ecob, R. (1987b) 'Towards more effective junior schooling: Further results from the ILEA's junior school project', *Forum* 29 (3): 70–3.

Mortimore, P., Sammons, P., Stoll, L., Lewis, D. & Ecob, R. (1987c) 'For effective class-room practices', *Forum* 30 (1): 8–11.

Mortimore, P., Sammons, P., Stoll, L., Lewis, D. & Ecob, R. (1988a) *School Matters: The Junior Years*. Wells, Somerset: Open Books. Reprinted 1995, London: Paul Chapman Publishing.

Mortimore, P., Sammons, P., Stoll, L., Ecob, R. & Lewis, D. (1988b) 'The effects of school membership on pupils' educational outcomes', *Research Papers in Education* 3 (1): 3–26.

Mortimore, P., Sammons, P., Stoll, L., Lewis, D. & Ecob, R. (1989) 'A response to McNamara', essay review (unpublished).

Mortimore, P., Sammons, P. & Thomas, S. (1994c) 'School effectiveness and value-added measures', *Assessment in Education* 1 (3): 315–32.

Mortimore, P. & Stone, C. (1991) 'Measuring educational quality', *British Journal of Educational Studies* 39 (1): 69–82.

Mowrer, O.H. (1960) *Learning Theory and the Symbolic Processes*. New York: Wylie.

Murphy, J. (1990) 'School effectiveness', paper presented at the International Conference on the Study of School Effectiveness and the Practice of School Improvement, Boston, MA.

Murphy, J. (1991) *Restructuring Schools: Capturing and Assessing the Phenomena*. New York: Teachers' College Press.

Murphy, J., Weil, M., Hallinger, P. & Mitman, A. (1982) 'Academic press: Translating high expectations into school policies and classroom practices', *Educational Leadership* 40 (3): 22–6.

Musgrove, F. & Taylor, P.H. (1972) 'Pupils expectations of teachers', in A. Morrison & D. McIntyre (eds.) *The Social Psychology of Teaching*, pp. 171–82. Harmondsworth: Penguin.

Myers, K. (1995) *School Improvement in Practice: Accounts from the 'Schools Make a Difference' Project*. London: Falmer Press.

Nash, R. (1973) *Classrooms Observed*. London: Routledge & Kegan Paul.

National Commission on Education (1993) *Learning to Succeed*. London: Heinemann.

National Commission on Education (1996) *Success Against the Odds: Effective Schools in Disadvantaged Areas*. London: Routledge.

National Union of Teachers (1979) 'Secondary findings stress the obvious', *The Teacher*, 30 March.

Needham, N. (1988) 'What makes good schools (surprise!)', *National Education Association Today* February: 17.

Neustatter, A. (1986) 'What makes a good school?', *Good Housekeeping*, March.

New Society (1986) 'Could do better', *New Society*, 18 April.

Newman, J.H. (1852) *The Idea of a University*. Indiana: University of Notre Dame Press.

Newsam, P. (1979) 'Teacher knows best after all', *Observer*, 25 March.

Northwest Regional Educational Laboratory (1984) *Onward to Excellence: Making Schools More Effective*. Portland, Oregon: NREL.

Northwest Regional Educational Laboratory (NREL) (1989) *Effective Schooling Practices: A Research Synthesis*, Portland, Oregon: Northwest Regional Educational Laboratory.

Northwest Regional Educational Laboratory (NREL) (1990) *Effective Schooling Practices Update*, Portland, OR: Northwest Regional Educational Laboratory.

Nunes, T., Schliemann, A.D. & Carraher, D.W. (1993) *Street Mathematics and School Mathematics*. Cambridge: Cambridge University Press.

Nunn, P. (1920) *Education: Its Data and First Principles*. London: Edward Arnold.

Nuttall, D.L. (1990) *Differences in Examination Performance*, RS 1277/90. London: Research and Statistics, Inner London Education Authority.

Nuttall, D.L. (1991) 'An instrument to be honed', *Times Educational Supplement*, 13 September.

Nuttall, D.L. (1992) 'Add value to league tables', *ISIS Magazine* 4, Spring: 14.

Nuttall, D.L. (1993) paper presented at the Conference of the Centre for Policy Studies.

Nuttall, D.L., Goldstein, H., Prosser, R. & Rasbash, J. (1989) 'Differential school effectiveness', in *International Journal of Education Research, Special Issue: Developments in School Effectiveness Research* 13 (7): 769–76.

Nuttall, D.L., Sammons, P. & Thomas, S. (1993) personal communication.

Nuttall, D.L., Sammons, P., Thomas, S. & Mortimore, P. (1992b) *Differential School Effectiveness: Departmental Variations in GCSE Attainment*, ESRC award R000234130. London: Institute of Education, University of London.

Nuttall, D.L., Thomas, S. & Goldstein, H. (1992a) *Report on Analysis of 1990 Examination Results*, Association of Metropolitan Authorities project 'Putting Examination Results in Context'. London: Centre for Educational Research, LSE.

O'Connor, M. (1980) 'Fifteen thousand hours that shook the academics', *Education Guardian*, 22 July.

OECD (1989) *The Quality of Education*. Paris; OECD.

OECD (1992) *New Technology and its Impact on Educational Buildings.* Paris: OECD.

OECD (1995) *Our Children at Risk.* Paris: OECD.

Ofsted (1992) *Standards and Quality in Education, 1992–1993.* London: HMSO.

Ofsted (1993) *Mathematics Key Stages 1, 2, 3 and 4, 1992–1994.* London: HMSO.

Olweus, D. (1991) 'Bully/victim problems among school children: Basic facts and effects of a school-based intervention programme', in D. Pepler & K. Rubin (eds.) *The Development and Treatment of Childhood Aggression*, pp. 411–88. Hove and London: Erlbaum.

Oppenheim, C. (1993) *Poverty: The Facts.* London: CPAG.

Osborne, A.F. & Milbank, J.E. (1987) *The Effects of Early Education.* Oxford: ClarendonPress.

Oswick, C. (1979) 'Less caning does not spoil the child', *Southend Evening Echo*, 27 March.

Ouston, J., Maughan, B. & Mortimore, P. (1979) 'School influences', in M. Rutter (ed.) *Developmental Psychiatry*, pp. 67–76. London: Heinemann.

Ouston, J., Maughan, B. & Rutter, M. (1991) 'Can schools change? II: Practice in six London secondary schools', *School Effectiveness and School Improvement* 2 (1): 3–13.

Owens, R.G. (1981) Letter to the Editor, *Educational Researcher*, January.

Paterson, L. & Goldstein, H. (1991) 'New statistical methods of analysing social structures: An introduction to multilevel models', *British Educational Research Journal* 17 (4): 387–93.

Paul, D.A. (1977) 'Change processes at the elementary, secondary, and post-secondary levels of education', in N. Nash & J. Culbertson (eds.) *Linking Processes in Educational Improvement.* Columbus, OH: University Council for Educational Administration.

Pearson, A. (1984) 'Competence: A normative analysis', in E.C. Short (ed.) *Competence: Inquiries into its Meaning and Acquisition in Educational Settings*, pp. 31–8. New York: University Press of America.

Peters, T. & Waterman, H. (1984) *In Search of Excellence.* New York: Warner Books.

Phillips, M. (1996) 'Inspectors only come under fire when they say schools are doing badly. No one complains about their methods when the results are good', *Observer*, 27 October.

Piaget, J. (1955) *The Construction of Reality and the Child* (trans. M. Cook). London: Routledge & Kegan Paul.

Piers, E.V. & Harris, D.B. (1964) 'Age and other correlates of self-concept in children', *Journal of Educational Psychology* 55 (2): 91–5.

Pilling D. & Pringle, M.K. (1978) *Controversial Issues in Child Development.* London: Paul Elek.

Plewis, I. (1997) Letter to the *Times Educational Supplement*, 9 May.

Porter, B. (1988) 'Effective schools make a big difference', *Burlington Spectator*, 4 May.

Power, M., Alderson, M., Phillipson, C., Schoenberg, E. & Morris, J. (1967) 'Delinquent schools?', *New Society* 264: 542–3.

Power, S. Whitty, G. & Youdell, D. (1995), *No Place to Learn: Homelessness and Education.* London: Shelter.

Preece, P. (1988) 'Misleading ways of expressing the magnitude of school effects', *Research Papers in Education* 3 (2): 97–8.

Preece, P. (1989) 'Pitfalls in research on school and teacher effectiveness', *Research Papers in Education* 4 (3): 48–69.

Proudford, C. & Baker, R. (1995) 'Schools that make a difference: A sociological perspective on effective schooling', *British Journal of Sociology of Education* 16 (3): 277–92.

Purkey, S. & Smith, M. (1983) 'Effective schools: A review', *Elementary School Journal* 83 (4): 427–52.

Purkey, S. & Smith, M. (1985) 'School reform', *Elementary School Journal* 83 (4): 427–52.

Quick, R. (1884) 'Universities and their relation to the training of teachers', Health Education Literature Conference on the Organisation of Intermediate and Higher Education, XVI, London.

Radical Statistics Education Group (1982) *Reading Between the Numbers: A Critical Guide to Educational Research*. London: BSSRS.

Raudenbush, S. (1989) 'The analysis of longitudinal, multilevel data', *International Journal of Educational Research, Special Issue: Developments in School Effectiveness Research* 13 (7): 721–40.

Redman, T. (1982) 'Preparation for college: A national approach', *Journal of Development and Remedial Education* 5: 3–5.

Resnick, L.B. (1987) 'Learning in school and out', *Educational Researcher* 1: 13–20.

Reynolds, D. (1974) 'Some do, some don't', *Times Educational Supplement*, 10 May.

Reynolds, D. (1975) 'When teachers and pupils refuse a truce: The secondary school and the generation of delinquency', in G. Mungham & G. Pearson (eds.) *British Working Class Youth Culture*, pp. 124–37. London: Routledge & Kegan Paul.

Reynolds, D. (1976) 'The delinquent school', in M. Hammersley & P. Woods (eds.) *The Process of Schooling*, pp. 217–29. London: Routledge & Kegan Paul.

Reynolds, D. (1982) 'The search for effective schools', *School Organisation* 2 (3): 215–37.

Reynolds, D. (ed.) (1985) *Studying School Effectiveness*. Lewes: Falmer Press.

Reynolds, D. (1988) 'Research on school and organisational effectiveness: The end of the beginning?', paper presented at the BEMAS Third Research Conference on Educational Management and Administration, Cardiff.

Reynolds, D. (1989) 'School effectiveness and school improvement: A review of the British literature', in D. Reynolds, B. Creemers & T. Peters (eds.) *School Effectiveness and Improvement*, pp. 11–29. Groningen: RION Institute for Educational Research / Cardiff: School of Education, University of Wales.

Reynolds, D. (1990a) 'Research on school and organisational effectiveness: The end of the beginning', in R. Saran & V. Trafford (eds.) *Research in Education Management and Policy: Retrospect and Prospect*, pp. 9–23. Lewes: Falmer Press.

Reynolds, D. (1990b) Paper given at the Conference of the International Congress for School Effectiveness and School Improvement, Van Leer Institute, Jerusalem.

Reynolds, D. (1992) 'School effectiveness and school improvement: An updated review of the British literature', in D. Reynolds & P. Cuttance (eds.) *School Effectiveness Research, Policy and Practice*, pp. 1–24. London: Cassell.

Reynolds, D. (1993) 'Linking school effectiveness knowledge and school improvement practice', in C. Dimmock (ed.) *School-Based Management and School Effectiveness*, pp. 185–200. London: Routledge.

Reynolds, D. (1995a) 'The effective school: An inaugural lecture', *Evaluation and Research in Education*, 9, 2, 57–73.

Reynolds, D. (1995b) *Failure Free Schooling*, Series 49. Melbourne: IARTV.

Reynolds, D. & Creemers, B. (1990) 'School effectiveness and school improvement: A mission statement', editorial, *School Effectiveness and School Improvement* 1 (1): 1–3.

Reynolds, D., Creemers, B. & Peters, T. (eds.) (1989) *School Effectiveness and Improvement: Proceedings of the First International Congress, London, 1988.* Groningen: RION Institute for Educational Research / Cardiff: School of Education, University of Wales.

Reynolds, D. & Cuttance, P. (eds.) (1992) *School Effectiveness: Research, Policy and Practice.* London; Cassell.

Reynolds, D. & Farrell, S. (1996) *Worlds Apart? A Review of International Surveys of Educational Achievement involving England*, Ofsted Reviews of Research. London: HMSO.

Reynolds, D., Hargreaves, A. & Blackstone, T. (1980) 'Fifteen Thousand Hours: A review symposium', *British Journal of Sociology of Education* 1 (2): 207–19.

Reynolds, D., Hopkins, D. & Stoll, L. (1993) 'Linking school effectiveness knowledge and school improvement practice: Towards a synergy', *School Effectiveness and School Improvement* 4: 37–58.

Reynolds, D., Jones, D. & St. Leger, S. (1976) 'Schools do make a difference', *New Society* 37 (721): 223–5.

Reynolds, D. & Packer, A. (1992) 'School effectiveness and school improvement in the 1990s', in D. Reynolds & P. Cuttance (eds.) *School Effectiveness: Research, Policy and Practice*, pp. 171–87. London: Cassell.

Reynolds, D., Sammons, P., Stoll, L. & Barber, M. (1994a) *School Effectiveness and School Improvement in the United Kingdom* (ICSEI Country Report), presented at the International Congress for School Effectiveness and Improvement, Leeuwarden, The Netherlands.

Reynolds, D., Sullivan, M. & Murgatroyd, S. (1987) *The Comprehensive Experiment.* Lewes: Falmer Press.

Reynolds, D., Teddlie, C., Creemers, B., Cheng, Y.C. (1994b) 'School effectiveness research: A review of the international literature', in D. Reynolds, B. Creemers, P. Nesselradt, E. Schaffer, S. Stringfield & C. Teddlie (eds.) *Advances in School Effectiveness Research and Practice*, pp. 25–51. Oxford: Pergamon.

Reynolds, D., Creemers, B. Nesselrodt, P., Schaffer, E. Stringfield, S. & Teddlie, C. (1994c) *Advances in School Effectiveness Research and Practice*, Oxford: Pergamon.

Reynolds, D., Davie, R. & Phillips, D. (1989b) 'The Cardiff Programme', *International Journal of Educational Research* 13 (7): 801–14.

Robertson, P., Sammons P. & Mortimore, P. (1996) *Improving School Effectiveness: A Project in Progress*, BERA Annual Conference, Lancaster.

Robinson, G. (1983) *Effective Schools: A Summary of Research.* Arlington, VA: Educational Research Seminar.

Robinson, P. (1997) *Literacy, Numeracy and Economic Performance.* London: Centre for Economic Performance/London School of Economics.

Roeder, P. & Sang, F. (1991) 'Uber die Institutionelle Verarbeitung von Leistungsunterschieden', *Zeitschrift f. Entwicklungspsychologie u. Pedagogische Psychologie* 23 (2): 159–70.

Rogers, R. (1979) 'How good schools can change children', *New Statesman*, 23 March.

Rosenthal, R. & Jacobson, L. (1968) *Pygmalion in the Classroom: Teacher Expectations and Pupils' Intellectual Development.* New York: Holt Rinehart & Winston.

Rowe, K.J. (1995) 'Factors affecting students' progress in reading: Key findings from a longitudinal study in literacy', *Teaching and Learning* 1 (2): 57–110.

Rowlands, C. (1979) 'Schools that harm the gifted', *Daily Mail*, 22 March.

Rowlands, C. (1986) 'School chiefs back return to three Rs', *Daily Mail*, 15 April.

Rubinstein, D. & Stoneman, C. (1970) *Education for Democracy*. Harmondsworth: Penguin.

Ruddock, J., Chaplain, R. & Wallace, G. (1996) *School Improvement: What Can Pupils Tell Us?* London: David Fulton.

Rutter, M. (1973) 'Why are London children so disturbed?', *Proceedings of the Royal Society of Medicine* 66: 1221–5.

Rutter, M. (1983) 'School effects on pupil progress: Research findings and policy implications', *Child Development* 54: 1–29.

Rutter, M., Cox, A., Tupling, C., Berger, M. & Yule, W. (1975) 'Attainment and adjustment in two geographical areas: I. The prevalence of psychiatric disorder', *British Journal of Psychiatry* 126: 493–509.

Rutter, M. & Madge, N. (1976) *Cycles of Disadvantage*. London: Heinemann.

Rutter, M., Maughan, B., Mortimore, P. & Ouston, J. (1979a) *Fifteen Thousand Hours: Secondary Schools and Their Effects on Children*. London: Open Books. Reprinted 1995, Paul Chapman Publishing.

Rutter, M., Maughan, B., Mortimore, P. & Ouston, J. (1979b) '*Fifteen Thousand Hours*, school influences on pupil progress: Research strategies and tactics', *Journal of Child Psychology and Psychiatry* 2 (4): 366–8.

Rutter, M., Maughan, B., Mortimore, P. & Ouston, J. (1980a) 'Educational criterion of success: A reply to Acton', *Educational Research* 22 (3): 170–4.

Rutter, M., Maughan, B., Mortimore, P. & Ouston, J. (1980b) 'The researchers' response', in *Bedford Way Papers 1*. London: Institute of Education.

Rutter, M., Tizard, J. & Whitmore, K. (eds.) (1970) *Education, Health and Behaviour*. London: Longman.

Rutter, M., Yule, W., Berger, M., Yule, B., Morton, J. & Bagley, C. (1974) 'Children of West Indian immigrants: I. Rates of behavioural deviance and of psychiatric disorder', *Journal of Child Psychology and Psychiatry* 15, 241–62.

Rutter, M., Yule, B., Quinton, D. & Berger, M. (1975) 'Adjustment and attainment in two geographical areas: III. Some factors accounting for area differences', *British Journal of Psychiatry* 125: 520–33.

Sammons, P. (1989a) 'Ethical issues and statistical work', in R. Burgess *Ethics of Educational Research*. Lewes: Falmer Press.

Sammons, P. (1989b) 'Measuring school effectiveness', in D. Reynolds, B. Creemers & T. Peters (eds.) *School Effectiveness and Improvement*, pp. 169–88. Cardiff: School of Education, University of Wales / Groningen, The Netherlands: RION Institute for Educational Research.

Sammons, P. (1993) *Measuring and Resourcing Educational Needs: Variations in LEAs' LMS Policies in Inner London,* Clare Market Paper, 6. London: Centre for Educational Research, London School of Economics.

Sammons, P. (1994) 'Findings from school effectiveness research: Some implications for improving the quality of schools', in P. Ribbins & E. Burridge (eds.) *Improving Education: Promoting Quality in Schools*, pp. 32–51. London: Cassell.

Sammons, P. (1995) 'Gender, ethnic and socio-economic differences in attainment and progress: A longitudinal analysis of student achievement over nine years', *British Educational Research Journal* 21 (4): 465–85.

Sammons, P. (1996) 'Complexities in the judgement of school effectiveness', *Educational Research and Evaluation* 2 (2): 113–49.

Sammons, P. (1998) 'Diversity in classrooms: Effects on educational outcomes', in D. Shorrocks-Taylor (ed.) *Directions in Educational Psychology*. London: Whurr.

Sammons, P., Hillman, J. & Mortimore, P. (1995e) *Key Characteristics of Effective Schools: A Review of School Effectiveness Research*. London: Institute of Education and Ofsted.

Sammons, P., Kysel, F. & Mortimore, P. (1983) 'Educational Priority Indices: A new perspective', *British Educational Research Journal* 9 (1): 27–40.

Sammons, P. & Mortimore, P. (1993) 'Differential school effectiveness project', paper prepared in connection with a study sponsored by the Economic and Social Research Council (ESRC).

Sammons, P., Mortimore, P. & Hillman, J (1996) 'A response to David Hamilton's reflections', *Forum* 31 (3): 88–90.

Sammons, P., Mortimore, P. & Thomas, S. (1993c) 'First weigh your ingredients', *The Independent*, November.

Sammons, P., Mortimore, P. & Thomas, S. (1996a) 'Do schools perform consistently across outcomes and areas?', in J. Gray, D. Reynolds, C. Fitz-Gibbon & D. Jesson (eds.) *Merging Traditions: The Future of Research on School Effectiveness and School Improvement*, pp. 3–29. London: Cassell.

Sammons, P. & Nuttall, D.L. (1992) 'Differential school effectiveness', paper presented to the British Educational Research Association Conference, Stirling.

Sammons, P., Nuttall, D.L. & Cuttance, P. (1993b) 'Differential school effectiveness: Results from a reanalysis of the Inner London Education Authority's junior school project data', *British Educational Research Journal* 19 (4): 381–405.

Sammons, P., Nuttall, D.L., Cuttance, P. & Thomas, S. (1995c) 'Continuity of school effects: A longitudinal analysis of primary and secondary school effects on GCSE performance', *School Effectiveness and School Improvement* 6 (4): 285–307.

Sammons, P. & Reynolds, D. (1997) 'A partisan evaluation: John Elliott on school effectiveness', *Cambridge Journal of Education* 27 (1): 123–6.

Sammons, P. & Stoll, L. (1988) *Measuring Primary Pupils' Self-concepts*. London: Research and Statistics, Inner London Education Authority.

Sammons, P., Thomas, S. & Mortimore. P. (1994a) *Value Added Approaches: Ways of Comparing Schools*. London: Institute of Education.

Sammons, P., Thomas, S. & Mortimore, P. (1995a) *Differential School Effectiveness: Departmental Variations in GCSE Attainment*, ESRC End of Award Report, R000 234130. London: Institute of Education.

Sammons, P., Thomas, S. & Mortimore, P. (1995b) 'Accounting for variations in academic effectiveness between schools and departments: Results from the "Differential Secondary School Effectiveness Project"—a three-year study of GCSE performance', paper presented at the European Conference on Educational Research/BERA Annual Conference, Bath. London: Institute of Education.

Sammons, P., Thomas, S. & Mortimore, P. (1996d) 'Promoting school and departmental effectiveness', *Management in Education* 10 (1): 22–4.

Sammons, P., Thomas, S. & Mortimore, P. (1996c) 'Differential school effectiveness: Departmental variations in GCSE attainment', paper presented at AERA Annual Conference, New York, *The School Field* 8 (1): 97–125.

Sammons, P., Thomas, S. & Mortimore, P. (1997a) *Forging Links: Effective Schools and Effective Departments*. London: Paul Chapman Publishing.

Sammons, P., Thomas, S. & Mortimore, P. (1997b) 'School and departmental effectiveness: Implications from a recent British study for policy, practice and future research', paper presented at ICSEI, Memphis. Chapter 9 in *Forging Links: Effective Schools and Effective Departments*. London: Paul Chapman Publishing.

Sammons, P., Thomas, S., Mortimore, P., Cairns, R. & Bausor, J. (1994b) 'Understanding the processes of school and departmental effectiveness', paper presented to the annual conference of the British Educational Research Association, Oxford.

Sammons, P., Thomas, S., Mortimore, P., Cairns, R., Bausor, J. & Walker, A. (1995d) 'Understanding school and departmental differences in academic effectiveness', paper presented at the International Congress for School Effectiveness and Improvement, Leeuwarden, The Netherlands.

Sammons, P., Thomas, S., Mortimore, P., Owen, C. & Pennell, H. (1994c) *Assessing School Effectiveness: Developing Measures to Put School Performance in Context*. London: Institute of Education/Ofsted.

Scheerens, J. (1990) 'School effectiveness and the development of process indicators of school functioning', *School Effectiveness and School Improvement* 1 (1): 61–80.

Scheerens, J. (1992) *Effective Schooling: Research, Theory and Practice*. London: Cassell.

Scheerens, J. (1993) 'Basic school effectiveness: Items for a research agenda', *School Effectiveness and School Improvement* 4: 17–36.

Scheerens, J. (1995) 'School Effectiveness as a research discipline', paper presented at the International Congress of School Effectiveness and School Improvement, Leeuwarden, The Netherlands.

Scheerens, J. & Bosker, R. (1997) *The Foundations of Educational Effectiveness*. Oxford: Elsevier Science.

Scheerens. J. & Creemers, B. (1989) (eds.) 'Conceptualizing school effectiveness', *International Journal of Educational Research* 13: 691–706.

Scheerens, J. & Creemers, B. (1989) (eds.) 'Developments in school effectiveness research', *International Journal of Educational Research* 13: 7.

Scheffler, I. (1967) 'Philosophical models of teaching', in R.S. Peters (ed.) *The Concept of Education*, pp. 120–34. New York: Humanities Press.

Schein, E. (1985) *Organizational Culture and Leadership*. San Francisco, CA: Jossey-Bass.

School Curriculum and Assessment Authority (1994) *Value Added Performance Indicators for Schools*. London: SCAA.

School Curriculum and Assessment Authority (1995) *The Value Added National Project: General and Technical Reports*. London: SCAA.

Shaw, D. (1986) 'Purge on schools: The ABC of good teaching', *Evening Standard*, 14 April.

Shipman, M. (1978) 'The presentation of examination results', *Contact* 20: 29–31.

Shipman, M. (1980) '*Fifteen Thousand Hours*: A review article', *Research in Education*, May.

Shipman, M. (1985) 'Developments in educational research', in M. Shipman (ed.) *Educational Research: Principles, Policies and Practices*, pp. 7–16. Lewes: Falmer Press.

Silver, H. (1994) *Good Schools, Effective Schools and Judgements and their Histories*. London: Cassell.

Simon, B. (1988) Research Report, *Forum* 30 (3): 95.

Sinclair, I.A.C. (1971) *Hostels for Probationers*. London: HMSO.

Sirotnik, K. (1985) 'School effectiveness: A bandwagon in search of a tune', *Education Administration Quarterly* 21 (2): 135–40.

Sizemore, B. (1987) 'The effective African American elementary school', in G. Noblit & W. Pink (eds.) *Context: Qualitative Studies*, pp. 175–202. Norwood, NJ: Ablex.

Skinner, B.F. (1938*)* *The Behaviour of Organisms*. New York: Appleton.

Slater, R. & Teddlie, C. (1992) 'Towards a theory of school effectiveness and leadership', *School Effectiveness and School Improvement* 3 (4): 247–57.

Slavin, R. (1996) *Education for All*. Lisse: Swets & Zeitlinger.

Slavin, R.E., Karweit, N.L., Dolan, L.J., Wasik, B.A. & Madden, N.A. (1993) 'Success for all: Longitudinal effects of a restructuring program for inner city elementary schools', *American Educational Research Journal* 30: 123–48.

Slavin, R.E., Karweit, N.L. & Madden, N.A. (1989) *Effective Programmes for Students at Risk*. Needham Heights: Allyn & Bacon.

Slavin, R.E., Madden, N.A., Dolan, L., Wasik, B., Ross, S. & Smith, L. (1994) 'Success for all: Longitudinal effects of systemic school by school reform in seven districts', paper presented at the annual conference of the American Educational Research Association, New Orleans.

Smith, D. & Tomlinson, S. (1989) *The School Effect*. London: Policy Studies Institute.

Smith, G. (1987) 'Whatever happened to educational priority areas?' *Oxford Review of Education* 13 (1).

Smith, T. & Noble, M. (1995) *Education Divides: Poverty and Schooling in the 1990s*. London: CPAG.

Smith, G., Smith, T. & Wright, G. (1997) 'Poverty and schooling: Choice, diversity or division?', in A. Walker & C. Walker (eds.) *Britain Divided: The Growth of Social Exclusion in the 1980s and 1990s*. London: CPAG.

Sofer, A. (1988) 'Matter of facts', *Times Educational Supplement*, 25 March.

Southworth, G. (1994) 'The learning school', in P. Ribbens & E. Burridge (eds.) *Improving Education: Promoting Quality in Schools*. London: Cassell.

Springfield, S. & Herman, R. (1995) *Assessment of the State of School Effectiveness Research in the United States of America*, ICSEI Country Reports. Leeuwarden, The Netherlands.

St John Brooks, C. (1979) 'Fifteen Thousand Hours', *New Society* 20: 493–4.

St John Brooks, C. (1988a) 'Quality of school lessens the effect of class', *Sunday Times*, 20 March.

St John Brooks, C. (1988b) 'Shedding light and optimism on the class of the future', *Sunday Times*, 27 March.

Stevens, A. (1979) 'When potted plants are better than discipline', *Observer*, 7 January.

Stevenson, M. & Shin-Ying, L. (1990) 'Contexts of achievement: A study of American, Chinese and Japanese children', *Monographs of the Society for Research in Child Development* 221: 55.

Stoll, L. (1992) 'Making Schools Matter: Linking Effectiveness and School Improvement in a Canadian School District', unpublished PhD thesis, University of London.

Stoll, L. & Fink, D. (1989) 'An effective schools project: The Halton approach', in D. Reynolds, D. Creemers & T. Peters (eds.) *School Effectiveness and Improvement: Proceedings of the First International Congress, London 1988*, pp. 286–99. Groningen, The Netherlands: RION Institute for Educational Research / Cardiff: School of Education, University of Wales.

Stoll, L. & Fink, D. (1993) 'Canadian Pioneers', *Managing Schools Today* 2 (6): 12–15.

Stoll, L. & Fink, D. (1996) *Changing Our Schools: Linking School Effectiveness and School Improvement.* Buckingham: Open University Press.

Stoll, L. & Mortimore, P. (1995) *School Effectiveness and School Improvement,* briefing paper. London: Institute of Education.

Stoll, L. & Myers, K. (1997) *No Quick Fixes: Perspectives on Schools in Difficulty.* London: Falmer Press.

Stoll, L. & Sammons, P. (1988) *Smiley: A Scale for Measuring Primary Pupils' Attitudes.* London: Research and Statistics, Inner London Education Authority.

Stoll, L. & Thomson, M. (1996) 'Moving together: A partnership approach to improvement', in P. Earley, B. Fidler & J. Ouston (eds.) *Improvement through Inspection: Complementary Approaches to School Development,* pp. 23–37. London: David Fulton.

Strachan, V. & Sammons, P. (1986) *ILEA Junior School Project: The Assessment of Creative Writing.* London: Research and Statistics, Inner London Education Authority.

Stringfield, S. & Teddlie, C. (1988) 'A time to summarize', *Educational Leadership* 46 (1): 43–9.

Stringfield, S., Teddlie, C., Wimpleberg, R. & Kirby, P. (1992) 'A five year follow-up of schools in the Louisiana school effectiveness study', in J. Bashi & Z. Sass (eds.) *School Effectiveness and Improvement, Proceedings of the Third International Congress for School Effectiveness,* pp. 381–414. Jerusalem: Magnes Press.

Swann Report (1985) *Education for All: The Report of the Committee of Inquiry into the Education of Children from Ethnic Minority Groups.* London: HMSO.

Sylva, K. & Hurry, J. (1995) *The Effectiveness of Reading Recovery and Phonological Training for Children with Reading Problems,* report prepared for the School Curriculum and Assessment Authority. London: Thomas Coram Research Unit, Institute of Education.

Taggart, B. (1993) 'School improvement: Catalyst for change', *Managing Schools Today* 2 (9): 12–15.

Taylor, B. (1990) *Case Studies in Effective Schools Research.* Dubuque, IA: Kendall/Hunt.

Taylor, F. (1988) 'What makes good schools?', *School Governor,* June.

Teddlie, C. (1994) 'The study of context in school effects research', in D. Reynolds, B. Creemers, P. Nesselradt, E. Schaffer, S. Stringfield & C. Teddlie (eds.) *Advances in School Effectiveness Research and Practice,* pp. 85–110. Oxford: Pergamon.

Teddlie, C., Falkowski, C., Stringfield, S., Deselle, S. & Garvue, R. (1984) *The Louisiana School Effectiveness Study, Phase 2.* Louisiana: Louisiana State Department of Education.

Teddlie, C., Kirby, P. & Stringfield, S. (1989) 'Effective versus ineffective schools: Observable differences in the classroom', *American Journal of Education* 97: 221–36.

Thomas, S. & Mortimore, P. (1994) *Report on Value Added Analysis of 1993 GCSE Examination Results in Lancashire.* London: Institute of Education.

Thomas, S. & Mortimore, P. (1995) *A Multilevel Analysis of the 1993 GCSE Examination Results in Lancashire,* final report. London: Institute of Education.

Thomas, S. & Mortimore, P. (1996) 'Comparison of value added models for secondary school effectiveness', *Research Papers in Education* 11 (1): 5–33.

Thomas, S. & Nuttall, D.L. (1992) 'An analysis of 1991 Key Stage 1 results in Dorset: Multilevel analysis of English, mathematics and science subjects level scores', *British Journal of Curriculum and Assessment* 3 (1): 18–20.

Thomas, S. & Nuttall, D.L. (1993) *An Analysis of 1992 Key Stage 1 Results in Lancashire—Final Report: A Multilevel Analysis of Total Subject Score, English Score and Mathematics Score.* London: Institute of Education.

Thomas, S., Nuttall, D.L. & Goldstein, H. (1992) 'Survey of 1992 A-level examination results', *Guardian*, 20 October.

Thomas, S., Nuttall, D.L. & Goldstein, H. (1993a) *Report on Analysis of 1991 Examination Results.* London: Association of Metropolitan Authorities.

Thomas, S., Nuttall, D.L. & Goldstein, H. (1993b) 'Survey of 1993 A-level examination results', *Guardian*, 30 November.

Thomas, S., Pan, H. & Goldstein, H. (1994) *Report on Analysis of 1992 Examination Results.* London: Association of Metropolitan Authorities.

Thomas, S., Sammons, P. & Mortimore, P. (1995) 'Differential secondary school effectiveness', paper presented at the BERA Annual Conference, Bath, *British Educational Research Journal* 23 (4): 451–69.

Thomas, S., Sammons, P., Mortimore, P. & Smees, R. (1997a) 'Stability and consistency in secondary schools' effects on students' GCSE outcomes over three years', *School Effectiveness and School Improvement* 9 (2): 169–97.

Thorndike, E.L. (1898) 'Animal intelligence', *Psychological Monograph* 1 (8): 300.

Thrupp, M. (1995) 'The school mix effect: The history of an enduring problem in educational research, policy and practice', *British Journal of Sociology of Education* 16: 183–203.

Thrupp, M. (1997a) 'The school mix effect: How social class composition of school intakes shapes school processes and student achievements', paper presented at the annual meeting of the American Education Research Association, Chicago.

Thrupp, M. (1997b) 'The art of the possible: Organising and managing high and low socio-economic schools', AERA paper, Chicago.

Times Educational Supplement (1986) Leader and articles by Sarah Bayliss, 18 April.

Times Educational Supplement (1996) 9 November.

Times Educational Supplement (1996) 'Inspectors to take account of deprivation', February.

Tizard, B. (1975) 'Varieties of residential nursery experience', in J. Tizard, I. Sinclair & R. Clarke (eds.) *Varieties of Residential Experience*, pp. 102–21. London: Routledge & Kegan Paul.

Tizard, B. (1980) '*Fifteen Thousand Hours*: A review', *Journal of Child Psychology and Psychiatry* 21 (4): 363–4.

Tizard, B., Blatchford, P., Burke, J., Farquhar, C. & Plewis, I. (1988) *Young Children at School in the Inner City.* Hove: Lawrence Erlbaum.

Tizard, B., Burgess, T., Francis, H., Goldstein, H., Young, M., Hewison, J. & Plewis, P. (1980), '*Fifteen Thousand Hours*: A discussion', *Bedford way Papers 1*. London: Institute of Education.

Tizard, B. & Rees, J. (1974) 'The development of children whose first two years of life were spent in institutional care', *Child development* 45: 92–9.

Tizard, J., Schofield, W. & Hewison, J. (1982) 'Symposium: Reading—collaboration between teachers and parents in assisting children's reading', *British Journal of Educational Psychology* 52: 1–15.

Tizard, J., Sinclair, I. & Clarke, R.V.G. (eds.) (1975) *Varieties of Residential Experiences.* London: Routledge & Kegan Paul.

Tizard, J. & Tizard, B. (1975) 'The institution as an environment for development', in H. Brown & R. Stevens (eds.) *Social Behaviour and Experience*, pp. 135–50. London: Open University Press.

Toews, J. & Murray-Barker, D. (1985) *The Baz Attack: The School Improvement Experience Utilising Effective Schools Research, 1981–85*. Calgary, Alberta: Bazalgette Junior High School.

Toft, M., Inman, S. & Whitty, G. (eds.) (1995) *Healthy Schools Are Effective Schools*. London: Health and Education Research Unit.

Tomlinson, J., Mortimore, P. & Sammons, P. (1988) 'Freedom and education: Ways of increasing openness and accountability', *Sheffield Papers In Education Management*. Sheffield: Sheffield City Polytechnic.

Tomlinson, S. (ed.) (1994) *Educational Reform and its Consequences*. London: IPPR/Rivers Oram Press.

Townsend, P. (1996) Comment quoted in Richards, H. 'Perspectives', *Times Higher Education Supplement*, p. 13, 30 August.

US Department of Education (1987) *What Works?* Washington, DC: US Department of Education.

Van de Grift, W. (1990) 'Educational leadership and academic achievement in elementary education', *School Effectiveness and School Improvement* 1: 26–40.

Van Velzen, W., Miles, M., Ekholm, M., Hameyer, U. & Robin, D. (1985) *Making School Improvement Work: A Conceptual Guide to Practice*. Leuven, Belgium: Acco Publishers.

Vygotsky, L. (1978) *Mind in Society*. Cambridge, MA: Harvard University Press.

Walberg, H. (1986) 'Synthesis of research on teaching', in M. Wittrock *Handbook of Research on Teaching* (third edition), pp. 214–29. New York: Macmillan.

Waldron, P. (1983) *Towards a More Effective School*. Banff, Alberta: Canadian Education Association .

Walker, A. & Walker, C. (eds.) (1997) *Britain Divided: The Growth of Social Exclusion in the 1980s and 1990s*. London: CPAG.

Wallace, M. & Hall, V. (1994) *Inside the SMT*. London: Paul Chapman Pupblishing.

Wang, M., Haertel, G. & Walberg, H. (1990) 'What influences learning?', *Journal of Educational Research* 84: 30–43.

Watkins, C. (1995) 'School behaviour', in *Viewpoint No 3*. London: Institute of Education.

Weber, G. (1971) *Inner-city Children Can Be Taught to Read: Four Successful Schools*. Washington, DC: Council for Basic Education.

Wedge, P. & Prosser, H. (1973) *Born to Fail?* London: Arrow Books.

Weikart, D.P. (1972) 'Relationship of curriculum, teaching and learning in pre-school education', in J.C. Stanley (ed.) *Preschool Programs for the Disadvantaged*. Baltimore: John Hopkins University Press.

White, J. (1997) 'Philosophical perspectives on school effectiveness and school improvement', in J. White & M. Barber (eds.) *Perspectives on School Effectiveness and School Improvement*, pp. 41–60. London: Institute of Education.

Whitehouse, A. (1979) 'Lessons for a perfect school', *Yorkshire Post*, 21 March.

Whitty, G. (1985) *Sociology and School Knowledge*. London: Methuen.

Whitty, G. (1992) 'Education, economy and national culture', in R. Bocock & K. Thompson (eds.) *Social and Cultural Forms of Modernity*, pp. 267–309. Buckingham: Open University Press.

Whitty, G. (1997a) 'Creating quasi-markets in education: A review of recent research on parental choice and school autonomy in three countries', *Review of Research in Education* 22 (18): 3–47.

Whitty, G. (1997b) 'School autonomy and parental choice: Consumer rights versus citizen rights in education policy in Britain', in D. Bridges (ed.) *Education, Autonomy and Democratic Citizenship in a Changing World.* London: Routledge.

Wilby, P. (1988) 'The myth exploded: Schools really do matter', *Independent*, 24 March.

Wilcox, B. & Gray, J. (1996) *Inspecting Schools: Holding Schools to Account and Helping Schools to Improve.* Buckingham: Open University Press.

Wilkinson, R. (1996) *Unhealthy Societies: The Afflictions of Inequality.* London: Routledge.

Wilkinson, R. (1997) *Unfair Shares: The Effects of Widening Income Differences on the Welfare of the Young.* London: Barnardos.

Willis, P. (1977) *Learning to Labour.* Farnborough: Saxon House.

Willms, J. (1985) 'The balance thesis: Contextual effects of ability on pupils' "O" grade examination results', *Oxford Review of Education* 11 (1): 33–41.

Willms, J. (1986) 'Social class segregation and its relationship to pupils' examination results in Scotland', *American Sociological Review* 51: 224–41.

Willms, J. (1987) 'Differences between Scottish education authorities in their examination attainment', *Oxford Review of Education* 13 (2): 211–32.

Willms, J. (1992) *Monitoring School Performance: A Guide for Educators.* London: Falmer Press.

Willms, J. & Cuttance, R. (1985) 'School effects in Scottish secondary schools', *British Journal of Sociology of Education* 6 (3): 287–306.

Willms, J. & Raudenbush, S. (1989) 'A longitudinal hierarchical linear model for estimating school effects and their stability', *Journal of Educational Measurement* 26 (3): 209–32.

Wilmott, P. & Hutchison, R. (1992) *Urban Trends 1.* London: Policy Studies Institute.

Winch, C. (1997) 'Accountability, controversy and school effectiveness research', in J. White & M. Barber (eds.) *Perspectives on School Effectiveness and School Improvement*, pp. 61–76. London: Institute of Education.

Wing, J. & Brown, G. (1970) *Institutionalism and Schizophrenia: A Comparative Study of Three Mental Hospitals, 1960–1968.* Cambridge: Cambridge University Press.

Winkley, D. (1988) 'Handle with care', *Times Educational Supplement*, 25 March.

Wittrock, M. (1986) *Handbook of Research on Teaching* (third edition). New York: Macmillan.

Witziers, B. (1994) 'Co-ordination in secondary schools and its implications for student achievement', paper presented at the annual conference of the American Educational Research Association, New Orleans.

Wood, D. (1993) 'The classroom of 2015', in *National Commission Briefings, Number 20.* London: National Commission on Education.

Wood, N. (1986) 'Go back to 3Rs, says top lefty', *Daily Express*, 15 April.

Wood, R. & Bandura, A. (1989) 'Impact of conceptions of ability on self-regulating mechanisms and complex decision-making', *Journal of Personality and Social Psychology* 56: 407–15.

Woodhead, C. (1997) 'Inspecting schools: The key to raising educational standards' ('The Last Word' lecture at the *Royal Geographical Society*, London).

Wragg, T. (1980) 'Second thoughts on the Rutter report', *Education*, 14 March.

Yelton, B., Miller, S. & Ruscoe, G. (1994) 'The stability of school effectiveness: Comparative path models', paper presented at the annual meeting of the American Educational Research Association, New Orleans.

Subject Index

academic emphasis 129; *see also* focus on learning
accountability 207, 214, 258, 293, 297
adaptive instruction 163
advantaged areas 138
age 51, 55, 58–59
Amendment to 1965 Education Act by Hawkins/Stafford (1988) 152
analysis and interpretation 69–95
approved schools (community homes) 13–17, 19
APU (Language Survey Team of the Assessment of Performance Unit) 53, 78
attainment *versus* progress 240, 332
attendance 38–41, 46, 53, 55, 83–84, 114–7, 274, 276
attitudes 4, 53, 55, 57–60, 65, 85–88, 114, 117–8, 151, 223, 275
attribution theory 164

background, family, controlling for 4, 19, 42, 52, 58, 71, 115, 152, 154–5, 160, 196–9, 203–4, 207–8, 240, 258–60, 273, 299–315
backward mapping 3, 116, 140, 169
balance of ability 40, 42, 47, 332
basic skills 29, 52, 57, 76, 115, 123, 149, 168, 189, 203, 211, 218, 258, 290, 295
see also core skills
Basic Skills Unit 323
Bedford Way Paper 238
behaviour 3, 37–38, 42, 46, 54–55, 57–59, 82, 87–88, 99, 114, 118–9, 151–2, 218, 276, 278, 280, 296
BERA (British Educational Research Association) 104
Black Paper, The 10
blame 142
Bloom-type mastery learning 129
BMT (National Foundation for Educational Research Basic Mathematics Test) 53, 75

British Educational Research Association Conference (1979) 47
buildings 17–18, 28, 42, 45, 280, 284, 296
Burntwood Agreement, The 279
Burntwood Secondary School 269–87

Carroll model, The 163
catchment area 25, 28, 153, 186, 212, 272
CATs (Cognitive Abilities Tests) 187–8
census 99, 186
Central Advisory Councils 254
Centre for School Improvement 266
challenge, intellectual 63, 334
change
    impetus for 142–3, 156
    through school improvement 305–6
Child at School form 82–85
choice of outcomes 321–2
Choice and Diversity 206
classroom teachers 228–30 and *passim*
cognitive
    outcomes 72–75, 80–82
    psychology 163
    versus non-cognitive outcomes 53–56, 60, 70–95, 121, 139, 150, 203
Cognitive Acceleration Through Science 266
Coleman Equal Opportunity Survey (1966) 151
collegiality 262, 281
Comer Programme 132
commitment 330
communications, level of 63–64, 282
competition for students 142
comprehensives 212, 333
consistent approaches 174
context, social 138, 192–3, 262, 295, 305, 308, 317, 334, 342
core skills 129
crime rates 205

culture (ethos) 41–44, 46, 65, 121, 216, 218, 220, 233, 261, 278–81, 284–5, 294, 296, 310, 341
curriculum 1, 3–5, 294; *see also* national curriculum

Dartington Research Unit 13–15
definitions of effectiveness 318–20
delinquency 17, 25–26, 28, 31, 38–42, 46, 100, 153
departments *see* subjects
Department for Education and Employment 226, 307
DES (Department of Education and Science) 129, 150
Desmond Nuttall Memorial Conference 179–94
DHT (deputy head teacher) 62–63, 197, 201, 291, 293
differential effectiveness 6, 190–2, 195–234, 323, 343
Differential School Effectiveness 185
dignity 342
disadvantaged students 2, 7, 45, 115, 123, 143–4, 150–1, 214, 274, 332
Drive Primary School 289–298
dropping-out 4, 144, 157

Early Years 304
Education Act (1922) 130
Education Action Zones 313
Education Reform Act (1988) 50, 130, 148, 158, 180, 205, 248, 251
Education, Science and Arts Select Committee 106
effective learning and teaching 161–177 and *passim*
eleven-plus exams 303
empirical research 322–3
ends and means 161
EPA (Educational Priority Area) 303
equity 3, 4, 144, 159, 200, 213, 218, 231, 236, 314, 323
ERT (Edinburgh Reading Test) 53, 72
examination results 2, 4, 33, 38–42, 46, 50, 114–5, 120, 139, 143, 154, 157, 303
exclusions 216

expectations ('self-efficacy') 119, 125–6, 151–2, 163, 166, 171–2, 277–80, 294, 297, 334–5
extra-curricular activities 277

failing schools 130, 195, 204, 206, 210, 216, 297, 327, 332, 337
feedback 207, 230, 279, 283, 293, 295, 341
Fifteen Thousand Hours: Secondary Schools and their Effects on Children 3, 4, 6, 9, 35–47, 98–103
focus on learning 278–9
Forging Links: Effective Schools and Effective Departments 195–234
Framework for Inspection 322
Freedom of Information Inquiry 184
FSM (entitlement to free school meals) 188, 274, 289, 303
further education 156, 204
Future Learning Centre 340

GCSE (General Certificate of Secondary Education) 4, 144, 182, 187, 190, 275 and *passim*
gender (sex) 50–52, 55, 58–60, 114, 155, 159, 191, 269–87, 301
GM (grant-maintained schools) 213, 233, 272, 283–4
goals 161, 215, 220, 311; *see also* targets
governors 47, 158, 270, 273, 290, 292
grammar schools 212
GRIDS (Schools' Council's Guidelines for Review and Institutional Development) 131
guidelines 63

Head Start programmes 127
High Scope Pre-school Programme 159, 304
higher education 156–7, 204
HoDs (heads of departments) 197, 201–3, 215, 224–7
Home Office Research Unit 16, 24, 31
homework 276–7, 279, 283
HT (head teacher, principal) 62, 99, 103–4, 121, 123, 141, 151–2, 197, 201–3, 215, 270, 273, 281–2, 290–3, 297

ICSEI (International Congress of School Effectiveness and Improvement) 105, 147–77, 182, 194, 239
ideology 251–2, 324
IIP (Investors in People) 262
ILEA (Inner London Education Authority) 155
improvement, school, and school effectiveness 6–7, 130, 145, 152–3, 156–7, 175–6, 205, 221–5, 241–2, 244, 257–67, 292–6, 299–315, 331–2, 334–5
Improving School Effectiveness 264
infant schools 155
information technology 309, 339
inner cities 302
inputs and outcomes 185
inspections 71, 121, 206, 214–7, 223, 258, 274, 290–3, 297–8, 336, 338–9
institutions other than schools 9–21
intakes (inputs) 3–4, 7, 26, 33, 37–9, 46, 51, 70–71, 115, 120, 143, 154, 156, 185, 196, 209–10, 275, 307, 331, 337
intelligence 36, 99, 153
international co-operation 145
internet 309, 342
interventions, preventative 129–33, 155, 157, 211, 296–7
involvement 41–42, 63, 125–8, 172–4, 220, 283, 334
IQ (intelligence quotient) 210
IQEA (Improving the Quality of Education for All) 250
ISEIC (International School Effectiveness and Improvement Centre) 182, 188, 194, 241, 265
ISIP (International School Improvement Project) 153, 260
ISIS (International School Improvement Study) 130
Isle of Wight/Inner London 27–28

JSP (Junior School Project) 50–67, 69–95; *see also* primary schools

Key Characteristics of Effective Schools 322
Key Stages 182, 298

Labour Literacy Taskforce 204, 311
language 52, 59
leadership 41, 62, 125, 151, 171, 201–2, 220–1, 277, 281–2, 285–6, 293, 334–5
Leadership Centre 335
league tables 181–4, 195, 200, 207–11, 214, 300, 318, 333
learning
 theory 162–4
 versus teaching 340
Learning to Succeed 269, 277
Learning Works: Widening Participation in Further Education 305
Lifetime Learning 312
LMS (local management of schools) 206, 210–11, 223
London Reading Test 53
Louisiana Study 170, 189

management 230, 282, 335
Managing Schools Today 241
market, social 251, 258, 299, 311, 336
mathematics 55–56, 59, 75–76, 119–20
Me at School measure 84
measuring outcomes 139
media, the 46–47, 97–112, 114
mental hospitals 11
methodology 7, 11, 30, 54–56, 69–95, 116, 120, 124, 138, 156, 169, 196, 241, 317–8, 320, 329
middle managers 224–5
minority communities 138
models for school improvement 141–5
monitoring 63, 126, 172, 211, 217–20, 222–3, 283, 294–5, 339
moral and practical attributes 148–51
motivation 150, 218, 294, 330, 342

national curriculum and assessment 130, 142, 180, 184, 206, 223, 262, 274, 290, 308–10, 336
National Center for Effective Schools Research and Development 152
National Children's Bureau 35, 301
National Commission on Education 245, 269–70, 277, 306
negative impact on development 113
new directions 329–45

New York Department of Educations's Office of Educational Improvement 119, 151
NFER (National Foundation for Educational Research) 24, 28
non-cognitive outcomes 82–88
Northern study, The 28–29
NPQSL (National Professional Qualification for Subject Leaders) 224
NREL (Northwest Regional Educational Laboratory) 119, 151, 169

Ofsted (Office for Standards in Education) 187–8, 193, 206, 214–7, 223, 226, 290–3, 318, 335
Oracle Schedule 54, 103
oracy *versus* other cognitive skills 80; *see also* speaking
organization 18, 28, 31, 33, 54
outcomes (whether it makes a difference) 6, 10, 24, 29, 31, 33, 37–40, 43, 45, 57–67, 114, 116–21, 130, 154, 156, 196, 207, 306, 339
outliers 197, 199–201, 209
Oxford University School Effectiveness Project 120

parental
    choice 25, 27, 38, 43–44, 130, 206, 213, 231–3, 333
    involvement 65, 233–4
    views 54, 103
partnership 262, 344
Pathways to Learning 313
personal and social development 115
personality 29
planning 230
Plowden Report 70
policies 54, 61, 133–5, 220–21, 274, 282
policy making 235–255
praise *see* rewards
Pre-Inspection Context Indicators 215
preparing for publication, recommendations on 111–2
primary schools 49–67, 69–95, 103–11, 289–298
prior attainment, controlling for 52–53, 56, 70–71, 186–8, 190–1, 193,

199–200, 203, 207, 210, 217, 259–60, 326, 331
private schools 333
privilege 50
probation hostels 11, 15–16
process-outcome model 20–21, 30, 140–1
processes (how the schools work) 6, 10, 24, 29–31, 37, 40–41, 43, 45, 60–66, 130, 141, 156, 169, 201, 204, 322
professional morale 330, 336
progress *versus* attainment 240, 332
Project Equality 157
PTA (Parent-Teacher Associations) 128
punishments 40, 44–45, 47, 126, 172, 276

quality
    of life, students' 40
    of teaching 227, 280, 294

race (ethnic group) 19, 36, 40, 50–52, 55, 59–60, 120, 122, 155, 159, 289, 191–2
Rand Corporation Study 152
reading 55–56, 59, 72–75, 99, 119–20
    versus mathematics 76
Reading Recovery Project 132, 211–2, 252, 266, 304
reception of educational research 97–112
record keeping 65
recruitment 330
relationships 14, 18, 33, 278, 296
religion 155
replies to criticisms 317–27
resources 114, 151, 264, 331, 337, 339
respect 19, 342
Restructuring Programmes 158
rewards 40, 42, 44, 47, 65, 126–7, 172, 276, 296, 338
role models 32, 166
RSEG (Radical Statistics Education Group) 110
rules, school 32, 276, 344
Rutter B behaviour scale 119

SCAA (School Curriculum and Assessment Authority) 208, 226, 247
School Development Planning 158, 170, 176

School Improvement Centre 250
School Improvement Network 265
School Matters: The Junior Years 6,
  49–67, 69–95, 103–11
secondary schools 35–47, 99–103,
  269–87
Secondary Transfer Study 103
selection 212–4
self-concept 53, 55, 58–60, 87–88, 126,
  134, 211, 218, 254–5, 334
self-evaluation 262
SES (socio-economic status) 2, 36, 40, 45,
  50–52, 55, 58–60, 114, 120–1, 123,
  150, 159, 192
setting (ability grouping) 228, 274
SIG (Special Interest Group at the
  American Educational Research
  Association) 137–46
sixth form 285
size 17, 42, 45, 62, 175, 274
Smiley attitude scale 85
SMT (senior management team) 201–2,
  215, 217, 221–5, 270, 273, 282, 285,
  293
social sciences 98
South Wales 26–27
speaking (oracy) 55, 78–80
special
  measures 292, 297
  needs 11, 132
  schools 156
stability (continuity) 61–62
statistical analysis 88–89, 92–95, 103,
  115, 138–40, 154, 194, 203, 238–9,
  317
streaming 228
students' life chances 320
styles, teaching 29–31, 40, 42, 98, 164,
  229–30
subjects (departments) 4, 198–202, 209,
  215, 225–7, 231, 260
Success for All 266, 304
support
  not blame 336–7
  teams 143, 216

tabulae rasae 1
talent 330

targets 295, 307; *see also* goals
Teacher Training for Effective Schools
  167
teachers'
  courses 265
  knowledge and skills (competence)
    166–7, 262, 335
  styles *see* styles, teaching
  training *see* training teachers
  views 221–2, 271–2
  see also classroom teachers; professional
    morale; quality of teaching
team approach 307
technical issues 137–46
theory, need for better 134, 157, 169,
  242–4, 327
Thomas Coram Research Unit 302
Three Wise Men (1992) 67
time, variations over 121, 217–8
time-on-task 151, 175, 334
Tower Hamlets 25
TQM (Total Quality Management) 262
trailing edge 204–5, 212
training teachers 295–6
Training and Enterprise councils 312
trust 296–7, 335, 342
TTA (Teacher Training Agency) 224

United Kingdom, The 153–5
United States General Accounting Office
  130–1
United States, The 151–3
universities, the role of the 250–54

value-added component 6, 115, 168,
  179–94, 207–9, 213, 215, 217, 259,
  275, 307, 314
Verbal Reasoning Test 53, 155, 184,
  190–1
views
  of governors 271–2
  of parents *see* parents' views
  of students 271–2
  of teachers *see* teachers' views
voluntary-aided schools 61

writing 55–56, 59, 77–78, 119–20
  versus reading and mathematics 78

CONTEXTS OF LEARNING
Classrooms, Schools and Society

1. *Education for All.* Robert E. Slavin
    1996.   ISBN 90 265 1472 7 (hardback)
            ISBN 90 265 1473 5 (paperback)

2. *The Road to Improvement: Reflections on School Effectiveness.* Peter
    Mortimore
    1998.   ISBN 90 265 1525 1 (hardback)
            ISBN 90 265 1526 X (paperback)

3. *Organizational Learning in Schools.* Edited by Kenneth Leithwood and
    Karen Seashore Louis
    1999.   ISBN 90 265 1539 1 (hardback)
            ISBN 90 265 1540 5 (paperback)